Routledge Revivals

An Edition of the Middle English Grammatical Texts

An Edition of the Middle English Grammatical Texts

Edited by
David Thomson

First published in 1984 by Garland Publishing, Inc.

This edition first published in 2019 by Routledge
2 Park Square, Milton Park, Abingdon, Oxon, OX14 4RN
and by Routledge
52 Vanderbilt Avenue, New York, NY 10017, USA

Routledge is an imprint of the Taylor & Francis Group, an informa business

© 1984 by David Thomson

All rights reserved. No part of this book may be reprinted or reproduced or utilised in any form or by any electronic, mechanical, or other means, now known or hereafter invented, including photocopying and recording, or in any information storage or retrieval system, without permission in writing from the publishers.

Publisher's Note
The publisher has gone to great lengths to ensure the quality of this reprint but points out that some imperfections in the original copies may be apparent.

Disclaimer
The publisher has made every effort to trace copyright holders and welcomes correspondence from those they have been unable to contact.
A Library of Congress record exists under ISBN:

ISBN 13: 978-0-367-19547-2 (hbk)
ISBN 13: 978-0-367-19548-9 (pbk)
ISBN 13: 978-0-429-20308-4 (ebk)

An Edition of the Middle English Grammatical Texts

Garland Medieval Texts
Number 8

Garland Medieval Texts

A.S.G. Edwards
General Editor

Number 1:
The Commonplace Book of Robert Reynes of Acle:
An Edition of Tanner MS 407
Edited by Cameron Louis

Number 2:
The Isle of Ladies
or The Ile of Pleasaunce
Edited by Anthony Jenkins

Number 3:
The Creacion of the World:
A Critical Edition and Translation
Edited and Translated by Paula Neuss

Number 4:
Scotish Feilde and Flodden Feilde:
Two Flodden Poems
Edited by Ian F. Baird

Number 5:
Joseph of Arimathea:
A Critical Edition
Edited by David A. Lawton

Number 6:
Colkelbie Sow *and*
The Talis of the Fyve Bestes
Edited by Gregory Kratzmann

Number 7:
King Horn:
An Edition Based on Cambridge
University Library Ms.Gg 4.27(2)
Edited by Rosamund Allen

Number 8:
An Edition of the Middle
English Grammatical Texts
Edited by David Thomson

An Edition of the Middle English Grammatical Texts

edited by
David Thomson

GARLAND PUBLISHING, INC.
NEW YORK & LONDON
1984

Copyright © 1984 by David Thomson
All rights reserved

Library of Congress Cataloging in Publication Data
Main entry under title:
An Edition of the Middle English grammatical texts.
  (Garland medieval texts ; no. 8)
  Includes bibliographical references.
  1. English language—Middle English, 1100–1500—
Grammar.   2. English language—Middle English, 1100–1500
—Texts.   I. Thomson, David, 1952–   II. Series.
    PE529.E3   1984   427'.02   83-20717
           ISBN 0-8240-9434-4

Printed on acid-free, 250-year-life paper
Manufactured in the United States of America

Contents

Preface • vii
References and Abbreviations • ix
Introduction • xi
Table of Writers, Dates and Provenances • xxxi
Texts of the *Accedence* • 1
Texts of the *Comparacio* • 65
Texts of the *Informacio* • 82
Texts of the *Formula* • 131
Texts of Other Treatises • 177
Notes • 221
Glossary • 281

Preface

With this edition I have completed my initial purpose of making available a working text and guide to the context of a group of treatises which have so far not played their full part in the study of the late Middle Ages. The edition should be regarded as a companion volume to my *Descriptive Catalogue of Middle English Grammatical Texts* (Garland, New York and London, 1979), where full information on the manuscripts and matters of background to the treatises will be found. The treatment of these in the present volume is correspondingly brief, but I have included here a fuller account of the use of English in the treatises than was possible in the *Catalogue* where the texts themselves were not before the reader.

As always I owe a debt of gratitude to many friends and colleagues, but in particular to Professor Eric Dobson, Dr. Nicholas Orme, and to the late Dr. R. W. Hunt, of whose work this is but an echo.

References and Abbreviations

A123 etc.	The texts are referred to by *siglum* and line number.
Bodl. Lib.	Bodleian Library, Oxford.
Brit. Lib.	British Library.
Catalogue	David Thomson, *A Descriptive Catalogue of Middle English Grammatical Texts* (New York and London, 1979).
C.U.L.	Cambridge University Library.
Doctrinale	D. Reichling (ed.), *Das Doctrinale des Alexander de Villa-Dei, Monumenta Germaniae paedagogica* xii (Berlin, 1893).
EETS, OS and ES	Early English Text Society, Original Series and Extra Series.
Graecismus	J. Wrobel (ed.), *Eberhardi Bethuniensis Graecismus* (Breslau, 1887).
Keil	H. Keil (ed.) *Grammatici Latini*, vols ii–iv (Leipzig, 1855–1864).
Lewis and Short	C. T. Lewis and C. Short (ed.), *A Latin Dictionary* (Oxford, 1894).
MED	H. Kurath, S. M. Kuhn, and J. Reidy (ed.), *Middle English Dictionary* (Ann Arbor, 1952–).
NLW	National Library of Wales.
OED	J. A. H. Murray, H. Bradley, W. A. Craigie and C. T. Onions (ed.), *The Oxford English Dictionary* . . . (Oxford, 1933).
OHS	Oxford Historical Society.
Pinborg	J. Pinborg, *Die Entwicklung der Sprachtheorie im Mittelalter, Beiträge zur*

	Geschichte der Philosophie und Theologie des Mittelalters xlii.2 (Münster, 1967).
STC²	W. A. Jackson, F. S. Ferguson, and K. F. Pantzer, *A Short-Title Catalogue of Books Printed in England . . . 1475–1640*, second edition, revised and enlarged (London, 1976).
Study	David Thomson, "A Study of the Middle English Treatises on Grammar," D.Phil. thesis, Oxford, 1977.
Thurot	C. Thurot, *Notices et extraits de divers manuscrits latins pour servir à l'histoire des doctrines grammaticales au moyen âge. Notices et extraits des manuscrits de la Bibliothèque impériale*, xxii.2 (Paris, 1868).

Introduction

After the Norman Conquest, English fell out of use as the language of elementary instruction in Latin grammar, and no grammatical texts in Middle English survive from before the closing years of the fourteenth century. Ranulf Higden, who died c.1363, was still able to complain in his *Polychronicon* that "pueri in scholis contra morem caeterarum nationum a primo Normannorum adventu, derelicto proprio vulgari, construere Gallice compelluntur."[1] But by 1385, when John of Trevisa reached this passage in his translation of Higden's work, the situation was different, and Trevisa adds the following note of his own:

> Þis manere was moche i-vsed to for firste deth (i.e., 1349) and is siþþe sumdel i-chaunged; for Iohn Cornwaile, a maister of grammer, chaunged þe lore in gramer scole and construccioun of Frensche in to Englische; and Richard Pencriche lerned þe manere techynge of hym and of[2] oþere men of Pencriche; so þat now, þe ȝere of oure Lorde a þowsand þre hundred and foure score and fyue, and of þe secounde kyng Richard after þe conquest nyne in alle þe gramere scoles of Engelond, children leueþ Frensche and construeþ and lerneþ on Englische.[3]

This John of Cornwall was a grammar master at Oxford, and his *Speculum gramaticale*, dated 1346, is written in Latin but shows the change in "lore" in its use of English examples alongside the Latin in the specimen sentences (*latinitates*), conjugation of verbs, and elsewhere. Cornwall's instruction was not given in the Arts Faculty but in the grammar schools which existed alongside the University and were regulated by it.[4] Although we must presume that these schools always enjoyed a position of prestige, the number of Oxford Masters of Grammar had sunk to two in the years 1360–80, and the sharp rise to twenty-two by the period 1440–60 reflects a revival which is closely connected with the new form of instruction.[5] As a further indication of this revival we may note that John of Trevisa certainly and the author of the general prologue to the revision of the Wycliffe Bible probably were Oxford men and show a significant and developed interest in grammar and the vernacular.

Of the Oxford grammar masters of this time one in particular, John Leylond—who taught from before c. 1401 to his death in 1428—gained a considerable reputation. Like Thomas Sampson, who taught what we might call "business studies" also on the fringe of the University,[6] he moved away from the concept of a single *summa* embracing his field of study to produce instead a series of short texts, perhaps representing his lectures, which lead the student through from elementary teaching up to more complex material. A natural first stage in this curriculum was the use of elementary treatises in English, and it seems likely that Leylond's production of these lies behind the treatises collected in this volume. The *Informacio* and *Comparacio* are certainly his work, the *Accedence* possibly so.[7] The *Formula* is a revision of the *Informacio*, perhaps representing an attempt by John Cobbow or another of Leylond's pupils to produce a collected account of their master's teaching on the elements of syntax. The remaining texts are not as directly connected with Leylond, although we may regard them as drawing their inspiration from him. The variation found within the different versions of Leylond's texts, and the presence of this second group of more loosely connected treatises, reflect the fact that the texts were working tools of instruction and as such open to amendment and revision by those using them, as well as misrepresentation by the pupils who noted them down.

By 1460–80 the production of the Middle English treatises on grammar had reached its peak, representing the successful dissemination of Leylond's innovation to the new wave of school foundations of the fifteenth century.[8] Among the treatises printed here are examples from Winchester (statutes 1400), Eton (founded 1440), and St. Anthony's, London (endowed 1441).[9] The same twenty-year period saw a corresponding fall in the number of Oxford grammar masters from twenty-two to eleven as the initiative passed to the new foundations. The decline in production of manuscript grammars after 1480 reflects the rapid spread of printed texts from c. 1482 onwards.[10] It is not to be supposed, however,

Introduction

that there was at first any marked break away from the manuscript tradition. To illustrate this, the following extracts from the earliest editions available in the Bodleian Library of the printed grammars should be compared with the openings of the *Accedence, Comparacio, Informacio* and text KK respectively.

Long Accidence. How many partis of reason ben there? Eyght. Whiche viij? Nowne, pronowne, verbe, aduerbe, participle, coniunction, preposition and interiection. How many ben declynyd and how many ben vndeclynyd? Four ben declynyd and four ben vndeclynyd. Whiche four ben declynyd? Nowne, pronowne, verbe and participle. Whiche four ben vndeclynyd? Aduerbe, coniunction, preposition and interiection. How many ben declynyd with case and how many without case? Thre ben declynyd with case and one without case. Whiche thre ben declynyd with case? Nowne, pronowne and participle ben declynyd with case, and verbe onely without case. How knowest a nown? For al maner thyng þat a man may see fele here or vnderstonde þat berith þe name of a thynge is a nowne.[11]

Gradus Comparationum. What nownys maketh comparison? All adiectyues welnere that betokenyth a thynge that may be made more or lesse as "feyre, feyrer, feyrest," "blacke, blacker, blackest." How many degreys of comparisons be ther? III. The pos(yt)yue, the comparatyue and the superlatyue. How know you the posytyue degre? For he is the grounde and the begynnyng of al other degres of comparison. How know you the comparatyue degre? For he passyth his posityue with this Englysshe "more" or his Englysshe endeth in "-r" as "more wyse" or "wyser." Howe knowe you the superlatyue degre? For he passyth his posityue with this Englysshe 'most' or his Englysshe endyth in '-yst' as 'moste feyre' or 'feyryst,' 'moste whyte' or 'whytyst.'[12]

Long Parvula. What shalt thou do whan thou hast an Englysshe to make in Latyn? I shal reherse myn Englysshe ones, twyes or thryes, and loke out my pryncypal, and aske þe questyon "who or what;" and the worde that answereth the questyon shall be the nominatyf case to þe verbe, excepte it be a verbe impersonall, as in this example: "The mayster techeth scolers." "Techeth" is þe verbe. Who techeth? The mayster techeth. This worde 'mayster' answereth to the questyon here, and therfore it shall be the nominatyf case, and the worde that cometh after þe verbe shall be the accusatyf case comynly, as *Magister docet me*.[13]

Sum, es, fui. This verbe *sum* hath xiiij compoundys:

Ad, subter, potis, ab, sub, in, inter, de, super, ob, pre, Pro, simul adiungas, *ex* et *per* teste Perotto.

Adsum, ades, Englysshed 'to be at, present, or by' is construyd comenly with an ablatyue case with this preposition *in*, and somtyme with a datyue case; Englysshed 'to helpe' or 'to fauer' is construyd also with a datyue case; but Englisshyd 'to come' he requirith no case of hym self; a(n)d somtyme he is vsyd for his primatiue.[14]

It is clear from this demonstration of continuity that the earliest printed grammars in English were not an innovation inspired by the Continental Renaissance, but were rather an essentially conservative and cautious business enterprise, giving the market what it had shown it wanted for the last hundred or so years and cashing in on the extra demand created by the foundation of new grammar schools away from the traditional centres of learning. Innovation and continental influence only begin to take a significant part in this elementary tradition in the next, sixteenth century, wave of development, represented by the work of Colet at St. Paul's School in London, and it only became the dominant influence in elementary education at large with the royal sponsorship of "Lily's Latin Grammar" by Henry VIII in 1540, and the evolution of a new and more thoroughly secular system or breed of grammar schools.

The development of an adequate vocabulary to talk about grammar was clearly a *sine qua non* for teaching in the vernacular, and this seems to have happened fairly quickly. The earliest English treatises are as developed in this respect as the later, and a number of non-grammatical texts written in the last quarter of the fourteenth century which use grammatical terms show—as we must expect—that the terminology was in use during the period between John of Cornwall's innovation and the first surviving written texts.

Three texts in particular are important in this respect: the general prologue to the revision of the Wycliffite Bible[15], John Trevisa's translation of *Bartholomaeus Anglicus de proprietatibus rerum*,[16] and passus IV lines 335–410 of the C text of *Piers Plowman*.[17] The texts are dated a1397, a1398 and a1387 respectively by the *Middle English Dictionary*. It is possible to make considerable speculations about this grouping of material, but the following points need to be made here: first, it shows the close connection between discussing grammar in English and translation into the vernacular at this time; second, it draws attention to the interest of Trevisa in particular in both these areas, which is supported by his comments on his slightly older fellow-Cornishman John of Cornwall (who may have been in Oxford while Trevisa was there); third it reminds us that the extensions of literacy with which the English treatises are bound up lead us directly to some of the best literature and bitterest religious controversy of the period.

The Bible prologue passage is an argument for "resolucion," or rephrasing into what the writer considered more straightforward or "open" syntax, in the process of translation, and it is important not only for the command of technical vocabulary it demonstrates but also for the specificity of its examples, as for instance the resolution of *"the maister redinge, I stonde"*[18] which relates closely to the treatment of the ablative absolute in the English texts, and shows a concern for the English phrasing which is not found in those texts, which prefer the Latinate construction for pedagogical reasons.

Trevisa shows a general willingness throughout the translation of the *De proprietatibus rerum* to talk about grammatical and etymological matters—and he is, of course, following his source in this—but two passages are of particular interest. First, in talking about the names of God he incidentally makes an extensive analysis—at times philosophical rather than grammatical—of the various types of noun, using English terminology which goes beyond that used in the grammars: *abstract, adiectiue, appropriat, concret, essencial, nocional, partitiue, personal, plural, positif, priuatiue, (of) respect, singuler, substantif* and *transumpt*.[19] Second, he chooses to exemplify the working of the human mind—as contrasted with that of angels—as follows:

> As if a childe knoweþ þat if þe nominatif case and þe verbe discordiþ in persone and in noumbre, þanne þe resoun is incongrue, as in þis manere: *puer sumus bonus*. Þanne take (for) on premis: no resoun is conger in þe whiche þe nominatif case and þe verbe discordith in noumbre and in persone. And take for þe oþir permis: in þis resoun, *puer sumus bonus*, þe nomi-

natif case and þe verbe discordeþ in noumbre and in persone. And make þi conclusioun in þis maner: *ergo þis resoun is not conger, puer sumus bonus.*[20]

The *Piers Plowman* passage takes a grammatical point as the basis for moralisation, as a tale from the *Gesta Romanorum*[21] and other fifteenth century compositions do also. The point in this case is the concord between nouns and adjectives, relatives and antecedents, and naturally Conscience casts God in the role of antecedent, man in that of relative. The king's reply to Conscience reflects the relative newness of the terminology involved:

> Quath the kynge to Conscience. "knowen ich wolde
> What is relacion rect. and indyrect after,
> And thanne adiectyf and substantif.for Englische was it
> neuere."[22]

Ælfric's careful neologisms for grammatical terminology were no longer current by this time, and the teachers of Latin in English characteristically do not follow his example, but draw most of their vocabulary from Latin, often by way of French which was in use earlier as a language of grammatical instruction (as in *accord, certain, (en)chesoun, conceiven, couplen, defaute, degre, double, failen, gendre, governen, gramere, lettre, ordre, passen, pouer, propre, qualite, resoun, supreme*). The scale of borrowing is an indication of an important debt which the lack of surviving Latin grammars written in French for English use in the fourteenth century or earlier tends to obscure.

The fact that a number of the terms used, especially in EE (such as *metonomia, silempsis, transicion, infinitacion, intransicion*) where the writer is being more adventurous, are still very Latinate, like the frequent Latin tags and general macaronic quality of some of the texts, reflects the jargon nature of the language used in the treatises. Similarly, only a small proportion of the technical vocabulary is drawn from existing English words used in new senses. Examples where this does seem to have happened include *bitoknen, deed, drauen out of, eking, honging, strength, take, turn* and *worthe*.

Surprisingly, however, much of the technical vocabulary appears in either straightforward or figurative senses in Middle English literary compositions from the time of *Piers Plowman* on-

Introduction

wards, as the references to the terms in the MED demonstrate, and their use was clearly not wholly limited to the schoolroom.

In order to teach Latin more effectively, the writers of the Middle English treatises consistently given English examples of the categories and accidents of Latin grammar, and in the more elementary treatises these categories and accidents are often defined only in this way, without mention of the Latin forms. Similarly, in the treatises on syntax, parallel English constructions appear alongside the Latin ones, and occasionally these are discussed in their own right. The status accorded Latin as a universal grammar by the modistic grammarians[23] makes this application of Latin categories to English a very natural step. The pedagogical advantages and theoretical naturalness of treating English in this way help to explain why so little independent analysis of English is found in the treatises, while on the other hand English is used, even when we might consider its application strained, to elucidate the Latin. The "Latins" and "vulgars" printed by Meech show the same tendency at work.[24] Meech's suggestion that the distortion of the English examples was deliberately intended to illustrate Latin word order is interesting in these terms.

Naturally, this degree of licence, and the application of Latin categories to the English language in general, produce a number of English examples and analyses which appear strange, as well as a number of interesting remarks about the English of the day, and I shall look at these in some detail. First, however, it may be helpful to give an outline of the extent to which the Latin categories and accidents are transferred to English.

Donatus' eight parts of speech—noun, pronoun, verb, adverb, participle, conjunction, preposition and interjection—are naturally applied to English, and the treatises show no signs of wishing to change this system. H22–5 (quoted below) is the only passage to deal with the article as such and even there it is treated only as an adjunct of the noun. This classification corresponds to Michael's system 1,[25] and as the list of its users which he gives shows, a large number of later grammarians continued to apply it to English.[26]

The noun is defined in terms of English at M13-19 and H22-5 and its number (A52-5, H1-5), case (A56, GG4-8) and person (C217-24, GG33-5) are discussed using English examples. The discussion of number makes no explicit reference to English morphology, but in the passage at H1-5 the separation of the examples into two groups—"man" and "chyld," "beest" and "boke"—implies an awareness that some English nouns form their plural with "-(i)s" while others do not. Case in English is equated with analytic constructions such as "to þe mayster," "o þou maister,"[27] and number noted in personal pronouns mainly. The difference between substantives and adjectives is illustrated with reference to English alone at C14-20, but the discussion at H22-5 goes further:

> Howe knowe ye a nowne substantyue? By hys Englysch and by hys Laten. In Englych he may stand w'owt an adiectyffe and comynly one of thes tokens go before hym as:
>
> | | man' | | halle' | | sone' |
> | --- | ------ | ---- | ------- | ----- | ------ |
> | 'a | chyld' | 'an | halter' | 'the | mone' |
> | | boke' | | hors' | | see'. |

Apart from recognising one role of the article[28] the writer has classified the English nouns according to their initial sound and their customary generic or specific reference ("man" customarily has generic and specific, "sone" only specific reference). The uniform use of words whose spelling begins with "h-" rather than a vowel for the "an" class is particularly interesting. The passage goes on to identify the Latin *hic, hec, hoc* as articles,[29] but this is not relevant to the English discussion, other than suggesting that the writer may have started with the English construction and then looked for a Latin parallel rather than *vice versa*. Finally, comparison in adjectives is discussed in terms of English (without reference to Latin at C30-7) and both the "-r," "-est" endings and the use of "more" and "most"/"least" are referred to. Quality and quantity in comparison are identified using only English examples at N5-9. B301-5 offers a syntactic analysis of the construction of the genitive with the superlative, using only an English example:

> Þat is to say, when þe genetyf may be changyd into þe same case þat þe superlatyf degre ys and þe superlatyf degre into þe posityf by trewe sentence, as þus: "The rose is fayryst of flovrys", hit may be changyd þus and þe sentence trewe: "Þe rose ys a feyre flovre."

Two accidentals of the verb—mood and tense—are also dealt with in terms of English in some detail. At A175-80 the English

Introduction

equivalents of the indicative, imperative, optative, conjunctive and infinitive moods are identified, the indicative and imperative by meaning, the optative by the use of "wold" or "schuld" (C403-4 adds "mote" and "at my wille"), the conjuctive by "yf," and the infinitive by "to" before the verb.[30] GG76-7 differs in its analysis in that "all swylk wordys 'swld,' 'cowde,' 'mwght,' 'wald,' 'ware' sal be coniunctif mode preterneperfite tens," presumably reflecting the realisation that there is no separate optative mood in Latin. The imperfect, perfect, pluperfect and future tenses are identified in the English verb at A217-25 by the presence or absence of "have," "had" and "shall," and it should be noted that the standard English equivalent for the imperfect tense in the treatises is "I loved" (cf. B215), with "I have loved" as the perfect, perhaps reflecting the Latin morphology as well as the still infrequent use of the progressive form.[31] The verbs are classified by voice, which is commonly discussed in terms of verbs meaning either "to do" or "to suffer," as it was by later grammarians,[32] but B156-60 includes a brief section identifying these classes in English on the basis of the presence of "am," "art," "ys," "was," "were" or "be" in the passive forms as Poole was later to do.[33] The treatises also identify impersonal verbs by their construction in English with "hyt" or "me" (T294-311), and this is dealt with in more detail below.

The present, past and future participles are identified at A249-269 by the presence of "-yng" (C498 adds "-and"), "i-" and "to" (C506-8 gives "for to (be)"), respectively. The equation of forms in "to . . ." with the future participle is paralleled at X212, where "Y am to drede þe mayster" translates *Ego sum qui timebo magistrum* where the Latin construction with relative pronoun and future verb is used because the participle is lacking. Lily makes a similar equivalence.[34] This point is discussed further below.

The remaining parts of speech receive less detailed attention in the treatises. The three degrees of the adverb in "-ly," "er/-ir" and "-est" are described—without reference to Latin—at C483-91. At FF10 we are told, "Thow shalt knowe a relatyue by thys synys "that," "whom" or "the wyche," and personal pronouns are identified in discussing person in the noun. The treatment of English prepositions is similarly mostly found in the discussions of case in the noun. FF26-8 applies the category of conjunction to "that" and also deals with its ambiguity in English:

Thys Ynglyss worde "that" ys a conyunctyon when he cannot be takyn for thys Ynglyss worde "the wyche," and ys a relatyue when he ys so takyn.

Finally, A324-6 illustrates the interjection with English examples such as "fy" and "out" rather than Latin ones, and the various interjection sections taken together give an interesting list of Middle English exclamations.

Some of these classifications are put together briefly at T32-9 (cf. LL73-80):

> "A chyrch ys a place þe whych Cristunnen mecull ben holdyn to love." Whych ys thy principall verbe in þis reson? "Ys" . . . What case ys "the chyrch"? Þe nominatif case. What parte of spech ys "the whych"? A relatif.

The English is not, however, normally treated as explicitly as this.

A note of caution must be sounded before leaving this subject. At T400-1 we read "For when y have a verbe in Englysh nevter lyke to a passif, where the passyue faylyth . . ." where the sense must be "For when I have a verb in an English sentence which is to be translated by a Latin neuter verb which is not used in the passive . . ." It is possible that elsewhere also we can read more into the texts than their writers intended.

Turning now to some of the difficulties and points of interest this application of Latin grammar creates in English, we note that in dealing with "synecdoche" (i.e., accusative of respect), there is a strong suspicion that the grammarians have created an English expression in order to exemplify the Latin. D146-50 reads:

> Also whanne I haue a noun betokenyng party of mannys body comyng in construccyon after a noun adiectyf, a verbe neutre or verbe passyf, the party of the body schall be accusatyf case, as "I whyte the face, ake the hede, am hurte the legge," *Ego albus faciem, doleo caput, ledor pedem* uel *tibiam*.

The English examples, like those at EE211-221, might be taken as just literal versions of the Latin along the lines of the "Latins" and "vulgars" printed by Meech[35] if it were not for the discussion at BB257-62:

> *Iohannes fractus manicam erubescit versare inter proceres.* This word *manicam* is the accusatif case, for whan this syne "the" commyth before ony part of the body and folowᵗ a nown

adiectif, verbe neuter or passif or any of thair participuls, the same part of the body shal be sett yn the accusatif case bi this figure sinotiges. (cf. HH492-503)

The English construction is spelled out in detail, but I have not been able to find any convincing evidence for its use in Middle English. *Piers Plowman* A 8.834 may be an example

> Blynde & bedrede, & broken here membris[36]

where "the" is recorded as a variant of "here," but it is perhaps easier to take "broken here membris" as an absolute clause with "here membris" as the subject of "broken": "Blind and bedridden, and their members broken."

The parallel example in *Seinte Iuliene*

> Ich habbe iblend men & ibroken ham þe schuldren & te schonken[37]

is also more easily analysed without employing synecdoche, in this case taking "ham" as a dative of disadvantage.

In a number of other places constructions which are native English are given a more elaborated treatment than their English use might justify, and this is particularly true of absolute, and some impersonal, constructions, which were part of the epistolary style of the period but less frequent in spoken English.[38] The emphasis they received in school may have helped this situation develop.

The treatises define English impersonal (strictly, "quasi-impersonal") verbs by the presence of "hit" or "me" before the verb. In the course of their discussions they offer the following examples. The Latin they are translating and a specimen reference are also given.

hit	befalles	interest	W247-8
	behose	oportet	W194-6
	delytit	(placet)	Z256
	forthynkus	penitet	T294-311
	heuyethe	tedet	V15-17
	noeys	tedet	T294-311
	plesith	(placet)	BB470
	rwes	miseret	T294-311
me	beleuthye	creditur	V15-17

loues	amatur	T294-311
redis	legitur	T294-311
syttis	sedetur	T14-15
teches	docetur	T294-311

All the construcitons with "hit" are recorded by the MED or OED except "Hyt heuythe my soule my lyf" at V15-17, which is translating Job 10.1 *Tedet animam meam vite me*. The writer seems to have disguised what is essentially a personal construction in English by giving it a preposed formal subject and following the Latin word order, in order to maintain the equivalence between Latin and English impersonals. Interestingly the Wycliffite Bible translation uses "it noȝeth" at this point.[39] The constructions with "me" are best explained as uses of the indefinite pronoun "man" in its reduced form, although the formal identity with the first person singular accusative which was used in such constructions as "me rueth"[40] may have been in the writers' minds. The example with "belouythe" is once again translating the Bible (Romans 10.10) and the Wycliffite translations have the same construction.[41] Further constructions with preposed "hit" are dealt with below.

The English treatises give a number of examples of English absolute clauses using past and present participles as equivalents of Latin ablative absolutes (e.g., U12-13, V12-13, Y300-304, BB383-4) and the English construction is analysed at X225-30:

> For when I haue and Englyssch ⸢(of)⸣ a schorte hangyng resun⸣ of a nown and a particypull or els a pronown and a participull or ellys a parycipull of a verbe inpersonall ⸢sett⸣ by hymsylfe and no word in þe reson sett owt or understonde of þe whech he may be gouer(n)d, hyt schall be sett in þe wheche he may be gouer(n)d, hyt schall be sett in þe ablatyff case absolute and be expownd by *dum* or by *cum*. (cf. U265-70)

Visser demonstrates convincingly that the absolute construction in English was in frequent enough written use by 1500 to be considered naturalized,[42] and as with the other more Latinate constructions it seems likely that the free use of English versions in the grammatical treatises helped it to take root. The example at EE17-19 is the only one to cause any difficulty: "My lorde comyng to contre hys bonde men gretlych dredyth," *Dominum meum venientem ad istas partes sui serui vehementer formidant*. The Latin example in this case is not an ablative absolute but an object phrase in the accusative dependent on *formidant*. The word-order of the English version has evidently been distorted in order to make it fit

Introduction

the Latin, producing—probably unintentionally—the appearance of an absolute phrase.

Finally, a number of constructions using the English infinitive are dealt with in the treatises. The use of the infinitive after the verb "to be" in place of the future participle in such constructions as "I am to drede þe mayster" (X212) has already been discussed. A similar usage but with impersonal subject is used at T198-203 and in similar passages in other texts to translate the gerund.[43]

> When the English of an infinitif mode comus aftyr *sum, es, fui* and *sum, es, fui* have no nominatif case before hym, I shall have a gerundif in -*dum* wᵗowte *ad* preposicion, as thus: "Hyt ys to wᵗstond owre enmys purposyng to destrye owre reme," *Resistendum est inimicis nostris proponentibus nostrum regnum adnichilare.* (T198-203)

The use of the impersonal "Hyt ys . . ." opening can perhaps be compared in terms of surface structure with the constructions with an anticipatory subject noted by Davis.[44] AA191-4 deals with the causal infinitive in English, which again translates a Latin gerund:[45]

> Whan I haue þe English of þe infinityve mode þat commyth in a reson and tellith the cause of the reson, I shall haue a gerundyve in -*dum* wᵗ a preposicion. Exemplum: *Viri vadunt ad bellum ad dimicandum.*

The infinitive was similarly used as the equivalent of the supine in -*um* expressing purpose with verbs of motion, and occasionally the same analysis was extended to cover the supine in -*u* (T215-224, see the note *ad loc.*), although the English in this case, which is, in Latin categories, closest to the gerund, is also labelled a present participle. The area of Latin gerunds, gerundives and participles and English "-ing" words and infinitives was one of considerable uncertainty it seems, and this is hardly surprising since there is no easy correlation between the languages at this point. Lily translates the gerundive in *legendis veteribus proficis* with a gerund, "In readinge olde Authors, thou doest profit," and gives "to love" as the equivalent of *amaturus* (which might explain why T215-224 uses the label infinitive for an "-ing" word).[46]

Editorial Procedure

The separate editions of each text, even where a number of versions of a treatise survive, reflect difficulties in applying "traditional" textual criticism of the form described by Maas[47] to establish the relationships between the texts. Such textual criticism is based on a number of clear assumptions about the texts with which it deals. First, it assumes that no text is a perfect copy of its exemplar; second, that the scribe of the transmitted text is nevertheless attempting to produce such a perfect copy and not introducing readings from either other witnesses or on his own authority; and third, that independent scribes copying independently do not err in common. Clearly, these assumptions are not always valid, but the textual critic believes that the texts with which he is concerned follow them sufficiently to make divergent evidence isolable.

The conditions under which the English treatises were written make the last two assumptions dangerous. Three factors seem important. First, the texts probably first took form in the lectures of John Leylond at Oxford. The texts of lectures of Thomas Sampson[48] and of the treatises on estate-management which were most likely delivered as lectures, though possibly not at Oxford,[49] display variation which reinforces the hypothesis that such lectures, repeated year by year, were repeatedly revised by those delivering them. In such a situation, copies of the lectures and their descendants are not effectively witnesses to a single original.

Second, the writers of the texts share the common tendency of fifteenth century scribes to edit their originals;[50] and this is reinforced by the practical nature of the texts, which invited each successive teacher and pupil to reconstruct the text to suit his own needs. Thus, Harvey writing on the estate-management treatises notes that "three of the texts—the *Seneschaucy*, the *Rules* and the *Husbandry*—were so drastically rearranged by some of their early copyists that even the basic plan of the original treatises is open to question."[51] Not only does the resultant increase in variation, contamination, emendation and coincident "error" (which is apparent even in a cursory glance at the texts) cloud the critic's view, but also the apparent change in the scribal ideal from the perfect copy to a personal edition makes the "recovery" of a single text, with the relegation of other readings to the status of sub-variants or errors, an inappropriate procedure.

Third, the presence of variant forms of the texts, often found within the covers of a single MS as are U and V, or parts of Y and CC, the constant availability of source texts such as the *Doctrinale* which

Introduction xxv

also have their own patterns of variation, and the evident intention of the scribes to improve their text if possible as already discussed, means that not only variation but convergent variation is likely to occur in quantities which will completely obscure the pattern of vertically transmitted error.

In such circumstances, it seems appropriate to present each version of the treatises as an entity, and to abandon textual criticism in the narrower sense, although the texts have been lightly emended by conjecture at points where they make nonsense or contain such errors and irregularities as would seriously mislead the modern reader, and where a better reading can be suggested; and in these cases I have naturally borne in mind parallel passages in the other texts.

The texts are substantially in the form in which they were presented in my Oxford doctoral thesis and retain the lineation given there and referred to in my *Catalogue*. The texts have, however, been re-collated with the manuscripts and a number of readings changed.

The spelling of the manuscripts is preserved unless it might cause grave misunderstanding, and in these cases the manuscript form is always given in a footnote. In English passages, where the writer does not differentiate the graphs of þ/y and ȝ/z I have silently introduced the distinction, but I have followed the manuscripts in using capital I throughout for modern I/J. Initial ff in the manuscripts is treated as if it were single f. Word division follows modern usage as far as possible except in the case of "a nother" and similar phrases where some texts consistently use the word division shown. Abbreviations are expanded silently except in the footnotes where the expansions are italicized. (This is a change of practice from my thesis where all expansions were marked.) Occasionally identical abbreviation marks give alternative expansions (e.g., per- and par-), but this is not the rule and abbreviations are normally expanded to a consistent form. Readers should therefore beware of taking -us plurals, for instance, too quickly as dialect markers. The final flourishes to words common in the fifteenth century are probably of no significance and have been ignored, although an exception is made of final flourished -r for -re and flourished -ll for -llis. W^t is, however, left abbreviated; expansion would be more suitable to the present edition but would dislocate the line numbering of the texts given in my thesis and used for reference in the *Catalogue*. Punctuation, capitalisation, italicization of Latin examples and layout in the texts are editorial. Folio ends are indicated by |. Where a guide letter has been left for the rubricator but no initial added, the letter is given in parentheses with a note.

Four varieties of brackets are employed as follows:

( )   enclose editorial additions unless otherwise noted.
< >   show loss of text due to physical damage ot the manuscript. I have supplied the loss conjecturally where possible.
[ ]   enclose deletions in the manuscript. I have removed all except lengthy deletions to the notes, as described below.
⌈ ⌉   enclose additions in the manuscript. These are probably in the main hand of the text at the point of addition, unless otherwise noted.

The footnotes record mostly difficulties of reading and alteration in the text. Reference is normally to the word immediately preceding the number referring to the footnote but to the whole of a bracketed passage. Where this is not the case or where confusion might arise the appropriate *lemma* is given in the notes and marked off with a square bracket. Where reference is to part of the preceding word the position of the part is shown by hyphens, so that a-, -a-, and -a indicate the beginning, middle and end of a word respectively. Where a note of cancellation is given no such position, the cancelled letters followed the word to which the reference number is attached. The following table illustrates the formulae adopted.

Text	Footnote	MS Reading
most[1]	-a *canc.*	most[a]
	a *canc.*	most [a]
	most] *canc.*	[most]
	a *added after* most	most ⌈a⌉
	MS *adds* a	most a
	MS molt	molt
	repeated	most most
	-o- *from* a	m[a] ⌈o⌉ st (by alteration etc.)
	a- *canc.*, MS *adds* a	[a]most a
	sic MS	most

Introduction   xxvii

NOTES

[1] C. Babington (ed.), *Polychronicon Ranulphi Higden monachi Cestrensis together witht he English translations of John Trevisa and of an unknown writer of the Fifteenth Century*, Rolls Series xli (London, 1865–86), vol. ii, p. 158.
[2] Babington's MS *a* produces better sense by omitting this word.
[3] *ibid.*, pp. 159f.
[4] See my article, "The Oxford Grammar Masters Revisited" in *Mediaeval Studies*, xlv (1983), pp. 298–310, on these masters and their instruction.
[5] This statistical information is derived from a computer printout available in the Bodleian Library listing grammar masters (and other categories of graduates) mentioned in A. B. Emden, *A Biographical Register of the University of Oxford to A.D. 1500* (Oxford, 1957–9).
[6] H. G. Richardson, *An Oxford Teacher of the Fifteenth Century*, reprinted with corrections from *Bulletin of the John Rylands Library* xxiii, pp. 436–57 (Manchester, 1939).
[7] For the evidence supporting these and other statements in this introduction, the reader is referred to my *Catalogue* of the texts and their manuscripts.
[8] For the foundations see N. I. Orme, *English Schools in the Middle Ages* (London, 1973), p. 194.
[9] Texts X, Z and F/AA/JJ respectively.
[10] The date of STC^2 23163.13, *Long Parvula*, probably the earliest extant printed grammar in English.
[11] Bodl. Lib. Douce D. 238(2) Ai^r = STC^2 23153.4
[12] Bodl. Lib. Arch. A.e. 37(2) Ai^r = STC^2 23155.4
[13] Bodl. Lib. Arch. A.e 37(1) Ai^v = STC^2 23164.
[14] Bodl. Lib. Arch. A.e 37(2) Aiii^r = STC^2 23155.4
[15] J. Forshall and F. Madden (eds.), *The Holy bible containing the Old and New Testaments . . . made from the Latin Vulgate by John Wycliffe and his followers* (Oxford, 1850).
[16] M. C. Seymour et al. (eds.), *"On the Properties of Things," John Trevisa's Translation of Bartholomeus Anglicus, "De proprietatibus rerum"* (Oxford, 1975).
[17] W. W. Skeat (ed.), *The Vision of William concerning Piers the Plowman . . . by William Langland* (London, 1886), vol. i, pp. 89–93.
[18] Forshall and Madden, *op. cit.*, vol. i, p. 57.
[19] Seymour et al., *op. cit.*, pp. 47–54.
[20] *Ibid.* p. 60.
[21] S. J. H. Herrtage (ed.), *The Early English Versions of the "Gesta Romanorum,"* EETS ES xxxiii (London, 1879), pp. 416–9.

[22] Skeat, *op. cit.*, C IV 343–5.
[23] G. L. Bursill-Hall, *Speculative Grammars of the Middle Ages, Approaches to Semiotics* xi (The Hague and Paris, 1971), p. 38.
[24] S. B. Meech, "John Drury and his English Writings," *Speculum* ix (1934), pp. 82–3.
[25] I. Michael, *English Grammatical Categories and the Tradition to 1800* (Cambridge 1970), p. 214.
[26] Cf. E. Vorlat, *The Development of English Grammatical Theory 1586–1737, with special reference to the Theory of Parts and Speech* (Leuven, 1975), pp. 49–55.
[27] Cf. *ibid.* p. 155.
[28] Cf. *ibid.* pp. 74–6.
[29] Cf. *ibid.* chapter 5.
[30] Cf. *ibid.* pp. 329–30.
[31] Cf. N. Davis, "Style and Stereotype in Early English Letters," *Leeds Studies in English* new series i (1967), p. 9, and the passage from Lily quoted by Vorlat, p. 304, with her comments on pp. 307–8.
[32] Vorlat, *op. cit.* pp. 227–8.
[33] *Ibid.* pp. 278–9.
[34] Quoted *ibid.* p. 352.
[35] Meech, *op. cit.* pp. 82–3.
[36] G. Kane (ed.), *Piers Plowman: the A version* (London), 1960), p. 355.
[37] S. T. O. d'Ardenne (ed.), *þe Liflade ant te Passiun of Seinte Iuliene*, EETS OS ccxlviii (London, 1961), p. 43.
[38] Davis, *op. cit.*, pp. 8–9.
[39] Forshall and Madden, *op. cit.*, vol. ii, p. 686.
[40] F. T. Visser, *An Historical Syntax of the English Language* (Leiden, 1963), p. 35.
[41] Forshall and Madden, *op. cit.*, vol. iv, p. 324.
[42] Visser, *op. cit.*, pp. 1149–58 and 1264–6.
[43] Cf. examples in Visser, *op. cit.*, pp. 48–63, dated from 1400–1535.
[44] Davis, *op. cit.*, p. 9.
[45] Cf. E. Einenkl, *Geschichte der englischen Sprache* ii, *Historische Syntax. Grundriss der germanischen Phiologie* vi, third ed. (Strassburg, 1916), pp. 16–17.
[46] The passage from Lily is quoted by Vorlat, *op. cit.*, p. 352.
[47] P. Maas, *Textual Criticism* translated by B. Flower (Oxford, 1958).
[48] I. D. O. Arnold, "Thomas Sampson and the *Orthographia Gallica*," *Medium Aevum* vi (1937), pp. 193–209.
[49] D. Oschinsky, "Medieval Treatises on Estate Management," *Economic History Review*, second series viii (1956) pp. 296–309; D. Oshinsky (ed.),

"Walter of Henley" and other treatises on Estate Management and Accounting (Oxford, 1971); P. D. A. Harvey, "Agricultural Treatises and Manorial Accounting in Medieval England," *Agricultural History Review* xx (1972), pp. 170–182.

[50] Cf. H. J. Chaytor, *From Script to Print* (Cambridge, 1945), p. 129; M. B. Parkes, "The Literacy of the Laity," *Literature and Western Civilisation*, ed. D. Daiches and A. K. Thorlby (London, 1973), vol. ii, p. 569; and on literary texts Kane, *op. cit.*, pp. 115–6; A. Brisendorff, *The Chaucer Tradition* (London and Copenhagen, 1925), pp. 59–60; J. M. Manly and E. Rickert, *The Text of the Canterbury Tales* (Chicago, 1940), vol. ii, p. 41; A. J. Bliss (ed.), *Sir Orfeo* (Oxford, 1966), p. xvii.

[51] Harvey, *op. cit.*, p. 170.

Table of Writers, Date and Provenances

This table summarises information from my *Catalogue*, where these matters receive full discussion, in order to provide a quick ready reference for users of the present volume. In particular it should be noted that the table makes no attempt to distinguish between the degrees of probability of its various entries, which vary between the conclusively proven and the plausibly conjectured.

A		s.xv^{med}	Basingwerk Abbey
B		s.xv^{med}	Basingwerk Abbey
C		s.xv^{med}	St. Alban's
D		s.xv^1	Battlefield College, Shrewsbury
E	John Leke	s.xv$^{3/4}$	North Creake, Norfolk
F		s.xv^2	St. Anthony's School, London
G	Stephen Bukherst	c.1416	Kent
H	Thomas Wriothesley	s.xv-xvi	London
J		s.xiv-xv	Oxford
K		c.1492-4	Hereford
L	Walter Pollard	1444-83	Exeter
M		s.xv$^{3/4}$	Oxford
N	Thomas Pennant	s.xv$^{3/4}$	Basingwerk Abbey
O		s.xv^{med}	Basingwerk Abbey
P	Hardgrave	c.1434/5	Beccles
Q		s.xv-xvi	Norfolk
R	Walter Pollard	1444-83	Exeter
S		s.xv$^{3/4}$	Oxford
T	John Edwards of Chirk	1480's	Valle Crucis Abbey
U	Thomas Pennant	s.xv$^{3/4}$	Basingwerk Abbey
V		s.xv^{med}	Basingwerk Abbey

Writers, Dates, and Provenances

W		c.1414	Oxford
X	John Rede & William Slyngysby	1467-c.1480	Winchester College
Y		s.xv^{med}	Exeter
Z	Wyllyam Hampshyre	1475-9	Eton College
AA	John Claveryng	s.xv^2	St. Anthony's School, London
BB		s.xv^{in}	
CC	Walter Pollard	1444-83	Exeter
DD		s.xv^{med}	Exeter
EE		s.xv^1	Battlefield College, Shrewsbury
FF		s.xvi^{in}	
GG		s.xiv-xv	Durham
HH	John Jones	c.1440	Exeter
JJ	John Claveryng	s.xv^2	St. Anthony's School, London
KK		c.1501	Oxford
LL	mag. F. Framton	s.xvi^{in}	

An Edition of the Middle English Grammatical Texts

TEXTS OF THE ACCEDENCE

A. Aberystwyth, N.L.W., MS Peniarth 356B, fols.54^v-57^v and 48^r

How mony partys of spech byn þer? VIII. Qwech viij?
Nown, pronowne, verbe, aduerbe, participul, coniunccion,
preposicion, interieccion. How mony byn declynet and how mony
byn vndeclynet? IIII byn declynet and iiij byn vndeclynet.
Wech iiij byn declynet? Nowne, pronowne, verbe and partycipull.
Wych iiij byn vndeclynet? Aduerbe, coniunccion, preposicion
and interieccion. How mony byn declynyt w^t case and how mony
w^{t}out case? III wyth case and on w^{t}out case. Wech iij wyth
case? Nowne, pronowne and partycipull. Wych on w^{t}out case?
Verbe allon.   10

How knos þu a nowne? For all þat I may fele, here or se
þat berys þe name of a thyng, þe name ⸢þerof⸣ ys a nowne. How
mony maners of nownus byn þer? II. Wych ij? A nowne
substantiue and a nowne adiectiue. How knos þu a nowne
substantiue? For hyt ys declynet w^t on articull or ij at þe
most in on case. How knos þu a nowne adiectiue? For hyt ys
declynet w^t iij artyculs or iij dyuers endyngus in on case.
Wych byn þi articuls? *Hic, hec, hoc*. Wych byn þi dyuers
endyngus? -Vs, -a, -vm; -r, -a, -vm, most comynly.

How mony thyngus longon to a now(n)? VI. Qwech vj?   20
Qualite, comparyson, gendyr, nowmbyr,[1] figur[2] and case. How
mony qualites byn[3] in a nowne? II. Wech ij? A propur and
a comyn. How knos þu a propur qualyte? For hys Englysch
acordys kyndle to on thynge, a(s) 'Ion', 'Robert'. How knos a
comyn qualyte? For hys Englysch acordys kyndly to mo thyngus
then to on, as 'a towne', 'a cyte'.

How mony degres of comparysons byn þer? III. Wych iiij?
Þe posytiue and comparatiue and þe superlatyue. How knos þu
þe positiue degre? For he setys þe grownd of all oþer degres
of comparisons and ys fowrmyt of non, as 'whyt', 'blak', 'rede'.   30
How knos þu þe comparatiue degre? For he passys hys posytiue
degre w^t þi(s) aduerbe *magis*, and hys Englysch endys in '-vr' as
'whyttur', 'blakyr', þat ys to say 'whyttyr: more whyt',
'blaker: more blak'. How knos þu þe superlatyue degre?[4]
For he passys hys posytyue degre w^t þis aduerbe *maxime*, and hys
Englysch endys in '-ist', as 'wyttyst', 'blakyst', þat ys to say
'wytyst: most wyt', 'blakyst: most blak'.

How mony gendyrs of nownus byn þer? VII. Qwech vij?

---

[1] MS nowmbys [2] 3 *canc*. [3] -n *from* m
[4] MS dregre

ACCEDENCE TEXT A

Þe masculyn, þe femyn, þe neuter, þe comyn of ij, þe comyn of
iij, þe dubyn and þe epycyn. How knos þu þe masculyn gendyr? 40
For hyt ys declynyt w^t *hyc* as *hyc maijster*. How knos þu þe
femyn gendyr? For hyt ys declynet w^t *hec* as *hec musa*. How
knos þe neuter gendyr? For hyt declynyt w^t *hoc* as *hoc scamnum*.
How knos þu þe comyn of ij gendyrs? For hyt declynyt w^t *hic*
and *hec* as nominatiuo *hic et hec sacerdos*. How knos þe comyn
of iij gendyrs? For hyt declynyt w^t *hic* and *hec* | and *hoc* as
nominatiuo *hic et hec et hoc felix*. How knos þu dubyn gendyr?
For hyt ys declynyt w^t *hic* and *hec* and a *vel* coniunccion comyng
bytwene as *hic vel hec dies*, for 'a day'. How knos þu þe
epycyn gendyr? For[1] vndyr on voyse and vndyr on articull he 50
comprehendys boþe þe male and þe female as *hic passer* for 'a
sparo' both þe he and þe hoo.

How mony nowmbyrs byn þer? II. Wech ij? Þe singuler
and þe plurell. How knos þu þe singuler nowmbyr? For he
spekys but of on thyng as 'mayster'. How knos þu þe plurell
nowmbyr? For he spekys of mo thyngus þe of on as 'maysters'.

How mony casus byn þer? VI. Wech vj? Þe nominatiue,
þe genytiue, þe datiue,[2] þe accusatiue, þe vocatiue and þe
ablatiue. How knos þu þe nominatiue case? For he comys
byfor þe verbe of serten person and certayn nowmbyr and may
vnsware to þi question 'wo or wat?'. How knos þu þe genytiue 60
case? For 'of' aftyr a nowne substantiue, verbe substantiue,
partitiue or distributyue, or superlatiue degre ys þe sygn[3] of
þe genytiue case; and also wen ij nownus substantiuis comyn
togedyr and þe ton be hauer of þe todyr þe hauer schall be þe
genitiue case. How knos þu þe datiue case? For 'to' befor
a nowne or a pronowne w^{t}out a preposicion ys þe syne of þe
datiue case. How knos þu þe accusatiue case? For þat casuell
word þat comys next aftyr þe[4] verbe transitiue, ⌈gerundyue⌉,[5]
partycipull or supyn most comynly schall be ⌈set in⌉[5] þe
accusatiue case. How knos þu þe vocatiue case? For he 70
clepus or callys ⌈or spekys to⌉[5]. How knos þu þe ablatiue case?
By my synys. Wych byn þi synus? 'Of' aftyr a nowne adie(c)tiue,
verbe adiectiue, gerundyue, partycypull or[6] supyn; 'throgh'
and 'w^t', 'fro', 'w^{t}out', 'then' and 'by' aftyr a comparaty(u)e
degre. 'In' w^{t}out 'to' ys þe syne of þe ablatiue case, and
wen 'in' and 'to' comyn togedyr hyt ys þe syne of þe accusatiue
case.

How mony declynsons of nownus byn þer? V. Wech v?
Þe fyrst, þe secund, þe iij, þe iiij, þe v. How knos þu þe
fyrst declynson of nownus? Þat ys of þe wech þe genitiue 80
and datiue case singuler, þe nominatiue and þe wocatiue plurell
endyn in -*e*; þe accusatiue in -*am*; þe accusatiue neuter as þe
nominatiue; wen þe nominatiue endys in -*a* or in -*am* þe
vocatiue schall be lyk hym, wen þe nominatiue endys in -*as* þe

---

[1] hyt ys declynyt wt *canc*. [2] MS da^i. *This form of abbreviation is frequent in the texts*. [3] MS syng
[4] MS þer [5] *Insertions in a lighter brown ink and a different hand*. [6] MS of

ACCEDENCE TEXT A

vocatiue schall end in -*a*; þe ablatiue in -*a* and oþer wyle in
-*am*; þe genitiue case plurell in -*arum*; þe datiue and þe
ablatiue in -*is* and oþer wyl in -*abus*; þe accusatiue in -*as*,
yf hyt be neuter in -*a*.

How knos þu secund declynson of nownus? Þat ys of þe
wech þe genitiue case singule(r) endis in -*i*; þe datiue and þe   90
ablatiue in -*o*; þe accusatiue in -*vm*; þe accusatiue neuter as
þe nominatiue; wen þe nominatiue (endys) in -*r* or in -*vm* þe
vocatiue schall be lyk hym, wen þe nominatiue endus in -*vs* þe
vocatiue schall end in -*e*, wen þe nominatiue endys in -*ius* yf
hyt be a propur name of a man þe vocatiue schall ende in -*i*,
þe nominatiue and þe vocatiue plurell in -*i* yf hyt be <nott a
man>; þe genitiue in -*orum*; þe | datyue and þe ablatiue in
-*is*; þe accusatiue in -*os*, yf hyt be neuter in -*a*.

How knos þu þe þryd[1] declynson of[2] nownus? Þat ys[3] of
þe wych þe genitiue case singuler endys in -*is*; þe datyue in   100
-*i*; þe accusatyue in -*em* or in -*im*; þe accusatiue neuter as
þe nominatiue; þe vocatiue schall be lyk þe nominatyue, þe
ablatiue in -*e* or in -*i*; þe nominatiue, þe accusatyue, þe
vocatiue case plurell in -*es*, yf þay be neuter in -*a*; þe
genitiue plurel in -*vm* or in -*ium*; þe datiue and þe ablatiue
in -*bus*.

How knos þe iiij declynson of nownus? Þat ys of þe wych
þe genitiue case singuler endys in -*vs*; þe datyue in -*vj*; þe
accusatiue in -*vm*; þe accusatiue neuter as þe nominatiue; þe
vocatiue schall be lyk þe nominatiue; þe ablatyue in -*v*; þe   110
nominatyue, þe accusatiue and þe vocatyue plurell in -*vs*, yf
þay be neutyr in -*a*; þe genitiue plurell in -*vum*; þe datiue
and þe ablatiue in -*ibus*.[4]

How knos þu þe v decly(n)son of nownus? Þat ys of þe wech
þe genitiue and þe datyue singuler endyn in -*ei*; þe accusatyue
in -*em*; þe vocatiue schall be lyk þe nominatiue; þe ablatiue
in -*e*; þe[5] nominatyue, þe[6] accusatyue, þe vocatyue plurell in
-*es*; þe genitiue plurell in -*erum*; þe datyue and þe ablatyue
in -*ebus*.

How knos þu a pronown? A pronowne ys a party of spech   120
þe wych ys set for a mon and resayuys certayn person and certen
nowmbyr. How mony pronownus byn þer? XV. Wech xv? *Ego*,
tu, *sui*, *ille*, *ipse*, *iste*, *hic* and *hijs*, *meus*, *tuus*, *suus*, *noster*
and *vester*, *nostras* and *vestras*. How mony byn primatyuis and
how mony byn dyriuatyuis? VIII by primatyuis and vij byn
dyriuatyuis. Wech viij byn primatyuis? *Ego*, *tu*, *sui*, *ille*,
ipse, *iste*, *hyc* and *hijs*. Wych vij byn dyryuatyuis? *Meus*, *tuus*,
suus, *noster* and *vester*, *nostras* and *vestras*. Why byn þay cald
primatyuis? For þay takyn hor bygynyng of no[7] oþer. Why by
þay[8] callyd dyryuatyuis? For þay takyn hor bygynyng of sum   130

---

[1] i- *canc.*   [2] *repeated*   [3] *of canc.*
[4] MS vbus   [5] *genitiui canc.*   [6] *genitiui canc.*
[7] -þ *canc.*   [8] *ℓ canc.*

ACCEDENCE TEXT A

oþer.

How mony¹ thyngus longon to a pronowne? VI. Qwech vj?
Qualite, gendyr, nowmbyr, figur, person and case. How mony
qualites of pronownus byn þer? II. Wych? A certayn and a
uncertayne. How knos þu a certayne qualite? A property by
þe wech me knos wedyr a pronowne ys of certayn person, as *ego*.
How knos þu a uncertayn qualite? A property by þe wech me knos
wedyr a pronowne² be of vncertayne person, as *ille*. How mony
gendyrs of pronowns byn þer? V. Wech v? Þe masculyn as
(*hic*), þe femyn as *hec*, þe neuter as *hoc*, þe comyn of ij as   *140*
hyc et hec nostras, þe comyn of iij as *ego, tu, sui*. How mony
persons of pronowns byn þer? III. Wech iij? Þe fyrst, þe
secund, þe iij. How knos þe fyrst person? For (he spekys)
of hymself, as *ego*. How knos þu þe secund person? For he
spekys to a noþer, as *tu*. How knos þu þe iij person? For
spekys of a noþer, as *ille*.

How mony declynsons³ of pronownus byn þer? IIII. Wech
iiij? Þe fyrst, | þe secund, þe iij, þe iiij. How knos þu
þe fyrst declynson of pronownus? Þat ys of þe wych þe genitiue
case singuler endys in -*i* and in -*is*, and þe datiue in -*i*.   *150*
How many pronowns has he? *Ego, tu, sui*. How knos þu þe ij
declynso(n) of pronownus? Þat ys of þe wech þe genitiue case
singuler endys in⁴ -*ius* and in -*ius*, þe datyue in -*i* or in -*c*.
How many pronownus has he? V. Quech v? *Ille, ipse, iste,
hic* and *hijs*; and viij nownus wᵗ hor compowndus, þat ys to say
vnus, vllus, totus, solus, alter, alius, quis et *vter*. How
knos þu þe iij declynson of pronownus? For þe genetiue case
singuler endys in -*i*⁵ or in -*e* and in -*i*, þe datiue in -*o*⁶ and
in -*e* and in -*o*. How mony pronownus has he? V. Wech v?
Meus, tuus, suus, noster and *vester*. How knos þu þe iiij   *160*
declynson of pronownus? For þe genytiue case singuler endys
in -*atis*, þe datiue in -*ati*. How mony pronownus byn þerof?
II. Wech ij? *Nostras* and *vestras*, and on nown, þat ys to say
cuias, -atis, -ati.

How knos þu a verbe? A party of spech þat ys declynet
wᵗ mod and tens, wᵗout case or articull, and betokyns 'ᶠto' do'
or 'to suffur' or 'to be'. How mony thyngus longon to a verbe?
VI. Wych vj? Mod, coniugacion, gendyr, nowmbyr,⁷ fygur, tyme
and person. How (mony) modys byn þer? V. Whech v? Þe
indicatiue, þe imperatiue, þe optatiue, þe coniunctiue an þe   *170*
infenytyue. How knos þu þe indicatiue mod? For he tellys
or askys. How knos þu þe imperatiue mod? For he byddus or
comawyndys. How knos þu optatiue mod? For he wylnys or
desyrus, and by þes iiij Latyn wordys *vtinam, ne, quatynus*
and *o si*. 'Wold' or 'schuld' schall serue to þe optatiue mod.
How knos þu þe coniunctiue mod? For he ioynus ij resons togedyr in on mater; and by þes viij Enghysch⁸ wordys 'yf',
'but', 'wen', 'wosumevyr', 'thagh', 'tyl' or 'aftyr' or 'euyr'

¹ -n- *from* y   ² pron- *from* prop-   ³ MS declynsonsons
⁴ MS *adds* Iu   ⁵ MS in   ⁶ in *canc.*
⁷ MS nownbyr   ⁸ *sic* MS

ACCEDENCE TEXT A

wyll serue to þe¹ coniunctyue mode. How knos þu þe infenytyue
mod? For 'to' before a verbe ys þe syne of þe infenytyue mode; 180
and also wen ij verbus² comyn togedyr wᵗout³ a relatyue or a
coniunccion betwene, þe latyr schall be þe infenytyue mode.

How mony coniugacionis byn þer? IIII. Wych iiij? Þe
fyrst, þe secund, þe iij, þe iiij. How knos þu þe fyrst
coniugacion? For hit has A long befor þis lettyr S or þis
sillabull -*ris* or -*re* in þe secund person singuler nowmbur
presentens of þe indycatyue mod, as *amas*, -*aris* vel -*are*.
How knos þu ij coniugacion? For hyt has E long before þis
lettyr S or <þis> sillabull -*ris* or -*re* in þe ij person singuler
nowmbur presentens of þe indicatiue mode, as *doces*, -*ceris* vel 190
docere. How knos þu þe iij coniugacion? For he (has) I |
schort by þis lettyr S or þis sillabull -*ris* or -*re* in þe secund
person singuler nowmbur presentens of þe indicatiue mod, as
legis, *legeris* vel -*re*. How knos þu þe iiij coniugacion?
For hyt ha(s) I long before þis lettyr S or þis sillabull -*ris*
or -*re* in þe ij person singuler nowmbyr presentens of indicatyue
mod, as *audis*, -*diris*⁴ vel -*re*.

How many gendyrs of verbys byn þer? V. Qwech v? Þe
acty(u)e, þe passyue, þe neuter, þe comyn and þe deponent.
How knos þu a uerbe actiue? For hyt endys in -*o* and may tak 200
-*r* apon O and mak of hym a passyue, as *amo*, *amor*. How knos
þu a verbe passyue? For he endys⁵ in -*r* and may do away þis
lettyr R and turne into hys actyue, as *amor*, *amo*. How knos
þu a verbe neuter? For he⁶ endys in -*o*⁷ and yf he tak R apon
-*o* yt ys no Latyn, as *sto*, *curo*. How knos þu a uerbe comyn?
For he has þe letter of þe passyue and þe signific(ac)ion
of þe actyue. How knos þu a uerbe depone(n)t? For he has
þe lettyr of þe passyue and þe significacion of þe actyue and
þe passyue boþe How many verbys comyn⁸ byn þer? All þat
byn contenyt in þe versus. Vnde versus: 210

> *Largior*, *experior*, *veneror*, *moror*, *osculor*, *hortor*,
> *Criminor*, *amplector* tibi sunt communia lector;
> Si bene conumeres, *interpretor*,⁹ *hospitor* addes.

How many tensus of verbys byn þer? V. Quech v? Þe
presentens, þe preterinperfitens, þe preterperfitens, þe
preterpluperfitens and þe futertens. How knos þu þe presentens?
For he spekys of þe tyme þat ys now. How knos þu þe
preterinperfitens? For he spekys of þe tym þat ys lytyll agon,
and comys wᵗ noþer of þe synes 'haue' ne 'had'. How knos þu
þe preterperfitens? For he spekys of þe tym þat ys perfytely 220
past, and comys wᵗ syne 'haue'. How knos þu þe preterpluperfitens? For he spekys of þe tym þat ys more þen
perfytly past, and comes wᵗ þis syne 'had'. How knos þu þe
futur tens? For he spekys of þe tym þat ys to com, and comys

---

¹ to þe] *repeated*   ² w- *canc*.   ³ a- *canc. before*
-out   ⁴ MS dire   ⁵ and *canc*.
⁶ *repeated*   ⁷ y *canc*.   ⁸ MS comys
⁹ MS interp⁽re⁾⁽:e⁾⁽i⁾tor

ACCEDENCE TEXT A

w^t þis syn 'schall'.

How knos þu aduerbe? A party of spech þat ys vndeclynyt,
þe wych ys cast to a verbe to declare and fulfyll þe
sygnific(ac)ion of þe verbe. How mony thyngus longon an
aduerbe? III. Wych? Significacion, comparyson and figur.
Aduerbs þat comyn of now(n)us adiectyuis of þe ij declynson   230
byn fowrmyt of þe datyue case singuler be chongyng of -o in -e
a(s) *docto*, *-te*; *doctissimo*, *-me*; *claro*, *-re*; *clarissimo*, *-me*.
Aduerbs þat comyn of nownus adiectyus of þe iij declynson byn
fowrmyt on þis maner of wyse. Yf þe nominatiue case singuler
end in *-ns* þay schall be fowrmyt of þe genitiue^1 singuler be
chongyng of *-tis* into *-ter*, as *sapientis*, *-ter*; *prudentis*, *-ter*.
All oþer takyn *-ter* in þe datiue case singuler, as *forti*, *-titer*;
veloci, *-ter*. |

How knos þu a partycypul? A party of spech þat^2 ys
declynet w^t case and articull and betokyns 'to do' or 'to suffyr' 240
or 'to be' as a verbe. How mony thyngus longon to a partycypull?
VI. Wech vj? Gendyr, case, tym, significacion, nowmbyr and
fygur. How mony gendyrs of partycypuls? IIII. Wech iiij?
Þe masculyn as *hyc lectus*, þe femyn as *hec lecta*, þe neuter as
hoc lectum, þe comyn of iij as *hic, hec, hoc legens*. How mony
tens of partycipuls byn þer? III. Wech iij? A partycypull
of þe presentens, a partycipull of þe^3 pretertens, (a partycypull
of þe futur tens and) a noþer of þe futur tens.

How knos þu a partycypull of þe presentens? By my Englysch
and by my Latyn. How by þi Englysch and how by þi Latyn?   250
Wen my Englysch endys^4 w^t '-yng' and my Latyn endys in *-ens* or
in *-ans* I schall haue a partycipull of þe presentens, as *amans*:
'louyng'; *docens*: 'techyng'. Wereof schall he be fowrmyt?
Of þe fyrst^5 person, singuler nowmbyr, preterinperfitens of þe
indicatyue mode, be chongyng of *-bam* into *N* and *S* as *amabam*,
chong *-bam* into *N* and *S* and then hyt wyll be *amans*, *docebam*,
chong *-bam* into *N*^{6} and *S* and þen hyt wyll be *docens*.

How knos þu a partycypull of þe pretertens? By my
Englysch and by my Latyn. How by þi Englysch and how by þi
Latyn? My Englysch schall bygyn w^t 'I' and my Latyn schall end   260
in *-tus* or in *-sus*, as *amatus*: 'i-louyt', *doctus*: 'i-taght'.
Of whom schall he be fowrmyt? Of^7 þe latyr supyn^8 be putyng
to þis lettyr *S* as *amatum*, *-tu*, put (to) þis letter *S* and hyt
wyll (be) *amatus*, *-ta*, *-tum*; *doctum*, *-tu*, put to þis lettyr
S and hyt wyll be *doctus*, *-a*, *-tum*.

How <knos þu a party>cypull of þe futur tens in *-rus*?
By my Englysh^9 and by my Latyn. How by þi Englisch and how
by þi Latyn?^{10} My Englysch schall bygyne w^{t11} 'to' and my Latyn
schall end in *-rus*, as *amaturus*: 'to luff'; *docturus*: 'to tech'.

^{1} *from* datyue ^{2} *-i prob. canc.* ^{3} futurt *canc.*
^{4} MS bygynus ^{5} supyn *canc.* ^{6} MS S
^{7} *repeated* ^{8} -n *from* m ^{9} -s- *from* g
^{10} bi *canc.* ^{11} to *and canc.*

ACCEDENCE TEXT A

Wereof schall he be fowrnyt? Of þe latyr supyn be[1] puttyng
to þis sillabull -*rus* as *amatum*, -*tu*[2], put to þis sillabull
-*rus* and þen hyt wyll be *amaturus* -*ra*, -*rum*; *doctum*, -*tu*,
put to þis sillabull -*rus* þen hyt wyll be *docturus*, -*ra*, -*rum*.
How knos a partycypull of þe last futur tens? By my Englysch
and by my Latyn. How by þi Englysch and how by þi Latyn?
My Englysch bygynys w^t 'to' and 'be' and my Latyn endys in
-*dus*, as *amandus*: 'to be louyt'; *docendus*: 'to be taght'.
Wereof schall he be fowrmyt? Of þe genitiue case singuler of
a partycypull of þe presentens be chongyng of -*tis* into -*dus*,
as nominatiuo *hic*, *hec*, *hoc*[3]*amans*, genitiuo *hui(u)s* -*tis*, chong
-*tis* into -*dus* and þen wyll hit (be) *amandus*, -*da*, -*dum*; *hic*,
hec, *hoc docens*, genitiuo *huius* -*tis*, chong -*tis* into -*dus*
and þen wyll hit | be *docendus*, -*da*, -*dum*.

    How many partycypuls longon to a uerbe actyue? II.
Wech ij? A partycypull of þe presentens in -*ens* or in -*ans*,
a partycypull of[4] þe futur in[5] -*rus*, as *amans*, *amaturus*. How
mony partycypuls longon to a verbe passyue? II. Wech ij? A[6]
partycipull of þe pretertens in -*tus* or in -*sus* and a futur
in -*dus*, as *amatus*, -*dus*. How many partycypuls longon to a
verbe neuter. II, as to an actyue. Wych ij? A partycypull
of þe presentens in -*ens* or in -*ans* and a futur in -*rus*, as *stans*,
staturus.[7] How many partycypuls longon to a uerbe deponent?
III. Wech iij? A partycyp(u)ll of þe presentens in -*ens* or in
-*ans* and a preter in -*tus* or in -*sus* and a futur in -*rus*, as
loquens, *loquutus*, *loquuturus*. How many particypuls longon to
a verbe comyne? IIII. Wech iiij? A partycypull of þe
presentens in -*ens* or in -*ans* and a preter in -*tus* or in -*sus*
and a futur in -*rus*[8] and a noþer in -*dus*, as *criminans*, -*atus*,
-*turus*, -*andus*. How many endyngus of partycipuls by þer?
VI. Wech vj? -*Ens*, -*a(n)s*, -*tus*,[9] -*sus*, -*rus*, -*dus*. Versus:

    -*Ens*, -*ans* presentis semper dic temporis esse;
    -*Tus*, -*sus* preteriti; -*rus*, -*dus* dic esse futuri;
    -*Ens*, -*ans*, -*rus* et agunt, -*tus*, -*sus*, -*dus* compaciuntur.

    How knos a coniunccion? A party of spech þat ys vndeclynet
and ionys oþer partys of spechys togedyr. How mony thyngus
longon to a coniunccion? III. Wech iij? Powere, fygur and
ordyr. <How mon>y powers of coniunccion byn þer? V. Wech v?
Sum be[10] copulatyuis, sum byn <disiunctiuis, sum> byn explatyuis,[11]
sum casuels and sum racionels.

    How knos þu a preposicion? A party of spech þe wech ys
vndeclynet and ys set before oþer partys of spechys togedyr in
apposicion and composicion. How many thyngus longon to a
preposicion? On. Wych? Case allon. How many casus wyl
he serue to? II. Wech ij? Þe accusatiue and þe ablatiue.
Wych byn þe preposicions þat wyll serue to þe accusatiue case?

270

280

290

300

310

---

[1] *l canc.*
[2] *l canc.*
[3] ara *canc.*
[4] MS or
[5] Ius *canc.*
[6] -s *canc.*
[7] MS stuturus
[8] MS Ius
[9] d *canc.*
[10] þer *canc.*
[11] MS adds sum explatyuis

ACCEDENCE TEXT A

All þat byn contenyt in þis leson of þe 'Donet': 'Da preposiciones¹ casus accusatiui, vt *ad, apud,* et cetera'. Wych by þe preposycions þat wyll serue to ablatiue case? All þat byn contenyt in þis lesson of þe 'Donet': 'Da preposiciones casus ablatiui, vt *a, ab, abs,* et cetera'. Wych byn þe preposycions þat wyll serue to boþe? All þat by co(n)tenet in þis lesson of þe 'Donet': 'Da vtriusque casus preposiciones, et cetera'. 320

How knos þu an interieccion? A party of spech þat ys vndeclynet² þe wech betokyns passion of a monus sole w^t a imperfyt³ voyse, as 'fy', 'out', 'alas' and 'waylaway'. How mony thyngus longon to a⁴ interieccion? On. Wych on? Significacion allon. How mony significacionus of interieccions byn (þer)? IIII. Wych iiij? Sum betokyns ioy, | sum betokyns so(row), sum wondyr and sum betokyns drede. 330

How mony concordys in gramer byn þer? V. Quech v? Þe⁵ fyrst betwene þe nominatiue case and þe verbe, þe secund betwene þe adiectyue and þe substantyue, þe iij betwene þe relatyue and þe antycedens, þe iiij betwen þe nowne partytyue and þe genitiue case þat folus, þe v betwene þe superlatyue degre and þe genitiue case þat folus. In how mony schall þe nominatyue case and þe verbe acord? In ij. Wech ij? Nowmbyr and person. In how mony schall þe nowne adiectyue and þe substantyue acord? In iij. Wech iij? Case, gendyr and nowmbyr. In how mony schall (þe) relatyue and þe antycedens acord? In iiij. Wech iij? Ge(n)dyr, nowmbyr⁶ and person. In how mony schall þe nowne partytiue and þe genytyue case þat folus acord? In on. Wech on? Gendyr allon. In how mony schall þe superlatyue degre and þe genytyue case þat folus acorde? In on. Wech on? Gendyr alon, et cetera. 340

Explicit expliciunt, ludere scriptor eat.⁷

---

¹ pre- *from* pro- ² MS declynet ³ w *canc.*
⁴ coniunccion on *canc.* ⁵ *from* þer ⁶ MS nownbyr
⁷ The *explicit* tag is in darker ink.

ACCEDENCE TEXT B

B. Aberystwyth, N.L.W., MS Peniarth 356B, fols. 163^r, 165^r-167^v

(H)<o>w^1 many maners of speche byn þer? VIII. Whiche viii?
Noun, pronoun, verbe, aduerbe, participle, conunccion,
preposicion, interieccion. How many of þes byn declyned and
how many byn vndeclined? Foure byn declyned and iiij byn
vndeclyned. Whiche foure byn declyned? Noun, pronoun, verbe
and partycyple. Whiche foure byn vndeclyned? Aduerbe,
coniunccion, preposicion and interieccion. How many byn
declyned w^t case and how many w^{t}owte case? III w^t case and
on w^{t}owte case: verbe only.

How knowe ȝe a noun? For þe Laten of eny þyng ys^2 a noun.   10
How many maner nounys byn þer? II. Whiche ij? A noun
substantyf and a noun adiectyf. How knowe ȝe a noun substantyf?
For he^3 may be vnderstond by hymselfe and ys declyned in Latyn
w^t on article or w^t ij at þe moste: (w^t on article) as *hic
magister* for 'a master', or w^t ij at þe moste in on case as *hic
et hec sacerdos*. How knowe ȝe a noun adiectyf? For hit may
not be vnderstond by hitself w^{t}owte helpe of a noder word owte
sette or vnderstond, and is declyned in Latyn w^t iij articles or
w^t iij dyuers endynges in on case as 'wys' and 'good': *hic et
hec et hoc sapiens*, *bonus*, *-na*, *-num*. And euery noun þat may   20
receyue comparyson is a noun adiectyf, as *senex, senior, iuuenis,
iunior*. How many articles byn þer? III. Whiche iii? *Hic,
hec, hoc*.

How many þynges fallen to a noun? VI. Whiche vj? Qualite,
comparison, gender, noumber, figure and case. How ys þis verbe
accidunt^4 declyned? *Accido, -dis, accidi, -dere, -dendi, -do,
-dum, accidens*. Of whom ys þis verbe *accido* y-componed? Of þis
preposicion *ad* and þis verbe *cado* by changyng *D* into *C* and *A*
into *I*. Why lakethe þis verbe *accido* þe supines? For all þe
componys of þis verbe *cado*, *-dis* lacken þe supynes but *occido*,   30
-dis, þe whiche makethe *occasum, -su* and *recido, -dis* makyng
recasum, -su. Versus:

A *-cido*^{5} composita renuerunt cuncta supina;
Occidit, occasum prebet, *recido*que *recasum*.

What ys a qualite accidentall in a noun? A qualyte
accidentall in a noun ys a propurte to acorde to on þyng kyndely
all only, and so hyt is a propur qualite as *Petrus, Willelmus,
Iohannes*, or to many and þen hit is a comyn qualite as *homo*.

A text of the *Comparacio* is inserted at this point, instead of
the short passage on comparison, and this is given as text O below.
The section on the noun continues on fol. 165^r after a lacuna
caused by a lost folio.

...<How know ȝe þe secund clynson of novnys? For þe genetyf

---

^{1} (H) - *guide letter* ^{2} *repeated* ^{3} MS ȝe
^{4} de *canc.* ^{5} A -cido] MS accido

ACCEDENCE TEXT B

case singler endyth in -*i*, þe datyf and þe ablatyf in -*o*, þe 40
accusatyf in -*vm*, þe accusatyf neuter ⟩¹ ⟨ as þe nominatyf.
When þe nominatyf case singler endithe in -*r* or þe neuter gendyr
þe (vocatyf) shall be like hym. When þe nominatyf case endyth
in -*vs* þe vocatyf shall end in -*e*. When þe nominatyf case
endithe in -*ius* ʒif hit be a propur name of a man þe vocityf
shall end in -*i*; the nominatyf and þe vocatyf plurell in -*i*,
ʒif þey be nevter in -*a*; þe genetyf in -*orum*; þe datyf and þe
ablatyf in -*ys*, þe accusatyf in -*os*, ʒif hit be neuter in -*a*.
Et declinentur hec nomina: *hic caminus, hec corulus, hoc collum,
hoc pellagus,*² *hic Vergilius, hic Laurentius, hoc iuger(um),*³ 50
hic Theseus. How know ʒe þe þryd clynson? For þe genetyf
case endyth in -*is*; þe datyf in -*i*, þe accusatyf in -*em* or
in -*im*; þe accusatyf neuter as þe nominatyf; þe vocatyf shall
be like þe nominatyf; þe ablatyf in -*e* or in -*i*; þe nominatyf,
þe accusatyf and þe vocatyf plurell in -*es*, ʒif þey be neuter
in -*a*, þe genetyf in -*vm* or in -*ium*; þe datyf and þe ablatyf
in -*bus*. How know ʒe þe fourthe declynson of novnys? For þe
genetyf case singler endithe in -*vs*; þe daty(f) in -*vj*; þe
accusatyf in -*vm*; þe accusatyf nevter as þe nominatyf; þe
vocatyf shall be like þe nominatyf: þe ablatyf in -*v*; þe 60
nominatyf, þe accusatyf and þe vocatyf plurell in -*vs*, ʒif þey
be nevter in -*a*; þe genetyf in -*vum*; þe daty(f) and þe
ablatyf in -*bus*. Et declinentur hec nomina: *hic arcus, hec
acus*; *hoc cornu*. How know ʒe þe v clynson of novnys? For þe
genetyf and þe datyf case singler endyn in -*ey*; þe accusatyf
in -*em*; þe vocatyf shall be like þe nominatyf; þe ablatyf in
-*e*: the nominatyf, þe accusatyf and þe vocatyf plurell in -*es*;
þe genetyf in -*erum*⁷; þe datyf and þe ablatyf in -*ebus*.
Et declinentur hec nomina: *hic meridies, hec*⁴
spes. 70

(H)ow⁵ know ʒe a pronowne? A pronoun is a maner of speche
declyned wᵗ case, þe whiche is sette for a propur noun and
receyuethe certeyn person. How many þyngus longeth to a pronoun?⁶
VI. Whiche vj? Qualite, gendir, noumbre, figure, person
and case. How many pronouns byn þer? XV. Whiche xv?
Ego, tu, sui, ille, ipse, iste, hic and *is*; *meus, tuus, suus,
noster, vester, nostras* and *vestras*. How many of þes byn
primytyfes and how many dryuatyfes? VIII byn primatyfes and
vij byn dryuatyfes. Whiche viij byn primitifes? *Ego, tu,
sui, ille, ipse, iste, hic* and *is*. Whiche vij byn dryuatyfes? 80
Meus, tuus, suus, noster, vester, nostras and *vestras*. Whiche
of þes primytyfes byn only demonstratyfes and how many relatyfes,
and how many byn oder while demonstratyfes and oder while
relatyfes? Foure byn only demonstratyfes. Whiche foure?
Ego, tu, hic and *iste*. Whiche byn only relatyfes? II. Whiche
ij? *Is* and *sui*.⁸ Whiche ij byn oder while demonstratyfes and
oder while relatyfes? *Ille, ipse*. When byn þey relatyfes and
when byn þey demonstratyfes? When þey byn putte in þe fyrste
clause of a reson þat a man speketh þen (þey) byn demonstratyfes,

---

¹ *Supplied to complete the sense.*   ² MS *pullagus*
³ *dubious reading*   ⁴ *from* he   ⁵ (H)-*guide letter*
⁶ ii *canc.*   ⁷ MS *ejum*   ⁸ MS *sue*

ACCEDENCE TEXT B

as when y sey: *Ille vel ipse currit*; | and when þey byn sette¹ 90
in þe secund clavse of a reson þat a man speketh þen þey byn
relatyfes, vt: *Iohannes (currit) et ille vel ipse est fessus*.
Vnde versus:

    Tantum demonstrant *ego*, *tu* simul *hic* simul *iste*;
    Et tantum referunt, si discimus, *is*que suique;
    Nunc monstrant, referunt, si discimus, *ille* vel *ipse*.

How many pronovnys haue þe uocatyf case and how many lackyn?
IIII haue and all þe oder lacken. Whiche iiij haue? *Tu*,²
meus, *noster* and *nostras*. Vnde versus:

    Quatuor exceptis pronomina nulla vocabis;   100
    Tu, *meus* et *noster*, *nostras*: hec sola vocantur.

How many pronovnys byn possessyues? V. Whiche v? *Meus*,
tuus, *suus*, *noster* and *vester*. How many of þes dryuittyfes
betokeneth only folke? II. Which ij? *Nostras* and *vestras*.

How many persons byn þer? III. Which iiij? Þe fyrst,
þe ij, þe iij. How know ȝe þe first person? For hit spekyth
of hitselfe all only, and þen hit ys (singler as *ego*, or ellys
as 'we', and þen hit ys) plurell as *nos*. How know ȝe þe ij
person? For hit spekyth to a noder by hitself, and þen hit
ys singler as *tu*, or ellys as 'ȝe', and þen hit ys plurel as *vos*. 110
How know ȝe þe þryd person? For speche ys made þerof betwene þe
fyrst person and þe secund by³ hitself, and þen hit ys singler
as *ille*, or ellys wᵗ oder, and þen hit is plurel as *illi*; and
euery word þat (is) declyned wᵗ case is þryd person, oute-take
ego, *nos*, *tu* and *vos* and her obliyquis, and þe vocatyf case.

    Terne persone generaliter omnis habetur
    Rectus, sed demas pronomina quatuor inde.
    Ista vocant rectos ad primam siue secundam,
    Sunt *ego*, *nos* prime; *tu*, *vos* quoque sumpto⁴ secunde:
    Pauper ego ludo, dum tu diues meditaris;   120
    Nos tuti loquimur, dum vos timidi taciatis.

How many clynsons of pronouns byn þer? IIII. Whiche iiij?
The first, þe secund, þe iij, þe iiij. How know ȝe þe fyrst
clynson of pronouns? For þe genetyf case singler endith in *-i*
or in *-is*, and þe datyf in *-j*. How many pronouns byn þer of
þat declynson? III. Which þre? *Ego*, *tu*, *sui*. How know ȝe
þe secund clynson of pronouns? For þe genetyf case singler
endyth in *-jus* or in *-jus*, and þe datyf in *-j* or in *-c*⁵. How
many pronouns byn þer of þat clynson? V. Whiche v? *Ille*,
ipse, *iste*, *hic* and *is*, and viij nounys wᵗ her compnouns þe   130
whiche byn conteyned in þes versus. Vnde versus:

    Vnus et vllus, vter, alter,⁶ nullus quoque neuter,

---

¹ *-t canc.*   ² *-i canc.*   ³ *MS byn*
⁴ *dubious reading. MS sūpto*   ⁵ *from cc*
⁶ *MS alius*

ACCEDENCE TEXT B

Totus dant (in) *-ius* genitiuos[1] addis *alius*.

How many of þes haue þe vocatyf case and how many lakyn? III haue and all (þat oder lacken. Which iij haue) þe vocatyf case? Þat byn *totus*, *solus* and *vnus* and all þat oder lacken. Vnde versus:

> Pone vocatiuos cum *totus*, *solus* et *vnus*;
> Sed non in reliquis quorum geniti(u)us in *-ius*. |

How know ȝe þe þryd clynson of pronouns? For þe genetyf case singler endyth ⌈in *-e* and⌉ in *-i*, and þe datyf in *-o* and in *-e* (and) in *-o*. How many pronouns byn þer of þat declynson? V. Whiche v? *Meus*, *tuus*, *suus*, *noster* and *vester*. How know ȝe þe iiij declynson of pronov(n)ys? For þe genetyf[2] endyth in *-atis* and þe datyf in *-ati*. How many pronouns byn þer of þat declynson? II. Which ij? *Nostras* and *vestras*. How many pronouns byn of[3] þe fyrst declynson, how many of þe ij, how many of þe þryd, and how many of þe iiij? Pre of þe fyrst, v[4] of þe ij, v of þe iij, ij of þe iiij. Versus: 140

> Sunt tria prime, sed solummodo[5] quinque secunde; 150
> Tercia quinque tenet inflexio, sed duo quarta.

(H)ow[6] know ȝe a verbe? A verbe ys maner of spech þe whiche is declyned w[t] mod and tens w[t]owte case and article and betokeneth 'to do' or 'to suffer'. How many þyngus longyth to a verbe? VII. Which vij? Mode, coniugacion, gendir, noumbre, figure, tyns and person. Whereby know ȝe a verbe when hit betokeneth 'to do' and when hit betokenethe 'to suffur'? When y haue eny of þes vj wordys 'am', 'art', 'ys', 'was', 'were' or 'be' my verbe betokeneth 'to suffer', and when y haue non of hem my verbe betokeneth 'to do'. How many maners of verbys byn 160 þer? V. Whiche v? A verbe actyf, passyf, nevter, comyn and deponent. How know ȝe a verbe actyf? For hit endyth[7] in *-o* and ma(y) be construed w[t] on oblike case of a resonable þyng and may take R vppon O and make of hym a passyf as *amo*, *amor*. How know ȝe a verbe passyf? For hit endyth in *-r* and may do away his R and turne into his actyf. How know ȝe a verbe neuter? For hit endith in *-o*, and yf hit take R uppon O hit is no Latyn, as *sto*, *curro*. How know ȝe a verbe comyn?[8] For hit endyth in *-r* and comyth of no verbe endyng in *-o*, and betokenethe 'to do' and 'to suffer' in euery person and noumbere. 170 How many byn þer? VIII. Whiche viij? Patent per versus:

> *Largior*, *experior*, *veneror*, *moror*, *osculor*, *ortor*,
> *Criminor*, *amplector* tibi sunt communia lector;
> *Stipulor* adiunges; *interpretor*, *hospitor* addas.

How know ȝe a verbe deponent? For hit endith in *-r* and comyth of no verbe þat endyth in *-o*, and betokeneth only 'to do' or

---

[1] MS genitiǫ [2] gr canc. [3] repeated
[4] ij canc. [5] MS (?) i from *-o* [6] (H) *-guide letter*
[7] n- canc. [8] MS conyn

ACCEDENCE TEXT B

only 'to suffur' in þe fyrst person and þe secund.

How many modys byn þer? V. Whiche v? Indicatyf mode, imperatyf, optatyf, coniunctyf, infenytyf. How know ȝe þe indicatyf mode? For hit s(h)owethe a reson sothe or fals and betokeneth askyng or tellyng. How know ȝe imperatyf mode? For hit biddithe or commandyth. How know ȝe þe optatyf mode? For hit willythe or desyryth, and þes iij Latyn wordus *vtinam*, *ne* and *o si*, (and þes ii Englysse wordys) 'wold' and 'shold', seruyn to þe optatyf mode. How know ȝe þe coniunctyf mod? For hit ioyneth a noder verbe to hymselfe or hymselfe to a noder verbe, and þes viij Englysse wordys | 'ȝif', 'but', 'when', 'whosoeuer', 'ȝowȝte',[1] 'till', 'after', or 'euer' shall serue to þe coniunctyf mode; and þes Latyn wordys conteyned in þes versus seruyn to coniunctyf mode. Versus: *190*

180

> *Si, quamuis, quamquam, tametsi, licet* atque *priusquam,*
> *Antequam* et *donec, vt, postquam* siue *quousque,*[2]
> *Cum, nisi, quin, acsi, quo*[3] coniu(n)gunt, tibi dico.
> Indicat et *quando*, sic setera dic *aliquando*.

How know ȝe infenytyf mode? For when two verbes comyn togedder wᵗowte a relatyf or a coniunccion, þe later verbe shall be infenytyf mode; and 'to' before a verbe ys syne of infynytyf mode, as *Iohannes amat audire doctrinam magistri*. How many coniugacions byn þer? IIII. Whiche iiij? Þe fyrst, as *amo*, *amor*; þe ij, as *doceo*, *-ceor*; þe iij as *lego*, *-gor*; þe iiij   *200* as *audio*, *audior*. How know ȝe þe fyrste coniungacion? For hit hath *A* long before *-re* in þe infenytyf mode, as *amare*, or *A* long before *-ris* in þe secu(n)d person singuler noumbre present tens indicatyf mode, as *amaris*. How know ȝe þe secund coniugacion? For hit hath *E* long before *-re* in þe infenityf mode, as *docere*. How know ȝe þe iij coniugacion? For hit hathe *E* shorte before þe *-re* in þe infenityf, as *legere*. How know ȝe þe fourthe coniugacion? For hit hath *I* long before *-re* in þe infenityf mode, as *audire*.

How many tens byn þer? V. Whiche v? The present tens,   *210* preterinperfitens, preterperfite tens, preterpluperfyte tens and futur tens. How know ȝe þe present tens? For hit spekyth of tyme þat ys nowe, as 'y loue'. How know ȝe þe preterinperfites tens? For hit betokeneth tyme þat ys not fully agon wᵗowte þes synes 'haue' or 'hadde', as 'I loued'. How know ȝe þe preterperfite tens? For hit betokeneth tyme þat is fully agon wᵗ þis syne 'haue', as '(I) haue louyd'. How know ȝe þe preterpluperfite tens? For hit betokenet tyme þat is long ago wᵗ þis sine 'hadde', as 'I hadde louyd'.[4] How know ȝe þe futur tens? For hit betokeneth tyme þat is to come   *220* wᵗ þes synes 'shall' or 'shull', as 'y shall loue'.

How many tens byn formed of þe preterperfite tens,

---

[1] *sic* MS   [2] MS quousqua*m*   [3] MS que
[4] MS bouyd

ACCEDENCE TEXT B

indicatyf mode? VI. Which vj? The preterpluperfite tens
of indicatyf mode, as *amauy*: change *I* into *E* and sette þer-to
-ram and þen hit is *amaueram*. The preterpluperfite tens of
þe optatyf mode, as *amauy*: put þer-to *S* and *-sem* and þen hit
is *amauissem*. The preterperfyte tens[1] of coniunctyf mode, as
amauy: change *I* to *E* and put þer-to *-rim* and þen hit ys *amauerim*.
The preterpluperfite tens of þat same mode, as *amauy*[2]: put þer-
to *S* and *-sem* and þen hit is *amauyssem*. The futur tens of þat   230
same mode, as *amauy*: change *I* into *E* and put þer-to *-ro* and
þen hit is *amauero*. The preterpluperfite tens of infinytyf
mode, as *docui*: put þer-to *S* and *-se*[3] and þen hit *docuisse*.[3]
How many of þes change *I* into *E*? Þre. Whiche þre? Þe
preterpluperfite of indicatyf mode, þe preterperfitetens and
þe futur tens of coniunctyf mode, as *legi*: change *I* into *E* and
put þer to *-ram*, *-rim*, *-ro* and þen |

    A folio is missing at this point.

    ...to accusatyf case and when to ablatyf case? When 'in'
and 'to' conyn[4] togedder, þen þey shall serue to accusatyf case;
and when 'in' comyth wytoute 'to' hit will serue to ablatyf case. 240
Vnde versus:

    'Into' vult quartum, sine[5] 'to' vult possere sextum:
    In campo curro si sis, bene dicis, in illo.
    Si sis exterius *in campum* sit tibi cursus.

When will *super* serue to accusatyf case and when to ablatyf case?
When *super* betokeneth 'vppon' w^{t}[6] towchyng þat will serue to
accusatyf cas, as 'Appuls hongyn on þe tre', *Poma pendunt (super)
pomum*; and when *super* betokeneth 'vppon' w^{t}oute towchyng þen hit
will serue to ablatyf case, as 'Þu shall go on myn erand', *Tu
ibis super meo negocio*. Vnde versus: 250

    Quando *super* signat *in*, *de*, sexto societur;
    Sed quarto seruet aliter quocumque locetur.

When will þes iiij preposicions *in*, <*sub*>, *super* and *subter* serue
to accusatyf case and when to ablatyf case? When þey betokyn
mouyng þen[7] þey will serue to accusatyf, vt *Vado subter sepem*, and
when þe(y) betokyn no mouyng þ<en> þey will serue to ablatyf case,
as 'Þe sheperd lythe vnder þe fold', *Pastor jacet sub <sepe*[8]>.
Vnde versus:

    Construe cum quarto *super*, *in*, *sub*, *subter* eundo,
    Ast ablatiuis predatos[9] construe stando.   260

    (H)ow[10] know ȝe an interieccion? An interieccion ys a
party of speche vndeclyned þat betokeneth passion of soule w^{t}
an vnperfete voys. How many þyngus longyn to a interieccion?

[1] *g canc.*	[2] MS *amāy*	[3] MS *adds -m*
[4] *sic* MS	[5] MS *sūe*	[6] *owte canc.*
[7] from þey	[8] *dubious reading*	[9] MS *predatis;*
a letter canc.	[10] (H)- *guide letter*	

ACCEDENCE TEXT B

On. Whiche on? Significacion only. Wherein is þe sygnificacion
of interieccion? Som in sorow as <he>w, 'alas'; som in gladnes
as *ouge*, 'well þe be'; som in drede as *attat*, 'owte owte'; som
in wondyr as *pape*, 'lord mercy'; som indignacion as *jachasis*.

(H)ow[1] many (a)cordes of gramer byn þer? V. Whiche v?
Þe fyrst betwene þe nominatyf case and his verbe, the ij betwene
þe adiectyf and his substantyf, the iij betwene þe relatyf and   270
his anticedent, the iiij betwene þe no<un> par(ti)tyf, dystry(butyf)
and þe genetyf case þat foloweth, the v betwene þe superlatyf
degre and þe genetyf case þat foloweth.

In how many shall þe nominatyf case and his verbe be
acorde? In two. In which <two>? In numbre and person.
Exemplum as 'My felawe redyth his lesson', *Socius meus legit
leccionem suam.*

<Persona>, numero recto verbum sociato.

In how many s<hall> þe adiectyf and þe substantyf acorde?
In iij. In which iij? In case, gendyr and noumbre, as   280
'Þis man ʒeue (me) a f<ayr ʒifte>', *Iste homo dedit mihi pulcrum
donum.* Vnde versus:

In casu, genere, numero da mobile fyxo.

In how many shall þe relatyf and þe anticedens acorde?
In iij. In which iij? Gendyr, noumbre and person.
Exemplum: 'Thys bred ys <mowldy>, þe whiche ys made of whete',
Iste panis est mucidus qui sit de frumento. Versus:

In numero[2], genere, persona consimilatum
Cum precedenti[3] fore dic debere relatum.

In how many shall þe <noun parti>tyf and þe noun distributyf 290
and þe genetyf case þat foloweth acorde? In (on). In whiche
on? In gendyr al only. Exemplum: 'My fadyr ys on of
creaturis', *Pater meus est vna creaturarum.* Versus:

Concordans genere[4] fore cum casu genetiuo
Dic partitiuum, veliti *Venit vna*[5] *sororum.*

What y(s) a noun partityf? An adiectyf þat betokeneth party
as *vnus, alius, quidam, vter, alter, vterque.* |

In how many shall þe superlatyf degre and þe genetyf case
þat foloweth acorde? In on. In whiche on? In gendyr only.
ʒif so be þat he be taker of þe signi(fi)cacion of þe superlatyf   300
degre - þat is to say, when þe genetyf may be changyd into þe
same case þat þe superlatyf degre ys and þe superlatyf degre
into þe posityf by trewe sentence, as þus: 'The rose is fayryst
of flovrys', hit may be changyd þus and þe sentence trewe:

---

[1] (H)- *guide letter*   [2] MS *adds* no(?)   [3] MS precedendo
eñti   [4] MS genito   [5] sorum *canc.*

ACCEDENCE TEXT B

'Þe rose ys a feyre flovre' - ȝe may all wey chese, when þe
genetyf case ys taker of þe significacion of þe superlatyf degre,
whedur ȝe will þat he acorde w^t þe substantyf þat gothe before
or w^t þe genetyf case þat cometh after in gendyr, as *Rosa est
pul(c)errima vel pulcerimus florum, Deus est optima vel optimus*[1]
rerum, Frater meus est sapientissimus vel sapientissima   310
creaturarum. But when þe genetyf case is not taker of þe
signi(fi)cacion of þe superlatyf degre he shall acorde only w^t
þe substantyf þat gothe before, vt *Iohannes est fortissimus
istius societatis.* Vnde versus:[2]

   Omne superlatum partitiue recitatum
   Semper vult generi genitiui par retineri,
   Vt pateat verum, *Deus est* dic *optima rerum.*
   Imo superlatum propria vi quando locatur
   Per genus hoc fixo precedenti similetur,
   Naso dat verum: *Quid agis pulcerrima rerum.*   320

 The beginning of a text of the *Informacio* follows, which is
given as text U below.

---

[1] ·z· *canc.*   [2] MS *adds a scribble*

ACCEDENCE TEXT C

C. Cambridge, St. John's College, MS F.26 (163), fols. 1r-12r

How many partes ben þere of reson? VIII. Qwech viij?
Nown, pronown, verbe, aduerbe, participyl, coniunccyon,
preposicyon and interieccyon. ʳHow many be declynyd and how
many be vndeclynyd? IIII be declynyd and iiij be vndeclynyd.
Qwech iiij be declyned? Nown, pronown, verbe and participyl.
And qwech iiij be vndeclynyd? Aduerbe, coniunccyon,
preposicyon and interieccyonˀ.[1] How many be declyned wit case
and how many wᵗowte case? Thre be declyned wit case and on
wᵗowte case. Qweche thre be declyned wᵗ case? Nown, pronown,
and participyl. And qwo wᵗowte case? Al only verbe.   10

Qwerby knowyst a nown? For al thyng þat may be seen,
herd oþer felt or beryth þe name of a thyng is a nown. How
many maneer of nownys ben þere? To. Qweche to? Nown
substantyf and nown adiectyf. Qwerby knowe ȝe a nown substantyf?
For he may stonde in a perfyth reson wᵗowtyn helpe of a noþer
wurd, as 'man', 'tre' or 'beest', and is declinyd in Latyin wᵗ
on artikyl or too at þe moost in o case, as nominatiuo *hic
magister*, or nominatiuo *hic et hec sacerdos*. Qwerby krowyst
a nown adiectyf? For he may not stonde alone in a perfyth
reson wᵗowtyn help of a noþer wurd, as 'qwyt', 'red', 'blak',   20
and is declyned in Latyn wᵗ iij articulys or iij dyuerse
endynggis in o case, as nominatiuo *hic et hec et hoc felix*,
or nominatiuo *bonus, bona, bonum*. How many articulys ben þere?
III. Qwech iij? *Hic, hec, hoc*. How many diuerse endynggis
ben þere? III. Qwech iij? -*Vs*, -*a* and -*vm* or ellys -*or*, -*a*
and -*vm*.

Qwat is a conparison? A lyknesse of thynggis þat may be
mad more or lesse wᵗ good sentence. How many degrees of
comparison ben þere? Thre. Qwech iij? The posityf, þe
comparatyf and þe superlatyf. Qwerby knowyst þe posityf   30
degre? For he is ground of al oþer grees of comparison, as
'fayir', 'fowl' and soch oþer. Qwerʳbyˀ knowyst þe comparatyf
degre? For he passyth hys posityf wᵗ þis aduerbe 'more' or
'lesse' and endyth in Englysch in '-r', as 'fayrer', 'fowler'
and soch oþer. Qwerby knowyst þe superlatyf degre? For he
passyth hys posityf wᵗ þis aduerbe 'most' or 'lest' and endyth
in Englysch in '-est', as 'fayrest', 'fowlest' and soch oþer.
Wyt qwat case wele þe comparatyf degre construe? Wyt ablatyf
case of bothe nowmberis wᵗowtyn a preposicyon, as *forcior illo*
vel *forcyor illis*, saue if *quam* come betwyn; þanne cuppelyth   40
he lyke case. Wᵗ qwat case wele þe superlatyf degre construe?
Wᵗ þe genityf case plurer, as *dignissima creaturarum*, or wᵗ þe
genityf si(n)guler of a nown collectyf. How many nown collectiuys
be þer? It is schewyd be þe verse. Vnde versus:

Sunt collectiua *populus, gens, plebs* quoque *turba*.

How many genderys of nown ben þere? VII. Qwech vij?
The masculyn, þe femynyne, þe neuter, þe comown of to, þe

[1] *added at foot of page*

ACCEDENCE TEXT C

comown of thre, þe dubyn and epycene. Qwerby knowyst þe
masculyn gender? For it is declyned w^t *hic*,[1] as nominatiuo
hic magister.[2] Qwerby knowyst þe feminyne gender? For it is   50
declyned w^t *hec*, as nominatiuo *hec musa*. Qwerby knowyst þe
neuter gender? For it is declyned w^t *hoc*, as nominatiuo *hoc
scamnum*. Qwerby knowyst þe comun (of) to gender? For it is
declyned w^t *hic* and *hec*, as *hic et hec sacerdos*. Qwerby
knowyst þe comun of thre gender? For it is declyned w^t *hic,
hec* and *hoc*, as *hic et hec et hoc felix*. Qwerby knowyst þe
duby gendyr? For (it) is declyned wit *hic vel hec*, as *hic
vel hec dies*. How many nownys be þere of þis gender? It
schew^t be þe vers:

    *Margo die*sque, *silex, finis, clunis* quoque *cortex*:   60
    Hec veteres vere dubij generis posuere.
    Singula sunt dubij sed sunt pluralia primi. |

Qwerby knowyst þe epicene gendyr? For vndyr on artikyl be
comprehendyd bothe male and femal, as *hic passer* 'a sparow',
hec aquila 'an egyl', *hec muscela* 'a wesyl' and *hic miluus*
'a puttock'. And foure wurdys þat folwyn in þe verse þat
sewyth be epicene gender:

    *Dama*que *pantera, grus, bubo* sunt epicena.

How many nowmberys ben þere? To. Qwech to? Singuler
and plurer. Qwerby knowyst singuler nowmbyr? For he spekyth   70
but of o thyng, as 'man'. Qwerby knowyst plurer nowmbyr?[3]
For he spekyth of many thynggis, as 'men'.

How many casys be þere? VI. Qwech vj? The nominatyf,
þe genityf, þe datyf, þe accusatyf, þe vocatyf and þe ablatyf.
Qwerby knowyst þe nominatyf case? For he comth beforn þe
verbe and doth or sufferyth þe dede of þe verbe. Qwerby
knowyst þe genityf case? For 'of' aftyr a nown substantyf,
verbe substantyf, nown partityf, nown distributyf or a superlatyf
degre is þe syne of genityf case. Qwerby knowyst datyf case?
For ⌈'to'⌉ beforn a casual wurd w^{t}owtyn a preposicyon is syne 80
of datyf case. Qwerby knowyst accusatyf case? For he comth
⌈aftyr⌉ þe verbe, gerundyf, participyl or suppyn þat betokenyth
'to do' and sufferyth þe dede of þe verbe; and also alle þe
wurdys in 'Da preposiciones casus accusatiui' serue to þe
accusatyf case. Qwerby knowyst vocatyf case? For he betokenyth
preying, biddyng or callyng. Qwerby knowyst ablatyf case?
For 'in', 'wit', 'fro', 'beforn' and 'aftyr' and alle þe wurdys
in 'Da preposiciones casus ablatiui' ar þe synes of ablatyf;
and also 'of' aftyr a propyr name or a nown adiectyf or a verbe
adiectyf, gerundyf, participyl or suppyn is þe syne of ablatyf   90
case. Vnde versus:

    Mobile vel proprium vel participans quoque verbum

---

[1] artikyl or to at þe most in o case *canc*.
[2] or nominatiuo hic et hec sacerdos *canc*.
[3] plurer nowmbyr *canc*.

ACCEDENCE TEXT C

Si sequitur sensus genitiui iungito sextum;
Cum reliquis sextum non iungas sed genitiuum.

How many declensons be þer? V. Qwech v? The furst,
þe secunde, þe thrydde, þe fourt, þe fyfte. Qwerby knowyst
þe secunde declenson? For þe genityf case singuler endyth in
-i; þe datyf in -o; þe accusatyf in -vm; þe vocatyf schal
be lyke þe nominatyf, saue qwan þe nominatyf endyth in -vs þe
vocatyf most comunly schal endyn in -e as nominatiuo *hic dominus*,100
vocatiuo *o domine*,|and qwanne þe nominatyf singuler of a
propyr name endyth in -*ius* þe vocatyf schal endyn in -*i* as
nominatiuo *hic Laurencius*, vocatiuo *o Laurenti*; *Vincencius*,
Vincenti; *Gregorius*, *Gregori*; and *filius* makyth vocatiuo
o filie vel *fili*; also in a neutyr gender þe nominatyf, þe
accusatyf and þe vocatyf schal acorde; þe ablatyf schal endyn
in -o; þe nominatyf and þe vocatyf plurer in -i; þe genityf
in -*horum*; þe datyf and þe ablatyf in -is; þe accusatyf ⌈in
-os⌉; and in a neutyr gendyr þe nominatyf, þe accusatyf and
þe vocatyf schal endyn in -a.   110

Qwerby knowyst þe furst declension of nown? For þe
genityf case singuler endyth in -e; þe datyf also; þe accusatyf
in -am; þe vocatyf schal be lyke þe nominatyf, saue if þe
nominatyf ende in -as þe vocatyf schal endyn in -a as nominatiuo
hic Thomas, vocatiuo *o Thoma*; þe ablatyf in -a; þe nominatyf
and þe vocatyf plurer in -e; þe genityf in -*arum*; and datyf
and þe ablatyf in -is, saue if þe feminyne be drawe out of þe
masculyn as *domina* is drawyn out of *dominus*, þanne schall þat
feminyne make þe datyf and þe ablatyf plurer in -abus as *domina*,
dominabus; and in a neutyr gender þe nominatyf, þe accusatyf 120
and þe vocatyf acordyn; ⌈þe accusatyf in -as⌉.[1] How many
newtyr genderys be of þat declenson? It is schewyd be þe
vers þat folwyn:

Pascha, polenta, iota, zizannia, mammona, manna
Sunt neutri generis et declinacio prima.

Qwerby knowyst þe thrydde declenson? For þe genityf case
singuler endyth in -is; þe datyf in -i; þe accusatyf in -em
or in -im; þe vocatyf lyke þe nominatyf; and in a neutyr
gender þe nominatyf, þe accusatyf and þe vocatyf acordyn; þe
ablatyf in -a or in -i; þe nominatyf, ⌈þe accusatyf⌉ and þe   130
vocatyf plurer in -es; þe genityf in -vm or in -ium; þe datyf
in -bus; and in a neutyr gender þe nominatyf, þe accusatyf and
þe vocatyf in -a; and þe ablatyf in -bus.

Qwerby knowyst þe fourt declenson? For þe nominatyf,
genityf and vocatyf singuler endyn in -vs; þe datyf in -vi;
þe accusatyf in -vm; and þe ablatyf in -v; the nominatyf, þe
accusatyf and þe vocatyf plurer in -vs; þe genityf in -vum;
þe datyf and þe ablatyf in -bus.

Qwerby knowyst þe fyft declenson of nown? For þe genityf

---

[1] Insertion signalled to this point, although by sense it belongs five lines earlier.

ACCEDENCE TEXT C

and datyf singuler endyn in -*ei*; þe accusatyf in -*em*; þe   140
vocatyf lyke þe nominatyf; þe ablatyf in -*e*; þe nominatyf,
þe accusatyf and þe vocatyf plurer in -*es*; þe genityf in -*erum*;
þe datyf and þe ablatyf in -*ebus*.

Nominatiuo *hec musa*, genitiuo *huius muse*, datiuo *huic muse*,
accusativo *hanc musam*, vocatiuo *o musa*, ablatiuo *ab hac musa*;
et pluraliter nominatiuo *hee muse*, genitiuo *harum -sarum*,
datiuo *hijs -sis*, accusatiuo *has -sas*, vocatiuo *o -se*,
ablatiuo *ab hijs musis*.

Nominatiuo *hec domina*, genitiuo *huius domine*, datiuo *huic
domine*, accusatiuo *hanc dominam*, vocatiuo *o domina*, ablatiuo   150
ab hac domina; et pluraliter nominatiuo *hee domine*, genitiuo
harum -arum, datiuo *hijs -abus*, | accusatiuo *has dominas*,
vocatiuo *o domine*, ablatiuo *ab hijs dominabus*.

Nominatiuo *hic Thomas*, genitiuo *huius Thome*, datiuo *huic
Thome*, accusatiuo[1] *hanc Thomam*, vocatiuo *o Thoma*, ablatiuo *ab
hac Thoma*.

Nominatiuo *hic magister*, genitiuo *huius -tri*, datiuo *huic
-tro*, accusatiuo *hunc -trum*, vocatiuo *o magister*, ablatiuo
ab hoc -tro; et pluraliter nominatiuo *hij magistri*, genitiuo
horum magistrorum, datiuo *hijs -tris*, accusatiuo *hos -tros*,   160
vocatiuo *o -tri*, ablatiuo *ab hiis -tris*.

Nominatiuo *hic dominus*, genitiuo *huius -ni*, datiuo *huic -no*,
accusatiuo *hunc dominum*, vocatiuo *o domine*, ablatiuo *ab hoc
domino*; et pluraliter nominatiuo *hij domini*, genitiuo *horum
dominorum*, datiuo *hijs dominis*, accusatiuo *hos dominos*,
vocatiuo *o domini*, ablatiuo *ab hijs dominis*.

Nominatiuo *hic Laurencius*, genitiuo *huius -cij*, datiuo
huic -cio, accusatiuo *hunc -cium*, vocatiuo *o Laurenti*, ablatiuo
ab hoc Laurencio.

Nominatiuo *hoc scamnum*, genitiuo *huius -ni*, datiuo *huic -no*, 170
accusatiuo *hoc scamnum*, vocatiuo *o -num*, ablatiuo *ab hoc scamno*;
et pluraliter nominatiuo *hec scamna*, genitiuo *horum -norum*.
datiuo *hijs -nis*, accusatiuo *hec scamna*, vocatiuo *o scamna*,
ablatiuo *ab hijs scamnis*.

Nominatiuo *hic et hec sacerdos*, genitiuo *huius sacerdotis*,
datiuo *huic sacerdoti*, accusatiuo *hunc et hanc sacerdotem*,
vocatiuo *o sacerdos*, ablatiuo *ab hoc et ab hac sacerdote* vel
sacerdoti; et pluraliter nominatiuo *hij et hee sacerdotes*,
genitiuo *horum et harum -tum*, datiuo *hijs -tibus*, accusatiuo
hos et has -dotes, vocatiuo *o -dotes*, ablatiuo *ab hijs -tibus*. 180

Nominatiuo *hic et hec et hoc felix*, genitiuo *huius felicis*,
datiuo *huic -ci*, accusatiuo *hunc et hanc felicem* et *hoc felix*,
vocatiuo *o felix*, ablatiuo *ab hoc et ab hac* et *ab*[2] *hoc felice*

---

[1] -t- from s   [2] -b from d

ACCEDENCE TEXT C

vel *felici*; et pluraliter nominatiuo *hij et hee felices* et *hec felicia*, genitiuo *horum et harum et horum felicium*, datiuo *hijs fe⌈li⌉cibus*, accusatiuo *hos et has felices* et *hec felicia*, vocatiuo *o felices* et *o felicia*, ablatiuo *ab hijs felicibus*.

Nominatiuo *hec manus*, genitiuo *huius -nus*, datiuo *huic -vi*, accusatiuo *hanc manum*, vocatiuo *o -nus*, ablatiuo *ab hac -nu*; et pluraliter nominatiuo *hee[1] manus*, genitiuo *harum manuum*, datiuo *hijs manibus*, accusatiuo *has manus*, vocatiuo *o manus*, ablatiuo *ab hijs manibus*.

Nominatiuo *hec res*, genitiuo *huius rei*, datiuo *huic rei*, accusatiuo *hanc rem*, vocatiuo *o res*, ablatiuo *ab hac re*; et pluraliter nominatiuo *hee res*, genitiuo *harum rerum*, datiuo *hijs rebus*, accusatiuo *has res*, vocatiuo *o res*, ablatiuo *ab hijs rebus*.

Qwerby knowyst a pronown? For he is set for a nown and signyfyith neer a moche as a nown, and oþer qwyle receyuyth certeyne person. How many maneer pronownnys be þer? XV. Qwech xv? *Ego, tu, sui, ille, ipse, iste, hic* and *is, meus, tuus, suus, noster* and *vester, nostras* and *vestras*. How many of þeise be primityuys and how many be[2] deriuatiuys? VIII be primitiuys and vij be diriuatiuys. Qwech viij be primitiuys? *Ego, tu, sui, ille, ipse, iste, hic* and *hijs*. And qwy be þi primitiuys? For þei take here begynnyng of noon oþer. Qwech be diriuatiuys? *Meus, tuus, suus, noster* and *vester, nostras* and *vestras*. And qwy be þei callyd diriuatiuys? For þei take here begynnyng of oþer, as of *me* comth *meus*, of *tu* comth *tuus*, of *sui* comth *suus*,[3] of | *nos* comth *noster* and *nostras*, and of *vos* comth *vester* and *vestras*. How many of theyse haue vocatyf case and how many wantyn? Fowre haue vocatyf case and alle oþer wantyn. Qwech iiij haue vocatyf case? *Tu, meus, noster* and *nostras*. Vnde versus:

Quatuor exceptis pronomina nulla vocabis;
Tu, meus et *noster, nostras*: hec sola vocantur.

How many personys be þer? Thre. Qwech iij? Þe furst, þe secunde, þe thrydde. Qwerby knowyst þe furst persone? For he spekyth of hymself as 'I' and 'we'. Qwerby knowyst þe secunde persone? For he spekyth to oþer as 'þu' or '3e'. Qwerby knowyst þe thrydde persone? For he spekyth of oþer as 'he' and 'þei'; and euery nown and euery pronown and euery participyl is þe thrydde persone owtakyn 'I' and 'we', 'þu' and '3e', and þe vocatyf case. Vnde versus:

Terne persone generaliter omnis habetur
Rectus; set demas pronomina quatuor inde.

How many declensons of pronown be there? IIII. Qwech iiij? The furst, þe secunde, þe thrydde, þe fourt. Qwerby

---

[1] MS h̄ [2] MS de [3] MS suu*u*s

ACCEDENCE TEXT C

knowyst þe furst declenson of pronown?¹ For þe genityf case
singuler endyth in *-i* or in *-is*, and þe datyf in *-i*. How many
pronownys hath he? Thre. Qwech iij? *Ego, tu, sui*.
Qwerby knowyst þe secunde declenson of pronown? For þe
genityf case singuler endyth in *-ius* or in *-ius*, and þe datyf
in *-i* or in *-c*.² How many pronownys hath he? V. Qwech v?
Ille, ipse, iste, hic and *is*; and viij nownnys wit here
componys qwech be *vnus, vllus, totus, solus, alter, alius,
quis* and *uter*. How many of theyse nownys haue vocatyf case
and how many wantyn? Thre haue vocatyf case and alle oþer
wantyn. Qwech iij be þo? *Vnus, totus* and *solus*. Vnde
versus:

    Pone vocatiuos cum *totus, solus* et *vnus*,
    Sed non in reliquis quorum genitiuus in *-ius*.

Qwerby knowyst þe thrydde declenson of pronown? For þe genityf
case singuler endyth in *-i* in *-e* and in *-i*, and þe datyf in *-o*
and in *-e* and in *-o*. How many pronownys hath he? V. Qwech
v? *Meus, tuus, suus, noster* and *vester*; and note wel þat
alle nown adiectiuys þat be declyned w^t thre dyuerse endynggys
be declyned aftyr þis declenson. Qwerby knowyst þe fourt
declenson? For þe genityf case singuler endyth in *-atis* and
þe datyf in *-ati*. How many pronownys hath he? To. Qwech
to? *Nostras* and *vestras*; and a nown interrogatyf qwech is
cuias, cuiatis. Qwat is *cuias* in Englysch? 'Of qwat folk'.
Qwat is *cuium* in Englysch? 'Of qwat thyng'. Qwat is *nostras*
in Englysch? 'A man or a woman of owre cuntre', and *vestras*
is 'a man or a woman of ȝour cuntre'. Versus:

    Cuias de gente, *cuium* de re petit apte. |

A note at the foot of fol.3^r informs us that, 'The nownys of
þis part be in þe lef folwyng'; and at the foot of fol.3^v we
are told to 'Turne ouyr to þe next lef'. The text of fol.4^{r-v}
is accordingly inserted at this point.

    Nominatiuo *ego*, genitiuo *mei* vel *mis*, datiuo *mihi*,
accusatiuo *me*, vocatiuo caret, ablatiuo *a me*; et pluraliter
nominativo *nos*, genitiuo *nostrum* vel *nostri*, datiuo *nobis*,
accusatiuo *nos*, vocatiuo caret, ablatiuo *a nobis*.

    Nominatiuo *tu*, genitiuo *tui* vel *tis*, datiuo *tibi*, accusatiuo
te, vocatiuo *o tu*, ablatiuo *a te*; et pluraliter nominatiuo *vos*,
genitiuo *vestrum* vel *vestri*, datiuo *vobis*, accusatiuo *vos*,
vocatiuo *o vos*, ablatiuo *a vobis*.

    Nominatiuo caret, genitiuo *sui*, datiuo *sibi*, accusatiuo *se*,
vocatiuo caret, ablatiuo *a se*; et pluraliter nominatiuo caret,
genitiuo *sui*, et cetera.

    Nominatiuo *ille*, *-la*, *-lud*; genitiuo *illius*; datiuo *illi*;
accusatiuo *illum*, *-lam*, *-lud*; vocatiuo caret; ablatiuo *illo*,

¹ MS prononown   ² MS ? e

ACCEDENCE TEXT C

-la, -lo; et pluraliter nominatiuo *illi, -le, -la*; genitiuo   270
illorum, -larum, -lorum; datiuo *illis*: accusatiuo *illos, -las*,
-la; vocatiuo caret; ablatiuo *ab hijs illis*.

Nominatiuo *ipse, ipsa, ipsum*; genitiuo *ipsius*; datiuo *ipsi*;
accusatiuo *ipsum, -am, ipsum*; vocatiuo caret; ablatiuo *ipso*,
-a, -o; et pluraliter nominatiuo *ipse, -e, -a*; genitiuo
ipsorum, -arum, -orum; datiuo *ipsis*; accusatiuo *ipsos, ipsas*,
-a; vocatiuo caret; ablatiuo *ab hijs ipsis*.

Nominatiuo *iste, -ta, -tud*; genitiuo *istius*; datiuo *isti*;
accusatiuo *istum, -tam, -tud*; vocatiuo caret; ablatiuo *isto*,
ista, -to; et pluraliter nominatiuo *isti, -te, -ta*; genitiuo   280
istorum, -arum, -orum; datiuo *istis*; accusatiuo *istos, -tas*,
-ta; vocatiuo caret; ablatiuo *ab hijs istis*.

Nominatiuo *hic, hec, hoc*; genitiuo *huius*; datiuo *huic*;
accusatiuo *hunc, hanc, hoc*; vocatiuo caret; ablatiuo *ab hoc*
et *ab hac* et *ab hoc*; et pluraliter nominatiuo *hij, hee, hec*;
genitiuo *horum, harum, horum*; datiuo *hijs*; accusatiuo *hos*,
has, hec; vocatiuo caret; ablatiuo *ab hijs*.

Nominatiuo *is, ea, id*; genitiuo *eius*; datiuo *ei*;
accusatiuo *eum, eam, id*; vocatiuo caret; ablatiuo *eo, ea, eo*;
et pluraliter nominatiuo *ei, ee, ea*; genitiuo *eorum, earum*,   290
eorum; datiuo *eis*; accusatiuo *eos, eas, ea*, vocatiuo caret;
ablatiuo *ab hijs eis*.

Nominatiuo *quis* vel *qui, que* vel *qua, quod* vel *quid*;
genitiuo *cuius*; datiuo *cui*; accusatiuo *quem, quam, quod* vel
quid; vocatiuo caret; ablatiuo *quo, qua, quo* vel *a qui*; et
pluraliter nominatiuo *qui, que, que* vel *qua*; genitiuo *quorum*,
quarum, quorum; datiuo *quis* vel *quibus*; accusatiuo *quos, quas*,
que vel *qua*; vocatiuo caret; ablatiuo *a quis* vel *a quibus*.

Nominatiuo *quidam, quedam, quoddam* vel *quiddam*; genitiuo
cuiusdam; datiuo *cuidam*; accusatiuo *quemdam, quamdam, quoddam*   300
vel *quiddam*; vocatiuo caret; ablatiuo *quodam, quadam, quodam*;
et pluraliter nominatiuo *quidam, quedam, quadam*; genitiuo
quorundam, quarundam, quorundam; datiuo *quibusdam*; accusatiuo
quosdam, quasdam, quadam; vocatiuo caret; ablatiuo[1] *ab hijs*
quibusdam.

Nominatiuo *vnus, vna, vnum*; genitiuo *vnius*; datiuo *vni*;
accusatiuo *vnum, -am, -um*; vocatiuo caret; ablatiuo *vne, -a, -um*; ablatiuo
vno, -a, -o; and it hath no plurer nowmbyr.

Nominatiuo *vllus, -a, -um*; genitiuo *v(l)lius*; datiuo *vlli*;
accusatiuo *vllum, vllam, vllum*; vocatiuo caret; ablatiuo *vllo*,   310
vlla, vllo; et pluraliter nominatiuo *vlli, vlle, vlla*;
genitiuo *vllorum, vllarum, vllorum*; datiuo *vllis*; accusatiuo
vllos, vllas, vlla; vocatiuo caret; ablatiuo *ab vllis*.

---

[1] *repeated*

ACCEDENCE TEXT C

Nominatiuo *meus, -a, -um*; genitiuo *mei, mee, -ei*; datiuo *meo,-ee, -o*; accusatiuo *meum, -am, -um*; vocatiuo *mi, -ea, -um*; ablatiuo *meo, -a, -o*; et pluraliter nominatiuo *mei, -ee, -a*; genitiuo *meorum, -arum, -orum*; datiuo *meis*; accusatiuo *meos, -as, -a*; vocatiuo *mei, -ee, -a*; ablatiuo *ab hijs meis*.

Nominatiuo *tuus, tua, tuum*; genitiuo *tui, tue, tui*; 320
datiuo *tuo, tue, tuo*; accusatiuo *tuum, -am, -um*; vocatiuo caret; ablatiuo *tuo, -a, -o*; et pluraliter nominatiuo *tui, -e, -a*; genitiuo *tuorum, -arum, -orum*; datiuo *tuis*; accusatiuo *tuos, -as, -a*; vocatiuo caret; ablatiuo *ab hijs tuis*.

Nominatiuo *suus, -a, suum*; genitiuo *sui, sue, sui*; datiuo *suo, -e, suo*;[1] accusatiuo *suum, -am, -um*; vocatiuo caret; ablatiuo *suo, -a, -o*; et pluraliter nominatiuo *sui, -e, -a*; genitiuo *suorum, -arum, -orum*; datiuo *suis*; accusatiuo *suos, -as, -a*; vocatiuo caret; ablatiuo *ab hijs suis*. |

Nominatiuo *noster, nostra, nostrum*; genitiuo *nostri, -e, -tri*; datiuo *nostro, -e, -o*; accusatiuo *nostrum, -am, -um*; 330
vocatiuo[2] *noster, nostra, nostrum*; ablatiuo *nostro, -a, -o*; et pluraliter nominatiuo *nostri, -e, -a*; genitiuo *nostrorum, nostrarum, nostrorum*; datiuo *nostris*;[3] accusatiuo *nostros, nostras, nostra*; vocatiuo *nostri, nostre, -a*; ablatiuo *ab hijs nostris*.

Nominatiuo *vester, vestra, vestrum*; genitiuo *vestri, -e, -i*; datiuo *vestro, -e, -o*; accusatiuo *vestrum, -am, -um*; vocatiuo caret; ablatiuo *vestro, vestra, vestro*; et pluraliter nominatiuo *vestri, -e, -a*; genitiuo *vestrorum, -arum, -orum*; 340
datiuo *vestris*; accusatiuo *vestros, -as, vestra*; vocatiuo caret; ablatiuo *ab hijs vestris*.

Nominatiuo *hic et hec nostras*; genitiuo *huius nostratis*; datiuo *huic nostrati*; accusatiuo *hunc et hanc nostratem*; vocatiuo *o nostras*; ablatiuo *ab hoc et ab hac nostrate* vel *nostrati*; et pluraliter nominatiuo *hij et hee nostrates*; genitiuo *horum et harum nostratum*; datiuo *hijs nostratibus*; accusatiuo *hos et has nostrates*; vocatiuo *o nostrates*; ablatiuo *ab hijs nostratibus*.

Nominatiuo *hic et hec vestras*; genitiuo *huius vestratis*; 350
datiuo *huic vestrati*; accusatiuo *hunc et hanc vestratem*; vocatiuo caret; ablatiuo *ab hoc et ab hac -te* vel *-ti*; et pluraliter nominatiuo *hij et hee vestrates*; genitiuo *horum et harum -tum*; datiuo *hijs -tibus*; accusatiuo *hos et has vestrates*; vocatiuo caret; ablatiuo *ab hijs vestratibus*. |

Qwerby knowyst a verbe? For it is declyned w^t moodd and tens and persone and betokenyth 'to do' or 'to suffyr' or 'to be'. How many maneer of verbys ben þere? V. Qwech v? Verbe actyf, verbe passyf, verbe neutyr, verbe deponent and

---

[1] MS so   [2] caret ablatiuo *canc*.   [3] -i- from o

ACCEDENCE TEXT C

verbe comowne. Qwerby knowyst a verbe actyf? For it endyth in 360
-o and may take -r vpon O and make of hym a passyf, as *amo* put -r
þer-to and þanne is *amor*. Qwerby knowyst a verbe passyf? For it
endyth in -r and may do awey -r and turne aȝen into hys actyf.
Qwerby knowyst a verbe neuter? For he endyth in -o and may noon
-r take vpon O nor make of hym no passyf. Qwerby knowyst a verbe
neutyr-passyf? For he endyth in -o lyk an actyf and hath þe
Englysch of þe passyf, as *fio, fis, factus sum, fieri*: 'to be mad'.
Qwerby knowyst a verbe neutyr (e)normal? For he folwyth no ryth
rewle of coniugacyon; and vndyrstonde þat a verbe neutyr qwech
hath þe lettyr and þe significacyon of an actyf may haue a passyf 370
voys in þe thrydde persone, as 'Þe weye is ronnyn', *Via
curritur*. Vnde versus:

> Neutrum quod transit in rem sermone carentem
> Ternam passiuam de se dat progredientem.

Qwerby knowyst a verbe deponent? For he endyth in -r lyke a
passyf and hath þe Englysch of[1] an actyf, as *loquor*: 'I speke';
and in þe thrydde persone he may haue a passyf voys; as 'Þe
lond is eryid', *Terra aratur*. Vnde versus:

> Et deponencium passiuum dat documentum:
> Sic *Sermo fatur* dicas, vt *Campus aratur*. 380

Qwerby knowyst a verbe comun? For it hath lettyr of þe passyf
and Englysch bothe of þe actyf and of þe passyf,[2] as 'I kysse
þe'. *Osculor te*; 'And I am kyssyd of the', *Et osculor a te*.
How many verbe comons be þer? As many as be conteyned in þe
verse þat folwyn:

> *Largior, experior, veneror, moror, osculor, ortor,
> Criminor, amplector*, tibi sunt communia lector;
> Si bene connumeres, *interpretor, hospitor* addes.

How ma(ys)t þu knowyn qwan þi verbe betokenyth 'to do' and
qwan 'to suffyr'?[3] Qwan I haue ony of þeise vi Englysch 390
wurdys, 'am', 'art', 'is', 'was', 'be' or 'were' joyned to a
verbe, thanne it betokenyth 'to suffyr'; and if noon of þo
vj wurdys be joyned to þe verbe than it betokenyth 'to do'.

How many modys be þer? V. Qwech v? Indicatyf,
imperatyf, optatyf,[4] coniunctyf and infenityf. Qwerby knowyst
indicatyf mood? For it schewyth tale soth or lees and
betokenyth askyng or tellyng; or qwanne I haue ony of theyse
thre synes in my Latyin *sicut, dum, quando*, þe verbe þat
folwyth schal be indicatyf mood. Vnde versus:

> Indicat. vt *quando, sicut, dum*, cetera plura. 400

Qwerby knowyst imperatyf mood? For it preyith, byddyth, or
co|mawndyth. Qwerby knowyst optatyf mood? For it welyth or

---

[1] MS on [2] MS passyth [3] MS suffyffyr
[4] MS octatyf

ACCEDENCE TEXT C

desiryth; and þeyse Englysch wurdys joyned to a verbe, 'wold',
'schold', 'mote' or 'at my wylle', and þeyse Latyin wurdys afor
a verbe, *vtinam, ne, quatinus, o si,* ar þe synes of optatyf mood.
Vnde versus:

'Wold', 'schold' dic opti., *vtinam, ne, quatinus, osi.*

Qwerby knowyst coniunctyf mood? For he is joyned to a noþer
verbe or a noþer verbe is joyned to hym; or qwan ony of þe Latyn[1]
wurdys þat folwyn in þe next come beforn a verbe, it schal be þe 410
coniunctyf mood.

Si, quamuis, quamquam tam(et)si, licet[2] atque *priusquam,
Antequam* an *donec, vt, postquam* siue *quousque,
Cum, nisi, quam, acsi, quo* coniungunt tibi dico.

Qwerby knowyst infenityf mood? For qwanne to verbis come
togeder w^towte a relatyf or a coniunccyon, þe lattar schal be
infenityf mood. Also þis lytel wurd 'to' beforn a verbe is syne
of infenityf mood, as 'to loue', 'to rede'.

How many tens be þere? V. Qwech fyue? The present
tens, þe pretyrtens vnperfyth, þe pretyrtens perfyth, þe[3]   420
pretyrtens pluperfyth and þe futur tens. Qwerby knowyst þe
present tens? For he spekyth of tyme þat is now, as *amo*:
'I loue'. Qwerby knowyst pretertens vnperfyth? For it spekyth
of tyme vnperfythly passyd, as *amabam*: 'I louede'. Qwerby
knowyst þe pretyrtens perfyth? For it spekyth of tyme perfythly
pasyd, and hath þis Englysch wurd 'haue', as *amaui*: 'I haue
louyd'. Qwerby knowyst þe pretyrtens pluperfyth? For it
spekyth of tyme more þan perfythly passyd, and hath þis Englysch
wurd 'hadde', as *amaueram*: 'I had louyd'. Qwerby knowyst þe
future tens? For it spekyth of tyme þat is to come, and   430
hath þis Englysch wurd 'schal', as *amabo*: 'I schal louyn'.

How many nowmberys be þer of verbe? The singuler nowmbyr
as *amo, amas, amat*; and þe plurer as *amamus, -atis, -ant*. How
many personys be þer of verbe? Thre. The furst as *amo,
amamus*, þe secunde as *amas, amatis*; and þe thrydde as *amat,
amant*.

How many coniugacyons be þere? Foure. Qweche iiij?
Þe furst, þe secunde, þe thrydde, þe fourt. Qwerby knowyst
þe furst coniugacyon? For it hath *A* long beforn þe *-re* in
þe infenityf actyf voys or in þe imperatyf mood passyf voys,   440
as *amare*. Qwerby knowyst þe secunde coniugacyon? For it hath
E long aforn þe *-re* in þe infenityf mood actyf voys or in þe
imperatyf mood passyf voys, as *docere*. Qwerby knowyst þe
thrydde coniugacyon? For it hath[4] *E* schort beforn þe *-re* in
þe infenityf mood actyf voys or in þe imperatyf mood passyf
voys, as *legere*. Qwerby knowyst þe fourt coniugacyon? For
it hath *I* long beforn þe *-re* in þe infenityf actyf voys or in

[1] -f *canc.*   [2] *tam(et)si, licet]* MS tam silicet
[3] per *canc.* [4] þe thrydde *canc.*

ACCEDENCE TEXT C

þe inperatyf mood passyf voys, as *audire*. Fro þeise rewlys be owtakyn alle verbe neutyr enormalys, for þei folow no ryth rewle of coniugacyon. Qwech be verbe neutyr enormalys? 450
Patet per versus: |

Sum, volo, fert et *edo* sunt enormal(i)a credo.

And note wel þat alle þe componys of þeyse verbys fayle ryth rewle of coniugacyon, saue too componys of *edo* qwech be *excedo* and *comedo*. Versus:

Cum cunctis natis; *edo* nata set excipiantur,
Excedo nam *comedo* regularia stare probantur.

And how many componys haue *sum*, *es*, *fui*? It is schewyd be þe versys folwyng:

Sum neutri generis est et sua cuncta creata 460
Quorum per metrum pateant tibi (cuncta) signata:
Adsum, sum presens; *absum*, dum cisto remotus;
Presum, preficio;   sed *possum*, robore tutus;
Subsum, subcumbo;   multis *obsum* quia nocendo;
Insum componens *intus*, sum dicere debes,
Hijs quibus *intersum*, me presentem, bene pendo;
Quod restat *superest*. Iam non tibi plurima pando.

Also fro þe rewle of coniugacyons be owtake many verbe defectiuys, as *queso*, 'I beseche', hath no more but *quesumus*; *aue*, 'heyl', hath no more but *auete*,[1] *aueto*, *auetote*; *salue*, 'heyl', hath   470
no more but *saluete*, *salueto*, *saluetote*; *vale*, 'farwel', hath no more but *valete*, *-to*, *valetote*; and *memento*, 'haue in mynde', hath no more but *mementote*.

Amo, amas, amam . . . .

Fols.5ᵛ line 20 to 10ᵛ line 20 contain paradigms of *amo, doceo, lego, audio, sum, possum, volo, nolo, malo, fero, edo* and *fio*, with their English equivalents. I have given only the beginning and end of this section here, and have omitted the remainder.

. . . . vt *facturus*, as 'for to be mad hereaftyr'.

And note wel for a rewle þat þe futur tens of indicatyf mood in þe thrydde and þe fourt coniugacyon turnyth *A* into *E* in alle personys singuler and plurer saue in þe furst persone of þe singuler nowmbyr, as *audiam*, *-es*, *-et*, and in þe futur tens of þe optatyf[2] mood and þe present tens of coniunctyf mood   480
he kepyth stylle *A* in alle personys, as *audiam*, *-as*, *-at*.

Qwerby knowyst an aduerbe? For he is cast to a verbe and fulfyllyth þe significacyon of þe verbe. How many degre of comparyson hath aduerbe? III. Þe posityf, þe comparatyf and þe superlatyf. How knowyst þe posityf degre of aduerbe?

---

[1] MS aueto   [2] MS oftatyf

27

ACCEDENCE TEXT C

For he endyth in Englysch most comunly in '-ly' as 'fayrly',
'goodly', 'swetely' and soche oþer. How knowyst þe comparatyf
degre? For ʰhe endyth in Englysch¹ in '-er' or in '-jr' as
'swetter', 'betyr'. How knowyst þe superlatyf degre? For
he endyth in Englysch in '-est' as 'fayrest', 'fowlest' and   490
soch othyr.

   Qwerby knowyst a participyl? For he takyth part of nown,
part of verbe and part of bothe. Qwat takyth he of nown?
Gendyr and case. Qwat of þe verbe? Tyme and significacyon.
And qwat of bothe? Nowmbyr and persone. How many tens be þer
of participyl? III. Qwech iij? Þe present tens, þe pretertens
and þe futur tens. Qwerby knowyst þe participyl of present tens?
For he endyth in Englysch in '-yng' or in '-and' as 'redyng',
'louand', and in Latyn in -ens or in -ans, as legens, amans.
Qwerby knowyst þe participyl of pretyrtens? For al soch scort   500
Englysch wurdys, 'loued', 'red', 'tawt', 'herd', arn synes of
þe pretertens of partici(pyl), and endyth in Latyin in -tus
or in -sus, as lectus, visus. Qwerby knowyst | a participyl of
þe futur tens? For if he be a participyl of þe actyf voys he
hath þe Englysch of þe infenityf mood of þe actyf voys and
endyth in Latyne in -rus, as lecturus, 'for to redyn'; and
if it be a participyl of þe passyf voys he hath þe Englysch of þe
infenityf mood of þe passyf voys, as legendus, 'for to be red'.

   How many participulys hath a verbe actyf? Too. Qwech ij?
On of þe present tens endyng in -ens or in -ans, as legens, amans;510
and a noþer of þe futur tens endyng in -rus, as lecturus, amaturus.
How many participulys hath a verbe passyf? Too. Qwech ij?
On of þe preter tens endyng in -tus or in -sus, as lectus,
visus; and a noþer of þe futur tens endyng in -dus, as legendus,
videndus. How many participul hath a verbe neutyr? Too.
Qwech ij? On of þe present tens endyng in -ens or in -ans, as
currens, stans; and a noþer of þe futur endyng in -rus, as
cursurus, staturus. How many participul hath a verbe deponent?
Thre. Qwech iij? On of þe present tens endyng in -ens or in
-ans, as loquens, auxilians; a noþer of þe pretertens endyng   520
in -tus or in -sus, as locutus, lapsus; and a participyl of þe
futur tens endyng in -rus, as locuturus. How many participul
hath a verbe comun? IIII. Qwech iiij? On of þe present
endyng in -ens or in -ans, as experiens, hortans; a noþer of
þe pretertens endyng in -tus, as expertus; and too futuris on
endyng in -rus, as hortaturus, and a noþer in -dus, as hortandus.
How many endynggis be þer of participyl? VI. Qweche vj?
Too of þe present tens endyng in -ens and in -ans; too of
pretertens endyng in -tus or in -sus; and too of þe futur
endyng in -rus or in -dus. Vnde versus: 530

     -Ens, -ans presentis semper dic temporis esse;
     -Tus, -sus preteriti; -rus, -dus dic esse futuri;
     -Ens, -ans, -rus et agunt, -tus, -sus, -dus et paciuntur.

   [(Q)werby knowyst a coniunccyon? For it joyneth or
disioyneth oþer partis of reson and ordeynyth in hem perfyth
sentence. Qweche (be) þe coniunccyons þat joynyn? Al þe

ACCEDENCE TEXT C

wurdys þat be in 'Da¹ copulatiuas'.]

Nominatiuo *hic et hec et hoc amans*; genitiuo *huius amantis*;
datiuo *huic amanti*; accusatiuo *hunc et hanc amantem* et *hoc amans*;
vocatiuo *o amans*; ablatiuo *ab hoc et ab hac et ab hoc amante* 540
vel *amanti*; et pluraliter nominatiuo *hij et hee amantes* et
hec amancia; genitiuo *horum et harum et horum amancium*;
datiuo *hijs amantibus*; accusatiuos *hos et has amantes* et *hec amancia*; vocatiuo *o amantes* et *o amancia*; ablatiuo *ab hijs amantibus.*

Nominatiuo *hic et hec et hoc legens*; genitiuo *huius -gentis*;
datiuo *huic -genti*; accusatiuo *hunc et hanc -gentem* et *hoc -gens*;
vocatiuo *o -gens*; ablatiuo *ab hoc et ab hac et ab hoc -gente*
vel *-ti*; et pluraliter nominatiuo *hij et hee -gentes* et *hec
-gencia*; genitiuo *horum et harum et horum -gencium*; (datiuo 550
hijs) *-tibus*; accusatiuo *hos et has -gentes* et *hec -gencia*;
vocatiuo *o -gentes* et *o -gencia*; ablatiuo *ab hijs legentibus.*

Nominatiuo *lectus, lecta, lectum*; genitiuo *lecti, -te,
-ti*; datiuo *lecto, -te, -to*; accusatiuo *lectum, lectam,
lectum*; vocatiuo *lecte, -ta, -tum*; ablatiuo *lecto, -ta, -to*;
et pluraliter nominatiuo *lecti, -te, -ta*; genitiuo *lectorum,
-tarum, -torum*; datiuo *lectis*; accusatiuo *lectos, -tas, -ta*;
vocatiuo *-ti, -te, -ta*; ablatiuo *ab his -tis.*

Nominatiuo *lecturus, -ra, -rum*; genitiuo *-ri, -re, -ri*;
datiuo *lecturo, -re, -ro*; accusatiuo *-rum, -ram, -rum*; 560
vocatiuo *-re, -ra, -rum*; ablatiuo *-ro, -ra, -ro*; et pluraliter
nominatiuo *lecturi, -re, -ra*; genitiuo *-rorum, -rarum, -rorum*;
datiuo *lecturis*; accusatiuo *-ros, -ras, -ra*; vocatiuo *-ri,
-re, -ra*; ablatiuo *ab hijs lecturis.* |

(N)ominatiuo *legendus, -genda, -gendum*; genitivo *-gendi,
-gende, -gendi*; datiuo *-do, -de, -do*; accusatiuo *-dum, -dam,
-dum*; vocatiuo *legende, -da, -dum*; ablatiuo *-do, -da, -do*;
et pluraliter nominatiuo *legendi, -de, -da*; genitiuo *-dorum,
-darum, -dorum*; datiuo *hijs legendis*; accusatiuo *legendos,
-das, -da*; vocatiuo *-di, -de, -da*; ablatiuo *ab hijs legendis.* 570

(Q)werby knowyst a coniunccyon? For it joyneth or
disioyneth oþer partys of reson and ordeynyth in hem perfyth
sentence. Qwech be þe coniunccyons þat ioynyn? Alle þe
wurdys þat be in 'Da copulatiuas'. And qwech be þo þat
disioynyn? Alle þe wurdys in 'Da disiunctiuas'. Qwat partys
of reson joyne þei or dis(i)oyne? Nownys, pronownys, verbys
and participulys. Qwan joyne þei or disioyne? Qwan ony
coniunccyons of joynyng or disioynyng come betwyn too nownys
or too pronownys or too verbis or too participulys. 'Da
copulatiuas vt² *et, que, atque, at, ac, ast.* Da disiunctiuas 580
vt *aut, ve, vel, ne, nec, an, neque.* Da expletiuas vt *quidem,
equidem, saltem, videlicet, quam(quam), quamuis, quoque, autem,
porro, licet, tamen, sin autem.* Da causales vt *si, etsi,*

¹ MS Das   ² MS adds que

ACCEDENCE TEXT C

eciamsi,[1] *siquidem, quando, quandoquidem, quin, quineciam, quatinus, sin, seu, siue, niue, nam, namque, ni, nisi, et enim,*[2] *ne, set, interea, quamobrem, presertim, item, itemque, ceterim, alioquin, preteria. Da racionales vt ita, itaque, enim et enimvero,*[3] *quia, quapropter, quoniam, quidem, quippe, nempe, ergo, ideo, igitur, silicet, videlicet, preteria, propterea, idcirco.'*

(Q)werby knowyst a preposicyon? For he is set beforn 590
oþer partys of reson and seruyth to certeyn case. To qwath
case seruyth a preposicyon?[4] To þe accusatyf case, to þe
ablatyf, or to boþin. Qweche preposicyons serue to þe accusatyf
case? Alle þe wurdys in 'Da preposicyones accusatiui'.
⌈Qwech preposicyons serue to þe ablatyf case? Alle þe wurdis
þat be in 'Da preposiciones casus ablatiui'. Qwech wurdes
serue to bothe casys? Alle þe wurdis þat be in 'Da vtriusque
casus preposiciones'. Qwan wyl 'in' serue to accusatyf case
and qwanne to þe ablatyf? Qwan 'in' comth w^t a 'to' it wyl
serue to þe accusatyf case, and qwan 'in' comth alone he wyl 600
serue to þe ablatyf case. Vnde versus:

> *In campo curro bene dicis si sis in illo;*
> *Si sis exterius in campum fit tibi cursus:*
> *'Into' vult quartum, sine 'to' iu(n)gito sextum.*⌉[5]

'Da preposiciones casus accusatiui. *Ad, aput, ante, aduersum, cis, citra, circum, circa, contra, erga, extra, inter, intra, infra, iuxta, ob, prope, propter, secundum, post, trans, vltra,* ⌈*preter*⌉, *supra, circiter, vsque, secus, penes.* Da preposiciones casus ablatiui. *A, ab, abs, cum, coram, clam, de, e, ex, pro, pre, palam, sine, absque, tenus.* Da vtriusque casus 610
preposiciones vt *in, sub, super* et *subter.'*

(Q)werby knowyst an interieccyon? For it lyth among oþer
partys of reson and betokenyth passyon of sowle w^t an vnperfyth
voyis, and betokenyth joye or sorow or dred or wunderyng or
indignacyon, as 'aha', 'alas', 'welawey', 'out out', 'owgh',
'so howgh', and soch oþer.

(H)ow many acordys ben þere of grameer? Fyue. Qwech v?
The furst betwyn þe nominatyf case and þe verbe; the secunde
betwyn þe substantyf and þe adiectyf; þe thredde þe relatyf
and þe antsedent; þe fowrt betwyn þe[6] superlatyf degre and þe 620
genityf case folwyng; þe fyfte be(twyn) þe nown partityf or þe
nown distributyf and þe genityf case þat folwit. In how many
acorde þe nominatyf case and þe verbe? In too. In qwech too?
In nowmbyr and persone. Vnde versus:

> *Vult in persona, numero rectus similari*
> *Cum personali verbo sibi voce sequente.*
> *Non pones rectum sine verbo, per Precianum,*

---

[1] MS *eciam. si.* [2] MS *ne*
[3] *et enimvero]* MS *etenim. vero*   [4] MS *adds* to
[5] *added at foot of page.*   [6] *re canc.*

ACCEDENCE TEXT C

Nec personale verbum pones sine recto. |

In how many schal þe substantyf and þe adiectyf acordyn?
In thre. In qwech iij? In gendyr, nowmbyr and case. 630
Vnde versus:

    Cum substantiuis tribus adiectiua locabis,
    In casu, genere, numero debes retinere.

In how many schal þe relatyf and þe antecedent acorde? In thre. In qwech thre? In gender, nowmbyr and persone.
Vnde versus:

    Antecedenti tribus hijs coniunge relatum
    Persona, numero; sit genus hijsque[1] datum.

In how many schal þe superlatyf degre and þe genityf case þat folwit acorde? In on. In qwech on? In gendyr. Vnde 640
versus:

    Omne superlatum partitiue recitatum
    Semper vult generi genitiuo sociari:
    Vt pateat verum sic: *Est Deus optima rerum.*
    Ymmo superlatum propria vi quando locatur
    Per genus hoc fixo precedenti famulatur.
    Naso dat[2] verum: *Quid agis dulcissime rerum.*

In how many schal þe nown partityf and þe genityf þat folwyt acorde? In on. In gendyr. Vnde versus:

    Conformes genere dic cum casu genitiuo 650
    Nunc partitiuum, veluti *Venit vna sororum.*
    Sic in gramatica dicas concordia quina.

---

[1] MS hijs quoque   [2] MS *adds* hoc

ACCEDENCE TEXT D

D. Cambridge, Trinity College, MS. O.5.4, fols. 4^v-6^v

This text of the *Accedence* forms part of a larger composite work, the remainder of which is given as text EE. The whole work has Latin section headings and marginal cross references to other parts of the manuscript. These are not reproduced here.

How many maner partyes of reson bu ther? Eyghte: noun, pronoun, verbe, aduerbe, participle, coniunccion, preposicion, interieccion. How many of these partyes be declynyd and how many vndeclynyd? Foure be declined, videlicet noun, pronoun, verbe and participle; and foure be vndeclined, videlicet aduerbe, coniunccion, preposicion, interieccion.

How knowyste a noun substantyf? A party of reson that betokenyth substaunce wyth qualite and is declined wyth case and article; and so the name of euery thyng in the world is 10 a noun substantyf. How many maner of nounes be ther? Tweyne: noun adiectyf and noune substantyf. How knowyst a noun substantyf? Euery word that is declined wyth on article or to atte moste, as *hic magister*, *hic et hec sacerdos*. How knowest a noun adiectyf? Euery word that is declined by thre articles or by thre diuerse endyngis in o case, as *hic et hec et hoc felix*, other as *bonus*, *-na*, *-num*. How many thyngis falleth to a noun? Sixe by the 'Donet': qualite, comparison, gendre, noumbre, fygure and case. How knowest a qualite in noun? A manere of knowyng by the whych me knowyth whether a 20 noun be propure or appellatyf, id est comyn. Propure, ut *Roma*; comyn, as *silua*.

How many degrees of compar(i)son be ther? Thre, videlicet posityf, comparatyf$^{(e)}$, superlatyf. How knowest the posytyf degre? A noun adiectyf that bytokenyth qualite or quantite wythoute eny echyng, as 'good', 'fayre', 'whyte', 'black'. How knowest the comparatyf degre? A noun adiectyf that bytokenyth qualite or quantite wyth sumwhat echyng, as 'betyr', 'werse'. How knoweste the superlatyf degre? A noun adiectyf that bytokenyth qualite or quantite wyth most echyng, as 30 'fayrest', 'foulest', 'best', 'worste'.

What case wyll the comparatyf degre haue aftur hym? An ablatyf case of eyther noumbre wythoute a preposicion, as 'I wyser than my brother am feyrour than al my felowes', *Ego sapiencior fratre meo sum pulchrior omnibus sociis meis*. Or ellys wyth a nominatyf case and thys coniunccion *quam* comyng bytwene wyth *sum*, *es*, *fui*, as *Sum sapiencior quam tu vna leccione*. Of what case of the posityf degre schall the comparatyf be formed? Other whyle of the genityf case and other whyle of the datvf case. When schall he be formed of the genityf case? Whenne 40 the noun of the posityf degre is the secunde declunson, as *albus*, *-ba*, *-bum*, genitiuo *albi*, addita *-or*, fit *albior*. Whenne of the datyf? Whenne the noun of the posytyf degre is the thridde declunson, as *hic et hec fortis et hoc forte* genitiuo *huius fortis*, datiuo *huic forti*, addita *-or*, fit *forcior*; $^{(}$sed

32

ACCEDENCE TEXT D

iuuenis facit *iunior*.¹

What case wole the superlatyf degre haue aftur hym? A
genityf case plurel other a genityf case singuler of a noun
collectyf, as *Ego pulcherimum animalium sum sapientissimus
istius comitiue*.¹ Of what case of the posytyf degre schall   50
the superlatyf be formed? Other whyle of the nominatyf case
and other whyle of the genityf. Whenne of the nominatyf case?
Whenne the nominatyf case endyth in -*r* onlych in singuler
noumbre, masculyn gendre, as *niger*, sette ther-to -*rimus*,
thenne hyt is *nigerimus*. How many be out-take of thys rewle?
Tweyne, videlicet *dexter* et *sinister* ⌈et *memor*⌉ that makyth the
superlatyf degre in -*timus*, as *dextimus* ⌈vel -*terrimus*⌉ et
sinistimus ⌈vel -*terrimus* et *memor*, *memorissimus*⌉. Versus:

    Cum tenet -*r* rectus -*rimus* est illi sociandus,
    Excipias *dexter* quod dat -*timus*² atque *sinister*.   60

Whenne schall he be formed of the genityf case? Whenne the
posityf endyth not in -*r* but in anothyr lettur, as *albus*,
-*ba*, -*bum*, genitiuo *albi*, sette to *S* and -*simus*, thenne hyt is
albissimus; ⌈but *maturus* maketh -*rimus*, *superus* -*rimus* and
vetus veterimus⌉. How many be oute-take of thys reule?
Fiue, wyth hure compounes. Whyche be they? *Facilis*,³
agilis, gracilis, humilis and *similis*, ⌈but *cessus* maketh
-*simus*⌉. How maketh they hure superlatyf? In -*limus*. Of
what case schall the superlatyf be formed? Of the nominatyf
case, as *facilis*, do awey the -*s* and sette ther-to -*imus* and   70
that makyth *facilimus*.

    Dant tibi quinque -*limus*⁴ signantur nomine *f-a-g-u-s*,
    Et sua composita tibi non sunt pretereunda.

How many gendres be in a noun? Seuene, videlicet masculin,
femynyn, neutre, comyn of tweyne, comyn of thre, dubie and epycen.
How knoweste the masculyn? For he is declynyd by *hic*, the
femynyn by *hec*, the neutre by *hoc*, the comyn of tweyn by *hic* and
hec, the comyn of thre that is declinid by *hic* and *hec* and *hoc*,
the epycen that word⁵ that bytokenyth the male and the female
vnder on article, as *hic passer* for the he sparwe and *hic*   80
passer for the heo sparowe. How knowyste the dubye gendre?
That word that is declined by *hic* and *hec* and *vel* coniunccion
goyng bytwene, as *hic vel hec dies*. How many nounes be ther
of dubye gendre? As many as be in these verse sewynge.
Versus:

    *Margo dies*que, *silex, cortex panter*aque, *dama*,
    Finis cum *clunis* dubium genus ista notabunt.
    Singula sunt dubii sed sunt pluralia primi.
    *Margo dies*que, *silex*,⁶ *cortex panter*aque, *dama*⁷.

---

¹ -mit- from met; W canc.   ² vel terimus added later and not part
of verse.   ³ possibly over an erasure   ⁴ que canc.
⁵ two letters canc.   ⁶ p canc.   ⁷ c canc.

ACCEDENCE TEXT D

Cum genere debes flectendo tenere. 90
Quamuis pro dubijs hec antiqui posuere,
*Dama*que *pantera* semper dicas epicena.

Bote alle these nounes be comyn gendyr of tweyne, out-take *pantera* et *dama* wheche ben epycen gendre by newe grammer.

    How many noumbres hastow? Tweyne, singuler and plurel.
How knowystow the singuler? That at bytokenyth o thynge.
How knowystowe the plurell? That at bytokenyth many thynges.
How many maners of figures hastow? Thre. Simple, compound
and decompound. How knowyst the symple? A party by the
whych me knowyth whether a word be or not, as *amo*. Compound? 100
Figure by the whych me knowyth whether a word be compounyd,
as *peramo*. Decompound? Whenne a word is compound of a word
that is compound byfore, as *magnanimitas*.

    How many case hastowe? Sixe, the nominatyf, genitif,
datyf, accusatyf, vocatyfe, ablatyf. How knoweste the nominatyf
case? A word that comyth byfore the verbe and the dede of the
verbe passyth oute of hym, that schall be nominatyf case. On
another maner a word that bytokenyth doyng or suffryng, the word
that doth or suffreth schall be nominatyf case, as 'The
maister sytteth on the benche', *Magister sedet super scannum*. 110

    How knoweste the genityf case? By my signes, as 'of'
aftur a noun substantyf, a noun partytyf, a distributyf, a
noun of superlatyf degre and aftur *sum*, *es*, *fui* be sygnes of
the genityf case. Ensample 'of' aftur a noun substantyf,
as 'The poynte of thys knyf is dulle', *Mucro istius cultelli
est obtusus*. Ensample aftur a noun partytyf, as 'Thys man is
on of creatures', *Iste homo est vna creaturarum*. Ensample
aftur a noun distributyf, as 'Euerych of vs schall haue hys
mede', *Quilibet nostrum habebit suum premium*. Ensample aftur
a noun of superlatyf degre, as, 'Thys man is fayrest of creatures', 120
Iste homo est pulcherima creaturarum. Ensample aftur *sum*, *es*,
fui, as 'Thys man is of fayre berynge', *Iste homo est pulchre
gesture*. How knowest the genityf case in another manere?
Whenne tweyne nounes substantyfys comyth togedyr and that on
be hauer of that other, the noun that bytokenyth hauer schall
be genityf case, as 'The maistres cloke is rede', *Armilausa
magistri est rubea*. Also wordes that bytokenyth emtynesse[1]
or fullenesse, byggyng or syllyng, reprehendyng or vndernymynge,
and verbes that|haue strengthe to constre wyth genityf case,
as *misereor*, *-reris*, *dominor*, *-raris* and other suche wyll 130
constrew w^t genityf case.

    How knowest datyf case? Whenne this Englysh 'to' comyth
byfor a noun, pronoun or participle, and no preposicion i-sette
for 'to', thenne schall 'to' be datyf case, as 'I ʒaf a peny
to a poure man', *Ego erogaui denarium pauperi*. Also wordes
that bytokenyth byddyng, hotyng or comaundyng, lycclynesse or
vnlicclynesse, euenesse or vneuenesse, profyt or vnprofyt wyll

[1] of *canc.*

ACCEDENCE TEXT D

constreu wyth datyf case, and verbes that haue strengthe to
constreu wyth datyf case, as *placeo*, *noceo* and other suche.

How knowest accusatyf case? Whenne I haue noun, pronoun   140
or participle comyng in a reson aftur a verbe, gerundyf,
participle or supyn and the dede of eny of hem passe into hym,
hit schall be accusatyf case. Ensample aftur a verbe, as
'I loue my mayster', *Amo meum magistrum*; *Laboro amando socium
meum*; *Sum amans fratrem meum*; *Vado amatum compatrem meum*.
Also whenne I haue a noun betokenyng party of mannys body comyng
in construccyon aftur a noun adiectyf, a verbe neutre or verbe
passyf, the party of the body schall be accusatyf case, as 'I
whyte[1] the face, ake the hede, am hurte the legge', *Ego albus
faciem, doleo caput, ledor pedem* uel *tibiam*. Also whenne I   150
haue eny preposicion that wole seruen to accusatyf case.

How knowest the vocatyf case? Whenne me clepyth or callyth,
as 'Wylyam come hydyr', *Willelme veni huc*.

How knowyste the ablatyf case? By my sygnes 'than' and
'by', 'wyth', 'in' and 'of', 'thorw', 'fro', and 'vnder' and
'for'; 'thanne' and 'by' aftur a comparatyf degre schall be
ablatyf case wythoute a preposicion. Ensample as 'I am wyser
thanne my brother by a dayes lernynge', *Sum sapiencior fratre
meo erudicione vnius diei*. 'Of' aftur a verbe gerundyf,
partyciple or supyn schal be ablatyf case wyth a preposicion,   160
as 'We be louyd of the maystre', *Nos diligimur a magistro* et
cetera. Also whenne I haue any preposicion that wol serue to
ablatyf case or any verbe that hath strengthe to constreu wyth
ablatyf case, as:

Vescitur et *fruitur*, et cetera.

Also wordes that bytokenyth fulness or emtynesse, byyng or
sellyng, reprehendyng or vndernymyng.

How many declynsones hastow in the noun? Fyve. The
fyrste is of the whych the genityf case singuler and datyf
endyth in *-e*, accusatif in *-am*, the vocatyf in *-a*, the ablatyf   170
in *-a*; the nominatyf plurel in *-e*, genityf in *-arum*, the datyf
in *-is*, the accusatyf in *-as*, the vocatyf in *-e*, the ablatyf in
-is. The secunde declynson is of the wheche ⌈the genityf
singuler endyth in *-i*, the datyf in *-o*, the accusatyf in *-vm*⌉;
whenne the ⌈nominatyf⌉ case endyth in *-r* or in *-m* the vocatyf
schall be lych hym; whenne the nominatyf endyth in *-vs*, the
vocatyf endyth in *-e*; and whenne ther is a propre name endyng
in *-ius* the vocatyf schall ende in *-i*; the ablatyf in *-o*.
The nominatyf plurell schall ende in *-i* or *-a*, the genityf in
-orum, the datyf in *-is*, the accusatyf in *-os* or in *-a*, the   180
vocatyf in *-i* or in *-a*, the ablatyf in *-is*. The thrydde
declynson is of the whych the genityf singuler endyth in *-is*,
the datyf in *-i*, the accusatyf in *-em* or in *-im*, the vocatyf
schal be lyche the nominatyf, the ablatyf in *-e* or in *-i*;

[1] I canc.

ACCEDENCE TEXT D

the nominatyf plurell in -*es* or in -*a*, the genityf in -*vm* or in -*ium*, the datyf in -*bus*, the accusatyf in -*es* or in -*a*, ⌠the vocatyf in -*es* or in -*a*⌡, the ablatyf in -*bus*. The fourthe declynson is of the which the genityf case singuler endyth in -*vs*, datyf in -*vi*, the accusatyf in -*vm*, the vocatyf in -*vs*, the ablatyf in -*v*; the nominatyf plurell in -*vs*, the genityf *190* in -*vum*, the datyf in -*bus*, the accusatyf in -*vs*, the vocatyf also, the ablatyf in -*bus*. The fyfthe declynson is of the which the genityf case singuler endyth in -*ei*, the datyf also, the accusatyf in -*em*, the vocatyf in -*es*, the ablatyf in -*e*; the nominatyf plurel in -*es*, ⌠the genityf plurel in -*erum*, the datyf in -*bus*, the accusatyf in -*es*,⌡ the vocatyf in -*es*, the ablatyf in -*bus*.

How knowest a pronoun? A party of reson[1] declynyd, the whych is sette for a propre name and reseueth certayn person. How many pronounes be ther? XV: *ego*, *tu*, *sui*, *ille*, *ipse*, *200* *iste*, *hic* and *is*, *meus*, *tuus*, *suus*, *noster* and *vester*, *nostras* and *vestras*. How many of these be prymytyuis and how many diriuatiuez? VIII be primitiues, videlicet *ego*, *tu*, *sui*, *ille*, *ipse*, *iste*, *hic* and *is*, and vij beth deriuatyfys, videlicet *meus*, *tuus*, *suus*, *noster* and *vester*, *nostras* and *vestras*. How many of these primityfys be demonstratyfys? *Ego*, *tu*, *iste* and *hic*. And wheche be onlych relatyfys? *Is* and *sui*. How many of these be othyr whyle relatyf and other whyle demonstratyf? Tweyne, videlicet *ille* and *ipse*. Whenne is *ipse* demonstratyf? Whenne *ipse* is y-sette wyth a substantyf in the same reson, as *210* *Ipse homo currit*. Butte whenne a reson cometh to-fore and another folwyth and *ipse* be sette in the reson folwyng wyth an *et* coniunccion sette byfore, thenne *ipse* is a relatyf, as *Vir currit et ipse monetur*. In the same manner schall *ille* be a relatyf and othyr whyle a demonstratyf. How many of these vij deriuatyfys be poscessiues? V, videlicet *meus*, *tuus*, *suus*, *noster* and *vester*; and *nostras* and *vestras* bytokenyth onlych folk.

How many thynges falleth to a pronoun? VI by the 'Donette', videlicet qualite, gendre, noumbre, figure, person *220* and case. Whyche be the qualitees in pronoun? A certeyn qualite and an vncerteyn. How knowest a certeyn qualite? A party by the wheche me knowyth whenne a pronoun is certeyn person, as *ego*. How the vncerteyn? A propurte by that me knowyth whenne a pronoun is of vncerteyn person, as *ille*. How many gendres hastow in pronoun? V, masculyn as *iste*, feminine as *ista*, neutre as *istud*, comyn of too as *hic et hec* *nostras*, -*atis*, comyn of thre, as *ego*, *tu*, *sui*. How many noumbres hastow in pronoun? Tweyne as in noun. How many figures haste in pronoun? Tweyne, the symple as *quis*, the *230* compoune as *quisquis*. How many persones hastow in pronoun? Thre in the singuler and thre in the plurell, as *ego*, *tu*, *sui*, *nos*, *vos*, *illi*. *Ego* and *nos* for the fyrste person, *tu* and *vos* for the secunde, *ille* and *illi* for the thrydde. How knowest the fyrst person of the pronoun? That that speketh of hemself.

[1] en *canc*.

ACCEDENCE TEXT D

How the secunde? That that speche is made to. How the
thrydde? That that speche is made of. And wyte well that
alle nounez, pronounez and participles be the thrydde person
out-take 'I' and 'thu', 'we' and 'ye', and the vocatyf case.
How many case hastow in pronoun? As many as in noun. 240

How many declynsons haste in pronoun? Foure. The
fyrste of the whych the genityf case singuler endyth in -*i*
or in -*is*, the datyf in -*i*. How many pronounez be ther of
the fyrste declynson? Thre, videlicet *ego, tu, sui*.[1] Which
is the secunde? Of the which the genityf case singuler endyth
in -*ius* vel -*ius*, the datyf in -*i* uel in -*c*. How many pronounez
hath he? Fyue, videlicet *ille, ipse, iste, hic* and *is*, and
viij nounes wyth hure compounez, videlicet *vnus, vllus, totus,
solus, alter* and *alius, quis* and *vter* et *eorum composita*.
How knowyst the thrydde declynson? Of the whych the genityf 250
case singuler endyth[2] in -*i* and in -*e* and in -*i*, the datyf in
-*o* and in -*e* and -*o*; and he hath v pronoues vndur (hym),
videlicet *meus, tuus, suus, noster* and *vester*. Wheche is the
furth? Of the whych the genityf case endyth in -*atis* and the
datyf in -*ati*; and he hath ij pronounes vndur hym, videlicet
nostras, -atis, and *vestras, -atis*, et vnum nomen *cuias, -iatis*. |

How many nounes of askynge haste? VIII, videlicet *quis,
qualis, quantus, cuius, cuias, quid, quotus* and *quot*. Wherof
asketh *quis*? Of substance, as 'Hoo techyth in the scole?
The mayster', *Quis docet in scola*? *Magister*. Wherof asketh 260
qualis? Of maner of thyng, as 'What maner man is thy fadyr?',
Qualis est pater tuus? 'A good man', *Bonus*; or ellys 'Such
as thy fadyr', *Talis qualis pater tuus est*. Wherof asketh
quantus? Of muchelnesse of thynge, as 'How moche is thy
brothur?', *Quantus est frater tuus*? 'As muche as thy fadyr',
Tantus quantus est pater tuus. Wherof asketh *cuius*? Of
possessyon of thyng, and thenne yif hyt bytokenyth possession
of a noun substantyf me schal answere by a genityf case, as
Cuius liber est iste? 'The maystres', *Magistri, Ricardi,
rectoris, vicarii*. Whenne hyt maketh askyng of possession of 270
a noun adiectyf, thenne me schall answere by a pronoun possessyf,
as 'Hoos cloke is thys?', *Cuius armilausa est ista*? *Mea, tua,
sua*. Et declinatur sic: nominatiuo, *cuius, -ia, -ium*;
accusatiuo *cuium, -ia, -ium*; ablatiuo *cuia*. Wherof asketh
cuias? Of a manere of folk, as 'Of what manere folk art thu?',
Cuias est tu? 'Englis', *Anglicus*, or 'Of Englis', *De anglicana
gente*. Wherof asketh *quid*? Of diuision of a thyng, as
'What thyng is a man?', *Quid est homo*? 'A dedlych best and
resonable', *Animal racionale*. *Quid est animal*? *Substancia
animata sencibilis*. Otherwhyle *quid* asketh of dede of the 280
verbe, as *Quid agit mater*? *Docet, legit* et cetera. Where⌈of⌉
asketh *quotus*? Of ordre, as 'How sytteth the mayster atte
mete?', *Quotus sedet magister in prandio*? 'The furste',
Primus homo et cetera. 'He sytte today as he satte yurstay',
Totus sedet hodie quotus sedebat heri. Other whyle of noumbre,
as[3] 'Wyth how many com the busshopp to toune?' And thenne

---

[1] W canc. with a paraph mark over it [2] in e and canc. [3] wh canc.

ACCEDENCE TEXT D

hyt is to answere by an ablatyf case absolute, as *Quotus venit episcopus ad villam*? *Se xx⁰, Se xl⁰* et cetera. Wherof asketh *quot*? Of noumbre, as 'How many scolers be in the scole?', *Quot scolares sunt in scola*? *XX, XLᵃ, C,* et cetera.   290

How knowest a verbe? A party of reson that bytokenyth doyng or suffryng and is declined wyth moode and tyme wᵗoute case, as 'I love the for I am loued of the', *Amo te quia amor a te*. How many thyngys falleth to a verbe? Seuene, videlicet moode, coniugacion, gendyr, noumbre, figure, tyme, and person. How many moodes bu ther? V. Wheche v? Indicatyf, imperatyf, optatyf, coniunctyf, and infinityf. How knowyst indicatyf mode? That at telleth or shewyth, that doth or hath do or shal do, suffreth or hath suffred or shall suffre, as 'I loue', *amo*; 'I am loued', *amor*. How knowyste imperatyf moode? That at   300 byddyth or commaundeth, as 'Go hens', *Vade hinc*. How knowyst the optatyf? That at wyllyth or desyryth, as 'God wolde that I were a good man', *Vtinam essem bonus homo*. Whyche be the wordes that serue to the optatyf mode? *Vtinam, ne, quatinus, o ci* and *o*. How knowyst the coniunctyf mode? That at is junyd to another mode wyth an *et* coniunccion. Wheche be the wordes of Englys that serue to the coniunctyf mode? 'Yif', 'thouȝ', 'bote', 'for te', 'that', 'whenne'. In Latyn *vt, si, cum, quamquam, quamuis, licet, nisi, quod, donec, quosque,* ⌈*priusquam, antequam, postquam, an, quando* ac *dum*, sicut et   310 cetera plura⌉¹. How knowest the infinityf mode? Whenne ther comyth two verbes togedre wythout and *et* coniunccion sette bytwene, the latter verbe schall be infinityf mode, as 'I here the mayster teche scolers', *Audio magistrum docere scolares*.

How many coniugacions hastowe? Foure. The fyrst ys that hath an *A* longe byfore the *-re* or the *-ri* in the infinityf mode, as *amare* or *amari*. How many be out-take of thys rule? Foure verbes actyues wyth hure passiues, videlicet *dare, venundare, pessundare* and *circumdare*. How knowest the secunde? That is the wheche hath an *E* longe byfor the *-re* or *-ri* in the   320 infinityf mode, as *docere* or *doceri*. How knowest the thrydde coniugacion? That at hath an *E* schorte in the secunde person indicatyf mode presentis temporis, as *legeris*, or in the infinityf mode, as *legere*. How knowyste the fourthe coniugacion? That at hath an *I* longe byfor the *-re* or *-ri* in the infinityf mode, as¹ *audire* uel *audiri*.

How many gendres haste of verbes? Fyue: actyf, passyf, neutre, comyn and deponent. How knowyste a verbe actyf? That at endyth in *-o* and bytokenyth doyng, and may make of hym a passyf, and be construyd wyth an accusatyf case of a resonable thyng,²   330 as 'I loue a man', *Diligo hominem*. How knowyste a verbe passyf? That at endyth in *-r* and is i-formed of an actyf and bytokenyth suffryng² and may be construyd wyth an ablatyf case of a resenable best, as 'I am loued of a man', *Diligor ab homine*. How knowyst a verbe neutre? That at endyth in *-o* as an actyf and bytokenyth doynge and suffryng and may not be construyd wyth an accusatyf case

¹ MS A- *from a*   ² MS *adds -is*

ACCEDENCE TEXT D

of a resenable beste, as *curro*, *vapulo*. How knowest a ve(r)be
commyn? That at endyth in -r as a verbe passyf and may bytokene
doyng or suffryng in diuerse reson, as 'I blame the for I am
blamed of the', *Criminor te quia criminor a te.* How many verbes   340
commyn bu ther? V, et cetera.

    Largior, experior, veneror, moror, osculor, ortor,
    Criminor, amplector tibi sunt communia, lector;
    Si bene connumeres, *interpretor* addere debes.

How knoweste a verbe deponent? That at endyth in -r as a
verbe comyn and bytokenyth onlych doyng or onlych suffryng,
as *loquor* and *nascor*.

    How many noumbres haste in the verbe? Tweyne: singuler
and plurell. The singuler as *lego*, the plurell as *legimus*.

    How many figures hastow in the verbe? Tweyne: symple   350
as *lego*, the compoun as *necligo*.

    How many tymes hastow in the verbe? Thre to make Latyn
by: the tyme that is now, the tyme that is a-goo, the tyme that
is to come. For hem in Englysh: 'I loue' for the tyme that
is now, 'I haue louyd' for the tyme that is a-goo, 'I schall
loue' for the tyme that is to com. How many tymes be ther in
declynson of the verbe? Fyue, that is the tyme that is nowe,
the tyme that is not fullych passed, the tyme that¹ is ⌈fullych⌉
passed, the tyme that ȝore is a-passed, the tyme that is to come.
For hem in Englysh:² ⌈I loue' for the tyme that is now, 'I   360
loued' for the tyme that nis not fullych passed, 'I haue loued'
for the tyme that is fullych passed, 'I ⌈hadde y⌉ -loued' for
the tyme that is more than a-go, 'I schall loue' for the tyme
that is to come.

    How many tymes be formed of the furst person of the tyme
that is fullych a-goo of the indicatyf mode? Thre. Whych
thre? The tyme that is more than a-passed in the same mode,
the tyme that is parfetly a-passyd in the coniunctyf mode, and
the tyme that is to come of the same mode; as *amaui*, chaungyth
the *I* into an *E*, thenne hyt schall be *amaue*, sette ther-to *-ram*   370
and thenne hyt is *amaueram*; or sette ther-to a *-rim* and thenne
hyt is *amauerim*; or sette there-to a *-ro* and thenne hyt is
amauero. How many be formed of the secunde person of the same
mode and tyme, singuler noumbre? Other thre. Whych thre?
The tyme that is ferre a-passyd of the coniunctyf mode, and the
tyme that is ferre a-passed of the optatyf mode, and the tyme
that is ferre a-passed of|the infinityf mode: as *amauisti*,
torne the *-ti* into a *-sem* and thenne hyt is *amauissem*; turne
the *-ti* into a *-se* and thenne hyt is *amauisse*. How many
persones be ther? III as in pronoun.   380

    How knowyste and aduerbe? A party of reson that is not
declinyd and is y-sette wyth the verbe and declareth the

¹ ȝore *canc*.   ² For them in Englysh *canc*.

ACCEDENCE TEXT D

significacion of the verbe. How many thyngys falleth to an
aduerbe? Thre: significacion, comparson and figure. The
significacions of the aduerbe be diuerse for summe be aduerbes
of place, and summe of tyme, as the 'Donet' declareth. How
many degrees of comparson bu ther in an aduerbe? Thre:
posytyf, comparatyf and superlatyf. How knoweste the posytyf
degre[1] of an aduerbe? That at bytokenyth qualite or quantite
wythoute eny echyng, as 'wyselych'. How knowyste the   390
comparatyf? That at bytokenyth qualite or quantite wyth
sumwhat echyng, as 'wyseloker'. How knowest the superlatyf?
That at bytokenyth qualite or quantite wyth aldermost echyng,
as 'wyselokest'. How many fygures haste in aduerbes? Tweyne:
simple as *docte*, the compoun as *indocte*.

How many reules haste to knowe whenne a propre name of a
place othyr of toun or cite schal be put in the stede of an
aduerbe? Foure. Whych foure? The furste is whenne I haue a
propre name of a toun or a place of the furst declynson or the
secunde, singuler noumbre, nouȝt i-compounyd, comyng in   400
construccion aftur a verbe, participle, gerundyf or suppyn
bytokenyng dwellyng in place, he schal be putte in the voys
of genityf case in stede of an aduerbe wythoute a preposicion,
as 'I dwelle atte Oxenford that dwellyd sumtyme at Yorke',
Moror Oxonie qui quondam moratus fui Eboraci. Whyche is the
secunde reule? Whenne I haue a propre name of a toun or cyte
or place of the thrydde declynson and singuler noumbre or furst
declynson and plurel noumbre nouȝt i-compounyd comyng in
construccion aftur a verbe, participle, gerundyf or suppyn he
schall be put in the voys of the ablatyf case wythoute any   410
preposicion, as *Sum Cartagine qui quondam fui Londonijs*.
Whych is the thrydde rule? Whenne I haue a propre name of a
toun or of a place nouȝt i-compounyd comyng[2] in construccion
aftur a verbe, participle, gerundyf or suppyn bytokenyng
sturyng into a place he schall be putte in voys of an accusatyf
case instede of an aduerbe, whatsoeuer declynson or noumbre so
he be. Whyche is the fourthe reule? That is whenne I haue
a propre name of toun or place nouȝt i-compounyd comyng in
construccion aftur a verbe, participle, gerundyf or suppyn
bytokenyng sturynge from a place, he schall be putte in the   420
voys of ablatyf case instede of an aduerbe, what noumbre or
what declynson euer he be. How many nounes appellatyfs
folwyth the same reule of these propre nounnes? Foure.
Whyche foure? *Domus*, *rus*, *humus* and *milicia*. Also the
propre names of contreys, tounes or places that be compouned
schul folwe the reule of nounes appellatiues, as 'I wynde
from Englond to Fraunce', *Vade de Anglia ad Franciam*; 'I come
fro Mounte Pelerz to[3] Bewmount, *Veni de Monte Pesulano ad
Bellum Montem*.

Of what case schal the aduerbe be formed? Other whyle   430
of the nominatyf case and other whyle of the datyf[4] case.
Whenne of the nominatyf case? Whenne my noune adiectyf

---

[1] an *canc*.   [2] bytwene *canc*.   [3] a stroke *canc*.
[4] from genityf

ACCEDENCE TEXT D

endyth in -*ens* or in -*ans*, as *sapiens*, do awey the -*s* and set there-to -*ter*, thenne hyt is *sapienter*. Whenne of the datyf case? Whenne my noune adiectyf is of the secunde declynson or the thrydde nouȝt endyng in -*ens* ne in -*ans*. Ensample of the secunde declynson, as *docto*, chaunge the -*o* into an -*e* and thenne hyt is *docte*; of the thrydde as *forti*,[1] sette there-to a -*ter* and thenne hyt wol be *fortiter*, et cetera.

How knowyste a partyciple? A party of reson that is declined and bytokenyth doyng or suffryng[2] wyth case and tyme wythoute mode. How many thyngis falleth to a participle? Sexe: case, gendre, noumbre, figure, tyme, an sygnificacion. Of case hyt is in the participle as hit is in the noun. How many gendres haste in the participle? Foure. Whyche be they? Masculyn, as *lectus*, feminine as *lecta*, neutre as *lectum*, comyn of thre as *hic et hec et hoc legens*. Noumbres and figures beth in the participle as in noun. 440

How many tymes haste in participle? Thre: the tyme that is now, the tyme that is a-goo, the tyme that is to come. How many endyngis haste in the tyme that is nowe? Tweyne: -*ens*, and -*ans*. How many of the tyme that is a-passyd? Other tweyne: -*tus*, and -*sus*. How many of the tyme that is to come? Other tweyne: -*rus*, and -*dus*. Vnde versus: 450

-*Ens*, -*ans* presentis semper dic temporis esse.
-*Tus*, -*sus* preteriti, -*rus*, -*dus* dicasque futuri.

How knowyst a partyciple of the tyme that is nowe? Whenne myn Englysh endyth[3] in '-ynge', thenne schal I haue a partyciple of the tyme that is now endyng in -*ens* or in -*ans*, as *sedens*, *amans*. How knowyste a participle of the tyme that is a-go? Whenne I haue thys lettre 'i-' comyng tofore a participle thenne I schall haue a participle of the tyme that is a-go endyng in -*tus* or -*sus*, as 'i-louid', 'i-sey', *amatus*, *visus*. How knowyst whenne thu schalt haue a participle of the future tens? Whenne thys sygne 'to' comyth bytwene the participle and *sum*, *es*, *fui*, thenne I schal haue a partyciple endyng in -*rus*, as 'I am to rede a lesson', *Ego sum lecturus leccionem*. Whenne schalte haue the participle endyng in -*dus* of future tens? Whenne 'to' and 'be' comyth togedre bytwene the participle and *sum*, *es*, *fui*, as 'I am to be louyd of the mayster', *Sum amandus a magistro*. 460

470

How many significaciones haste in the participle? Fyue: actyf, passyf, neuter, comyn, and deponent, as hyt declareth in the verbes. How many participles comyth of a verbe actyf? Tweyne, as *amans*, *amaturus*. How many of a verbe passyf? Tweyne, as *amatus*, *amandus*. Of a verbe neutre? Other tweyn, as *stans*, *staturus*. Of a verbe comyn? Foure, as *largiens*, *largiturus*, *largitus*, *largiendus*. Of a verbe deponent? Thre, as *loquens*, *loqutus*, *loquturus*. Of what party of the 'Donet'

---

[1] do awey the I and *canc*.   [2] MS suffryng*is*
[3] -th *from* ng

ACCEDENCE TEXT D

schall the participle endyng in -*ens* or -*ans* be formed? Of 480
the furst person of the pretert inperfyt tens, indicatyf mode
and singuler noumbre, as *amabam*, -*bam* conuersa in *N* et *S*, fit
amans. Wherof schall the participle endyng in -*tus* or -*sus*
be formed? Of the laste suppyn, as *amatu*, set ther-to[1] an -*s*
and thenne hit is *amatus*. Wherof is the participle endyng in
-*rus* i-formed? Of the laste suppyn, as *amatu*, sette ther-to a
-*rus* and thenne hyt is *amaturus*. Wherof schal the participle
endyng in -*dus* be formed? Of the participle of the tyme that
is now of the genitif case, as *amantis*, do awey the -*tis* and
set ther-to a -*dus*, and thenne hyt is *amandus*. 490

How knowest a coniunccion? A party of reson that is not
declynyd and wole joyne tweyne nomynatyf case in rewarde of a
verbe, other ellys twey verbes in reward of a nominatyf case.
How many thyngis falleth to a coniunccion? Thre. Whych thre?
Power, figure and ordur. How many spyces hath the power of
coniunccion? Fyue, by the 'Donet': copulatyf, disiunctyf,
expletyf, racionel, and causell. How knowest a coniunccion
copulatyf? That at joynyth|twey nominatyf case singuler in
reward of a verbe plurell, as 'I and thu beth in the scole',
Ego et tu sumus in scola. How knowyst a coniunccion disiunctyf? 500
That at joynyth twey nominatyf case singuler in reward of a verbe
singuler, as 'I or my felowe haue spende a peny', *Ego uel
socius meus expendidit denarium*. Her knowe for a generall
reule that whenne *vel* coniunccion comyth bytwene twey nominatyf
case the verbe that is folwyng schall acorde wyth the latter
nominatyf case and nouȝt wyth the furst, as *Ego uel tu curris*.
How knowest a coniunccion expletyf? That at fulfylleth the
sentence of a reson that is folwyng, as 'I forsothe haue souped,
thu forsothe not', *Ego quidem cenaui tu vero non*. How knowest
a coniunccion causell? That at bytokenyth cheson of that at is 510
folwyng, as 'Thu hast trespasyd therfor thu schalt be betyn',
Tu deliquisti ideo verberaberis. How knowest a coniunccion
racionell? That at bytokenyth reson of that at is folwyng
othyr of that byfore, as 'For thu art my frende I loue the well',
Quia tu es meus amicus diligo te. The ordre of coniunccion
stondyth on these maners. Sume schull be set byfore, as *at*,
ac, *ast*, and summe byhynde, as *que*, *ve*, *autem*, and summe buth
comyn, as *ergo*, *ideo*, *igitur*. In coniunccion buth tweyne
figures: the simple as *nam*, the compoun as *namque* et cetera.

How knowest a preposicion? A party of reson that is not 520
declinyd and seruith to accusatyf case and ablatyf. How many
thyngis falleth to a preposicion? On onlych. Wheche on?
Case. How many case? Tweyne: accusatyf and ablatyf.
Wheche beth the preposicion that seruyth to accusatyf case?
As many as be conteynyd in thys demaunde of the 'Donet': 'Da
preposiciones casus accusatiui'. Wheche beth hy that seruyth
to the ablatyf case? As[2] many as beth conteynyd in 'Da
preposiciones casus ablatiui, et cetera'. How many seruyth
to bothe case? Foure: *in*, *sub*, *super*, *subter*.

---

[1] a rus *canc.*   [2] A- *from* a

ACCEDENCE TEXT D

How knowyste an interieccion? A party of reson that   530
bytokenyth talente of a mannys thou3te and is not declinyd,
as 'fy', 'hay'. How many thyngys falleth to an interieccion?
Onlych significacion. How many spyces hath the sygnificacion
of interieccion? Foure: myrthe, as 'to gooderhele', as
euax; sorwe, as *heu*; drede, as 'haa', id est *metum*; wondryng,
as *pape*, id est *miror*, et cetera.

ACCEDENCE TEXT E

E. London, British Library, MS Add. 12,195, fol.66^r

(H)ow many partys of reson ben þer? VIII. Qwych viij?
Nown, pronown, uerbe, aduerbe, partycipyll, coniunccion,
preposicion, interiection. How many arn declynyd and how
many arn vndeclynyd? IIII arn declynyd and iiij arn
vndeclynyd. Qwych iiij arn declynyd? Nown, pronown
uerbe and partycipyll. Qwych iiij arn vndeclynyd? Aduerbe,
coniunccion, preposycyon and interieccion. How many arn
declynyd w^t case^1 and how many w^{t}owt case? III w^t case and
I w^{t}owt case. Qwych iij w^t case? Nown, pronown and
partycypyll. Qwych on w^{t}owte case? Verbe alone.   10

How know ȝe a nown? For all þat I may see or fele or
know þat beryth þe name of a thyng is a nown, as *homo* for
'a man', *corpus* for 'a body', *anima* for 'a sowle' and all so
lyke. How many maner of nownys ben þer? II. Q(wich) ii?
A nown substantyf and a nown adiectyf. How ken ȝe a nown
substantyf? For it may stond<e>

Does not continue on other side of leaf or elsewhere in
the manuscript.

---

^{1} abbreviated ca$_9$, which is normally Latin 'casus', but this
scribe interchanges the fully written out 'case' with this
abbreviation.

44

ACCEDENCE TEXT F

F. London, British Library, MS Add. 37,075, fols.1ʳ-6ᵛ

H<ow man>y partis of reson be þer? VII<I>. Whiche viij?
Nown, pronown, verbe, a<duer>be, participill, coniunccion,
preposicion and int<er>ieccion. How many be declyned and how
many be vndeclyned? IIII be declyned and iiij be vndeclyned.
Whiche iiij be declyned? Nown, pronown, verbe and participill.
Whiche iiij be vndeclyned? Aduerbe, coniunccion, preposicion
and interieccion. Howe many be declyned wᵗ case and how many
wᵗowt case? III be declyned wᵗ case and oon wᵗowt case.
Whiche iij be declyned wᵗ case? Nown, pronown and participill.
Which oon wᵗout case? Verbe only. 10

Howe know þu a nown? For all þat I may see, here, fele
or vndirstande þat beryth þe name of a thyng is a nown. How
many thyngys longe to a nown? VI. Whiche vj? Qualite,
comparison, gendyr, nowmber, figure and case. How many manere
of nowmys be þer? II. Whiche ij? A nown substantyf and a
nown adiectyffe. How know þu a nown substantyffe? For he
may stonde by hymmself wᵗout þe helpe of a nodyr worde and is
declyned in Laten wᵗ oon artikyll as *hic magister* or wᵗ ij at
the most as *hic et hec sacerdos*. How know þu a nown
adiectyve?| <For he may not stonde by hymself wᵗout þe help>e 20
of a noþer worde and is <declyned in Laten wᵗ iij a>rtikyllis
as *hic et hec et hoc felix*, or wᵗ iij <di>uerse endyngis as
bonus, -a, -um.

How many degrees of comparison be þer? III. Whiche iij?
Þe positive, þe comparatyve and þe superlatyve. How know þu
þe posityve degree? For he is grounnde of all odyr degrees of
comparison, as 'wyse'. How know þu the comparatyve degree?
For he passith þe posityve degree wᵗ þis aduerbe *magis* as
'more wyse' or 'wyser'. How know þu the superlatyve degree?
For he passith þe posityve wᵗ þis aduerbe *valde* or *maxime*, as 30
'most wyse' or 'wysest'.

How many gendirs be þer? VII. Whiche vij? Þe
masculyn, þe femynyn, þe newter, þe comyn of ij, þe comyn of
iij, þe dubyn and þe episcen. How know þu the masculyn gendyr?
For he is declyned wᵗ *hic* as *hic magister*. How know þu the
femynyn gendyr? For he is declyned wᵗ *hec* as *hec musa*. How
know þu þe newter gendyr? For he is declyned wᵗ *hoc* as *hoc
scammum*. How know þu þe comyn of ij? For he is declyned wᵗ
hic and *hec* as *hic et hec sacerdos*. How know þu þe comyn of
iij? For he is declyned wᵗ *hic, hec, hoc* as *hic et hec et hoc* 40
felix. How know þu the dubyn gendir? For he is declyned ⸢wᵗ
hic and *hec*¹ and a¹ *vel* comyng betwen as *hic*|<*vel hec dies*.
How know þu> episcen gendyr? For vndyr on voys and <on
ar>ticull he comprehendeth male and female, as *hic passer* for
'a sparow'.

How many nowmbyrs ben þer? II. Whiche ij? Syngulere
and plurell. How know ye the singulere nombyr? For he spekyth

¹ vel *canc*.

ACCEDENCE TEXT F

of on þynge, as 'a man'. How know ye the plurell? For he
spekyth of moo thyngis þan of on, as 'men'.

How many case ben þer? VI. Whiche vi? Nominatyff, 50
genetyff, datyff, accusatyff, vocatyff and ablatyff. How know
ye þe nominatiff case? For he comyth byfore þe verbe and
answeryth to þis question 'who or what?'. How know ye þe
genityff case? For 'of' aftyr a nown substantyff, verbe
substantyffe, nown partityff, distributyff, comparatyff or
superlatyff degree is signe off þe genityff case. How know
ye þe datyff case? For 'to' before a nown or a pronown is
signe of the datyff case. How know ye the accusatyff case?
For he comyth aftyr the verbe. How know ye þe vocatyff case?
For he callith or spekyth to. How know ye the ablatyff case? 60
By my signes. Which be thoo? 'In', 'w^t', 'throw', 'for',
or 'froo', 'þan' and 'by' aftyr a comparatyff degree, be the
signes of the ablatyff case.

How many declensons of nowmys ben þer? V. Whiche v?
The fyrst, þe secunde,|<th>e iij^d, the iiij<th, the v^{te}.
How know ye the fyrst declenson? For the g>enityf case
singuler <endyth in -e, and also the dat>yff case, as nominatiuo
hec musa, genitiuo *huius -se*, datiuo *huic muse*. How know ye
the secunde declenson? For þe genityff case singulere endyth
in -*i* and þe datyff in -*o*, as nominatiuo *hic magister*, genitiuo 70
huius magistri, datiuo *huic magistro*. How know ye the iij^d
declenson? For þe genityff case singuler endith in -*is*, the
datyff in -*i*, as *hic et hec sacerdos*, genitiuo *huius –dotis*,
datiuo *huic sacerdoti*. How know ye the iiijth declenson?
For the genityff case synguler endyth in -*vs*, the datyff in
-*vi*, as nominatiuo *hec manus*, genitiuo *huius manus*, datiuo
huic manui. How know ye the v^{te} declenson? For þe genityff
case singulere endith in -*ei*, the datyff also, as nominatiuo
hec species, genitiuo *huius speciei*, datiuo *huic speciei*.

How know ye a pronown? For he is sett for a propir nown 80
and sumtyme receuyth certeyn person. How many thyngis longe
to a pronown? VI. Whiche vj? Qualite, gendyr, numbyr,
figure, person and case. How many pronownnys ben þer? XV.
Whiche xv? *Ego, tu, sui, ille, ipse, iste, hic* and *is*;
meus, tuus, suus, noster and *vester, nostras* and *vestras*.
How many be primatiuis, how many be deriuatiuis? VIII be
primatiuis and vij be deryuatiuis. Whiche viij be primatiuis?
Ego, tu, sui, ille, ipse, iste|<*hic* and *is*.> Which <vii be
deriu>atiuis? *Meus, tuus, suus, noster* and *vester, nostras*
and *vestras*. How many haue the vocatyff case and how many 90
want? IIII haue the vocatyff case and all oþer want. Whiche
iiij haue þe vocatyff case? *Tu, meus, noster* and *vestras*,
and all oþer want.

How many persǫnns ben þer? III. Which iij? The first,
the secund, þe iij^d. How know ye the first? For he spekyth
of hymmselfe, as 'I' or 'we'. How know ye the secund? For
he spekyth to a noþer, as 'þu' or 'ye'. How know ye the iij^d?
For all nownnys and pronownnys and participillis be þe iij^d

46

ACCEDENCE TEXT F

person, owte-take *ego*, *nos*, *tu* and *vos* w^t her obliquis and the
vocatyff case.   100

How many declensons be there? IIII. Whiche iiij? Þe
fyrst, the secund, the iij^d, the iiijth. How know ye the
first declenson? For þe genityff case singulere endith in *-i*
or in *-is*, the datyff in *-i*, as nominatiuo *ego*, genitiuo *mei*
vel *mis*, datiuo *michi*. How many pronownns be of þis declenson?
III. Which iij? *Ego, tu, sui*. How know ye the secund
declenson of pronownns? For the genityff case singulere endith
in *-ius* or in *-ius*, the datyff in *-i* or in *-c*, as *illius, eius,*
illi, huic. How many pronownns be of þis declenson? V.
Whiche v? *Ille, ipse, iste, hic* and *is*. How many nownnnys?   110
VIII. Whiche viij? *Vnus, ullus, totus, solus, alter, alius,*
quis and *vter*|w^t her compownys. <How know ye the iij^d
declenson> of pronownnnys? For þe <genitiff> case singuler
⌐<endith>⌐ in *-i* or in *-e*, the datyff in *-o* or in *-e*, as
nominatiuo *meus, -a, -um*, genitiuo *mei, mee, -i*, datiuo *meo,*
-e, -o. How many pronownnnys be of þis declenson? V.
Whiche v? *Meus, tuus, suus, noster* and *vester*. How know
ye the iiijth declenson of pronowns? For the genityff case
singulere endyth in *-atis*, the datyff in *-ati*, as *hic et hec*
nostras, genitiuo *huius nostratis*, datiuo *huic nostrati*.   120
How many pronownnys be of this declenson? II. Whiche ij?
Nostras and *vestras*.

How know ye a verbe? For he is declyned w^t mode and tens
w^{t}owt case and articull, and betokenyth 'to do' or 'to suffyr'
or 'to be'. How many thyngis long to a uerbe? VII. Whiche
vij? Mode, coniugacion, gender, numbyr, fygure, tens and
person. How many modys be þer? V. Whiche v? Indicatyff,
imperatyff, optatyff, co(n)iunctyff and infinityff. How know
ye the indicatyff mode? For he shewith a reson trew or false
by the wey of askyng or of tellyng. How know ye the imperatyff   130
mode? For he byddith or commanndith. How know ye the
optatyff mode? For he willith or desyrith. How know ye the
coniunctyff mode? For he joynyth mode to mode, tens to tens.
How know ye the infinityff mode? For 'to' byfore a verbe is
signe of the infenityff|<mode; and when ij uerbys come>
togedyr w^{t}owt a relatyff <or a> coniunccion þe latter shall be
þe infenytiff mode.

How many coniugacions ben þer? IIII. Whiche iiij?
Þe fyrst, the secunde, the iij^d, the fourth. How know ye the
first? For he hath *A* long byfore the *-re* yn the infenityff   140
mode, as *amare*. How know ye the secunde? For he hath *E*
long byfore the *-re* in the infenytiff mode, as *docere*. How
know ye iij^d? For he hath *E* schorte byfore the *-re* in the
infinityff mode, as *legere*. How know ye the fourth? For
he hath *I* long byfore the *-re* in the infinityff mode, as *audire*.

How many gendyrs be þer of verbis? V. Which v? Actyff,
passyff, neuter, deponent and commyn. How know ye a verbe
actyff? For he endith in *-o* and may take *R* upon *-o* and make
of hym a passyff. How know ye a uerbe passyff? For he endith

ACCEDENCE TEXT F

in -*r* and may do awey þe -*r* and turn ynto his actyff. How 150
know ye a uerbe neuter? For he endith in -*o* and may not take
R upon -*o* nor make of hym a passyf. How know ye a uerbe
deponent? For he hath the letter of þe passyff and þe
significacion of þe actyff, and iiij participillis as *loquens,
locutus, locuturus*. How know ye a uerbe comyn? For he
endith in -*r* and hath the significacion of the actyff and
passiff both, and iiij participillis as *criminans,|criminatus,
criminaturus, (criminandus)*.

<How> many nownbyrs be þer? II. Whiche ij? Singuler
and plurell. Whiche is þe singuler? All þat commyth afore 160
'et pluraliter'. Which is the plurell? All þat commyth
aftyr 'et pluraliter'.

How many tens be þer? V. Which v? Þe present, þe
preterinperfit, þe preterperfit, þe preterpluperfit and þe
future. Howe know ye the present tens? For he spekyth of
the tyme þat is now, as *amo*, 'I loue'. How know ye the
preterinperfitens? For he spekyth of þe tyme þat is past
w^{t}owt this signe 'haue' or 'had', as *amabam*, 'I louyd'. How
know ye the preterperfit? For he spekyth of the tyme þat is
past w^t þis signe 'haue' as *amaui*, 'I haue louyd'. How 170
know ye the preterpluperfitens? For he spekyth of the tyme
þat is past w^t þis signe 'had', as *amaueram*, 'I had louyd'.
How know ye the future tens? For he spekyth of the tyme þat
is to come w^t þis signe 'schall', as futuro *amabo*, 'I shall
loue'.

How many persons ben þer? III. Which iij? Þe fyrst,
þe secund, þe iij^d. Which is the fyrst? The first worde,
as *amo*. Which is þe secunde? The secunde worde, as *amas*.
Whiche is þe iij^d? Þe iij^d worde, as *amat*.

How know ye an aduerbe? For he is set nere þe uerbe and 180
declarith his significacion. How many thyngis long to an
aduerbe? III. Whiche iij? Significacion,|compariso<n
and figure. How> many degreys of comparisons be þer off
<aduerb>ys? III. Which iij? Þe posytyff, as *docte*, þe
comparatyff, as *doctius*, þe superlatyff, as *doctissime*.

How know ye a participill? For he takyth parte off a
nown, parte of uerbe, parte of bothe. What takith he of nown?
Gendyr and case. What off a uerbe? Tens and significacion.
What of bothe? Nombyr and figure. How many tens be þer of
participillis? IIII. Whiche iiij? A participill of þe 190
presentens, a participill of þe pretertens, a participill of
the first future, a participill off þe last future. How know
ye a participill off þe presentens? For his Englissh endith
in '-yng', as 'louyng', and his Laten ende in -*ens* or
in -*ans*, as *legens, amans*. How know ye a participill of þe
pretertens? For þis is his Englissh: 'louyd', 'tauȝth',
'herde'; and his Laten schall ende in -*tus* or in -*sus*, as
amatus, visus. How know ye a participill of þe first
future? For his Englissh begynnyth w^t 'to' w^{t}owt 'be',

ACCEDENCE TEXT F

as 'to loue', and his Laten schall ende in -*rus*, as *amaturus*. 200
How know ye a participill of þe last future? For his Englissh
begynnyth w^t 'to' and 'be' after, as 'to be louyd', and his
Laten shall ende in -*dus*, as *amandus*.

Of whom is a participill of þe presentens i-formyd? Of
þe first person syngulere of þe preterinperfitens of þe
indicatyff mode by channgyng -*bam* into *N*|<and *S*, as *amabam*,
change -*bam* into *N*> and *S* it is *aman*<*s*. Of whom is a participill>
of þe pretertens i-formed? Of þe latter suppyne of þe verbe
bye puttyng to -*s*, as *lectu*, put to -*s*, it is *lectus*. Off
whom is a participill of þe fyrst future i-formyd? Of þe 210
latter suppyn of þe verbe be puttyng to -*rus*, as *lectu*, put
to -*rus*,¹ it is *lecturus*. Of whom is a participill of the
last future formed? Of þe genityff case, singulere nowmbyr
of þe participill of þe presentens by channgyng -*tis* into -*dus*,
as *legentis* channge -*tis* into -*dus*, it is *legendus*.

How know ye a coniunccion? For he joynyth odyr partis
of reson togedyr in ordyr. How many thyngis long to a
coniunccion? III. Whiche iij? Poure, figure and² ordyr.
How many maner of coniunccions ben þer? V. Whiche v?
Copulatyff, disiunctyff, expletyff, casuall, racionall. 220
Whiche be copulatyffis? All þat ben in þis verse, 'Da
copulatiuas'. Whiche be disiunctiuis? All þat ben in þis
verse, 'Da disiunctiuas'. Whiche be expletiuis? Alle þat
ben in þis verse, 'Da explatiuas'. Whiche be causallys?
Alle þat ben in þis verse, 'Da causales'. Whiche ben
racionallis? All þat ben in þis verse, 'Da racionales'.

How know ye a preposicion? For he is sett byfore oþer
partys of reson in apposicion or in composicion. How many
thyngis long to a preposicion? On. Whiche on? Case only.
To how many case seruyth a preposicion?| <II. Which ii? 230
The accusatyff> or þe ablatyff. Whiche ser<ue to the
accusat>yff case and whiche to the ablatyff case? All þat
ben in þis verse, 'Da preposiciones casus accusatiui', serue
to þe accusatyff case; all þat ben in þis verse, 'Da
preposiciones casus ablatiui', serue to þe ablatyff case;
and all þat ben in þis verse, 'Da vtriusque', will serue to
both case.

How know ye an interieccion? For he betokenyth passion
of a mannys soule vndyr an vnperfite voyce, as of joy, woo,
wondyr, drede or indignacion. 240

How many concordis of grammer ben þer? V. Which³ v?
The first bytwene þe nominatyff case and the verbe, the
secunde bytwene the adiectyff and the substantyff, the iij^d
bytwene þe relatyff and þe antecedent, the iiij^th bytwen þe
nowm partityff or distributyff and þe genityff case þat
folowith, the v^te bytwene the superlatyff degree and þe
genityff case þat folwyth. In how many shall þe nominatyff

---

¹ -r from D   ² odyr canc.   ³ v(?) canc.

ACCEDENCE TEXT F

case and þe uerbe acorde? In ii. Whiche ij? In nombyr
and person. In how many shall þe adiectyff and þe substantyff
accorde? In iij. Whiche iij? In case, gendyr and nombyr. In 250
how many shall þe relatyff and þe antecedent accorde? In iij.
Which iij? In gendyr, nommbyr and person. In how many
shall the nown partityff or distributyff accorde w^t þe
genityff|case þat folowyth? <In on. Whiche on? In>
gendyr only. In how many shall þe superlatyff degre accorde
w^t þe genityff þat folowyth? In on. Whiche on? In
gendir only. Explicit.

ACCEDENCE TEXT G

G. London, Public Record Office, MS C.47/34/13, fols.22ʳ-23ʳ

The manuscript is badly damaged at this point by water. The
following text is based on a transcript made under ultra-violet
light.

'Hwo' to-for de verbe ys nominatyf case; 'hwat' eft(er)
de verbe ys acusatyf cas<e; 'hwat'> efter dys verbe *sum*, *e(s)*,
fui ys nominatyft case; 'of' genetyf; 'to' datyf case; on
(of)¹ þi <signes> 'yn', 'by', 'wyt', 'dorwe' and 'fro' schal
cerue to ablatyf case. 'Of' efter a nown substantyf, partatyf,
superlatyf degre, 'of' efter a dicion sy<nfyyt fulnesse> or
foydnesse schal cerue to genityf case. 'Of' efter þis verbe
of *sum*, *es*, *fui* schal <cerue to> genetyf case. 'Of' efter a
verbe, 'of' efter a particypille, 'of' efter a gerundyf, 'of'
efter <a supyn> schal cerue to ablatyf case wyt *a* preposiscion.   10
'Þane' efter a comparatyf degre² s<chal cerue> to ablatyf case.

How manye tens beyt þer? Fy(v)e. Wyche fy(v)e?
Presentens, pretert inperfectens, preterperfectens, perfectens,
futur tens. How³ knowyst þu de presentens? For hyt synf<yyt
de tyme> þat ys nuw. How knowyst þu de preteryt imper(fe)ctens?
For hyt synfyyt <de tyme nat fully a-gon>. How k<no>wys þu de
preteryt perfecte(n)s? For hyt synfyyt de tyme þat ys
alþer-varnyst a-go. How k(n)owyst þu de preteryt
plusquamperfectens? For hyt synfyyt <de> tyme þat ys a aldyr-
varnyst a-go. How k(n)owyst de futur tens? For hyt synfyyt<de>   20
tyme⁴ þat ys to comyne.

How ma(n)y modis beyt þer? Fyue. Wyche fyve?⁵
Indicatyf mod, inperatyf mod<e>, optatyf mode, coniunctyf
mod, infyntyf mod. How k(n)owyst þu indicatyf mod<e>?
For he schewyt oþer actyt. How knowyst þu de⁶ ⌈inperatyf⌉
mod? For hyt hotyt <...>. How k(n)owyst þu optatyf mod?
For hyt wyllyt oþer desyryt. How k(n)owyst þu coniunctyf
mod? For hyt ys y-junyd be c,⁷ oþer by *cum* oþer by eny oþer
coniunccion þat schal cerue to coniunctyf mod. How knowyst
þu infynytyf mod? For w<hen> þer comyt two verbys yn a   30
reyson de latter schal be infynytyf mod.|

<How> manye concordanys byt þer? Dre. On betwene þe
nominatyf case and de werbe, <a> nodyr betwene de aiectyf and
de substantyf, and a noþer be þe relatyf and de anteced<ent>.
In how manye hauyt de nominatyf case and de verbe acorde?
In two. In weche two? Yn numbyr and persam. Yn how manye
hauyt de aiectyf and de substantyf acorde? Ym dre. In
weche dre? In numbyr and⁸ gendyr and case. Yn how manye
hauyt de relatyf⁹ and de ancedent to acorde? In dre. In
wyche dre? In gendyr, numbyr <and> persowne.   40

Ech patisipul þat endit yn '-yngge' as 'louyngg' ys

¹ *on* (of)] MS o.   ² MS þegre   ³ many *canc.*
⁴ MS tyne   ⁵ -u- *from* e   ⁶ infynytyf *canc.*
⁷ *sic* MS   ⁸ persun *canc.*   ⁹ MS leralatyf

51

ACCEDENCE TEXT G

presentens of <...> participyl þat shal ende yn Latyn yn
-ens vel -ans as *legens*, <a>*mans*. Ech particpyl synfyn 'y-do'
ys pretertens[1] þat ende in Latyn <in> -*tus* vel in -*sus*, ut
lectus, *visus*. Ech participyl synfyn 'to[2] ⌈be do⌉' <ys fu>ture
tens of participyl and þat schal yn Latyn yn -*rus*, as *lecturus*,
⌈*visurus*⌉. <Ech> participyl[3] synfyn '⌈for⌉ to be do' ys future
tens of participyl and þat schal ende in Latyn in[4] -*dus*,
vt ⌈*legendus*⌉, *amandus*.

    Ech ayectyf[5] þat hendyt in '-yngge' as 'louyngge',   50
'redyng' ys presentens p<articip>ul and þat schal ⌈ende⌉ yn
Latin yn -*ens* oþer -*ans*, vt *legens*, *amans*. <. . .>|

    Hywyche ys þe knowlychyng of de forste clensun? <......>
Wyche? Þe veche þe gentif casce singuler endyt yn <-*e*, þe
datif> also, þe acusatif yn -*am*, þe vocatyf schel be leche de
<nominatyf, þe> ablatyf in -*a*. <......>

---

[1] *i canc.*   [2] *ys canc.*   [3] *þat endit canc.*
[4] *repeated*   [5] *heche adiectyf added above the line*

ACCEDENCE TEXT H

H. Norwich, Norfolk Record Office, Colman MS 111, (fol.1^v of medieval MS A)

...the plurale numbre in Latyn allso. A word yn Englysch ys synglar numbre whan he spekyth but of one thyng, as 'a$\{^{man'}_{chyld'}$', 'a$\{^{beest'}_{boke'}$'. A word in Englysch ys plurall numbre whan he spekyth of many thyngys, as $\{^{'men'}_{'childurn'}$, $\{^{'beestis'}_{'bookys'}$. Numbre in a substantyue ys known by hys Englysch.

Ther be v gendres, the:

The $\left\{\begin{array}{l}\text{masculyn}\\\text{femynyn}\\\text{neutur}\\\text{comyn of ij}\\\text{comyn of thre}\end{array}\right\}$ gendre   10

All wordys declyned only w^t thys artykyll *hic* be masculyn gendur, as nominatiuo *hic*$\{^{magister}_{dignus}$. *Hic* ys artykyll of the masculyn gendre. Allso all wordys þat be declyned w^t *hec* be femynyn gendre, as nominatiuo *hec*$\{^{musa}_{toga}$. *Hec* ys artykyll of the femynyn gendre. All wordys declyned w^t *hoc* be neutur gendur, as nominatiuo *hoc*$\{^{scamnum}_{corpus}$. *Hoc* ys artykyll of the neutur gendre. *Hec* in the plurall numbre ys the neutur gendre. All wordys declyned w^t *hic* and *hec* be the comyn gendre of ij, as *hic*, *hec*$\{^{sacerdos}_{aduena}$. All wordys of the forsayd gendres be   20 nownys substantyues.

How knowe ye a nowne substantyue? By hys Englysch and by hys Laten. In Englych he may stand w^{t}owt an adiectyffe and comynly one of thes^1 tokens go before hym as:

'a$\{^{man'}_{chyld'}_{boke'}$' 'an$\{^{halle'}_{halter'}_{hors'}$' 'the$\{^{sone'}_{mone'}_{see'}$'

In Latyn he ys declyned w^t one artykyll,^{2} as nominatiuo *hic* $\{^{magister}_{dominus}$, *hec*$\{^{musa}_{vestis}$, *hoc*$\{^{scamnum}_{corpus}$; w^t ij artykyllis, as nominatiuo *hic*, *hec*$\{^{aduena}_{sacerdos}$. All wordys declyned w^t iij artykyllys be the comyn gendre of iij, as nominatiuo *hic*, *hec*, *hoc*$\{^{vetus}_{felix}$; nominatiuo *hic*, *hec*$\{^{doctior}_{vtilis}$ et *hoc*$\{^{doctius}_{vtilius}$$_3$;   30

---

^{1} -e- from y ^{2} or w^t canc. ^{3} -ius from e

53

ACCEDENCE TEXT H

hic, hec omnis et *hoc omne*; *hic, hec melior* et *hoc -lius*; and all such be adiectyuys of the third declynacion.

How knowne ye a nowne adiectyue? By hys Englych and by hys Latyn....

ACCEDENCE TEXT J

J. Oxford, Bodleian Library, MS Digby 26, fols.63^r, 63^v, 5^v, 62^v

Qweche[1] is þe knoulaching of þe first declinesone? Þis is hit of quom þe genitif and þe datif cas singuler, þe nominatif and þe vocatif cas pluril enden in -*e*, þe accusatif in -*am*, þe vocatif shal be lyk to þe nominatif, þe ablatif in -*a*, þe genitif pluril in -*arum*, þe datif and þe ablatif in -*is*, þe accusatif in -*as*.|

Qwech is þe knoulaching of þe secunde declinisonne? Þis is hit of quom þe genitif cas singuler, þe nominatif and þe vocatif cas plurel enden en -*i*, ⸢þe datif and þe ablatif enden in -*o*,⸣ þe accusatif cas singler in -*vm*. Quen þe nominatif cas singler endes in -*r* þe vocatif shal be lik to hit. Quen hit endes in -*vs* þe vocatif shal enden in -*e*. Quen hit endes in -*ivs* þe vocatif shal enden in -*i* and hit be a propre noune. Þe genitif plurel in -*orum*, þe datif and þe ablatif in -*is*, þe accusatif in -*os*.|

Quech is þe knoulaching of þe thrid declineson? This is hit of quome þe genetif cas singlere endes in -*is*, þe datif in -*i*, þe accusatif in -*em* or in -*im*, þe vocatif shal be lik to þe nominatif, þe ablatif in -*e* or in -*i*; þe nominatif and þe accusatif and þe vocatif casus plurel enden in -*es*, þe genitif cas plurel in -*vm* or in -*ium*, þe datif and þe ablatif in -*bus*. ⸢Versus. Qweche is the knoulac⸣|

Qweche is þe. Qweche is the know.|

10

20

---

[1] MS *adds* Qweche is *on the preceding line.*

ACCEDENCE TEXT K

K. Oxford, Bodleian Library, MS Douce 103, fols.53ʳ-57aʳ

How mony partyse of speche ben þer? VIII. Wyche viij?
Nowne, pronowne, verbe, aduerbe, partycypull, coniunccion,
preposicion and interieccion. How mony byth declynd and how
mony byn vndeclynd? IIII byn declynd and iiij byn vndeclynd.
Weche iiij byn declynd and wyche iiij byn vndeclynd? Nowne,
pronowne, verbe and partycypull byn declynd, aduerbe,
coniunccion, preposicion and interieccion byn vndeclynd. How
mony byn declynd wᵗ case and how mony wᵗowte case? III byn
declynd wᵗ case and j wᵗowte case. Wychy iij wᵗ case, wychy
j wᵗowte case? Nowne, pronowne and partycypull wᵗ case,   *10*
verbe o(n)ylie wᵗowte case.

How knowyst¹ a nowne? A nowne ys all maner of thyng þat
y may see, fele or hondyll or beryth þe name of a thyng, þe
name þerof ys a now(n)e. How mony maner of nownys byn there? II.
Wyche ij? Nowne substantyfe and nowne adiectyfe. How knowyst
a nowne substantyfe? For he ys y-declynd wᵗ j artycull or ij
at þe most. How knowyst a nowne adiectyfe? For he ys declynd
wᵗ iij artyculs or wᵗ iij dyuerse yendyngys. Wyche² byn þe
artyculys? *Hic, hec* and *hoc*. Wyche byn þe iij dyuerse
yndyngys? *-Vs, -a* and *-vm*. How? As *bonus, bona, bonum*   *20*
for 'goode'.

How mony nomburs³ byn there? II. Wyche to? The
synguler nombur and the plurell now(m)bur. How knowyst the syngler
nowmbur? For he spekyth of on thyng,|as 'mon' or 'beste'.
How knowyst the plurell nombur? For he spekyth of mony
theyngis, as ('men') or 'bestis'.

How mony degreys of comparsons byn there? III. Wyche
iij? The posityff degre, the comparatyf degree and the
superatyf degree. How knowyst thow the posytyf degree?
For he ys begynner and growndere of all oþer degreys of   *30*
comparsonys and þey byn formyd of hym and he ys not of them.
How knowyst the comparatyf degre? For he endyth yn '-r', as
'fayryre', 'lyngyr', 'schortyre'. How knowyst the superatyf
degre? For he endyth⁴ yn '-ys' as 'feyryste', 'lengyst',
'schortys'.

How mony persons byn there? III. Wyche iij? 'I'
and 'we' the fyrst person, 'þu' and 'ȝe' the secund person.
All oþer byn þe iij person excepte the vocatyf case. How
knowyst the fyrste person? For he spekyth of hymsylfe, as
'y' or 'we'. How knowyst the ij person? For he spekyth to a   *40*
oþer as 'þu' or 'ȝe'. How knowyst the iij person? For he
spekyth of a oþer as 'he' or 'they'.

How mony gendrys byn there? VII. Wyche vij? Masculyn
gender, femynin gender, neuter gendur, and commyn of two, commyn
(of) iij, dubyn gendur and ypsen gendur. How knowyst masculyn

---

¹ a partycipull *canc.*   ² h *canc.*   ³ h *canc.*
⁴ ys *canc.*

ACCEDENCE TEXT K

gendur? For he ys declyned w^t *hic* as *hic magister*. The
femynin w^t *hec* as *hec musa*. The neuter w^t *hoc* as *hoc scannum*.[1]
The commyn of two w^t *hic* and *hec* as *hic et hec sacerdos*. The
commen of iij w^t *hic*, *hec* et *hoc* (as *hic*, *hec* et *hoc*) *felyx*.
(How knowyst) the dubyn gendur? For he ys declynyd w^t *hic*, 50
hec and *vel* conjuncion betwene, as *hic vel hec dies*. | How
knowyst the epcyn gendur? For vndur oon artycul he
comprehendyth bothe male and female, as *hic pascer*, *hec aquila*.

    How mony nowmburs byn there? II. Wyche ij? Syngulere
and plurell. How knowyst þe synguler nowmbur? For he spekyth
but of on thyng, as 'a mon' or 'beste'. How knowyst þe
plurel[2] nowmber? For he spekyth of mo thyngis then of on,
as 'men' or 'bestis'.

    How mony cases byn the(r)? VI. Wyche vj? Nominatyfe
case, genetyfe case, the datyfe case, accusatyfe case, the 60
vocatyfe case and the ablatyfe case. How knowyst the
nominatyfe case? For he cumyt afore the verbe and askyt thys
questyon 'Who or wat?' How knowyst the genytyfe case?
For 'of' after a nowne substantyfe, verbe substantyfe, nowne
partyfe, nowne dystrybutyfe or a superlatyfe degre byn the
synes of the genytyfe case. How knowyst the datyfe case?
For 'to' before a nowne or a pronowne wyttoty remewyng ys the
senys of the datyfe case. How knowyst the accusatyfe case?
For he cumyth aftur the verbe and onseryth to thys questyon
'Whom or what?'. How knowyst the wocatyfe case? For he 70
clepyth or callyth or spekyth to. How knowyst the ablatyfe
case? By my synes. Wyche byn they? 'Yn' and 'wyth',
'throʒe', 'fro' and 'by' and ('than') after a comparatyf
⌈de⌉gre ys the synes of the ablatyfe case.|

    How mony declynsuns of now(n)ys? V. Wyche v? The furst,
the ij, the iij, the iiij, the v. How knowyst the furst?
For the genityfe case synguler endyth yn -*e* and datyfe also.
How knowyst the ij? For[3] þe genityfe synguler endyth yn -*i*
and datyfe and the ablatyfe yn -*o*. How knowyst the iij? For
the genityfe ⌈case⌉ synguler endyth yn -*ys*, the datyfe yn -*i*. 80
How knowyst the iijj? For the genityfe case synguler endyth
in -*vs*, the datyfe yn -*vj*. How knowyst the v? For the
genityfe case synguler endyth yn -*ei* and the datyfe also.[4]

    How mony persuns byn there? III. Wyche iij? The
furst, the ij, the iij. How knowyst the i persone? For he
spekyth of hymselfe as 'I' o(r) 'we'. How knowyst the ij
persone? For he spekyth of a nodur as 'thou' or 'ʒe'. How
knowyst the iij persone? For he spekyth of a nodure as 'he'
or 'they'.

    How knowyst a pronowne? For he ys a parte of speche 90
declynyd w^t case þe wyche ys seyt for a propur name of a man
and resewyth to hym certey(n) personys. How mony pronowys

[1] *sic* MS   [2] MS pluler   [3] -o- from e
[4] MS adds How knowyst

ACCEDENCE TEXT K

byn there? XV. Wyche xv? *Ego, tu, sui, ille, ipse, (iste), hic* and *his, meus, tuus, suus, noster* and *vester, nostras* and *vestras*. How mony byn the primityfis and how mony byn the deruatwes? VIII byn þe primitywes and vij|byn deruatywes. Wyche viij byn primitywes? *Ego, tu, sui, ille, ipse, iste, hic* and *js*. Wych vij byn deruatywes? *Meus, tuus, suus, noster* and *vester, nostras* and *vestras*.

How mony declynsonis of pronownes byn there? IIII. *100*
Wych iiij? The j, the ij, the iij, and the iiij. How knowyst the i? For the genytyf case synguler endyth yn *-i* or yn *-ys*, the datyfe yn *-i*. How mony pronownes conteynyth he?[1] III. Wych iij? *Ego, tu, sui*. How knowyst the ij? For the genytyfe case synguler endyth yn *-i(u)s* or yn *-ius*, the datyfe yn *-i* or yn *-c*. How knowyst the iij? For the genytyfy[2] case synguler endyth yn *-i* or yn *-e* and yn *-i* and the datyfe yn *-o* or in *-e* or in *-o*. How mony pronownes conteynyth he? V. Wych v? *Meus, tuus, suus, noster, vester*. How knowyst iiij? For the genytyfy case synguler endyth in *110*
-atis and datyfe in *-ati*. How mony pronownes conteyneth he? II. Wych ij? *Nostras* and *vestras*. And how many nownes? On. Wych on? *Cugeas, -ati(s)*.

How knowyst a verbe? For he ys a party of speche declyned[3] w{t} mode, tyme and coniugacion, w{t}owte case or arty(c)le, betokynyng 'to do', or sufferyng (or) 'to be'. How mony maner of verbis byn there? V. Wych v? Verbe actyfy, verbe passyfy, verbe neuter, verbe deponent and verbe commyn.|

How knowyst a verbe actyfy? For he endyth in *-o* and betokenyth[4] 'to do', and may take *-r* apon[5] *O* and make of hym *120*
a passyf, as *amo, amor*. How knowyst a verbe passyf? For he endyth yn *-r* and betokenyth 'to suffure' and may do away ys *-r* fro ys *O* and turne ayene[6] into ys actyfy, as *amor, amo*. How knowyst a verbe neuter? For he endyth in *-o* and may not take *-r* appon *O* ne constur w{t} hys accusatyf case *hominem* aftur hym. How knowyst a verbe deponent? For he endyth in *-r* as a verbe passyf and hath the Englyssche of the actyfy. How knowyst a verbe comyn? For he endyth in *-r* as a verbe passyf and hath the Englyssche of þe actyf and of the passyf booth.

How[7] mony coniugacions byn there? IIII. Wych iiij? *130*
The i as *amo*, ⌐*-as*⌐, *amor*, ⌐*-aris*⌐; the ij as *doceo, doces, doceor, -ris*; the iij as *lego, -gis, legor, -ris*; the iiij as *audio, -dis, audior, -ris*. How knowyst the i? For he hath A long before the *-re* infenityf mode, afore the *-ris* indicatyf mode, as *amare* vel *amaris*. How knowyst the ij? For he hath a E long before the *-re* infenityf mode, before the *-ris* indicatyf mode, as *docere* vel *-ris*. How knowyst the iij? For he hath a E schorte before the *-re* infenityf[8] mode, before the *-ris* indicatyf mode, as *legere* vel *-ris*. How knowyst

---

[1] MS the [2] -t- from f [3] MS edeclyd
[4] to do *canc.* after be- [5] -p- from o [6] I *canc.* after a-
[7] knowyst *canc.* [8] MS Indicatyf

ACCEDENCE TEXT K

the iiij? For he hath a I long|before ⌈the⌉ -*re* infynityf   140
mode, before the -*ris* indecatyf mode, as *audire* vel -*ris*.

How mony modis byn there? V. Wyche¹ v? Indicatyf
mode, imperatyf mode,² optatyf mode, coniunctyf mode, and
infenityf mode. How knowyst indicatyf mode? For he tellyt
or sowyt and hath no syne of no nothyre mode. How knowyst
imperatyf mode? For he byddyth or commawndyth. How knowyst
the optatyf mode? For he well or desyryt, and by ys ij synys
'wolde' or 'sculde'. How knowyst the coniunctyf mode? By
my synys. Wych byn they? *Si, cum, licet, quamvis, quamqua*(*m*)
and othyre coniunctions moo wyll haue coniunctyf mode aftur hym.   150
How knowyst infenityf mode? For whan ij verbys commyth
togedur wᵗout a relatyf or a coniunccion betwene, the later
verbe schall be the infenityf mode.

How mony tymes byn there? V. Wych v? The tyme þat
ys noo, the tyme that ys nott fulliche a-gonne, and the tyme
that ys a-gon, the tyme that (is) more then a-goon, and the tyme
that ys to cum. How knowyst the tyme that ys no? For he
betokynth the tyme þat ys no, as *amo*, 'y loue'. How knowyst
the tyme þat ys not folych a-gon? For he betokynyt the tyme
þat ys not fullych a-gon, as *am*(*a*)*bam*, 'y louyd'. How knowyst the 160
tyme þat ys a-gon? For he betokynyd the tyme þat ys a-gon, as
amaui, 'y haue louyd'. How knowyst the tyme þat ys to cum?
For he betokynyd the tyme þat ys to³ cum, as *amabo*, 'I schal
loue'.|

How knowyst an aduerbe? For he ys a party of spech
vnndeclynyd, the wych ys caste to a uerbe and makyth playne
and fulfyllyth syngnyfycacion of the verbe.

How knowyst a partycypull? For he ys a party of spech
declynyd⁴ wᵗ case and takyth parte of a nowne, party of a verbe,
and party of both two. What takyth of a nowne? Gendur and   170
case. What of a verbe? Tyme and syngnificacion. What of
both to? Nombur and fugur.

How mony maner partycypull byn there? IIII. Wych iiij?
The partycypull of the tyme þat ys now, the partycypull of tyme
þat ys⁵ a-gon, the partycypull ⌈of the⌉ tyme þat ys to cum
actyf, the partycypull of the tyme þat ys to cum passyf.
How knowyst the partycypull of the tyme þat ys noo? For he
endyth in '-yng' yn Englyssch, as 'louyng', 'techyng', 'redyng',
'heryng', and endyth yn -*ens* or yn -*ans* yn Latyn. Whereof
schall he be formyd? Of the furst person synguler nowbur of   180
the tyme þat ys nott fullych a-gon, as *amabam*, change -*bam* to
N and⁶ *S* and make nominatiuo *hic, hec, hoc amans*. How knowyst
the partycypull ⌈of⁷⌉ tyme þat ys gon? For he begynnyth be
'i' yn Englysse as 'y-louyd', 'y-tauӡth', 'y-radde', 'y-herde',
and endyth yn -*tus* or ⌈yn -*sus*⌉ yn⁸ Laten, as *amatus, doctus*,

¹ -c- *from* h   ² MS mᵒ *as elsewhere*   ³ ci *canc.*
⁴ MS edclynyd   ⁵ to cum *canc.*   ⁶ MS or
⁷ MS *adds* tyme   ⁸ lar *canc.*

59

ACCEDENCE TEXT K

lectus, auditus. Whereof schall he be formyd? Of the later suppyne, as *lectu*, sett ther-to *-s* and make *lectus, -a, -um*. How knowyst the partycypull of the tyme þat ys to cum actyf? For he[1] begynnyth as 'to'[2] yn Englysse, as 'to loue', 'to| teche' et cetera, and endyth yn Laten yn *-rus*, as *amaturus, docturus*. Whereof schall he be formyd? Of the latur suppyn, as *lectu*, set there-to *-rus* and make *lecturus*. How knowyst the partycypull (of the tyme) þat ys to cum passyfe? For he begynnyth[3] 'to be' yn Englysse, as 'to be louyd', 'to be ta3th', 'to be rad', 'to be harde', and schall endyth yn *-dus* in Laten, as *amandus, docendus, legendus, audiendus*. Whereof schall he be formyd? Of the genityf case synguler of the partycypull of the (tyme) that ys nou, as *legentis*, change the *-tis* into *-dus* and make *legendus, -da, -dum*.

How knowyst a coniunccion? For he ys a party of speche vndeclynyd, the wych cowpullyth or dyscowpulyth all othere partes of[4] speche yn ordur.

How knowyst a preposicion? For he ys a party of speche vndeclynyd the wych ys set before or beendyth yn apocycyon or yn compocycyon, and odur wyle seruyth to accusatyf case and odur wyle to ablatyf case and odur wyle to both too.

How knowyst an interieccyon? For[5] he ys a party of speke vndeclynyd the wych shew^t a monnys wyll w^t a vnperfytt voyce, as wondur, drede or merwell.

190

200

---

[1] be *canc*.
[2] MS *adds* be
[3] w^t *canc*.
[4] se *canc*.
[5] y *canc*.

ACCEDENCE TEXT L

L. Oxford, Bodleian Library, MS Rawl. D.328, fols. 119^r, 120^r, 121^r, 122^r, 123^r, 124^r-125^r, 126^r

The following text was begun and abandoned on six successive folios, and the end of the text was also partially repeated.

[How many partes of spech be ther? VIII. Which viij? Nowne, pronowne, verbe, adverbe, participill, coniunccion, preposicion and interieccion. How many beth declyned w^t c]|

[(H)^{1}ow many partes of spech be ther? VIII. Which viij? Nowne, pronowne, verbe, adverbe, participill, co<niun>ccion, preposicion and inteieccion. How many]| 5

[(H)^{1}ow many partes of spech be ther? VIII. Which viij? Nown, prownene, verbe, adverbe, participill, coniunccion, preposicion and interieccion. How many beth declend w^t cas]|

[(H)^{1}ow many partes of spech be ther? VIII. Which viij?   10
Nowne, pronowne, verbe, adverbe, coniunccion, preposicion and interiecco]|

[(H)^{1}ow many partes of spech be ther? VIII. Which viij? Nowne, pronowne, verbe, adverbe, participill, coniunccion, preposicion and interieccion. How many beth declened w^t case   15
and how many w^t

Ow many]|

How many partes of spech be ther? VIII. Which viij? Nowne, pronowne, verbe, adverbe, participill, coniunccion, preposicion and interieccion. How many beth declyned and how many beth vndeclyned? IIII beth declyned and iiij beth   20
vndeclyned. Which iiij beth declyned? Nowne, pronowne, verbe and participill. Which iiij beth vndeclyned? Adverbe, coniunccion, preposicion and interieccion. How many beth declyned w^t case and how many w^{t}out case? III beth declyned w^t case and on w^{t}out case. Which iij w^t case? Nowne, pronowne and participill. Which on w^{t}out case? Verbe only.

How knowist thow a nowne? For all thyng that I may se or fele or vndirstond that bereth the name of a thyng the name therof ys a nowne. How many maner of nownys be ther? II. Which ij? A nowne substantif and a nowne adiect(i)f. How   30
knowist thow a nowne substantif? For he may stonde by hymself w^{t}out the help of a nother worde and is declyned yn Latyn w^t on articule as *hic magister*, whith ij att the most as *hic et hec sacerdos*. How knowist a nown adiectif? For he may not stond by hymsilf w^{t}out the help of a nother worde and is declyned yn Latyn w^t iij articulis in on case as *hic et hec et hoc felix*|or hels whith iij diuers endyngys in oon case as nominatiuo *bonus, -a, -um*.

^{1} (H)- *guide letter*

61

ACCEDENCE TEXT L

How many thyngys belongeth to a nowne? VI. Which vj?
Qualite, comparacion, gender, number, figure and (case). 40
How many degreys of comparison be ther? III. Which iij?
The positif degre, the comparatif degre and the superlatif
degre. How knowist thow the positif degre? For he ys
funder and grownder[1] of all other degreys of comparson[2] w^{t}out
makyng more or lasse, as 'fayre', 'white', 'blacke'.
How knowist thow the positif degre|...

The text breaks off here and resumes on fol. 125^r in the
discussion of the declensions of pronowns.

of thys declynson? III. Which iij? *Ego, tu, sui*.
How[3] knowist thow the secunde declynson of pronownys? For
the genitif case singuler endeth in *-ius* or in *-ius*, the[4]
datif in *-i* or in *-c*. How many be ther of that declynson? V. 50
Which v? *Ille, ipse, iste, hic* and *hijs*. How knowist thow
the iij^{de} declenson of pronownys? For the genitif case
singuler endeth in *-i*, in *-e*, and in *-i*, the datif in *-o*, in
-e, and in *-o*. How many pronownys be ther of that declenson? V.
Which v? *Meus, tuus, suus, noster* and *vester*.|

of this declenson? III. Which iij? *Ego, tu, sui*. How
many be ther of this declenson?

---

[1] and grownder *repeated*   [2] *-s- from* o   [3] w- *canc.*
[4] *repeated*

ACCEDENCE TEXT M

M. Worcester Cathedral, MS F.123, fol.99^v

Incipit hic Liber Accidencium secundum vsum magistri Iohannis
Leylond

(H)ow mony maners of speche byn ther? VIII. Whiche viij?
Nowne, pronowne, verbe, aduerbe, participul, coniunccion,
preposicion and interiection. How mony of these byn declyned
and how mony byn vndeclyned? IIII byn declyned and iiij byn
vndeclined. Whiche iiij byn declyned? Nowne, pronowne,
verbe and participull. Whiche iiij byn vndeclyned? Aduerbe,
coniunction, preposicion and interiection. How mony byn
declyned w^t case and how mony w^{t}oute case? III w^t case, and   10
i w^{t}oute case. Whiche iij w^t case? Nowne, pronowne and
participul. Whiche i w^{t}oute case? Verbe only.

How knowest a no<wn>e? Of euery thing that is in this
world or out of this world the name is a nowne, as 'man',
'angel', 'vertue', etcetera. Whad maner of speche 'a man'?
A nowne. Whiso? For hit berith the name of a thing that is
in this world. 'Hevyn': whad maner of speche? A nowne.
Whi so? For hit beryth the name of a thing that is out of
this world.

How mony maner nownys byn ther? II. Whiche ij? A   20
nowne substantyf and an nowne adiectyf. How knoest þu a nowne
substantyf? For he may stand by hymself w^{t}oute helpe of
another wurd, and is declyned in Latyne^1 w^t one artycul of ij
at the moost in one case, as nominatiuo *hic magister*, for
'a mastyr', nominatiuo *hic, hec sacerdos*, for
'a pryst'. How knowest þu a nowne adiectyf? For he may
not stande by|hymself w^{t}oute help of another word and is
declyned w^t iij articlys, or w^t iij diuerse endyngis in one
case: w^t iij articlys as nominatiuo *hic, hec, hoc felix*;
w^t iij diuerse endingis as nominatiuo *bonus, -a, -um*. And   30
also euery nowne that may receyue comparson is a nowne
adiectif, as *senex, senior*; *iuuenis, iunior*.

How mony articlys byn ther? Thre. Whiche iij? *Hic,
hec* and *hoc*.

How mony thingis longyn to a nowne? VI. Whiche vj?
Qualite, comparson, gendur, nowmbur, figure and case.

Qualiter declinatur *accidunt? Accido, -is, -di, accidere,
accidendi, -do, -dum, accidens*; et componitur de *ad* et *cado,
-is*, et omnia composita huius verbi *cado, -dis* carent supinis,
preter *occido, -is* quod facit *occasum, -su*, et *resido, -is*,   40
quod facit *recasum, -su*. Vnde versus:

A *cado* composita renuerunt cuncta supinis;
Occidit occasum, recido dat iure re<c>asum.

---

^{1} and is declyned in Latyne] repeated

ACCEDENCE TEXT M

De qualitate nominis

Whad is a qualite accidental in a nowne? A propurte kyndely according to on al only, and so hit is a propur qualite as *Petrus*, or to mony, and so hit comyn as *homo*.

A text of the *Comparacio* is inserted at this point, and this is given as text S below.

TEXTS OF THE COMPARACIO

N. Aberystwyth, N.L.W., MS Peniarth 356B, fol.9^v

(Q)what is a comparison? A lyknes of diueris thyngus in a certen accedens. What maner of nownes may receyue þat lykenes? Nownes adiectiues betokenyng qualite or quantite that may be made more or lasse wyt a good sentens, as 'wyse', 'whyte', 'longe', 'chorte'. Qwhat is a qualite in a comparison? A thyng þat comes to þe body and passes away froo þe body and þe body nothur more ne lasse, as 'wys', 'fayre', 'conyng'.[1] Qwhat is a quantite[2] in a comparison? A thyng þat betokens lytulnes or meculnes, as 'chorte', 'long', 'lytull', 'mykule'. How mony degres of comparyson ben ther? III. Wheche iij? The posityue, þe comparat(i)ue and þe superlatyfe. How knowes þu the posityfe degre? For hyt betoknes qualite or quantete wytout[3] makyng more or lasse, and setys gronde of all oder degres of comparisons, and is formet of none oder, as 'wyse', 'wyte', 'long', 'chorte'.

10

---

[1] y canc. after -y-   [2] MS qualite   [3] MS wyt

COMPARACIO TEXT O

O. Aberystwyth, N.L.W., MS Peniarth 356B, fols.163ʳ-164ᵛ

The following text is inserted in a version of the *Accedence*,
given as text B above, where it replaces the section on comparison.
It probably ended on the folio lost after fol.164ᵛ.

What is a comparison? A comparison ys a likenes of dyuers
þynges in a certeyn accidens. What nounys may receyue þat
comparison? Nownys adiectyfes betokenyng qualite or quantite
þat may be made more or lesse by good sentence. Vnde versus:

> Est adiectiuis¹ graduum collacio talis,
> Dum valet augeri sua proprietas minuive.

What is a qualite in comparioson? A þynge þat comethe to þe
body and passethe awey fro þe body and þe body neuer þe more ne
þe les, as 'wys', 'feyr', 'connyng'. What ys a quantite in
camparison? A þyng þat betokenethe litelnesse or mechelnesse   10
and may not be take aweye wᵗovte makyng more or lesse, as
'long', 'shorte', 'brode'.

How many greys of comparison byn þer? III. Whiche iij?
Þe posityf, comparatyf and þe superlatyf. How knowe ȝe þe
posityf degre? Fo<r> he betokenethe qualite or|quantite and
ys þe ground of all oder degreis of comparison, as 'wys', 'white',
'long', 'shorte'. Whereof ys þe posityf formed? The posityf
degre is not formed but of hym byn formed all oder degreis of
comparison. Wᵗ what case will þe posityf degre be construed
after hym? Wᵗ no case² by þe strengthe of hys degre.   20

How know ȝe þe comparatyf degre? For he passethe his
posityf wyt þis aduerbe *magis*, and endithe in Englisse in 'ir',
as 'whitur', 'blacker', þat is to sey 'whittur: more white',
'blacker: mor blacke'. Whereof ys þe comparatyf y-formed?
Of hys posityf. Of what case? Oder while of þe genetif
case and oder while of þe datyf case. Vnde versus:³

> Si tibi declinet positiuum norma secunde,
> Taliter inde gradum debes formare secundum:
> I breuies, quem dat geniti(u)us, et *or* superaddas.
> Terne consimule formabunt more datiui.   30
> Inde *sinisterior*, hinc et *iunior* excipiuntur.
> Iungis *amicus*, *beneficus*, sic *magnificus*que,
> *Mirificus* sed *honerificus* coniungitur istis,
> Et sic *munificus*, sit 'Catholicon' tibi testis,
> Et *potis* et *nequam* que dant aliam tibi formam.

When is he formed of þe genetyf case? When þe noun of
þe posityf degre is þe fyrst declynson and þe secund, þen þe
comparatyf degre shall be formed of þe genytyf case singler in
-*i* puttyng þer to þis sillable -*or* as *albi*, -*ior*;⁴ *docti*, *doctior*.
Wheder shall ȝe sey *doctior*, sownyng *T* afore *I* or þis lettur   40

---

¹ MS adiectius   ² *an illegible word canc.*   ³ Declinet terna
positiuos norma secunda *added in a lighter ink*   ⁴ de(?) *canc.*

COMPARACIO TEXT O

C? (C) By what rule? For when þer comnyn two fowellis
nexte after þis letter T, 3if þe firste be I þe T shall haue
þe sowne of C but S go nexte before T, as *questio*, or X, as
mixtio, or H be put betwene, as *Mathias*. Vnde versus:

Bine vocales T quandocumque secuntur,
I prior est quarum, tunc T pro C resonabit
S nisi precedat vt *questio*, vel nisi presit
X vt *mixtio*, vel nisi H fortasse sequatur.

Whan is he formed of þe datyf case? When þe noun of þe
posityf degre is þe þryd declynson, þen þe comparatyf schall   50
be formed of þe datyf case singler of his posityf in -*i* bi
puttynge to þis sillable -*or*, as *debili, debilior*; *forti,
fortior*. How many byn owte-sette of þe first party of þis
rule? This noun *sinister* makyng *sinisterior*, and all þe
novnis of þe posityf degre þat haue a vowell before -*vs*
lacken þe comparatyf degre, in þe stede of þe which comparatyf
is take þe posityf w^t þis aduerbe *magis*, as *pius, magis pius,
pijssimus; idoneus, magis idoneus, idonijssimus; arduus,
magis arduus, arduissimus*. Vnde versus:|

Quod fit -*ius* vel -*vis*, (-*eus*) aut -*vus*, -*or* caruere: 60
Per *magis* et primum quod comparat instituere.

How maken þese v nownys *bonus, malus, magnus, paruus* and
multus com(pa)ryson? Vnruly. How is þat? *Bonus* maketh
melior and *optimus; malus, peior, pessimus; magnus, maior,
maximus; paruus, minor, minimus; multus, plurimus; multa,
plurima; multum, plurimum*. Versus:

Res bona, res melior, res optima; res mala, peior,
Pessima; res magna, res maior, maxima rerum;
Parua, minor, minima dic, *multus*,[1] *plurimus* addens:
Plurimus et *multus*[1] sic comparat absque secundo.   70

How many byn owte-sette of þe secund party of þe rule?
This noun *iuuenis* makyng *iunior*, and novnys hauyng a vowell
afore -*is*: *tenuis* þe which lacketh þe comparatyf degre,
potys makyth *potior*, and *nequam* makyth *nequior*. What gendur
ys euery noun of þe comparatyf degre? Comyn gendyr of þre,
but þis nown *senior* þe which is only masculyn gendyr, as *hic
senior*. Vnde versus:

Comparati(u)us in -*or* semper communis[2] habetur,
Mas. tantum *senior* cui feminium prohibetur.
-*Or* mutabit in -*vs* neutrum, *senior* remouemus.   80

Whiche nounys of posityf degre haue þe comparatyf and
lacken þe superlatyf? Pa(te)nt per versus:

Ante, senex, iuuenis, adolessens: quattuor ista
Sola quidem solis vtuntur comparatiuis.

---

[1] MS mult*is*   [2] MS commun*us*

COMPARACIO TEXT O

Proximus addatur, Ianuensis testificatur.

Whiche novnys of þe comparaty(f) degre byn euyn as many sillables as þe posityf degre? Patent per versus:

Voce gradus medij superant primos nisi quini:
Iunior et *maior*, *peior*, *prior* et *minor*. Ista
Et non plura suis equalia sunt positiuis.   90
Plus minus est vno, sint hec in pectoris imo.

Whiche novnys byn take oder while in þe posityf and oder while in þe superlatyf? Patent per versus:

Proximus, *extremus*, quibus *intimus* atque *supremus*,
Infimus addatur: duplex gradus hijs tribuatur.
Postremus sequitur, autoribus vt reperitur.

What[1] case will þe comparatyf degre after hym? Ablatyf case w[t]owte a preposicion; or *quam* commyng betwene will cowpel case. Vnde versus:

Det medio gradui sextum casum bene iungi   100
Nominis aduerbi: *Sum doctior insipienti*.

How know ȝe þe superlatyf degre? For hit passeth his[2] posytyf w[t] þis aduerbe *maxime* and endithe in Englisse in '-yste' a(s) 'wisyst',[3] 'blackyst',[3] þat ys to sey 'wisist[3]:| most[3] wyse', 'blackyst[3]: most[3] blacke'. Whereof ys þe superlatyf degre y-formed? Of his positif. Of what case? Oder while of þe nominatyf case, oder while of þe genetyf case. When shall he be formed of þe nominatyf case?[4] When þe posytyf endith in *R* lettur of what declynson soeuer hit be, þen þe superlatyf shall be formed of þe nominatyf by puttyng   110
to of -*rimus*, vt *pulcer*, *pulcerimus*; *miser*, *miserimus*; *paupe(r)*, *pauperimus*. When shall þe superlatyf be formed of þe genetyf of his posityf degre? When novnys of þe posityf degre of þe fyrst declynson and þe secund endyn in -*vs* in þe nominatyf case, þen þe superlatyf shall be formed of þe genetyf case singler endyng in -*i* puttyng to *S* and -*simus*, as *clari*, *clarissimus*; *docti*, *doctissimus*; oute-take þes v novnys *bonus*, *malus*, *magnus*, *paruus* and *multus*[5] þat haue superlatifes oute of rule as þes versus showen: *Res bona*, *res melior et cetera*. And when þe noun of þe posityf degre   120
ys þrid declynson þen þe superlatyf degre shall be formed of þe genetyf case by[6] puttyng to -*simus*, vt *fortis*, *fortyssimus*. Vnde versus:

-*Vs*que secunda tenens superante(m) de genetiuo
Sic format: iunges *S* atque -*simus* superaddes;
In terna forma -*simus* addes cum genetiuo.
Sed cum *R* recti sibi vult -*rimus* associari.

---

[1] *a stroke canc.*   [2] *body canc.*
[3] *these words end with an 'er' abbreviation in MS*
[4] *I(?) canc.*   [5] *MS multis*   [6] *pt canc.*

COMPARACIO TEXT O

How formyn þes vj novnys *nuperus, vetus, maturus, dexter, sinister* and *memor*[1] þe superlatyf degre? Thes twey novnys *nuperus* and *maturus* changyn *-vs* into *-rimus*, as *maturus*, change   *130* þe *-vs* into *-rimus* and þen hit is *maturimus*;[2] *nuperus*, change þe *-vs* into *-rimus* and þen hit is *nuperimus*. But þis noun *vetus* changith *-tus* into *-ter* and taketh þer-to *-rimus*, as *vetus*, change *-tus* into *-ter* and þen hit ys *veter*, put þer-to *-rimus* and þen hit ys *veterrimus*. Þes two novnys *dexter* and *sinister* make þe superlatyf degre in *-rimus* and *-timus*, as *dexter, dextimus, dexterimus*; *sinister, sinistimus, sinisterimus*. Þis noun *memor* aʒenst þe rule makythe *memorissimus*. Vnde versus:

> Cum rectus dabit *R* poteris *-rimus* addere semper;
> *Nuperus* atque *vetus*, *maturus* eis societur.   *140*
> In *-rimus* atque *-timus* *dexter*ve *sinister* habetur,
> Et *memor* excipitur: *memorissimus* hinc reperitur.

How formys þes v nownys *agilis, gracilis, humilis, similis* and *facilis* þe superlatyf degre? Of þe nominatyf case, by puttyng away *-is* and puttyng to *-limus*, as *agilis*, do away *-is* and þer leuyth *agil*; put þer-to *-limus* and þen hit is *agillimus*. Vnde versus:

> Dant tibi quinque *-limus* que sistunt nomine *f-a-g-u-s*:
> Hec *agilis, gracilis, humilis, similis facilis*que
> Et sua composita sumunt *-limus*, *LL* duplicata.   *150*

What case construith þe superlatyf w^t? W^t genityf case plurell, or w^t genytyf case singler of a noun collectyf or of a noun þat betokeneth multitude in þe singeler noumbre, as: *Frater meus est sapientissimus istius societatis; Deus est optima rerum. Pater meus est doctissimus istius ville.* Versus:|

(A folio is lost at this point.)

---

[1] MS *adds* of   [2] MS *adds* But þis noun [vetus]

COMPARACIO TEXT P.

P. Cambridge University Library, MS Add. 2830, fols.54ᵛ-56ᵛ

De comparacionib<us>

Qwhat is a comparison? A liknes of diuerse thyngis
in a certeyn accidens, as 'Iohn is wys, Thomas is wysere þan
he, William is wysest þan alle'. *Iohannes est sapiens,
Thomas est sapiencior, Willelmus est sapientissimus omnium
illorum.* Qhat ⌈maner⌉ of nownys may receyue þat liknes?
Nown adiectiuis betokenyng qualite or quantite þat may be maad
moore or lesse wᵗ good centense, as 'qwhit', 'blak', 'wis',
'lewde', 'schort'. Qwhat is a qualite in ⌈a⌉ comparison? A
thyng þat comyth to þe bodi and passyth awey from þe bodi ⌈and   10
þe body⌉ is noþer more nor lesse, as 'fayr', 'fowl', 'qwyth',
'blak', 'lewde', 'louyng' and so of alle oþere. Qwhat is a
quantite in a comparison? A thyng þat betokenyth lytilnes
or mekilnes, as 'long', 'schort', 'litil', 'mekil'.

De gradibus comparacionis

How many degreis ben þer of comparison? Thre. Whech
thre? Posityf, comparatif and þe superlatyf. How knowe ȝe
þe positif degre? For it betokenyth qualite or quantite
wᵗoutyn makyng more or lesse, and settyth þe grownd of alle
oþere degreis of of comparison, as 'wys', 'qwyth', 'long',   20
'schort'. How knowe ȝe þe comparatif degre? For it passith
his positif degre wᵗ þis aduerbe *magis* and endyth in ⌈þis⌉
Englych ⌈word⌉¹ '-er', as 'wyttur',² 'blaker', þat is to sey
'wyttur: more wyth', 'blakur: more blak'. How knowe ȝe þe
superlatif degre? For it passith his positif³ ⌈and his
comparatif⌉⁴ wᵗ þis aduerbe *maxime* and endyth in ⌈þis⌉ Englych⁵
'-est', as 'wytiest', 'blakest: most blak'.⁶ Qwerof is þe
positif degre formyd? The positif degre is not formyd but of
hym ben formyd in dyuerse (weis þe) oþere degreis of comparison.

Whereof is þe comparatif degre formyd? Of his positif.   30
Of what case of þe positif degre? Oþer qwile of þe genytif
case and oþer qwile of þe datif case. How and qwenne of þe
genytif case? If þe nown of þe positif degre be of þe ferste
declenson and of þe secunde þan þe nown comparatif xal ben
formyd of þe genitif case singuler endyng in -*i* be puttyng to
þis sillabille|*or*, as *doctus, docti, doctior; clarus, clari,
clarior*. And is declynyd on þis maner wise: *hic et hec
doctior et hoc doctius*, genetiuo *huius doccioris*, datiuo *huic
doctiori*. When is he formyd of þe datif case? When þe
nown of þe posityf degre is of þe þredde declension þan þe   40
comparatif degre xal be formyd of þe datif case singuler endyng
on -*i* puttyng to þis sillabil *or*, as *debili, debilior*; *forti
forcior*. Owt of þe ferste party of þis rewle is out-take
sinister makyng *sinisterior*; and alle þe nownys of þe positif
degre þat haue a vowel before -*vs* or -*is* lakken þe comparatif
degre, in þe stede of þe wheche is takyn þe positif degre wᵗ

¹ j *canc*.   ² MS wyttus   ³ degre *canc*.
⁴ In left margin   ⁵ in *canc*.   ⁶ MS blakest

COMPARACIO TEXT P

þis aduerbe *magis*, as *pius, magis pius, piissimus*; *arduus, magis arduus, arduissimus*; *idoneus, magis idoneus, idonissimus*; *tenuis, magis tenuis, tenuissimus.* Versus:

> Quod fit *-jus* vel *-vus, -eus* aut *-vis -or* caruere,   50
> Per *magis* et primum quod comparant[1] instituere.

And þese v nownys *bonus, malus, magnus, paruus* and *multus* han here comparatif degreis onrewlely, as þese vers schewyn:

> *Res bona, res melior, res optima; res mala,*[2] *peior, Pessima; res magna, res maior, maxima rerum.*
> *Parua, minor, minima* dic, *multus,*[3] *plurimus* addens;
> *Plurimus* et *multus* se comparant[4] absque secundo.

Out of þe secunde party of þis rewle is out-takyn *juuenis* makyng *iunior*, and nownys hauyng a vowel before *-is* as *tenuis* þe lakken þe comparatif degreis, and *potis*[5] makyng *pocior* and *nequam*   60
indeclinable makyng *nequior*.

Whereof is þe superlatif degre formyd? Of his positif. Of quat case of his positif degre? Other qwile of þe nominatif and oþer qwile of þe genytif case. Whenne xal þe superlatif degre ben formyd of þe nominatif case of his positif degre? Qwen þe nown of þe positif degre endyth in *R* lettere of quat declenson þat euere he be, þan þe nown superlatif xal be formyd of þe no(m)i(n)atif case singuler, masculine gender be puttyng[6] to *-rimus*, as *pulcher*: put þer-to *-rimus* and þan it (is) *pulcherimus, -a, -um*; *miser, mise|rimus*; *satur, saturrimus*;   70
pauper, pauperrimus. And out-take *dexter* makyng *dextimus* and *sinister* makyng *sinistimus* and *memor* makyng *memorissimus*. Vnde versus:

> Cum tenet *R* rectus *-rimus* est illi sociandus,
> Excipies *dexter* faciens *-timus* atque *sinister*,
> Et *memor* excipitur, *memorissimus* hinc reperitur.

And alle þese v nownys *agilis, gracilis, vmilis, similis* and *facilis* and here compownys formyn here superlatif degreis of þe nominatif case puttyng awey *-is* and set þer-to *-limus*, as *agilis*: do awey *-is* and set þer-to *-limus* and þan it is   80
agillimus; and so of alle othere. Versus:

> Hec *agilis, gracilis, vmilis, similis facilis*que
> Rite superlata de rectis dant[7] fore nata.
> Demis[8] *-is* a recto, *-limus* addis, *agillimus* esto,
> Sic bene formatum quis duplex *ll* sit aratum.

Whenne xal þe superlatif degre be formyd of þe genytif case of his positif degre? Qwen þe nown of þe positif degre is of þe ferste declenson and of þe secunde endyng in *-vs*, in

[1] sic MS   [2] MS male   [3] MS mult*s*
[4] sic MS   [5] MS potus   [6] MS adds -o
[7] MS dantur   [8] MS Nemis

COMPARACIO TEXT P

-*a* and in -*vm* þe superlatif degre xal be formyd of þe genytif
case synguler endyng in -*i* puttyng þer-to *S* and -*simus*, as
clarus, clari, clarissimus; *doctus, docti, doctissimus*;
out-take þese v nownys *bonus, malus, magnus, paruus* and *multus*
þe qweche haue þe superlatiues out of þe rewle as þese vers
schewyn:

> *Res bona, res melior, res optima* et cetera.

And also out-take *nuperus* makyng *nuperrimus* all only and
maturus makyng *maturrimus* onrewly and *maturrissimus* rewly.
Versus:

> -*V*sque secunda tenens[1] superantem de genetiuo
> Sic format: iunges *S* atque -*simus* superaddes
> *Res bona, res melior, res optima*; *res mala*,[2] *peior*,
> *Pessimus*; *res magna, res maior, maxima rerum*;
> *Parua, minor, minima* dic; *multus*,[3] *plurimus* addens:
> *Plurimus* et *multus* se comparant[4] absque secundo.
> *Nuperus* adde -*rimus* sed non -*simus* hoc reperimus,
> Dat -*rimus* atque -*simus* maturus et hoc bene scimus.|

Also nown positiuus of þe thred declenson þe qweche han
superlatiuis wᵗoutyn endyng in -*r* and wᵗoute þese v nownys
agilis, gracilis, vmilis, similis, facilis wᵗ here compownys,
and *vetus* makyng *veterimus* takyn to here genitif case singuler
-*simus* and makyn here superlatiuis degreis, as *fortis,
fortissimus*; *felicis, felicissimus*. Versus:

> In terna formo -*simus* addens cum genitiuo,
> Sed tamen -*r* recti sibi uult -*rimus* asociari,
> Et *vetus* adiunge formando *veterimus* inde.
> Dant tibi quinque -*limus* que signant nomine *f-a-g-u-s*:
> Hec *agilis, gracilis, vmilis, similis facilis*que
> Et sua composita, que dant -*limus*, *ll* dupplicata.

Wᵗ what case construit þe posityf degre? Wᵗ non case
because of his degre but because of his significacion he may
be construid wᵗ alle heme gouernyng, out-take þe nominatif and
þe vocatif; wᵗ a genytif vt *Rex est dignus laudis*, wᵗ a datif
vt *Ego sum similis patri meo*, wᵗ an acusatif ex vi sinotheges
vt *Sum albus faciem*, wᵗ an ablatif vt *Pater meus est diues auro*.

Wᵗ what case xal þe comparatif degre be construid wᵗ
because of his degre? Wᵗ an ablatif case of eyþer nownbre
wᵗoute a preposicion, and wᵗ a nominatif case *quam* aduerbe
comyng betwyn, vt *Sum doctior socio meo* vel *socijs meis*, vel
doctior quam socius meus vel *quam socij mei*. Also a nown of
þe comparatif degre because[5] of his significacion may be
construid wᵗ alle swych case as wel as his positif degre be
construid wᵗ, and þer-to beryth wytnesse þese vers of Garlond.
Versus:

---

[1] Superla *canc.* [2] MS *male* [3] MS *multis*
[4] *sic* MS [5] -*u-from* j

COMPARACIO TEXT P

Quam uult naturam gradus offerri sibi casus,
Illam fructuram uult quisque secundus et vnus.

Wyth a nominatif case *quam aduerbe comyng betwyn*, vt *Ego sum doctior quam socius meus*, w^t a genytif case vt *Magister est dignior laudis hostiario suo*, w^t a datif case vt *Sum similior patri meo quam matri mee*, w^t an acusatif case ex vi sinotheges vt *Sum albior faciem sorore mea*, w^t a vocatif case *quam aduerbe*   140
comyng betwyn vt *O Iohannes melior quam pulcher, grossior quam alte, tu es amabilis* vel *amandus*, w^t an ablatif case vt *Pater meus est diuitior*[1] *auro patre tuo*.

Wyth what case xal þe superlatif degre be construid w^t because of his degre? W^t a genytif case plurer betoknyng mo thyngis|þan ij, vt *Ego sum doctissimus omnium sociorum meorum*, or w^t a genytif case singuler of a nown collectif or of a nown of place, vt *Rex est valentissimus gentis sue vel potentissimus regni sui*; *Iohannes est pauperrimus istius plebis et miserimus huius ville*. Also for cause of his   150
significacion he may be construid w^t alle swyche case as wel as his positif degre be construid and þer-to beryth wytnesse þese vers of Garlond:

Quam uult naturam gradus et cetera.

With a genytif case vt *Sum doctissimus gramatice omnium hic presencium*; w^t a datif case vt *Sum simillimus patri meo omnium filiorum suorum*, w^t an acusatif case vt *Sum albissimus faciem omnium fratrum meorum*, w^t an ablatif case vt *Sum dignissimus laude omnium sociorum meorum*.

Expliciunt Comparaciones **quod Hardgraue de B.**   160

Positiuis

How formist þu an aduerbe of þe positif degre? Oþer qwile of þe genytif case and oþer qwile of þe datyf case and oþer qwile of þe nominatif case. Quanne of þe genytif case? Quan þe positif degre is of þe ferste declenson and þe secunde, as nominatiuo *doctus, -a, -um*; genitiuo *docti, -te, -ti*. *Docte*, feminyn gender, is þe aduerbe. Quan of þe datif case? Quan þe positif degre is þe thredde declenson, as nominatiuo *hic, hec fortis* and *hoc -te*; genitiuo *huius fortis*; datiuo *huic forti*. Put þer-to a *-ter* and þan it is *fortiter*. Quan   170
of þe nominatif case? Quan þe positif degre endit in *-ns* or in *-rs*. As how? As nominatiuo *hic, hec, hoc sapiens*: turne þis *-s* into a *-ter* and þanne[2] it (is) *sapienter*. Nominatiuo *hic, hec, hoc solers*: turne þis *-s* into a *-ter* and þan it is *solerter*.

Comparatiuis[3]

How formist þu an aduerbe of þe comparatif degre? Of þe

[1] MS diues   [2] MS þananne   [3] MS comparatig

COMPARACIO TEXT P

nominatif case, neuter gender, singuler nounbre, as nominatiuo *hic, hec docior* et *hoc -cius*. *Doccius* is þe aduerbe.

Superlatiuis *180*

How formist þu an aduerbe of þe superlatif degre? Of þe genityf case, feminyn gendre, singuler noumbre, as nominatiuo *doctissimus, -a, -um*; genitiuo *doctissimi, doctissime, doctissimi*. *Doctissime* is þe aduerbe.

COMPARACIO TEXT Q

Q. Oxford, Bodleian Library, Printed Book Douce D.238(2), fols. B5^v-B6^r

The text begins at the foot of fol.B5^v after the colophon of the printed text.

-Ram, *-rim*, *-ro* mutant *I* ⌈in *E*⌉, *-sem*, *-sem*, *-se* retinent *I*.|

Wat ys a comparyson? A lykenes. What nowys may receyue þat lykenes? Nownys adiectyfys betokynyng qualite or quantite. Qwhat ys a qualite? A thyng that comys to þe body and passus awey fro þe body and makys þe body nodyr more ne lesse, as 'fayr', 'fowole', 'qwyght', 'blake'. Qwath ys a quantyte? A thyng þat betokynyth meculnesse or leytylnesse, as 'long', 'schorth', 'brod'.

How many degreys of comparysons ben there? III. Qwych iij? Þe posytyf degre, the comparatyf degre, þe superlatyf 10
degre. How know ȝe þe posytyf degre? For yt settys grownd off all odyr degreys of comparysons, as 'wyse'. How know ȝe þe comparatyf degre? For yt passyt þe posityff degre w^t þis aduerbe 'more' as 'more wyse' or 'wyser'. How know ȝe þe superlatyf degre? W^t thys aduerbe 'most' as 'most wyse' or 'wysest'.

W^t qwhat case wyll þe posytyff degre constriu w^t? W^{t1} ⌈no⌉ case thowrow þe vertu^2 of hys howyn kynde. W^t qwat case wyll þe comparatyff degre constriu w^t? W^t þe ablatyff case w^{t}owt a *quam*, or ellys w^t a *quam* þat wyll copyll lyke case, as 20
Ego sum doccior Wyllelmo vel *quam Willelmus*. W^t qwath case wyll þe superlatyf degre constriu w^t? W^t þe genityff plurell betokenyng many thyng, as *Ego sum doctissimus poetarum*, or ellys w^t þe genityf case singuler of a nowne collectyf þat betokynyth as mekyl in þe singuler numbyr as a nodyr nowne dothe in þe plurell numbyr, as *populus*, *gens*; and theis beyn nownys collectywys þat beyn conteynyd in þis verse:

Sunt collectiua *populus*, *gens*, *plebs* quoque *turba*.

What xal ȝe doo when ȝe xall make a comparyson? I xall declyne my posytyff degre be hymself, my comparatyf degre be 30
hymself and my superlatyff degre be hymself. I xall declyne my posytyf degre to I cum at a case þat endys as nominatiuo *doctus*, *-a*, *-um*, genitiuo *docti*; do ther-to an *-or* and then ys yt *doccior*, and then ys my comparatyf degre made. As *docti*, do þer-to an *S* and a *-simus* an þen ys *doctissimus* and þen ys my superlatyf degre made.|

---

^{1} þe uocatyf *canc*. ^{2} *a stroke canc.*

COMPARACIO TEXT R

R. Oxford, Bodleian Library, MS Rawlinson D 328, fols.80ʳ-83ʳ

This text is included in a version of the *Formula*, given below as text CC.

How many degreys of comparson ben þer? III. Wych iij? Þe positiue degre, þe comparatiue degre and þe superlatiue. Wherof ys þe positiue degre y-furmyd? He ys not y-furmyd, but al oþer degreys of comparson byt furmyd of hym and he[1] of noþer.

De furmacione comparatiui gradus

Wherof ys þe comparatiue degre y-furmyd? Owth of hijs positiue. Of what case? Oþer wyse of þe genitiue case and oþer of þe datiue case. When ys he y-furmyd owth of þe genitiue case and when of þe datiue? When þe nowne of þe positiue degre ys þe[2] fyrst declinson and þe iij^{de} þan þe comparatiue schall be furmyd of þe genitiue case singuler endyng in *-i* settyng to þis sillabill[3] *-or*, as nominatiuo *albus, -a, -um*, genitiue *albi, -e, -i*, settyng to þis sillabyll *-or* and then hit wol be nominatiue *hic et hec albior et hoc albius*.

De datiuo casu

When ys he y-furmyd oute of þe datiue case? When þe nowne of þe positiue degre ys þe iij^{de} declynson and then[4] þe comparatiue schall be furmyd of þe datiue case singuler puttyng to thys sillabyll *-or*, as nominatiuo *hic et hec fortis et hoc forte*, genitiuo *huius fortis*, datiuo *huic forti*, put to þis silabill *-or* and then hit wol be nominatiuo *hic et hec forcior et hoc forcius*. Þe furmacion of both casus of both said byth contaynid yn thes verse. Vnde[5] versus:|

Si tibi declinet positiuum norma secunde
Taliter inde gradum debes[6] formare secundum:
I breuias quem dat genetiue et -or superaddes.
Terne consimili formabunt more datiuj;
Iunior inde, gradum *susterior*[7] cape *dexterior*que,
Quod tibi prebet, *-icus* hijs iungas, testis *amicus*.

De excepcionibus furmacione a genitiuo[8]
casu comparatiui gradus

Oute of þe fyrst rule bith accept thes v nownys: *bonus, malus, magnus, paruus* and *multus*, þe which makyth comparson oute of rule as thes maner wyse: *bonus,*[9] *melior, optimus; bona, melior, optima; bonum, melius, optimum; malus, peior, pessimus; mala*[10]*,peior, pessima; malum, peius, pessimum;*

[1] MS be
hit wolbe nominatiue *canc.*
[5] vnde *canc.*
[8] s *canc.*
[2] fry *canc.*

[6] -s from t
[9] MS bonuus
[3] or *and* then
[4] MS ther
[7] sic MS
[10] MS male

76

COMPARACIO TEXT R

*magnus, maior, maximum; magna, maior, maxima; magnum, maius,
maximum; paruus, minor, minimus; parua, minor, minima;* 40
*paruum, minus, minimum; multus, plurimus; multa, plurima;
multum, plus, plurimum.*

Res bona, res melior, res optima; res ⌈mala, peior⌉,[1]
Pessima; res magna, res maior, maxima rerum;
Parua, minor, minima dic, multus,[2] plurimus addens;
Plurimus et multus[2] sic comparat absque secundo.

Also oute[3] of þis fyrst rule bith accept thes v nownys
magnificus, murificus, munificus, benificus and *honorificus*,[4] |
þe which lackyth[5] þe comparatiue degre, and they berowith of
old positiuis þat be not in vse as *magnificens, mirificens,* 50
beneficens and *honorificens*. Magnificen\<s\>
makyth *magnificencior, mirificens* makyth *mirificencior,
benificens* makyth *benificencior, honorificens* makyth
honorificencior. And also bith accept all nownys of þe ij^de
declinson, *amicus* makyth *ami⌈ci⌉cior, inimicus* makyth
inimicicior, þe whych makyth owte of rule as h(i)t ys y-sayd
abow yn thys verse. Vnde versus:

Si tibi decline(t), et cetera.
Iunior inde, *senesterior*[6] cape *dexterior*que,
Quod tibi prebet, *-icus* hijs iungas, testis *amicus*. 60

**Item excipiuntur a formacione comparatiuj gradus a
genetiuo casu suj positiuj nomina que sequntur**

Also byth accept of þe fyrst rule all nownys havyng a fowle
next afor *-vs,* þe whych lackyth þe comparatiue degre, in whos
stede ys take þe positiue degre w^t þis aduerbe *magis,* as *idoneus,*
(*magis idoneus*), *idonissimus, pius,*[7] *magis pius, piissimus.*

Que per *-eus* vel *-ius, -vis* aut *-vus or* caruere,
Per *magis* et primum quod comparat instituere.

**Item excipiuntur a formacione comparatiuj gradus a
genitiuo casu suj positiui nomina que secuntur** 70

Oute of þe ij^de rule ys accept this nowne *iuuenis* þe which
makyth *iunior* as hit is shewid abow yn þis verse.

Si tibi declinet positiuum, et cetera. |

Also byth accept thys ij nownys *nequam* and *potus.*
Nequam[8] makyth *nequior, nequissimus; potis*[9] makyth *pocior,
potissimus.* Also byth accept of þe ij^de rule nownys of þe
iij^de declinson endyng in *-is* havyng a fowle next before
-is þe which lackyth þe comparatiue degre and beth[10] fulfellid
by there positiuis w^t thys aduerbe *magis,* as *tenuis, magis*

---

[1] This line glossed in English [2] MS multis [3] MS outo
[4] The adjectives glossed in English [5] MS laclyth
[6] pa canc. [7] MS paruus [8] Si tibi declinet canc. (an earlier note) [9] MS potus [10] MS heth

COMPARACIO TEXT R

tenuis, tenuiss⁽i⁾me, and other mo as hit is shewid abow in thys verse: 80

Que per *-eus* vel *-ius, -vis* aut *-vus,* et cetera.

The comparatiue degre excidith his positiuis by on sillabyll or ij, except thys nownys þat byth contaynid yn these verse, and ys lasse þen his[1] positiue as thes comparatiue degre plus.

Voce gradus medij superant primos[2] nisi quini:
Iunior et *maior,*[3] *peior, prior* et *minor* ista.
Hec et non plura suis equalia sunt positiuis,
Plus minus est primo; sunt hec in pectoris imo. 90

All comparatiuis endyng in *-or* byth þe comyn[4] gender of to, as nominatiuo *hic et hec fortior et hoc fortius,* and makyth þe ablatiue case singuler in *-e*[5] and in *-i* except ⁽comparatiue degre⁾ *senior,* þe whyche ys þe masculyn gender all only and makyth þe ablatiue case synguler in *-e* only. Vnde versus:

Comparatiuus[6] in *-or* semper communis habetur,
Mas. tantum *senior* cui feminium prohibetur.
Adiectiua *senex, senior*que simul recitentur;
Hic tantum sumunt, generis tamen omnis habentur.
-I vel *-e* postulat *-or,* sed dic tantum *seni*⁽o⁾*re*. 100

De formacione superlatiui gradus

⁽Of⁾ when ys superlatiue degre y-furmyd? Owt of hys p<ositif>.| Of what case? Wother whyle of the nominatiue case and woþ<er> whyle of þe genytiue case and woþer whyle of datiue case. When hys y-furmyd owte ⁽of⁾ þe nominatiue case? When þ<e> nown of[7] þe positiue degre yndyth in *R* letter w<hat> declenson þat euer he be, þe schal þe superlatiue degre be fu<r>myd owte of[7] þe nominatiue case indyng in *-r* putyn<g> ther-to þis sillabil[8] *-rymus,* as *pulcher* sette to a *-rim<us>* and then hyt wyll be *pulcherimus; niger,* 110
nigerimus; pauper, pauperimus.

Cum rectus tenet *-r* poteris *-rimus* addere semper;
⁽*Nuperus* atque *vetus, maturus detero* iungis.⁾
In *-rimus* atque *-timus dexter*ve *sinister*[10] habetur;
Et *memor* excipitur,[11] *memorissimus* hunc reperitur.

Oute of thys rule ys accept *dexter* makyn *dextimus* ⁽and⁾ *senister* maken *senistimus,* but when they makyth *dexterimus* and *senisterimus* then þey byth not accept, and *memor* ys acce<pt> þe whych makyth *memorissimus*; and also byth accept iiij superlatiuis *nuperimus, maturimus, veterimus* ⁽and⁾ *dexterimus*[9] 120

[1] h- from y
[2] MS primus
[3] -i- from g
[4] MS ?comyng
[5] ex canc.
[6] MS Comparatiuis
[7] repeated
[8] sy canc.
[9] *sic* MS
[10] si- from se
[11] MS exciperitur

78

COMPARACIO TEXT R

þe whych comyth of nownys not endyng in -r and makyth -rimus, as of[1] nuperus, nuperimus; maturus, materimus, vetus, veterimus;[2] dexter, dexterimus; and thys excepcions byth[3] sa⸢i⸥d abow in thes verse:

Cum rectus tenet -r, et cetera.

De formacione superlatiuj gradus a genitiuo[4] casu.

When ys þe superlatiue degre y-furmyth oute of þe genytiue case? When þe nowne of þe positiue degre ys þe fyrst declynson and þe secunde endyng not in -r, than þe superlatiue shall be furmyth oute of þe genitiui case synguler endyng in -i, puttyng 130
ther-to S and -simus, as nominatiuo doctus, -a, -um, genitiuo docti, -e, -i put to S and -simus, and then hit wol be nominatiuo doctissim<us>, ⸢-a, -um⸥; clari, clarissimus; albi, albissimus⸥.|

**Excepcio formacionis superlatiui
gradus a genitiuo casu**

Oute of thys rule bith accept thes x nownys said before: bonus, malus, magnus, paruus and multus,[5] magnificus, murificus, minificus, beneficus and honorificus, and also byth accept thes ij nownis nuperus and maturus þe which makyth þe 140
superlitiue degre in -rimus as hit is shewid abow in these verse:

Cum rectus tenet -r, et cetera.

Also byth accept thys nowne proximus, for he may be ⸢both⸥ positiue (and) superlatiue: when he is idem quod propinquus,[6] -a, -um[7] then he ys þe positiue, and when he ys idem quod prope w^t his[8] aduerbe maxime then he ys þe superlatiue degre.

De formacione superlatiui gradus a datiuo casu

When ys þe superlatiue degre y-formyd oute of þe datiue case? When þe nowne of þe positiue degre ys þe iij^de declynson 150
endyng not in -r, then shall þe superlatiue degre be formyd oute of þe datiue case by puttyng a S[9] ⸢and⸥ -simus as nominatiuo hic et hec fortis et hoc forte, genitiuo huius fortis, datiuo huic forti; forti, put to a S[9] and -simus and then hit wol be nominatiuo fortissimus,[10] -a, -um; felici, put to S and -simus and hit wol be filicissimus, -a, -um.

**Excepcio formacionis superlatiuj
gradus de datiuo casu**

Oute of thys rule bith accept thes v nownys: agilis,

---

[1] nuperimus ⸢nuperus(?)⸥ canc.   [2] Nuperus, maturus and vetus are glossed in English   [3] MS hyth   [4] sa canc.
[5] MS multis   [6] MS proxinuus   [7] a minim canc. after -u-
[8] -s from t   [9] a S] MS as   [10] -ti- from tu

COMPARACIO TEXT R

gracilis,[1] *facilis, humilis* and *similis*, þe which byth furmyd   160
oute of þe nominatiue case synguler chaungyng -*is* into a -*limus*
and then hit wol be *agillimus*, -*ma*, -*um*, and so of oþer mo.

Dant tibi quinque -*limus* que signa⌈n⌉t nomine *f-a-g-u-s*:
Hec[2] *agilis, gracilis, humilis, similis facilis*que
Et sua composita que duplici sunt *ll* habenda.|

Item alie excepcionis

And also bith accept þes v nownys (*ante, subter*), *senex,*
iuuenis[3] and *adolescens*, þe which lackyth þe superlatiue degre.

Ante, senex, iuuenis, adolescens, subter et addis:
Sola quidem solis vtuntur comparatiuis.   170

Item alie excepcionis

Also byth accept thes þat bith contaynyd yn these verse
folowyng: when they bith of þe positiue degre then þey lackyth
þe superlatiue degre, and when they bith superlatiue degre
then they comyth of aduerbe as hit is shewid by these verse.
Vnde versus:

Proximus, extremus, quibus *intimus* adde, *supremus,*
Infimus addatur: duplex gradus hijs tribuatur.
Postremus sequitur, autoribus vt reperitur.

All thes aduerbis,[4] preposicions þat bith conteynid yn   180
these verses folowyng[5] bith put yn þe stede of þe positiue
degre.

Bis septem dicas aduerbia prepo(s)itasve
Quas nostri patres posuere loco positiui:
Ante, citra, prope, post, extra, supra et *infra*
*Intra, nuper, osis vltra*que, *pridem penitus*que.
Dicit *osis* Grecus, *ocior* parit[6] in⌈de⌉ Latinus.[7]
Addere *pene* quidam seu *penes*[8] addere querunt.

Ante, anterior	*Intra, interior, intimus.*
Citra, citerior.	*Nuper, nuperior.*[10] 190
Prope, propior, proximus.	*Osis, ocior.*
Post, posterior, postremus.	*Vltra, ulterior, ultimus.*
Extra, exterior, extremus.	*Pridem, prior, primus.*
Supra, superior, supremus.[9]	*Penitus, penituor.*[11]
Infra, inferior, infimus.	*Sepe, sepior, sepissimus.*

---

[1] *glossed in English*   [2] -e- *from* i   [3] *ad* canc.
[4] -i- *from* e   [5] MS felowyng   [6] -i- *from* e
[7] -u- *from* i   [8] -es *from as*   [9] -re- *from* er
[10] *from* nuperimus   [11] *sic* MS

COMPARACIO TEXT S

S. Worcester Cathedral, MS F.123, fols.99vb-100ra

This text is inserted in a copy of the *Accedence*, given as text M above. It has been erased and the following text and tentative reconstruction is based on a transcription made under ultra-violet light.

De comparacione

How <mony> deg<res of comparison ben ther? III.> Whiche <iij? Þe posityf, þe> compar<a>tyf <and þe superlatyf.> How knowest þu <þe positif degr>e? <For it betokenyth qualite or quantite .....> 1ls <w^{t}owt makyng more or less, and settyth þe grownd> of <alle oþere degres of comparison, as 'wys', 'white', 'long', 'short'>. How <kn>owist <þu þe> comparatif deg<re? For it passith his positif degre with þis aduerbe *magis* and his Englisshe endyth in '-er' as 'whitter', 'blacker'>: f<or to say 'whitter:> more wh<ite', 'blacker: more black'.> How knowest <þu þe superlat>if de<gre?> For he p<a>ss<yth> his pos<itif degre w^t þis aduerbe *maxime*> and his Englisshe <endyth in '-ist', as> 'whittist', 'bl<ackist': for to say 'whittist:> mo<st> white', 'bla<cki>st: <m>os<t b>lacke'.   10

De <...>tate comparacionis

Whad is a comparson? A lykenes of <diuers> thyngv<s. Whad maner> of nownes <may receyue þat lykenes?> Nownus <ad>ecty<ves betokening qualite or quantite> th<at may>e be made (more) or lasse by goode sent<ence>.| 20

De qualitate in comparacione

Whad is a qualite in comparson? A thing that longyth to the body, and passith away fro the body, and the body is nowther more ne lasse, as 'wise', 'feyr', 'connyng'.

De quantitate in comparacione

Whad is a quantite in comparson? A thing that betokenyth lytelnis or myche(lni)s as[1] 'short', 'long', 'lytel', 'mychel'.[2]

De formacione graduum comparacionis

Wherof is the posityf degre y-formed? The posityf degre is not y-formed but alle other degrees of comparson byn formed   30
of hym. Of whom is the comparatyf degre formed? Of his posityf degre. Of whad case of his posityf degre? Other while of the g<e>nitif case and other while of the datif case. Whenne is he formed of <the genitif case and when> of the <datif case?>

The rest of the folio is cut away.

[1] *repeated*   [2] MS mychest

81

TEXTS OF THE INFORMACIO

T. Aberystwyth, N.L.W., MS NLW 423D, fols.11^v-17^r

In how mony maner of wyse shall þu bygyn to mak Latten
and to construe by ryȝtwyse ordyr of construccion? In v.
In whych v? By a vocatif case, by a nominatif or sumwhat
set yn þe stytt of a nominatif case and a verbe of certayn person,
by an ablatif case absolute, and a verbe inpersonell. How
bygynne[1] ȝe by a vocatif case to mak your Latten? As 'Willam[2]
make fyre', *Willelme fac ignem*. How by a nominatif case and
a verbe of certayn person? As 'Þe mayster syttis yn þe
scole', *Magister sedet in scola*. How by sumwhat sett yn þe
stud of a nominatif case? As 'To dyne betyme shall comfort   10
monys hert', *Iantari tempestiue confortabit humanum cor*. How
by an ablatif case absolute? As 'The mayster techyng yn þe
scole, (I am agayste)', *Magistro docente in scola, ego sum
perteritus*. How by a verbe inpersonell? As 'Me syttis
yn the scole', *Sedetur in scola*.

What shall þu doo when thow hast a matter to mak Latten
by? I shall loke owte my principall werbe personell and loke
whedyr hyt[3] betokyns 'to do' or 'to suffre'; and yf hyt
betokyns 'to doo' the doer shal be nominatif case and þe
suffrer sech case as þe verbe wyll have aftyr hym; and yf my[4]   20
principall verbe personall betokyn to suffre the suffrer shal
be nominatif case and þe doer ablatif case w^t *a* preposicion;
and yf my principall verbe be a verbe inpersonell y shal begyn
att hyt to make my Latten and to constyr. How shall þu know,
yf þer be mony verbys yn a matter, whych ys thy principall
verbe? Euermore the furst verbe ys my principall verbe, butt
yf hyt com nexte to a relatif or ellys be lyk to an infinitif
mode. Whereby knowystow when hyt comys nexte to a relatif?
When hyt comys nexte to thys English worde[5] 'that' or 'the whych'.
Whereby knowystow when hyt ys lyke to an infinitif mode? When   30
y have þis syne[6] 'to' as 'to love' or 'to be lovyd'.

Sequitur latinitas

'A chyrch ys a place þe whych Cristunnen mecull ben holdyn
to love.' Whych ys thy principall verbe in þis reson? 'Ys'.
When *sum, es, fui* ys thy principall verbe how shall þu know
whych ys þi nominatif case? By þis Englysh 'Whoo or what?',
as 'Whoo or what ys? The chyrch (ys)'. What case ys 'the
chyrch'? Þe nominatif case. What parte of spech ys 'the

---

[1] MS bygyme
[4] verbe *canc*.

[2] MS willm^a
[5] w(?) *canc*.

[3] b *canc*.
[6] as *canc*.

INFORMACIO TEXT T

whych'? A relatif. What has a relatif? Antecedent.¹
Whereby knowystow an antecedent? For hyt goys before the   40
relatif and ys rehersid of the relatif. How knowystow a
relatif? For hyt makys rehersyng of thyngis sayd before.
What case, what gendyr, what nowmbur shall the relatif be?
Such case, such gendur, such nowmbre as the anticedent shul be
yf he stode þer as þe relatif stondis, and þe relatif were putt
away. Aliter sic: what case shall þe relatif be when þer
comys a nominatif case betwene the relatif and þe verbe?
Then þe relatif shal be such case as the verbe wyll have aftyr
hym. And yf þer com no nominatif case betwene the relatif
and the verbe, then the relatif shal be nominatif case to the   50
verbe, butt yf the verbe be a verbe inpersonell. Then the
relatif shal be such case as the verbe inpersonell wyl be
construet w^t. Is that soth all way? Ye, but yf that verbe
inpersonell have hys casuell word aftyr hym. Then þe relatif
shal be such case as the infinitif mode wyll have aftyr hym.
How shall thow say on Latten thys English before sayd?
Ecclesia est locus quem Christiani tenentur multum diligere.
Quem: what² gendur? Masculin gendur? Why soo? For to the
nexte antecedent shall þe relatif be refert, butt yf the sentens
let, as in thys Latten: *Canis tuus occidit ouem meam quem ego*   60
occidam. Thys relatif *quem* accordis w^t the furst anticedent
in gendur and nott w^t the later by enchosyn of the sentens.

*Ibo ad locum qui*³ vel *quod est nouum castrum.* What
gendur is *qui* vel *quod*? The masculin gendyr and newtur.
Why soo? For when y have a relatif sett betwene ij nownus
substantiuis of diuers gendyrs longyng both to on thyng hyt
may acorde w^t aythyr substantif in gendur. Vnde versus:

    Quando relatiuum generum casus variorum
    Inter se claudunt qui rem spectant ad eandem,
    Per genus hoc poterit vtrilibet assimilari: 70
    Est pia stirps Iesse quem Christum dicimus esse.

Vtinam essem episcopus, qui vocor Wilelm(u)s, sub spe
releuandi paupertatem amicorum meorum. Episcopus: what case?
The nominatif case. Why soo? For|*sum, es, fui* ys a verbe
copulatif and wyll cowpull lyk case. What maner of verbus
haue strenght to cowpull lyke case? Verbys substantiuis
and uerbus vocatiuus and verbus havyng here strength. How
mony verbus substantiuis bene þer? III. Whych iij?
Sum, fio, existo. Vnde versus:

    Ars substantiua tria dat tantummodo verba: 80
    Sum simul *existo, fio,* nil amplius addo.

How mony verbys vocatiuis byn þer? V. Whych v? Patent
per versus:

    Quinque vocatiua dicas tantummodo verba:

---

¹ MS añtecedent *as elsewhere*   ² case *canc.*   ³ q *canc.*

INFORMACIO TEXT T

Nominor, appellor sic *nuncupor* et[1] *voco, dicor.*

What maner of verbus haue strength to cowpyll case, owte-take verbus substantiuis and verbys vocatiuis and verbys havyng here strength? Verbus passiuis, ut *Ordinor acolitus, Teneor sapiens*; and verbus as þei were passiuis, ut *Vapulo ignarus*; and verbus betokenyng stuping or[2] meuyng of bodi, ut *Curro celer*, or meuyng of saule, ut *Meditor sapiens*; and verbus þat betokynyng rest, *90* ut *Sedeo tristis*; and verbus þat betokyn semyng, ut *Appareo bonus, Immineo celsus*.

De genitiuo

Istud doleum est plenum vini vel *vino*, vel *vacuum -ni* vel *-no*. (*Vini* vel *vino*): what case? Genitif and þe ablatif. Why soo? For all nownus adiectiuis betokynyng fulnes or emtines wyll constur w^t þe genitif and þe ablatif. Vnde versus:

Que plenum signant vel que vacuata figurant
Iunguntur sextis, ut scribitur, et genitiuis:
Vini vel *(vi)no duo dolea plena videto.*   *100*

De verbis personalibus constructis cum genitiuis

Abstineo irarum vel *desino viciorum*. *Irarum* and *viciorum*: what case? Genitif case. Why soo? For thes ij verbys *desino* and *abstineo* wyll consture w^t genitif case ex vi transicionis personalis. Versus:

Desinit, abstineo genitiuis iungere curo.

Dominor huius ville vel *huic ville cuius incolarum* vel *incolis miserebor*. What casus *ville, incolarum* vel *incolis*? Genitif and datif. Why soo? For *dominor, -aris* and *miserior, -eris* wyll consture w^t genitif and[3] datif, ex vi transicionis *110* personalis. Versus:

Da *dominor* ternis *misereri* siue secundis.
Et sibi vult iungi iiij^{tum} casum *misereri*:
Nostri vel *nobis* vel *nos Ihesu misereri.*

De verbis personalibus indifferenter constructis cum genitiuis, accusatiuis et ablatiuis|

Ricardus et Willelmus indigent diuine gracie, diuinam graciam vel *diuinia gracia*. *Diuine gracie, diuinam graciam* vel *diuina gracia*: what case? Genitif, accusatif and þe ablatif. Why soo? For thes ij verbys *egeo, -es*; *indigeo*, *120* *-es* wyll construe w^t genitif, accusatif and ablatif.

Des iiij^{tis}, sextis *eget, indiget* et genitiuis:
Indigeo rem, re coniunge *rei, mihi care,*
In quem respicias. Hoc ass(er)it ipse Papias.

---

[1] vod *canc.*   [2] mvw *canc.*   [3] ablatif *canc.*

INFORMACIO TEXT T

Indigent: what nowmbur? Plurell nowmbur. Why soo? For ij nominatif case singler w^t an *et* coniunccion betwene wyll have the verbe plurell, and ij nownus singler wyth an *et* coniunccion betwene wyll have a relatif plurell.

De verbis personalibus constructis cum datiuis

Obuiemus regi et regine venientibus Oxonia. Regi et 130
regine: what case? Datif case. Why soo? For all verbus conteynyng yn thes versus wyll construe w^t datif case:

Obuio, parco, placet, noceo, respondeo, seruit,
Precipit, opponit, concludo, iunge datiuis,
Supplicat, arridet, faueo, vaco, proficit, heret,
Subuenit addatur, *succurrit, propiciatur,*
Congruit, compacior, confert, succedit, adulor,
Insidet, imponit, conuicior, improperabit,
Sufficit, aspirat, valedico, gratulor, astat,
Imminet ac *equipollet* vel *obedit* et *obstat,* 140
Occurrit, restat et *cedo,* quando locvm dat,
Derogo, condoleo, preiudico, detraho, defert,
Suppetit hijs iungas. Que *sunt* componit, eis das.[1]
Hec et quamplura ternis coniungere cura.

De verbis constructis cum duobus accusatiuis

Postulo Deum graciam bene discendi, qui doceor gramaticam.
Graciam: what case? Accusatif case. Why soo? For all þe verbus contenyng yn þes versus '*Postulo, posco, peto*' woll construe w^t dowbyll accusatif case betokonyng dyuerse thyngus. *Gramaticam*: what case? Accusatif case. Why soo? For all 150
þe verbys[2] passiuis comyng of the actiuis þe whych bene construet w^t dowbyll accusatif case may construe w^t þe latter accusatif case. Vnde versus:

Postulo, posco, peto, doceo, rogo, flagito, celo,
Exuo cum *vestit, monet, induo, calceo, cingo*:[3]
Accusatiuos geminos hec verba requirunt,
Passiuis quorum postremus iungitur horum.

De verbis constructis cum ablatiuis

Vtor rubeo capicio. Capicio: what case? Ablatif case. Why soo? For all the verbus contenit in þes versus wull 160
construe w^t ablatif case. Vnde versus:

Vescitur et *fruitur, caret, vtitur* atque *potitur*;
Hec ablatiuos[4] transicione regunt.
Hijs iungas *fungor,* et *deficio* sociatur.

How mony yndyngis of gerundiuis byn þer? III. Whych iij? *-Di, -do, -dum.* Whereby knowystow a gerundif in *-di*?

---

[1] MS dat [2] actiuis *canc.* [3] MS cigno
[4] ms *adds* in

INFORMACIO TEXT T

When y have a word like to an infinitif mode comyng aftyr
tempus or *est* or a nowne substantif y shall have a gerundif
in *-di*. Exemplum: 'Masse y-done hit ys tyme to brek owre
fast'. Latinum: *Missa finita tempus est soluendi nostrum* 170
ieiunium. I shall have a gerundif in *-di* as þus: 'The Pope
has power to assoyle Cristunnen leuyng in God of here synnys',
Noster Papa habet potestatem absoluendi Christianos confitentes[1]
in Deo de suis peccatis. Whereby knowystow a gerundif in *-do*?
In ij maners. In whych ij maners? When þis English 'in'
comus before a worde that yndyth yn '-yng' w^{t}owte a substantif
sett to hym y shall have a gerundif in *-do* w^t thys preposicion
in, as thus: 'In feghtyng mony men byn wondit, mony mamed and
mony slayn', *In dimicando quamplurimi homines sunt vulnerati
et quamplurimi mutilati et quamplurimi occisi; In discendo* 180
gramaticam sapienciam. Whereby knowystow a gerundif in *-do*
in the secunt maner of wyse? Whe(n) the English of a
participull of the presentens comus aftyr a substantif y may
ches[2] whedur y wyll have a gerundif in *-do* or a participull of
the presentens, as thus: 'The mayster ys buse yn the scole
ynformyng hys discipuls, of the whych he reseuys euery yere
grete vauntache', *Magister est assiduus in scola (in)formans* vel
informando suos discipulos de quibus recipit annuatim magnum[3]
*emolumentum; Mercatores multum lucrantur et diuites efficiuntur
care vendendo* vel *vendentes.* | Whereby knowystow a gerundif in 190
-dum? In ij maners. In whych ij maners? Oþer whyle w^t *ad*
preposicion and other whyle w^{t}owte *ad* preposicion. When shall
y have a gerundif in *-dum* w^t *ad* preposicion? When the English
of an infinitif mode comus aftyr a reson and tellus the cause
of the reson y shall have a gerundif in *-dum* w^t *ad* preposicion,
as thus: 'Men goon to battell to feʒte w^t here enmys', *Viri
vadunt ad bellum ad dimicandum cum suis inimicis*. When shall
y have a gerundif in *-dum* w^{t}owte *ad* preposicion?˙ When the
English of an infinitif mode comus aftyr *sum, es, fui*, and *sum,
es, fui* have no nominatif case before hym, I shall have a 200
gerundif in *-dum* w^{t}owte *ad* preposicion, as thus: 'Hyt ys to
w^{t}stond owre enmys purposyng to destrye owre reme', *Resistendum
est inimicis nostris proponentibus nostrum regnum adnichilare*.

De supinis

*Intendo ire oppositum scolaribus quos bene respondentes
sum intime dilecturus. Ire*: what mode? Infinitif mode.
Why soo? For when ij verbus comyn togedur w^{t}owte a relatif
or a coniunction comyng betwene, þe later verbe shal be infinitif
mode. *Oppositum*: what maner of spech? The furst suppin.
Why soo? For when y have an Englysh of an infinitif mode 210
suyng a verbe betokynyng bodely meuyng to any thyng to be done
or to be suffirte y shall have the furst suppin, vt *Vado lectum
libros, Vado doctum a magistro*. How mony yndyng of suppins
byn þer? II. Whych ij? *-Tum* and *-tu*, as *amatum, amatu*.
Whereby knowystow the furst suppin comyng in spech? When a
worde lyke to an infinitif mode comus aftyr a verbe betokynyng
bedely mevyng to any thyng to be done or to be suffrete I shall

[1] *sic* MS   [2] MS sech   [3] s *canc*.

86

INFORMACIO TEXT T

have the furst suppin, as *Vado lectum libros*, *Vado doctum a magistro*. Whereby knowystow the latter suppin? When y have a worde lyke to a participull of the presentens comyng before 220 a verbe that betokyns bodely mevyng from any thyng to be done or to be suffrete y shall have þe latter suppin, as *Venio lectu libros*, *Venio doctu a magistro*. Vnde versus:

Post motus verbum bene ponis vtrumque supinum,
Ad loca vult primum, *de* vult signare secundum;
Vt *Vado lectum*, *dormitum*, siue *comestum*;|
Vt *Venio lectu*, *dormitu*, siue *comestu*.
Ast infinitum si non signat tibi motum,
Vt *Cupio legere*, *Volo ludere*, *Curo docere*.

And when y have an English lyke to an infinitif mode 230 that shulde be set in the furst suppin, where þe furst suppin falyth y shall take þis nowne *locus* w^t thys preposicion *ad* and the futur tens of the same verbe þat the supin should com of w^t þis aduerbe *vbi*. Exemplum: *Vado ad locum vbi addiscam gramaticam*. And yf þer com a nowne betokenyng place before an English lyke to an infinitif mode þat shuld be sette in þe furst suppin, where the supin falyth y shall take þis aduerbe *vbi* w^t the futur tens of the same verbe that the suppin shulde come of, (vt) in hoc exemplo: *Vado Oxoniam vbi (a)discam gramaticam*. And when y have an English lyke to an infinitif mode that shulde 240 be sette in the latyr supin, where the latter supin falyth y shall take thys nowne *locus* w^t thys preposicion *a* and the preterperfitens of the same verbe that the supin shuld come of w^t thys aduerbe *vbi*, ut in hoc exemplo: *Veni a loco vbi addidici gramaticam*. And yf þer come a nowne betokynyng place before an English lyke to an infinitif mode þat shuld be sett yn the latter suppin, where þe lattyr suppin falyth y shall take þis aduerbe *vbi* w^t the preterperfitens of the same verbe þat the supin shuld come of, vt in hoc exemplo: *Veni Oxonis vbi addidici gramaticam*. 250

Dilecturus: what maner of spech? A participull of the futur tens yndyng in *-rus*. Why soo? For when y have an English like to an infinitif mode betokynyng 'to do' suyng thys verbe *sum*, *es*, *fui*, hyt shal be sette[1] in a participull of the futur tens yndyng in *-rus*, vt *Sum amaturus magistrum meum*. And yf hyt betokyn 'to suffyr' hyt shal be sette in þe participull of the futur tens yndyng in *-dus*, ut *Sum amandus a magistro*.

De ablatiuo casu absoluto

Magistro docente pueri proficiunt. *Magistro*: what case? 260 Ablatif case. Why soo? For when y have a reson of a nown or a pronowne and a participull (and) no word sette furth ne vndyrstond of the whych eny word of that reson may be gouernit, hyt shal be sette in the ablatif case absolute, ut|*Sole oriente veni ad scolas*; *Sole occidente tempus est dissoluendi scolas*;

---

[1] hyt shal be sette] *repeated*

INFORMACIO TEXT T

*Pluuia*¹ *pluente veni ad villam*. In how mony maner may the ablatif case absolute be expount? By ij. By whych ij? By *dum* or by *cum*. By *dum* as *Me vidente tu cecidisti*, id est, *Dum ego vidi tu cecidisti*; by *cum* *Augusto imperante Alexandria deuicta est*, id est, *Cum Augustus erat imperator Alexandria* 270 *deuicta est*. Vnde versus:

Per *dum* vel per *cum* sexti resolucio detur,
Huius namque rei Precianus testis habetur.
Per *quia, quando, si,* poterit racione resolui.

De sinodoche

Michi Roberto fracto caput medicina proficiet. *Caput*: what case? Þe accusatif case. Why soo? For when y have a nowne adiectif, verbe neuter or passif, or any of here participuls, gerundiuis, or supinis betokynyng all comyng in a reson before a worde þat betokyns party of þat all, hyt shal be280 sette in the accusatif case and be gouernit of þis figure: sinodoche. Exemplum de nomine adiectiuo: *Sum albus faciem*. Exemplum de verbo neutro ut *Doleo caput*. Exemplum de verbo passiuo ut *Frangor caput*. Exemplum de participio ut *Sum fractus caput*. Exemplum de gerundiuo: *Non habeo voluntatem frangendi caput*. Exemplum de supino: *Vado fractum caput*.

Adiectiua regunt passiuaque verbaque neutra
Accusatiuos, per sinodochen sibi iunctos,
Cum partis toti tribuantur proprietate(s):
Alba comas, dolet Anna caput; *crus frangitur illa*. 290
Participans iunges: ut² *Femina compta capillos*,
Hijsque gerundiua coniunges atque supina.

De verbis (in)personalibus

How knowystow a verbe inpersonall? For hyt hath noþer nowmbur ne person ne nominatif case before hym, but he ys declint in þe voice of the iij person singler and comus in English wᵗ on of these ij synys 'hyt' or 'me'. How mony maner of verbys inpersonall byn þer? II. Whych ij? Verbys inpersonalls of the actif voice and verbys inpersonalls of the passif voice. How knowystow a verbe inpersonall of the actif 300 voice? By my English and by my Latten. How by thyn English?³ My English shal begyn wᵗ 'hyt' as 'hyt|forthynkus', 'hyt noeys', 'hyt rwes'. How by thy Latten? My Latten shall ynde in -*t* as *penitet, tetet, miseret, pudet* and *piget*. How shall þow fynd owte thy principall verbe inpersonall of the actif voice? Aftur the iij person singler nowmbyr of a verbe of þe actif voice, as *iuuat, dilectat, penitet, oportet*. How knowystow a verbe inpersonall of the passif voice? By my English and by my Latten. How by thy English? My English shal begynne wᵗ 'me' as 'me loues', 'me redis', 'me teches'. How by thy 310 Latten? My Latten shall ynd in -*r* as *amatur, legitur, docetur*. A quibus verbis descendunt verba impersonalia? A verbis

¹ MS Pluuiam   ² MS vel   ³ sha *canc*.

INFORMACIO TEXT T

actiuis et a verbis neutris actiua signantibus.

Semper ab actiuis impersonale creatur,
Vel neutris (illis) quibus actio significatur.

Et sciendum est quod a verbis passiuis deponentibus et
communibus non discendunt impersonalia.

A deponenti communi vel pacienti
Inpersonale nomquam dicemus haberi.

What case may all the verbus impersonells of þe actif   320
voice construe w^t? Þe datif case, owtak xiij of þe whych v
may construe w^t accusatif case and genitif, and thay bene þes:
penitet, tetet, miseret, pudet and *piget*; and v wyth þe
accusatif case al only, and þai bene thes: *iuuat, decet,
delectat, oportet* and *latet*; and iij w^t genitif case and
ablatif, and they bene þes: *interest, refert* and *est* when þey
bene sette for *pertinet*.

De verbis impersonalibus constructis cum genitiuo

Penitet me tui. Me: what case? Accusatif case. Why
soo? For thes v verbys *penitet, tedet, miseret, pudet* and *piget*   330
wyll construe w^t genitif case and accusatif case; w^t accusatif
of þat thyng that doth the dede of þe verbe and w^t genitif case
of that thyng þat the dede of þe verbe ys done fore.

Penitet et *tetet, miseret, pudet* et *piget*; ista
Accusatiuum poscunt simul et genitiuum,
Natura primum sed transicione secundum.

Libet mihi comedere. Mihi: what case? Datif case. Why
soo? For all the verbys conteineit in þes versus wyll construe
w^t datif case. Versus:

Hec *libet* atque *licet, placet* et *liquet, accidit* inde,   340
Congruit, euenit (et) *contingit* (et) *expedit* adde,|
Pertinet, incumbit, vacat (et) *cedit,* quoque *prestat*
Cum reliquis paribus poteris coniungere ternis.

Iuuat me studium exercere. Me: what case? Þe accusatif case.
Why soo? For all þe verbus contenit in these versus woll
construe w^t accusatif case. Versus:

Quarto iunge *iuuat, decet* ac *dilectat, oportet,*
Et *latet* illorum numero vult associari:
Me decet esse ducem; *Monachum decet esse priorem*;
Et *Me delectat fore moriginum,* vel *oportet.*   350
Me de velle tuo, te deque meo latet, Hugo.
Me de velle tuo latet, O pulcherima virgo.

How is *iuuat* declind? *Iuua(t), iuuit, -are, -di, -do, -dum,
iuuans.* Why ys *iuuat* soo declind? For when y have a verbe
to be declind personell or impersonell y shal begyne att the

89

presentens of the indicatif mode and ioyn to the gerundyuys and þe supynys and then to þe participuls.

De declinacione huius verbi iuuat

Secundum 'Quod est impersonale actiue vocis?': verbo impersonali indicatiuo modo *iuuat*, preterito inperfecto   360
iuuabat, preterito perfecto *iuuit*, preterito plusquamperfecto *iuuerat*, futuro *iuuabit*; inperatiuo modo *iuuet*, futuro *iuuato*; optatiuo modo *vtinam iuuaret*, preterito perfecto et plusquam *vtinam iuuisset*, futuro *vtinam iuuet*; coniunctiuo modo *cum iuuet*, preterito inperfecto *cum iuuaret*, preterito perfecto *cum iuuerit*, preterito plusquamperfecto *cum iuuisset*, futuro *cum iuuerit*; infinitiuo modo *iuuare*, preterito perfecto et plusquamperfecto *iuuisse*, futuro *iutum ire*. Gerundia vel participalia verba sunt hec: *-di, -do, -dum*. Vnicum participium trahitur ab hoc verbo impersonali presentis temporis, ut *iuuaris*. 370

How many participuls longen to a verbe impersonell of the actif voice? On. Whych on? A participull of the presentens, as of thys verbe *penitet* comus *penitens*, owt-take ij impersonells the whych haue ij participuls, a present (and) a preter, as of þis verbe *miseret* comus *miserens*, and *misertum*, and of thys verbe *tedet* comus *tedens* and *pertesum*. Vnde versus:

Tedet pertesum flectet, *miseret*que *misertum*;
Actiue vocis reliquis non attribuatur
Preteritum tale, Precianus testificatur.|

Hec est differentia inter *iuuat* personale et *iuuat*   380
impersonale. *Iuuat* personale est actiuum, idem est quod *auxiliari, delectari*; et *iuuat* impersonale est neutrum, et idem est quod *delecta(t)*. Vnde versus:

Est *iuuat* actiuum *delector* et *auxiliatur*;[1]
Impersonale *iuuat* est *delectat* vbique.

De interest

Interest mea clerici iugiter studere et addicere. Mea: what case? Ablatif case. Why soo? For *interest, refert* and *est* sett for *pertinet* woll constru w^t genitif of all casuels partes, owtake v genitius case of þj[2] pronowns principals, þat   390
is to say *mei, tui, sui, nostri* and *vestri*, and on genitif case of a nowne, þat ys to say *cuius, -a, -um*, in the stud of the whych þe forsayd verbys byn construyd w^t ablatif case, femyn gendur, singler nowmbur, sayng apon þis wyse: *Mea, tua, sua, nostra* and *vestra* and *cuia interest*, in the whych is vndyrstondyd *re* or *vtilitate* for here substantiuis.

De hoc verbo impersonali obuiatur

Obuiatur mihi a scolari bono socio. Obuiatur: what maner

---

[1] MS auxiliator   [2] MS iij

INFORMACIO TEXT T

of spech? A verbe impersonell. Why ys thys Englysh made by
a verbe impersonell? For when y have a verbe in Englysh nevter 400
lyke to a passif, where the passyue faylyth y shall take the
verbe impersonell of such mode and such tens as the passif
semus to be, and that þat semus to be nominatif case¹ y shall
turne into such case as the verbe wyll have aftur hym. *Bono
socio*: what case? Ablatif case. Why soo? For all casuels
wordis longyng to one thyng comyng fast togedur shal be sett
in on case.

    How shall þu say on Latten: 'The mayster betis me'?
By thys verbe *vapulo*: *Vapulo a magistro*. Why soo? For when
y haue an English of actif significacion þat oth to be made 410
be a verbe neutur-passif, þat worde þe whych semus to be
nominatif case y shall turne into an ablatif case w^t a
preposicion, or ellis into a datif case when y have þis verbe
nubo, -is, as: *Nubo tibi*; and all þe (verbus that ben contenyd
in thes uersus ben) verbus neutris-passiuis. Vnde versus:

    *Exulo, vapulo, veneo, fio, nubo licet*que²
    Sensum passiui sub voce gerunt aliena.|

Verba neutropassiua sunt quinque que patent per versus:

    *Audeo*³ cum *soleo, fio* cum *gaudeo, fido,*
    Quinque puer numero neutropassiua tibi do. 420

    Indicatiuo modo, tempore presenti *amatur*, preterito
inperfecto *amabatur*, preterito perfecto *amatum est* vel *fuit*,
preterito plusquamperfecto *amatum erat* vel *fuerat*, futuro
amabitur; imperatiuo modo *ametur*, futuro *amator*; optatiuo
modo *vtinam amaretur*, preterito perfecto et plusquamperfecto
vtinam -atum esset vel *fuisset*, futuro *vtinam amaretur*;
coniunctiuo modo *cum amaretur*, preterito inperfecto *cum
amaretur*, preterito perfecto *cum amatum sit* vel *fuerit*,
preterito plusquamperfecto *cum amatum esset* vel *fuisset*,
futuro *cum amatum erit* vel *fuerit*; infinitiuo modo *amari*; 430
preterito perfecto et plusquamperfecto *-atum esse* vel *-atum
fuisse*, futuro *-atum iri*. Gerundia vel participalia verba
sunt hec: *amandi, -do, -dum, -atum, -atu*. Vnicum participium
trahitur ab hoc verbo impersonali ut nominatiuo *hoc amatum*,
accusatiuo *hoc -atum*, ablatiuo *ab hoc amato*.

De temporibus formatis a preterito perfecto modi indicatiui

    How mony tensys byn þer formed of the preterperfitens of
the indicatif mode? VI. Whych vj? Þe preterpluperfitens
of þe same mode, and þe preterperfitens and pluperfitens of þe
optatif mode, and þe preterperfitens and pluperfitens and þe 440
futur tens of þe coniunctif mode, and the preterperfitens and
pluperfitens of þe infinitif mode. How many turnyn *I* vnto *E*
and how mony holdyn *I* styll? III turnyn *I* vnto *E* and iij
holdyn *I* styll. Whych iij turnyn *I* vnto *E*? Þe preterpluper-

¹ to þe verbe *canc.*   ² MS liceo   ³ Exulo vapulo *canc. before* Audeo

91

INFORMACIO TEXT T

fitens of þe indicatif mode and þe preterperfitens and þe futur tens of þe coniunctif mode. As how? As *legi*, turne *I* vnto *E* and do þer-to a *-ram* and then hit ys *legeram*, *-as*, *-at*; *legi*, turne *I* vnto *E* and do þer-to a *-rim* and hyt hys *legerim*, *-is*, *-it*; *legi*, turne *I* vnto *E* and do þer-to a *-ro* and þen hyt ys *legero*, *-is*, *-it*. Whych iij holdyn I styll? Þe preterperfitens 450 and pluperfitens of þe optatif mode, and þe preterpluperfitens of the coniunctif mode, and þe preterperfitens and pluperfitens of the infinitif mode, as *legi*, do þer-to *S* and *-sem* and then hyt ys *legissem*; *legi*, do þer-to *S* and *-se* and then hyt ys *legisse*.

Explicit *Informacio* secundum Leylond. Rosa flos florum sic Leylond gramaticorum.

INFORMACIO TEXT U

U. Aberystwyth, N.L.W. MS Peniarth 356B, fols.1r-9v

Inn how mony manerys schall þu begynne to make <Laten>
by ryghtffull ordur of construction? By v. Wheche v? By
a <vo>catyve case, by a nominatyue case, by sumqwat sett in þe
stydde of the nominatyue case, by an ablatiue case absolute,
and by a uerbe impersonell. How b<y> a vocatiue case? As
'Wyllyam[1] make þe fyre', *Willelme fac ignem*. How be a
nominatyue case and a verbe of certen persan? As 'The
maister syttis in the scole', *Magister sedet in scola*. How
be sumwhat sett in stydde of þe nominatyue case? As 'To
dyne tymele schall[2] comfe<rt> monnus hert', *Iantari tempestiue*   10
confortabit humanum cor.[3] How by an ablatyue case absolute?
As 'The maister techyng in th<e> scole, I am agayste',
Magistro docente in scola ego sum perteritus. How be a uerbe
impersonell? As 'Me syttis in the scole', *Sedetur <in scola>*.

What scall thow do when thow hast an Englyche to mak<e> a
Laten? I schall fyrst loke owt my pri⸢n⸣cypall uerbe personell,
and loke whedur hytt betokon 'to do' or 'to suffur'. And yff
hytt betokon 'to do' the doer schall be the nominat<yue> case
and the sufferer seche case as the uerbe wyll haue aftyr hym.
And yff my princypall uerbe pers<onel> betokon 'to suffur',   20
the suffurer schall be þe nominatyue <case> and the doer the
ablatyue case w^t *a* prepocicion, yff þer <be>|<d>oer in the reson.
And yff[4] my pry(n)cypall uerbe be a uerbe impers<o>nell, I schall
begynne at hymne to make Laten and to constrew. How schall thow
know, yff þer be mone uerbys in a reson, wheche ys thy prymcypall
uerbe? Euermore the fyrste ys my prymcypall uerbe, but yff hyt
come next to a relatyue or ellys be lyke to an infenetyue
mode. Whereby knowus þu when hyt comys next to a relatyue?
When hyt comys next thys Englyche worde 'that' or 'the weche'.
Whereby knouus þu when hytt is lyke to an infenetyue mode?   30
When I haue thys Englyche 'to' or 'to be', as 'to love' or
'to be loved'.

'(A)[5] chirche is a place the wheche Crystyn menne bem
mecull holdon to loue.' Wheche ys thy pry(n)cypall uerbe in
þis reson? 'Is'. When þis uerbe *sum, es, fui* is thy
pry(n)cypall uerbe, how schall þu knoo wheche ys thy nominatyue
case? By þis Englyche worde 'Whoo or what?', as 'Whoo or
what ys? The chirche is.' What case 'the chirche'? The
nominatyue case. What parte of speche is 'the whech'? A
nown relatyue. What hase a relatyue? An antecedent.   40
Whereby knouus þu an antecedent? For hyt gouus beffore the
relatyue and ys rehersytt of the relatyue. How knouus thow
a relatyue? Fo hytt makys rehersyng of[6] thyngus sayd or
spokyn beffore. What case, what gendur, what nowumbour schall
the relatyue be? Seche case, seche gendur, seche nowumbour
as the antecedent schulde be yff he <stod>e þer as relatyue
stoumdus and the relatyue wheyr[7] put away. <Wh>at case schall
the relatyue be when þer comys a nominatyue <ca>se betwene þe

[1] -m *from* n   [2] cow(?) *canc*.   [3] -da *erased?*   [4] þer b *canc*.
[5] *guide letter*   [6] a(?) *canc*.   [7] *a stroke canc*.

93

INFORMACIO TEXT U

relatyue and the uerbe?[1] | Then the relatyue schall be seche
case as the uerbe wy<ll> have aftyr hym. And yf there come no   50
nominatyue case betwene the relatyue and þe verbe, then the
relatyue schall be þe nominatyue case to þe uerbe, but yf the
uerbe be a uerbe inpersonell. Then the relatyue schall be
suche case as þe uerbe inpersonell woll be construid wyth.
Is that sothe all way? ʒey, but yf the uerbe inpersonel
haue hys casuell worde afftyr hym. Then the relatyue schal
be suche case as the infenytyue mode wyll haue after hym.
How schall thou say on Latyn þe Englysch before sayd?
Ecclesia est locus quem Christiani tenentur[2] *multum diligere.*
Quem: qwat gendur? The masculyn gendur? Why so? For to   60
the nexte antecedent schal the relatyffe be referrit, but yf
the sentens lett, as in thys Latyn: *Canis tuus occidit ovem*
meam quem ego oc<i>dam. Thys relatyue *quem* acordys with the
fyrst antecedent and noʒt wyth the latur, be enchesum of the
sentens.

   (I)bo[3] *ad locum qui* vel *quod est nouum caustrum.* Qwat
gendur is *qui* vel *quod*? The masclyn gendur and the[4] neutur.
Why so? For qwen I haue a relatyue sette betwene[5] ij nown<ys>
substantyues of dyuerse gendur,[6] hyt may acorde wyht aythyr
substantyve in gendur. Vnde versus: 70

        Quando relatiuum generum casus variorum
        Inter se claudunt qui[7] rem spectant ad eandem,
        (Per genus hoc poterit vtrilibet assimilari):
        Est pia stirps Iesse quem Christum dicimus esse. |

   Vtinam essem episcopus, qui vocor Willelmus, sub spe
releuandi paupertatem amicorum meorum. Episcopus: what
case? The nominatyffe case. Why so? For *sum, es, fui* is
a verbe copulatyue and wyl copul[8] (lyke) case. What maner of
verbis haue strenght to cowpull lyke case? Verbys substantyves,
uerbes vocatyves, and uerbys hauyng (hor) strenght. How mony   80
uerbes substantyues ben þer? III. Wyche iij? *Sum, fio*
and *existo*. Vnde uersus:

        Ars subst(ant)iua tria dat tantummodo[9] uerba:
        Sum simul *existo, fio*, nil amplius addo.

How mony verbys vocatyves bene there? V. Wyche v? Pateat
per uersus:

        Quinque vocatiua[10] dicas tantummodo[9] uerba:
        Nominor, appellor, sic[11] *nuncupor* et *voco, dicor*;
        Ast adiectiua fore dicas cetera verba.

What maner of uerbys haue strenght to cowpull lyke case,   90

---

[1] and the uerbe] *repeated at beginning of fol.* 2ʳ.
[2] MS tonentur   [3] (I) - *guide letter*   [4] no *canc.*
[5] t *canc.*   [6] lo *canc.*   [7] MS quia
[8] -atyue *canc.* [9] MS tantomodo   [10] MS vacatiua
[11] MS sit

INFORMACIO TEXT U

out-takyn verbys substantyuis and uerbys vocatyuis? Verbys
passyvys, vt *Ordinor acolitus, Tenior sapiens*; and uerbys as
were passyuis,[1] vt *Vapulo ignarus*; and uerbys betokenyng
strenght or mevyng of soule, vt *Meditor sapiens*; and uerbys
þat betokenyng rest, vt *Sedio tristis*; and uerbys that
betokening semyng, vt *Aperio bonus, Emineo excelsus*.

(I)stud[2] *dolium est plenum vini* vel *vino.* *Vini* vel *-no*;
what case? The genetiue case and þe ablatyffe.| Why soo?
For all nownus adiectyuis þat betokyn (fulnes) or emtenes wyll
connstrw whyt the genitiue case and þe ablatyuiffe. Vnde   100
versus:

> Que plenum signant vel que vacuata figurant
> Iunguntur sextis, vt scribitur, et genetiuis:
> *Vini* vel *vino duo dolia plena videto.*[3]

(D)esino[4] *viciorum et abstenio irarum. Irarum et viciorum:*
what case? The genitiue case. Why so? For thes ij verbys
desino and *abstenio* will constrw whit the genetyffe case ex vi
transicionis personalis. Vnde uersus:

> *Desino, abstenio* genitiuis iungere curo.

Dominor huius ville vel *huic ville cuius incolorum,*   110
incolis vel *incolas miserebor. Huius* vel *huic ville*: what
case? The genitiue and the datiue. Whi so? For *dominor,*
-naris and *miserior, misereris* wyll constrw wyth the genetyue
case and þe datyue[5] ex vi transicionis personalis, and[6] wyth
the accusatiue ex vi transicionis. Vnde uersus:

> Do *dominor* ternis *misereri* siue secundis,
> Et sibi vult iungi quartum casum *misereri*:
> *Nostri* vel *nobis* vel *nos Ihesu misereri.*

Ricardus et Willelmus indigent diuine gracie, diuinam
graciam vel *diuina gracia. Diuine gracie, diuinam graciam* vel   120
diuina gracia: what case? The genetyue case,[7] the accusatyue
and the ablatyue. Why so? For theys uerbys *egeo, eges* and
indigeo, -ges wyll constrew wyth the genetyffe case, þe
accusatyue case and the ablatyue. Vnde uersus:|

> Des quartis, sextis *eget, indiget* et genetiuis:
> *Indegio rem, re*, coniunge *rei, mihi care*,
> *In quem respicias.* Hoc asserit ipse Papias.

Indigent: what nowumbour? The plurell now<m>bor. Why so?
Fo(r) ij nominatyue case syngler wyth an *et* coniunccion comyng
betwene wyll haue a uerbe plurell; and ij substantyuis syngler   130
wyth an *et* coniunccion betwene wyll haue an adiectiue plurell;
and ij antecedens syngler whyt an *et* coniunccion comyng betwene

---

[1] as thay were *canc*. [2] (I)- *guide letter* [3] -i- *from* e *or* c
[4] (D)- *guide letter*; I *canc*. [5] MS accusatyue
[6] the *canc*. [7] w *canc*.

95

INFORMACIO TEXT U

wyll haue a relatyue plurell.

(O)buiemus regi et regine venientibus Oxoniam qui sunt
digniscimi[1] creaturarum. Regi et regine: what case? Þe
datyue case. Why so? For all the uerbys þat ben contenyt
in thys uersus wyll constrew w[t] þe datyue case. Vnde uersus:

> Obuio, parco, placet, noceo, respondio, servit,
> Precipit, opponit, concludo, iunge[2] datiuis,
> Supplicat, aridet, faueo, vaco,[3] proficit, herit,   140
> Subvenit addatur, succurrit, propiciatur,
> Congruo, conpacior, comfert, succedit, adulor,
> Incidet, imponit, conuicior, improperabit,[4]
> Suffecit, aspirat, valedico, gratulor, astat,
> Imminet ac equipollet, alludit, obedit et obstat,
> Occurrit,[5] sedit, restat, et quando locum dat,|
> Derogo,[6] condolio, preiudico, detraho, differt,
> Suppetit his iungas. Que sum componit, eis das.
> Hec et quamplura ternis coniungere cura.

(P)ostulo[7] Deum graciam bene discendi qui doce(o)r   150
gramaticam. Gra(ciam):[8] what case? The accusatyue case.
Why so? For all the uerbis þat ben contenyd in thys versus
wyll constrew wyth a[9] dowbull accusatyue case betokenyng diuers
thyng. Gramaticam: what case? The accusatiue[10] case. Why
so? For all the[11] uerbys passyuis comyng of verbes actiues the
wyche ben constrwd wyth a dowbull accusatiue[12] case may be
constrewed wyth a latur accusatyue case. Vnde versus:

> Postulo, posco, peto, doceo, rogo, flagito, celo,
> Exuo, cum vestit, monet, induo, calceo, cingo:
> Accusatiuos geminos hec uerba requirunt.   160
> Passiuis quorum postremus[13] iungitur horum.
> Istis iungantur hec omnia que similantur,[14]
> Que poscant, colant, ornantque rogantque magistrant.

(U)tor rubio capicio. Capicio: qwath case? The
ablatyue case. Why soo? For all the uerbys that be
contenyt in[15] thys versus wyll constru wyth the ablatyue case.
Vnde uersus:

> Vescitur et fruitur, caret, vtitur atque potitur:
> Hec ablatiuos[16] transicione regunt.|
> Hijs iungas fvngor, et difficio sociatur.   170

How mony endynges of gerundyues ben there? III. Qwech
iij? -Di, -do and -dum. When schall þu haue a gerundyue in
-di in comyn speche? When the Englych of an infenetyue mode

---

[1] -i from a   [2] MS imge   [3] MS vacuo
[4] MS Impropererabit   [5] Ress canc.   [6] MS derigo
[7] (P)- guide letter   [8] MS gra[maticam], with the correction not
completed   [9] dol canc.   [10] a stroke canc.
[11] the repeated   [12] a stroke canc.   [13] MS pastremus
[14] MS similianatur   [15] uer canc.   [16] MS ablatiuis

INFORMACIO TEXT U

comys after *tempus* and *est* or ellys aftyr a nowne substan<tyue>
I schall haue a gerundyue in *-di*. Exemplum: 'Masse endytte,
hyt ys tyme to breke oure faste', *Missa fenita, tempus est
dyssoluendi ieiunium nostrum*. I schall haue a gerundyue in
-di after a nowne substantyue, as thus: 'Oure Pape hasse power
to assoyle Crystyn men leuyng in God of her synnys', *Noster
Papa habet potestatem absoluendi Christianos in Deo confidentes   180
de peccatis suis*. Qwereby knous thow (when) a gerundyue in *-doo*
schall come in speche? In ij maners of wyse. In wych ij?
When the Englisch 'in' comys before the Englych of a
par(ti)cipull of the precentens wythowt a substantyue set to
hym, I shall haue a gerundyue in *-do*, as thus: 'In feȝtyng
mony men ben wondyd and mony maymnyd and slayn', *In dimicando
quamplurimi*[1] *homines sunt uulnerati quamplurimi mutilati et
quamplurimi occisi*. When schall I haue a gerundyue in *-do* in
the[2] secunde maner of wyse? When the Englysch of a participull
of precent tens commys fer after a nowne substantyue, I may   190
chose whedur I wyll haue a gerundyue or a participull of the
precent tens, as 'The maister is bese in the scole in-
formyng hys dysypuls, of the qwech he resayuis|yerly grete
auantage', *Magister est assiduus in scola informando* vel
*informannte suos dissipulos, de quibus recipit annu(a)tim
magnum emol<umen>tum*. When schall I haue a gerundyue in *-dum*
in comyn speche? In ij manerys. In wheche ij? Oþer whyle
w^t *ad* prepocicium and oþer whyle w^{t}owt *ad* prepocicicm. When
þe Englysch of a infenetiue mode commys after a resom and
tellus the cause of the resun I schall haue a gerundyue in   200
dum w^t *ad* prepociciom, as: 'Men gonn to batell to feȝth w^t
hor enimys', *Viri vadunt ad bellum ad dim<i>candum cum suis
inimicis*. When schall I haue a gerundyue in *-dum* w^{t}owt an
ad prepocicion? When þe Englysch of an infenetiue mode comys
after *sum, es, fui* and *sum, es, fui* ha<ue> no nominatiue case
before hym, I schall haue a gerundyffe w^{t}owt *ad* prepocicion,
as thus: 'Hyt ys to w^{t}stonde owr enmys purposyng to dystrye
our reaume.' *Resistendum est inimicis nostris proponentibus
adnichilare regnum nostrum.*

 (I)ntendo[3] *ire oppositum scolaribus quos bene respondentes*   210
sum intime dilecturus. Ire: what mode? Infenetyffe mode.
Why so? For when ij verbis comyn togedur w^{t}out a relatyue
or a coniunction betwene, the lattyr schall be the infenetyue
mode. *Oppositum*: what maner of speche? The fyrst supyn.
Why so? For when I haue an Englych of an infenetyue mode
suyng a uerbe betokenyng bodeli mevyng to any thyng to be done
or to be suffurd, I schall haue þe first supyn, as *Vado lectum
libros*; *Vado doctum a magistro*. How mony endyngys of supynnys
ben þer? II. Whiche ij? *-Vm* and *-v*, as *amatum, -tu*. When
schall I haue the fyrst supyn in comyn speche? When|the   220
Englyshe of an infenetyue mode comys after a verbe betokenyng
bodely meuyng to any thynge to be done or to be suffur(d), I
schall haue the fyrst supyn, as *Vado lectum libros*; *Vado
doctum a magistro*. And iff hyt betoken bodeli meuyng from any
thynge to be done or suffurt I schall haue the latyr supyn, as

---

[1] MS quamplurimus   [2] MS adds ij   [3] (I)- *guide letter*

97

INFORMACIO TEXT U

Vado lectu libros; *Vado doctu a magistro*. Vnde uersus:

    Post motus uerbum bene ponis vtrumque supinum,
    Ad loca vult primum, de vult signare secundum;
    Vt *Vado lectum, dormitum* siue *commestum*[1];
    Vt *Venio lectu, dormitu* siue *commestu*.   230
    Ast infenitum si non signat[2] tibi motum,
    Vt *Cupio legere, Volo ludere, Curo docere*.

    (A)nd[3] also when I haue a worde like to an infenetyue mode or a participull suyng a nowne endyng in -*ilis*, hyt schall be set in the latur supyn. Exemplum vt *Ista latinitas est difficilis compositu*. And when I haue an Englyche like to an infenetyue mode that schulde be sette in þe fyrste supyn, where the supyn faylys I schall take þis nowne *locus* w^t þis prepocicion *ad* and the fetur tens of the same uerbe þat þe supyn schulde (come) of w^t þis aduerbe *vbi*. Exemplum: *Vado ad locum vbi*   240
adiscam gramaticam. And iff þer comme a nowne betokenyng place before a word lyke to an infenetiue mode that schulde be set in the fyrst supyn, where the supyn faylys I schall take þis aduerbe *vbi* and the fetur tens of the same uerbe þat the supyn schulde come of, vt in hoc exemplo: *Vado Oxoniam vbi adiscam gramaticam*. And when I haue an Englyche like to an infenetyue mode that schulde be sette in the latur supyn, wheyr þe supyn faylys I schall take þis nowne *locus*|w^t þis prepocicion *a* and the pretyrperfytens of the same uerbe þ<at> the supyn schulde comme of w^t thys aduerbe *vbi*, vt in hoc   250
exemplo: *Veny a loco vbi adidici gramaticam*. And iff þer come a nowne betokenyng place before an Englyche lyke to an infe⌈ne⌉tyue mode that schulde be sette in the later supyn, where the supyn failis I schall take þis aduerbe *vbi* and the preterperfitens of þe[4] same uerbe þat þe supyn schulde come of, vt in hoc exemplo: *Veni Oxonia vbi adidici gramaticam*.

    Dilecturus: what maner of speche? A participull of the futur tens endyng in -*rus*. Why so? For when I haue on Englyche lyke to an infenetyue mode betokenyng 'to do' suyng þis uerbe *sum, es, fui* hyt schall be sett in a participull in   260
-*rus*, vt *Sum*[5] *amaturus magistrum meum*. And iff hyt betokon 'to suffur' hyt schall be sett in a participull of þe fetur tens endyng in -*dus*, vt *Sum amandus a magistro meo*.

    (M)*agistro*[6] *docente pueri proficiunt*. *Magistro*: what case? The ablatyue case absolute. Why so? For when I haue a resun of a nowne or a pronowne and a participull and noo worde furthe sett ne vnderstondin, of the wheche that reson may be gouerned, hyt schall be sett in þe ablatyue case absolu<te>, as thus: 'The sonne rysyng I come to[7] scole',
Sole oriente veni ad scolas. *Sole occidente tempus est*   270
dissoluendi scolas. *Plu(u)ia pluente veni ad villam*. In how mony manerys schall the ablatyue case absolute ⌈be⌉

---

[1] Ast Infenitum si non signet tibi motum *canc.*   [2] MS signēt
[3] (A)- *guide letter*   [4] th *canc.*   [5] ame(?) *canc.*
[6] (M)- *guide letter*   [7] scho *canc.*

INFORMACIO TEXT U

expowned? In[1] ij. Wheche ij? By *dum* and by *cum*. By
⌈*dum*⌉ as thus: *Me vidente tu secidisti*, id est: *Dum ego vidi
tu cecidisti*. By *cum* as: *Augusto imperante Alexandria diuicta
est*, id est: *Cum Augu<stus> erat imperator Alexandria deuicta
est*. Vnde uersus:|

    Per *dum* vel per *cum* sexti resolucio detur,
    Hujus[2] namque rei Precianus testis habetur.
    Per *quia, quando, (si)*, poterit racione resolui.   280

    (M)ichi[3] *Roberto fracto caput medicina proficiet*.
Caput: what case? The accusatyue case. Why soo? For
when I haue a nowne adiectyue, uerbe neutur, passyue, or hony
of hor participuls, gerundyuis or supynnis betokenyng all,
comyng in a resun before a wourde that betokenys part of that
all, that worde þat betokenus parte of that all schall be set
in þe accusatyue case and be gouerned be thys fegur: synodoges.
Exemplum de nomine adiectiuo, vt *Sum albus faciem*. Exemplvm
de uerbo nevtro vt *Doleo caput*. Exemplum[4] de passiuo vt
Frangor tebias. Exemplum[5] de gerundiuo vt *Habeo voluntatem*   290
frangendi caput. Exemplum de supino vt *Vado fractum caput*.
Vnde uersus:

    Adiectiua regunt passiuaque uerbaque neutra
    Accusatiuos, per sinodochen sibi iunctos,
    Cum partis toti tribuantur proprietates,
    Aut e conuerso: mox hinc exempla videto.

    How knous þu a uerbe inpersonell? For hyt hase nothur
nowumbur ne person ne no no(m)i(n)atyue case and is declynyd
in þe voyce of the iij person singler nowumbor and comys in
Englyche w[t] one of thes synis 'hyt' or 'me'. How mony manerys   300
of uerbys inpersonellis ben þer? II. Wheche ij? Uerbis
impersonellys of[6] actyue voyce and verbis impersonellis of the
passiue voyce. How[7] knowus þu a uerbe impersonell of the
actyue uoyce? By my Englyche and by my Laten. How by thy
Englyche and how by þi Laten? My Englyche schall begynne w[t]
'hyt', as 'hyt forthynkys', 'hyt ruis'. How by Latyn? My
Laten schall emde in -*t* as *penitet, tedet, miseret*. How
schall þu fymde out a uerbe impersonell of the actyue voyce?
After the iij person singuler|nowmbur of a uerbe of the
actyue voyce, as *iuuat, dilectat, oportet*. How knous thow   310
a uerbe impersonell of the passyue uoyce? By my Englyche and
by my Laten. How by Englyche and how by þi Laten? When my
Englyche schall begynne w[t] 'me' as 'me loves', 'me redys',
'me techis'. How by þi Laten? My Laten schall emde in -*r*
as *amatur, legitur, docetur*. A quibus ⌈*uerbis*⌉ descendunt
uerba impersonalia? A uerbis actiuis et a uerbis neutris
actum significantibus. Vnde uersus:

    Semper ab actiuis impersonale creatur,

[1] t *canc*.   [2] MS hugis   [3] (M) *guide letter*
[4] MS Exempliūn[i]   [5] MS exemlplum   [6] and verbis *canc*.
[7] *illegible word canc*.

INFORMACIO TEXT U

Vel neutris illis quibus accio significatur.

Et sciendum est quod a uerbis passiuis deponentibus et 320
commvnibus non descendunt impersonalia. Vnde uersus:

> Impersonale numquam de iure creatur
> A deponenti communi vel pacienti,
> Aut neutris illis quibus passio¹ significatur,
> Defectum cuius supplere valet *aliquis, quis.*

Wyth what case may all the uerbis imperson(e)llis of the actyue voyce construe? W^t the datyue case, out-takyn xiij² of the wheche v may construe w^t the accusatyue case, and thay bem theis: *penitet, tedet, miseret, pudet* and *piget*; and v w^t þe accusatyue case, and thay bem thes: *iuuat, decet,* 330 *delectat, oportet* and *latet*; and iij w^t the genitiue case and the ablatyue, and thay bem thes: *interest, refert* and *est* when hyt ys sette for *pertinet.*

(P)enitet³ *me tui. Me*: what case? The accusatyue case. Why? Thes v uerbys *penitet, tedet, miseret, pudet* and *piget* wyll construe w^t the genityue case and the accusatyue case; w^t the accusatyue case of that thynge that dose the dede of the uerbe, and wythe the genetyue case of that thynge that the dede of the uerbe is done fore. Vnde versus:|

> *Penitet* (et) *tedet, miseret, pudet* et *piget*: ista 340
> Accusatiuos poscunt simul et genetiuos,
> Natura primum sed transescione secundum.

Libet michi comedere. Michi: what case? The datyue case. Whi soo? For all the uerbys that bem contende in thes uersus will construe w^t the datyue case. Vnde uersus:

> Hec *libet* atque *licet, placet* et *liquet, accidit* inde,
> *Congruet, euenet* et *contingit* et *expedit* adde,
> *Pertinet, incumbit, vacat* et *cedit*, quoque *prestat*
> Cum reliquis paribus potest associare datiuis.

Iuuat me studium excercere. Me: what case? The 350 accusatiue case. Why so? For all the uerbs þat bene contenid in þes uersus wyll constru w^t þe accusatiue case. Vnde versus:

> Quarto iunge *iuuat, decet* ac⁴ *delectat, oportet,*
> Et *latet* illorum numero vult associari:
> *Me decet esse ducem*; *Monachum iuuat esse priorem*;
> Et *Me delectat fore morigervm,* vel *oportet.*
> *Me de uelle tuo, de teque meo latet,* Hugo.
> *Me de velle tuo latet, O pulcherima uirgo.*

How ys⁵ *iuuat* declynid? *Iuuat, iuuit, iuuare, -di, -do, -dum, iuuans*. Why ys *iuuat* so declyned? For when I haue a 360

¹ MS accio   ² MS x[v]iij   ³ (P)- *guide letter*
⁴ h- *canc.*   ⁵ h- *canc.*

INFORMACIO TEXT U

uerbe to be declynyd personell or impersonell I schall begenne
at the presentens of the indicatiue mode and then to[1] the
preterperfitens and then to the infenetiue mode, and then to the 363
gerundyu<is> and then to the supynnys and then to þe 363a
partycipuls. Declina[2] secunddum 'Quod est inpersonale actiue 364
vocis?'.[3] Indicatiuo modo tempore presenti *iuuat*, preterito
inperfecto *iuuabat*, preterito perfecto *iuuit*, preterito
plusquamperfecto *iuuerat*, futuro *iuuabit*; inperatiuo modo
iuuet, futuro *iuuato*; optatiuo modo *vtinam iuuaret*, preterito
perfecto et plusquamperfecto *vtinam iuuisset*, futuro *vtinam
iuuet*; coniunctiuo modo *cum iuuet*,|preterito inperfecto *cum* 370
iuuaret, preterito perfecto *cum iuueret*,[4] preterito plusquamperfecto[5] *cum iuuisset*, futuro *cum iuuerit*, infenetiuo modo
iuuare, preterito perfecto et plusquamperfecto *iuuisse*,
futuro caret. Vnicum participium trahatur ab hoc uerbo
impers(on)ali[6] temporis tantum presentis, vt *iuuans*.

How mony participuls[7] longon to a uerbe impersonell of
the actiue voyce? One. Wheche one? A participull of the
presentens, as of thys verbe *penitet* commys *penitens*, out-takyn
ij impersonels þe haue ij participuls, a precent and a preterit,
as of thys uerbe *miseret* comys *miserens* and *misertum*, and of 380
þis uerbe *tedet* comys *tedens* and *pertesum*. Vnde versus:

Tedet pertesum flectet, *miseret*que *misertum*;
Actiue vocis reliquis non attribuatur
Pretoritum tale, Precianus testificatur.

Hec est differentia inter *iuuat* personale et *iuuat*
impersonale. *Iuuat*[8] personale est actiuum, et id(em) est quod
auxiliari, *delectari*; et *iuuat* impersonale est neutrum, et
id(em) est quod *dilectat*. Vnde uersus:

Est *iuuat* actiuum *delector* et *auxiliatur*;[9]
Impersonale *iuuat* est *dilectat* vbique. 390

Interest mea clerici iugiter adiscere et studere. *Mea*:
what case?[10] The ablatiue case. Why so? For *interest*, *refert*
and *est* when hyt ys sett for *pertenet* will constru w^t the
genetiue case of all partis casuellys, out-taken v genetiue
casus of v pronownus primatiuis, þat ys to say *mei, tui, sui,
nostri* and *uestri*, and one genetiue case of a nowne, that ys
to say *cuius, -ia, -um*, in the styd of þe whyche þe foresayd
uerbs bem construid w^t þe ablatiue case, femyn gendur,
singuler nowumbur of hor possessiuis[11], sayng|on thys wyse: *Mea,
tua, sua, nostra* and <*vest*>*ra* and *cuia interest*, in the styd of 400
the whyche ys vndurstondon *re* or *vtilitate* for hor substantyuis.

Obuiatur michi a scolari bono socio. *Obuiatur*: what
maner of speche? A uerbe inpersonell. Why ys thys Englych

---

[1] þe *canc.*   [2] MS Ốeclina   [3] MS voces
[4] -et *from* rt   [5] per- *from* pre-   [6] MS *adds* presentis
[7] MS par- *from* pre- *which was not cancelled*   [8] est a(?) *canc.*
[9] MS auxiliator   [10] case *canc.*   [11] MS passiuis

101

made by a uerbe impersonell? For when I haue a uerbe neuter
in Englych lyke to a passiue, where the passiue faylys I schall
take the uerbe impersonell of seche mode and tens as the passyue[1]
semys[2] to be, and þat as semys to be the nominatiue case[3] I schall
turne onto seche case as the uerbe impersonell wyll haue after
hymme. *Bono socio*: what case? The ablatiue case. Why soo?
For all casuell[4] wordis comyng fast togedur vndur the syne of[5]   410
a lyke case schall be sett in one case.

How schall þu say on Laten, 'The maister betes me'? By
thys uerbe *vapulo*. *Vapulo a magistro*. Who so? For when I
haue a Englyche of an actyfe syngnificacion þat ogh to be made
be a uerbe neuter-passyue, þat as semys to be þe nominatiue case
I schall turne into the ablatiue case, or els into þe datiue
case when I haue thys uerbe *nubo*,[6] -*bis*, as: *Nubo tibi*. And
all that bem contenyd in thes uersus bem uerbys neutur-passiuis.
Vnde uersus:

> *Exulo, vapulo, veneo, fio, licet* quoque *nubo*   420
> Sensum passiui sub voce gerunt aliena.

Verba neutra-passiuia sunt quinque que patent per uersus:

> *Audeo* cum *soleo, fio*[7] cum *gaudeo, fido,*
> Quinque puer numero neutro-passiua tibi do.

Indicatiuo modo, in the schewyng maner, tempore presenti
amatur, preterito inperfecto *amabatur*, preterit(o) perfecto
amatum est vel *fuit,*|preterito plusquamperfecto *amatum erat*
vel *fuerat*, futuro *amabitur*, imperatiuo modo *ametur*, futuro
amator; optatiuo modo *vtinam amaretur*, preterito perfecto et
plusquamperfecto *vtinam amatum esset*[8] vel *fuisset*, futuro   430
vtinam ametur; coniu(n)ctiuo modo *cum ametur*, preterito
inperfecto *cum amaretur*, preterito perfecto *cum amatum sit*
vel *fuerit*, preterito plusquamperfecto *cum amatum esset* vel
fuisset, futuro *cum amatum erit* vel *fuerit*; infenetiuo modo
amari, preterito perfecto et plusquamperfecto *amatum esse* vel
amatum fuisse, futuro *amatum iri*. Gerundi(u)a vel participalia
uerba sunt hec: -*di*, -*do*, -*dum*, -*atum*, -*tu*. Vnicum
participium trahitur ab hoc uerbo impersonali vt nominatiuo
hoc amatum, accusatiuo *hoc amatum*, ablatiuo *ab hoc amato*.

How mony tens bem formyd of the preterperfitens of the   440
indicatiue mode? VI. Wheche vj? The preterpluperfitens
of the same mode and the preterpluperfitens of the optatiue[9]
mode, the preterperfitens, preterpluperfitens and the fvtur tens
of the coniunctiue mode, and preterplvperfitens of the infenetiue
mode. How mony of thes turnun[10] the *I* into *E* and how mony holden
I stylle? III turnun *I* into *E* and iij holden stylle the *I*.
Whe(che) iij turnun *I* in to *E*? The preterpluperfitens of the

[1] -s *canc.*   [2] MS samys   [3] sc *canc.*
[4] -s *canc.*   [5] the *canc.*   [6] -v- *from* o
[7] a stroke *canc.* [8] f *canc.*   [9] m^e *canc.*
[10] MS Turniun

INFORMACIO TEXT U

same mode, the preterperfitens and futur tens of the coniunctiue
mode, as *legi*, turne *I* into *E* and¹ put þer-to a -*ram* and then
hyt wyll be *legeram*; *legi*, turne *I* into *E* and put þer-to a   450
-*rym* and then hyt wyll be *legerim*; *legi*, turne *I* into *E* and
put þer-to a -*ro* and then hyt wyll be *legero*. Wheche iij
holdyn styll the *I*? The preterplvperfitens of the optatiue
mode, the preterplvperfitens of the coniunctiue mode, the
preterplvperfitens of the infenetiue mode, as: *legi*, put
þer-to *S* and -*sem* and then hyt wyll be *legissem*;   *legi*, put
þer-to *S* and² -*se* and then hyt wyll be *legisse*. |

  Explicit³ *Introduccio Puerorum*, quod ⌈**Wylliam Tholoyd**⌉.⁴
Ihesus amen.⁵ **Explicit quod Ihed.**⁶

---

¹ t *canc.*   ² *a stroke canc.*   ³ MS *adds* Exp *on*
preceding line above Introduccio   ⁴ *written over an*
erased name   ⁵ E *canc.*   ⁶ *doubtful reading*

103

INFORMACIO TEXT V

V. Aberystwyth, N.L.W. MS Peniarth 356B, fols.167^v-168^r

This incomplete version of the *Informacio* follows on without
a break from text B.

(I)n[1] how many maner shall ȝe begynne to construe and to
make a Latyn by þe ryȝtfull order of construccion? In iiij.
In which iiij? By þe vocatyf ȝyf hit be in þe reson, by þe
nominatyf or somwhat sette in þe stede of þe nominatyf and by
a verbe of certeyn person, by þe ablatyf case absolute, and
by a verbe inpersonell. How by þe vocatyf case? As 'Willum
make a fyre', *W(i)llelme fac ignem*. How by a nominatyf case
and a verbe of certeyn person? As 'Ion ys hys name',[2]
Iohannes est nomen eius. How by somwhat y-sette in þe stede
of þe nominatyf? As 'To rede and not to vnderstond is to   10
despyce', *Legere et (non) inteligere est negligere*. How by
þe ablatyf case absolute? As 'Þe spowse comyng a wys
mady(n) redy whent w^t hym to þe weddyng', *Weniente sponso
prude(n)s virgo preparita introiuit cum eo ad nupcias.* How
by a verbe inpersonell? As 'Hyt heuyethe my soule my lyf',
Tedet animam meam vite me. 'In hert me belouythe to ryȝtwesnes',
Corde creditur ad iusticiam. Vnde versus:

   Quatuor ecce modis construccio recta paratur:
   Quinto vel recto casu, rectore soluto,
   Impersonali, sic *Condecet*[3] atque *parari*.   20

 What shall ȝe do when ȝe[4] haue an Englishe to make a Latyn?
I (s)hall loke oute þe prinspall verbe and loke whedyr hit
betokyn 'to do' or 'to suffer', and ȝyf hit betokyn 'to do' þe
doer shall be nominatyf case and þe sufferar shall be suche case
as þe verbe will haue after hym, and ȝyf my prynspall verbe
betokyn 'to suffer' þe sufferar shall be nominatyf case and
þe doer shall be ablatyf w^t *a* preposicion ȝyf þer be doer.
And ȝif þe prinspall verbe be a verbe inpersonell y shall
begynne at hym to make|my Laten and constru. How shall ȝe
know, if þer be many verbys in a reson, which is þe prinspall   30
verbe? Euermore þe fyrst ys þe prynspall verbe, but hit cum
nexte after þe relatyf or be like to an infinityf mode.
Whereby know ȝe when hit cometh nexte after a relatyf? When
hit cometh nexte after þis English word 'þat' or 'þe which'.
Whereby know ȝe when hit is like an infinityf mode? When y
haue þis syne 'to' as 'to teche', 'to[5] rede'.

 'A chyrche ys a holy place þe which Cristyn men byn meche
y-hold to loue.' Whiche ys þe prinspall verbe? *Sum, es, fui.*
How shall ȝe know which

The text breaks off incomplete at this point.

---

[1] (I)- *guide letter*   [2] MS nane   [3] MS condocet
[4] an *canc.*   [5] MS -r *canc.*

INFORMACIO TEXT W

W. Lincoln Cathedral Library, MS 88, fols. 91ᵛ-95ʳ (margins)

(I)n[1] how mone maners shal þu begynne to make a Latyn an to construe? In foure. Qweche foure? First be a vocatif case, by a nominatif case, or sumqwat set in þo stede of a nominatif case, be an ablatif case absolute, an be a verbe inpersonil. Qwat shal þu do qwen þu hase a Englissh to make a Latyn? I shal loke to my principall verbe an loke if he betoken 'to do' or 'suffer', and if he betoken 'to do' þo doer shall be nominatif case an þo suffrer seche case as þo verbe wil haue aftur hym, vt *Amo magistrum*; and if my verbe betoken 'to suffer' þo suffrer shal be nominatif case an þo doer ablatif case with a preposicione, vt *Amor a magistro*; and if my principall verbe be a verbe inpersonil at hym I shal begyn to make a Latyn an to construe, vt *Oportet me adiscere*. Qwat shal þu do, if þu haue mone verbes in a reson, to knowe þi principal verbe? Euermore my first verbe is my principal verbe but if hit come next a relatif, vt *Magister qui sedet legit*, other ellis be like an infinitif mode, vt *Amare magistrum est naturale*.

Qwat parte of reson is þis noun 'qweche'? A noun relatif. Qwat hase a relatif? An antecedent; ⌜and hit is taker (of) an antecedent⌝. (Querby knowes an antecedent?) For hit gos before þo relatif and is reherset of þo relatif. Querby knowes a relatif? For hit makes rehersyngis of thing spoken of before. If þu haue mone antecedentz in a reson to qweche shal þi relatif be referret? Euermore to þo next, but if þo sentence let as in þis Latyn: *Canis tuus occidit ouem meam quem ego occidam*. Þis relatif quem acordes to þo forther[2] an not to þo latur because of þo sentence. Qwat shal þu do if þi relatif be set betwen two antecedents of diuers gendur longing both to one thing?[3] Þen hit shal acord to ayther in gendur, vt *Ibo ad locum qui* vel *quod est nouum castrum*; and if þer come a nominatif case betwene|þo relatif an þo verbe þen þo relatif shal be sech case as þo verbe wil haue aftur hym, vt *Video magistrum quem tu vides*; and if þer come noe nominatif case betwene þo relatif an þo verbe þe þo relatif shal be nominatif case to þo verbe but if hit be a verbe inpersonil, þen þo relatif shal be sech case as þo verbe inpersonil wil haue aftur hym, ⌜as *Cuius interest legere libros* et cetera,⌝ but if he haue his casuel word aftur hym, for þen þo relatif shal be seche case as þo infinitif mode[4] wil haue aftur hym, ⌜as *Quem interest magistri* <   >.⌝

Vtinam essem episcopus qui vocor Ricardus. Episcopus: qwat case? Nominatif case. Qwi so? For *sum, es, fui* is a verbe copulatif an wil coupell like case; and verbes substantiuis (also), as is open be versus. Versus:[5]

Ars substantiua tria dat tantummodo verba:
Sum simul existo, fio, nil amplius addo.

---

[1] (I)- *guide letter* [2] MS ferth [3] MS thingis
[4] MS mede [5] *in margin, as elsewhere below.*

105

INFORMACIO TEXT W

Qwat verbes also wil coupul like case? Verbes vocatiuus,
vt *Ego vocor Ricardus*. Versus:

> Quinque vocatiua dicas tantummodo verba: 50
> *Nominor, appellor* sic *nuncupor* et *voco, dicor,*

Qwat maner verbes out-taken verbes substantiues an verbes
vocatiues haue strength to coupul like case? Hit is to say
þat uerbis passiues as *Ordinor acolitus*, verbis as hit were
passiues as *Vapulo ignarus*, verbis betokenyng sterynk or
meuynk of bode or saule vt *Curro velox, Meditor tacitus,* an
verbes betokenyng rest vt *Appareo bonus*. Versus:

> *Elegor, experior, interpretor* atque *doce(t)ur,*
> *Vado, iacet, sedeo, venio, sto, dormio, curro,*
> *Eminet, apparet, vigilo, preparo* quoque *surgo.* 60

Ricardus desinit viciorum, abstinens irarum, et indiget
dolii, -lium vel -lio pleni, plenum vel -no vini vel -no et
tamen dominatur huius ville et miseretur ciuitis, iconomis
ibidem residentibus. Qwat case *viciorum* and *irarum*? Genitif
case. Qwi so? For *desino* and *abstineo* wil construe with
genitif case, vt per versus patet:

> *Desinit, abstineo* genitiuis iungere curo.

Qwat case *dolij, -lium* an *-lio*? Genitif case, accusatif case
and ablatif case. Qwi so? For *egeo* and *indigeo* wil construe
with genitif case, accusatif case and ablatif case, as is knowen 70
be versus. Versus:

> Des quartis, sextis *eget, indiget* ac genitiuis:
> *Indigeo rem, re, indigeo rei, michi care.*

Qwat case *vini* vel *vino*? Genitif case and ablatif case.
Qwy so? For *vacuus* an *plenus* betokenyng fulnes or emthenes[1]
wul constru with genitif case and ablatif case, vt patet per
versus:

> Que plenum signant et que vacuata[2] figurant
> Hec ablatiuis coniunges vel genitiuis:
> *Vini* vel *(vi)no* duo dolia plena videto. 80

Qwat case *ville* and *iconomorum* and *iconomis*? Genitif case an
datif case. Qwi so? For *dominor, -aris* an *misereor, -eris*
wil constru with genitif case an datif case. Versus:

> Do *dominor* ternis *misereri* siue secundis.

Ricardus obuiabit domino suo. Qwat case *domino*?
Datif case. Qwy so? For *obuio, -as* and all his felawes
contenet in þese versus wil constru with datif case. Versus:

---

[1] MS themenes   [2] MS vacuater

INFORMACIO TEXT W

Obuio, parco, placet, noceo, respondeo, seruit,
Precipit, opponit, concludo, *iunge datiuis,*
Supplicat, arridet,[1] *faueo, vaco, proficit, heret,*   90
Subuenit addatur, *succurrit, propiciatur,*
Congruo, conpacior, confert, succedit, adulor,
Insidit, inponit, conuicior, inproperabit,
Sufficit, expirat, maledico, regracior, exstat,
Imminet ac *equipollet* vel *obedit* et *obstat,*
Occurrit, restat et *sedit,* quando locum dat,
Derrogo, condoleo, preiudico, detraho, defert;
Suppetit hijs iungas. Que *sum* componit, eis das.
Hec et quamplura ternis coniungere cura.

Postulo te graciam qui doceor gramaticam. Qwat case   100
gracium an *gramaticam*? Accusatif case. Qwi so? For all
suying in versus wil constru with doubul accusatif case in þo
actif voice, an with sengle in þo passif. Versus:

Postulo, posco, peto, doceo, rogo, flagito, celo,
Exuo cum *vestit, monet, induo, calceo, singo*:
Accusatiuos geminos hec verba requirunt,
Et cum passiuis illorum iungitur vnus.

Vtor rubio capicio. Capicio: qwat case? Ablatif case.
Qwi so? For all verbes contenet in þese versus suyng wil
constru with ablatif case. Versus: 110

Vescitur et *fruitur, caret, vtitur* atque *potitur;*
Hec ablatiuos transicione regunt.
Hijs iungas[2] *fungor* et *deficio* sociatur,
Et *gaudet*|casum sibi sextum[3] poscit habere.

Tempus est iantandi. Iantandi: qwat parte of reson?
A gerundif. How mone endyngis of gerundifes ar þer? Þre.
Qweche þre? *-Di, -do, -dum.* Qwen shal þu (haue) a gerundif
in *-di*? Qwen the Englissh of an infinitif mode comes aftur
tempus or *est* or a noun substantyf I shal haue a gerundyf in
-di, vt *Missa fenita tempus est dissoluendi ieiunium nostrum.*   120
Aftur a noun substantyf I shal haue a gerundyf in *-di*, vt
Noster papa habet potestatem absoluendi Christianos in Domino
confitentes.[4] Qwen shal þu haue a gerundyf in *-do*? In two
maners, for qwen this Englissh 'in' comes byfore a participull
of the present tempus with ⌈oute⌉ a substantyf set with him I
shal haue a gerundyf in *-do*, as *In dimicando multi viri sunt*
occisi. Þe second maner qwen 'in' before[5] a participul of
the present tempus comes aftur a participull or aftur an
adiectyf I may chose quether I will haue a gerundyf in *-do*
oþer a participull of the present tempus, as þus: *Magister*   130
est assiduus informando vel *informans suos discipulos.*

    I shal haue a gerundyf in *-dum* in two maners, oþer quile
with a preposicion quen the Englissh of an infinityf mode

---

[1] vac *canc*.   [2] MS *iungor*   [3] MS *silems*
[4] *sic* MS   [5] from *of*

INFORMACIO TEXT W

comes aftur a reson ande telles the cause of the reson, vt
Viri tendunt ad bellum ad dimicandum cum suis inimicis, ande
withoute a preposicion qwen this Englisshe of an infinityf
mode comes aftur *sum, es, fui* ande *sum, es, fui* hase[1] (no)
nominatyf case byfore hym; I shall haue a gerundyf in -*dum*,
vt sic: *Resistendum est inimicis nostris proponentibus ad-
nichilandum regnum*. Qwat cases asken participullis, gerundiues   140
or suppines? Suche case as the verbes that þai comen of.
Versus:

    Omne gerundiuum|sic participansque supinum -
    Casus ista petunt quos sua verba regunt.

    Vado visum sacrific(e)m. *Visum*: qwat part? A noun
supin. How mone endyngis of supyns ar þer? Two. Qweche
two? -*V* and -*vm*, as *lectum, lectu*. Qwerby shal þu know
þe first supyn? Be þo Englisshe of an infinitif mode suyng
a verbe betokenyng steryng to ane thing to be done, hit shal
be set in þo first[2] supyn, as *Vado lectum Virgilium*; and if   150
hit betoken bodely mevynk fro ane think to be done hit shal
be set in þo later supy(n), as *Venio lectu Virgilium*. Versus:

    Prima supina dabit post signans ad loca verbum;
    Deque loco venit, postremum pone supinum.

    Qwen I haue an Englissh like to an infinitif mode þat
shuld be set in þo first supin, þer þe supyn fayles I shal
take þis noun *locus* with þis preposicion *ad* and þe future
tempus of þe verbe that þe supyn shuld come of with þis
aduerbe *vbi* as þus: *Vado ad locum vbi adiscam gramaticam*;
other a noun betokeninge a place byfore þe infinityf mode þen   160
thus: *Vado Oxoniam vbi adiscam gramaticam*. Quat shal þu do
if þi latur suppyn fayle? I shal take þis noun *locus* other
a noun betokening place with þis preposicion *a* and þis
aduerbe *vbi* as þus: *Veni a loco vbi addidici gramaticam*.

    Magistro docente Iohannes stat. *Magistro*: qwat case?
Ablatif case absolute. Qwy so? For qwen I haue ⌈an Englissh
of⌉ a noun or a pronoun and a participul set forth other
vnderstonden ⌈an⌉ no wort set forthe ny vnderstonden of the
quech the worte of þe reson may be gouernet of, hit shall be
set in þe ablatif case absolute. Howe many maners may þe   170
ablatif case absolute be exponet? Be two, be *cum* and by
dum. Be *dum* vt *Me vidente cecidisti*, id est *Dum ego vidi
cecidisti*; be *cum* vt *Augusto imperante Alexandrea domita est*,
id est *Cum Augustus erit imperator*.

    Per *cum* vel per *dum* sexti resolucio detur,
    Huius namque rei Prescianus|testis habetur.

    Michi Ricardo fracto caput medicina proficit. *Capud*:
qwat case? Accusatyf case. Qwy so? For qwen I haue a
noun adiectyf, verbe neutur or passif or any of hor participuls,

---

[1] *a word canc.*   [2] *from* latter

gerundiues or suppines betokening al comynge in a reson before   180
a worte betokening parte of that al, that worde þat betokenesse
party of þat al shal be sette in the accusatyf case and be
gouernet by þis figure synodoges, vt *Sum albus faciem, Doleo
capud, Frangor caput, Sum fractus caput, H(ab)eo voluntatem
frangendi caput, Vado fractum caput.* Versus:

> Adiectiua regunt passiuaque verbaque neutra
> Accusatiuos, per synodochen sibi iunctos:
> *Alba comasque caput dolet hec, et rumpitur aurem.*
> Participans iunges, ut *Femina compta capillos,*
> Atque gerundiua coniunges ymo supina.   190

Qwerby knowes þu a verbe impersonill? For he hase
nouther nowmbur ni person ny no(m)i(n)atyf case, and is
declinet in þe voyce of the thridde person, and comes in
Englissh with one of these sygnes 'hit' or 'me', as 'Hit
behose me to lorne', *Oportet (me adiscere).* 'Me redes',
Legitur. How many maners of verbes inpersonill ar there?
II, that is to say one of the actyf voyce for hit endes in
a *T* lettere as *oportet,* ande another of the passyf voyce for
hit endes in *R* lettere as *opponitur.* Qwat case will al
verbes inpersonill of the actyf voyce construe with? With datyf   200
case, outaken xiij of the qwech v will construe with accusatif
case, and þay are knowen by versus:

> Quarto iunge *iuuat, decet,* (ac) *dilectat, oportet,*
> Et *latet* illorum numero uult associari.

And v will construe with accusatif case ande genitif case, as
Penitet me tui, and tho ar knowen by versus:|

> *Penitet* et *tedet, miseret, pudet* et *pyget*:   ista
> Accusatiuos poscunt simul et genitiuos,
> Natura primum sed tran(sicione) secundum.[1]

And thre, that is to say *interest, refert* and *est* set for   210
pertinet, and þai will construe with[2] genityf case of al
parte that beris case as thus: *Interest Willelmi studeri,*
oute-taken þe genityf case of v pronouns primitiues, videlicet
mei, tui, sui, nostri and *vestri,* in the stede of the queche
þese verbes will construe with ablatif case, feminine gendur
ande singler nowmbur ⸢of þaire possessiues⸣ on þis wyse:
Interest mea, tua, sua, nostra and *vestra,* in þe quech is
vnderstonden for hor substanti(u)es *re* vel *vtilitate,* and þo
ar knowen by versus:

> *Inter.,*[3] *refert,*[4] *est* genitiuis iungere prodest,   220
> Sed possessiua demas pronomina quina,
> Vt[5] *Refert nostra* dicas, *Refert* quoque *vestra.*

A verbe inpersonil is declinet in þe voyse of þe þrid

---

[1] *(?) from* sic   [2] repeated   [3] MS Interest
[4] MS adds et   [5] MS Vtque

INFORMACIO TEXT W

person, as *interest, intererat, in(ter)fuit, -rat, intererit*,
and on participul longyng to a verbe inpersonil of þe actyf
voyse as *penitens, iuuans*, outaken ij, þat is to witte of
miserat comes *meserens* and *misertum*, and of *tedet* comes *tedens*
and *pertesum est*.

Tedet pertesum flectet *miseret*que *misertum*;
Actiue vocis reliquis non attribuatur   230
Preteritum tale, Presianus testificatur.

Obuiabatur michi a scolari bono socio. Qwat party of
reson is *obuiabatur*? A verbe inpersonil of þe passyf voyse.
Qwat shal þu do quen þu hase a verbe neutur, þe Englissh like
a passyf, þer þe passyf fayles? I shal take a^1|verbe
inpersonil of þe passyf voyce of sech mode and sech temps as
þe passyf semes to be and þat þat semes to be no(m)i(n)atyf
case I shal cupil into sech case as the^2 verbe will
haue aftur him. *Bono socio* is ablatif case, for that þat
longes to on thing comyng fast togeder shal be set in one case. 240
By þis verbe *vapulo* þu shal say 'The meistur betys me',
Vapulo a magistro, for qwen I haue the Englissh of an actyf
sygnificacion þat ogh to be made be a verbe neutur-passyf,
þat the quech semes to be a no(m)i(n)atyf case I shal turne
into an ablatif case with a preposicion, or elles into a
datyf case qwen I haue þis verb *nubo, -is*: 'to be weddet',
as þus: 'Hit befalles me þe mayre son to wed þi doghtur',
Interest filie tue nubere filio^3 *maioris.* Que sunt verba
neutra-passiua? Patet per versus, et sub actiua^4 voce
passiuam habens significacionem.   250

*Exulo, vapulo, veneo, fio, nubo licet*que
Sensum passiui sub voce gerunt aliena.

Que su(n)t verba neutro-passiua? Dico quod illa que habent
circumlocutionem in preteritis ad modum passiuorum.

Audeo cum *soleo, fio* cum *gaudeo, fido*:
Quinque, puer, numero neutro-passiua tibi do.

Hit is to wit þat verbes inpersonil of þe passyf voyce^5
makyn *iri* in þe finitif mode, as *oppositum iri*, 2 gerundiues
þai han and ⌐one⌐ participle, as no(minatiuo) *hoc amatum*,
accusatiuo *hoc amatum*, (ablatiuo) *ab hoc amato.*   260

---

^{1} *repeated* ^{2} MS *adds* pfit ^{3} MS filie
^{4} MS actiuam ^{5} of þe þrid person as verbes inpersonill
of þe actyf voice *canc.*

INFORMACIO TEXT X

X. Oxford, Bodleian Library, MS Hatton 58, fols.46ʳ-54ᵛ

(W)hat schalt thow doo whan thow hast an Englysch to
make yn Latyn? I schall reherse myne Englysche onys, ij
or iij, and loke owt my principall verbe and loke whether (he)
betoken 'to do' or 'to suffer' or 'to be'; and[1] yf he
betokyn 'to do' þe doyr schall be þe nominatiff case to þe
verbe and þe sufferer schall be suche case as þe verbe wyll
haue after hym; and hit betoken '<to> suffer' the sufferer
schall be þe nominatiff case to þe verbe <a>nd þe doer schall
be þe ablatyff case wᵗ a preposicion. How knowest þi
pryncipall verbe yf þer com moo ⸌ve(r)bs⸍[2] than on<e> yn a   10
reson?[3] Euermore my first verbe ys my principall uerbe but
yf h<e> com ny a relatyff or a coniunccyon or be lyke to an
infinityff mode. Whereby knowest whan þi pryncipall verbe
commyth ny a r<a>latyff? Euermore when þer commy<th> any of
thes English wordis 'þat', 'whom', or 'þe wheche'. Whareby
knowest whann he ys lyke to an infinityff mode? Whan y haue
ony of these signes 'to' or 'to be' byfore a verbe as 'to loue'
⸌or⸍ 'to be louyd'.

Latinitas

'A cherch ys a place the wheche Cristyn men bethe[4] bound<en>   20
to loue.' Whyche ys þi pryncipall verbe yn thys reson?
<'Ys'.> Whan a verbe personall ys thy principall verbe,
how schall þu know his[5] nominatyff case? By thys[6] questyon
'Wo or what?', as 'Who or whatt ys?', 'A cherche ys'. 'A
cherche':[7] what case? Þe nominatiff case. Why so?
For he commyth byfore þe verbe, et cetera. What hathe a
relatyff? And antecedent. How knowest þu an antecedent?
For hee gothe byfore þe relatyff and ys rehersed of þe relatyff.
How knowest a relatyff? For he rehersit thyngis þat be
spokyn of afore. When there cometh a[8] |nominatyff case   30
bytwene þe ralatyff and þe verbe, þe ralatyff schall be suche
case as verbe wyll haue after hym, and yf there come noo[9]
nominatiff case bytwene[10] þe ralatyff and þe verbe[11] þe relatyff
schall be þe no(m)i(n)atyff case to þe verbe.

Ecclesia est locus quem Christiani multum tenentur diligere.
Quem: what gender? Þe masculyn gender. Why? For when I
haue a nown relatyff folowynge ij antecedentis of diuerse
gender hauyng both reward to oone thynge, þe relatyff schall
acorde wᵗ þe latter and not wᵗ þe fyrst antecedent, for to my
nyxte substantyue schall myne adiectiue be bere and to myne   40
nyxte antecedent schall my relatyff be referred, but yf the
sentens lette hyt as in thys Latyn: *Canis tuus occidit ouem*
meam, quem ego interficiam. This relatyff *quem* acordith wᵗ

[1] perhaps *canc.*
changes to the text
[4] moche *canc.*
[7] ys a place *canc.*
foot of folio
after by-

[2] in another hand, as are most of the
[3] yn a reson] perhaps *canc.*
[5] -i- from y   [6] -s] perhaps *canc.*
[8] Qwat ys þe rowle of þe relatyf added at
[9] nat *canc.*   [10] thene *canc.*
[11] personall *canc.*

111

INFORMACIO TEXT X

þe fyrst antecedent and not w^t þe latter bycause of þe sentens.

Ibo ad locum qui uel *quod est nouum castellum.* What gender ys *qui* uel *quod*? The masculyn gender or þe neuter gender. Why? For when I haue a relatyff y-sett bytwene ij antecedens of diuerse gender longyng bothe to oone thyng, þe¹ ⌈relatyfe⌉ may acorde w^t bothe² in gender. Vnde versus:

> Quando relatiuum generum casus variorum   50
> Inter se claudu(n)t qui rem spectant ad eandem,|
> Per genus hoc poterit vtrilibet associari:
> Est pia stirps Iesse quem Christum nouimus esse.

*Ego sum ille qui*³ *sedeo* uel *qui sedet*. Why seyst thow *qui sedeo* uel ⌈*qui*⌉ *sedet*? For (wen) thys relatiff *qui*, *que*, *quod* commyth nexte a pronown of the iij person y-sett after a verbe substantiff, þe relatyff w^t þe verbe folowyng may be þe iij person or suche person as þe nominatiff case before the verbe substantyff, as *Tu es ille qui sedes* uell *qui sedet*; and wen hit folowyt nexte a nown, þe relatyff w^t þe verbe   60
folowyng schal be oonly the iij person,⁴ as *Ego sum homo qui sedet*. Hec Petrus Helias.

Vtinam essem episcopus qui vocor Iohannes sub spe releuandi paupertatem amicorum meorum. Episcopus: what case? Þe nominatiff case. Why? For *sum, es, fui* is a verbe copulatiff and wyll copull like case.⁵ What maner of verbis wyll copull like case? Responsio: verbis substantiuis, verbis vocatiuis and verbis þat hathe strenkth. How many verbis substantiuis be þer? III. Wheche iij? *Sum, sisto* and *maneo*. Vnde versus: 70

> *Sum, sisto, maneo* quasisubstantiua vocantur
> Et que consimilem sensum r⌈e⌉tinere probantur,
> Ast adiectiua tibi cetera uerba notentur.

How many verbis vocatiuis be þer? V. Wheche v? *Nominor, -ris; appellor, -aris; nuncupor, -paris; vocor, -aris* and *dicor, -ris*. Versus:

> Quinque vocatiua dicas tantummodo uerba:
> *Nominor, appellor* sic *nuncupor* et *voco, dicor*
> Et *vocor*: hec similes⁶ semper poscunt sibi casus.|

What maner of verbis hath strength to copull like case   80
owt-take verbis substantiuys and verbis vocatiuis? Responsio: verbis passiuis, as *Ordinor acolitus, Teneor sapiens*; and verbis as they were passiuis as *Fio prudens, Vapulo ignarus*; ⌈and verbys þat be ⌈to⌉ keyns semyng, as *Apario bonus*;⌉ and verbis betokenyng bodeli ⌈strength or soffer⌉⁷ as *Curro velox*;

¹ þ *added above* þ-   ² *antecedentis indeferently canc.*
³ -i *from* e   ⁴ *only added after* person
⁵ MS *adds* Responsio verbis *perhaps subpunctuated.*
⁶ sensum retinere probantur *canc.*   ⁷ *from* meuyngge

INFORMACIO TEXT X

and verbis þat betokenyng bodely rest as *Sedeo tristis.*
Dormio quietus; a(n)d verbis þat be(to)kenn strenght of
manys sowle as *Meditor tacitus, Emineo peritus.*

    Dominor huius ville abstinens irarum inter seruos meos.
Huius ville: what case? Þe genitiff case.[1] Why? For   90
þes iij verbis *dominor, -raris*; *miserior, -ris* and *abstineo,*
-es wyll be construyd w^t a genityff case.

    Abstineo, dominor, miserere cum genitiuo
    Iunges: *Abstineo panis, Miserere dolentis,*
    Dominor et ville bonus heres iure parentis.

Irarum: what case? The genityff case. Why? For euery
participyll, gerundife or supyn wyl be construed w^t þat same
case þat þe verbe wyll þat he comyth (of). Vnde versus:

    Iudex quo(s)cumque serie casus imitatur,
    Illos tocius verbi flexus comitatur,   100
    Iunge gerundiua cum participante, suppina.

    Ista scola est plena puerorum uel *pueris. Puerorum* uel
pueris: what case? Þe genityff case and þe ablatiff. Why?
For[2] all nownys adiectiuis betokenyng|havyng or (w)antyng,
fulnesse or amtynesse, and all þe adiectiuis þat hathe þe
significacion of a participull of a verbe passiue, may be
construyd w^t a genityff case and a ablatyff case.

    Nomen quod retinet passiuum significatum
    Do genitis, sextis: poterunt exempli(fi)care
    Plenus uel *uacuus, (in)dignus, pauper, egenus.*   110

    Ricardus et Robartus egent gracia[3] *diuina,*[3] *graciam diuinam*
uel *gracie diuine* et cetera. What case? Þe genityff case,
accusatyff and the ablatyff. Why? For al verbis conteyned
in þes verseys wyll be construyd w^t a genytyff, accusatyff,
abla(tyff).

    Des iiij^{tis} sextis *eget, indiget,* et genitiuis,
    Ut noscas verum *Res indigeo* quoque *rerum,*
    Indigio bobus ad rura colenda duobus.

    Memento mei cum[4] *tibi bene fuerit. Mei*: what case?
Þe genityue case. Why? For al ⌈verbeys⌉ betokenyng mynd   120
as *recordor*, foryetyng as *obliuscor*, presyng as *laudo*, blamyng
as *culpo* wyll be construed w^t a genityffe and a[5] ablatyff.

    Verbum significans obliuisci, memorari,
    Quarto cum genito sextove petit sociari,
    Aut accusare, reprehendere siue monere,
    Necnon damnare signans uel vituperare.
    Arguo te sceleris, Accuso ⌈sic⌉ *leuitatis,*

---

[1] þe genitiff case *canc.*   [2] euery *canc.*
[3] -a *from* -e   [4] *from* causa   [5] an *added after* a

INFORMACIO TEXT X

Accuso, dampnor bene dicitur *impietatis.*
Cum precij verbis tu casibus vtere sextis,|
Cum¹ quibus, et si uis, vti poteris genitiuis.   130

Obviemus episcopo Cantuariensi. Episcopo: what case?
Datyff case. Why? For these verbis þat be conteyned in
þes versus wyll construe wᵗ a datyff case. Vnde versus:²

Obuio, parco, placet, noceo, respondeo, seruit,
Precipit, opponit, concludo,³ *iunge datiuis,*
Supplicat, aridet, faueo, vaco, proficit, erit,
Subuenit addatur, *succurrit, propiciatur,*
Congruit, conpacior, confert, succidit, adulor,
Incidit, imponit, conuicior, improperabit,
Sufficit, asspirat, obtempero, gratulor, asstat,   140
*Imminet, equiualet, alludet, obedit*⁴ et *obstat,*⁵
Occurit, restat, et *cedit,* quando locum dat,
Insidior, fido, pateo, minor et *valedico.*
Derogo, condoleo, preiudico, detraho, defert,
Suppetit hiis iungas. Que *sum* componit, eis das.
Hec et quamplura ternis coniungere cura.

Postulo te graciam qui docior gramaticam. Graciam:
what case? Þe accusatyff case. Why so? For all verbis
þat betokeneth 'to aske',⁶ 'to teche', 'to pray' or 'to beseche' wyll be construyd wᵗ a dowbyll accusatyff þat betokeneth   150
diuers thyngis. *Gramaticam*: what case? Þe accusatif case.
Why? For all⁷ þe passiuis|commynng of actiuis that be
construyd ⌈wᵗ a dobyll accusatyf case⁸ there passiuis
wyll be construyd⌉ wᵗ þe latter of them, and suche ⌈as⌉ be
⌈in⌉ þe verse. Vnde⁹ versus:

Postulo, posco, peto, doceo, rogo, flagito, celo,
Exuo cum *vestit, monet, induo, calcio, cingo*:
Accusatiuos geminos hec verba requirunt,
Et cum passiuis posttremus iungitur horum.

Vtor rubio capicio. Capicio: what case? Ablatyff.   160
Why so? For all verbis conteyned in these versus wyll be
construyd wᵗ an ablatyff case. Vnde versus:

Vescitur et *fruitur, caret, vtitur* atque *potitur*:
Hec ablatiuos transsicione regunt.
Hijs iungas *fungor,* et *deficio* sociatur.

Hec est deferencia inter *fruor, vtor,*¹⁰ *fungor, pocior, poteris*

---

¹ Interdum si sit certum precium dabo iiijᵗᵒ *added at top of page*
² *These verses and the next have English glosses to the verbs cited,*
mostly in later hands.   ³ -o *from* it   ⁴ -i- *from* e
⁵ *over an erasure*   ⁶ yng *added after* to aske
⁷ verbis *canc.*   ⁸ and *added after* case
⁹ suche ⌈as⌉ be ⌈in⌉ þe uerse. Vnde] *perhaps canc.*
¹⁰ pocior *canc.*

114

INFORMACIO TEXT X

uel *potiris*. Vnde versus:

> Diuinis fruimur, exo⌈p⌉tatisque potimur,
> Vtimur vtilibus, fungimur offici⌈i⌉s,
> Vescimur ac escis et potu delicijsque. 170

Intendo ire oppositum scolaribus quos bene respondentes intime sum delecturus. *Ire*: what mode? The infinytyf mode. Why? For when ij verbis, et cetera. *Oppositum*: what part of reson? The fyrst supyn. Why? For when y haue and Englyssh of a infinityff mode commyng after a verbe, partycypull, gerundyff or supyn betokenyng mevyng or steryng|to a place where eny thynng to be do hyt schall be sett in þe fyrst supyn or gerundive in *-dum*, as *Vado lectum* vel *ad legendum*. And yf hit betokyn mevyng fro a place where enythyng was to be do or to be sufferyd hit schall be sett in þe latter supyn or 180 gerundyff in *-do*, as *Venio lectu* vel *a legendo*. Versus:

> Post motus verbum bene ponis vtrumque supinum:
> *Ad loca* vult primum, *de* vult signare secundum,
> Vt *Vado lectum, dormitum* siue *comestum*,
> Vt *Venio lectu, dormitu* siue *comestu*.
> Ast infenitum si non[1] signet tibi motum,
> Vt *Cupio legere, Volo ludere, Spero docere*.

'I go to lerne gramer': *Vado ad locum vbi discam gramaticam*.[2] Why seyst þu *ad locum*? For when y haue and Englyssh of þe infynytyff mode that schold be sett in þe fyrst supyn where 190 the supyn faylyth y schall take this preposicion *ad* and thys nown *locum* and thys aduerbe *vbi* and the futer tens of þe same verbe that the supyn schold com of; exemplum vt supra. And yf a nown propir be(to)ken place cum before and Englissch of a infinitiff mode that schold be set in þe fyrst supyn where the supyn faylythe y schall take this aduerbe *vbi* and þe futer tens of þe same verbe ⌈þat⌉ the supyn schold come of, a⌈s⌉ *Veni Cicestriam vbi discam gramaticam*. And yf y haue and Englyssch like to and infinityff mode that schold be sett in latter (supyn where the supyn) faylyth y schal take this[3] 200 aduerbe *vbi* w^t þe preterperfitens of þe same verbe that þe supyn|scholld come of, as *Veni Oxonia vbi dedici gramaticam*. *Dilecturus*: what part of reson? A particyull ⌈of þe fyr(s)t futer⌉ in *-rus*. Why? For when y haue and Englis of a infinitiff mode folowyng this verbe *sum, es, fui*, yf hyt be of þe actyue voyce yt schal be sett in þe participull of þe futer tens in *-rus*, as *Sum delecturus magistrum meum*, and yf hit be of þe passiue voyce hit schall be sett in þe participull ⌈of þe last futer⌉ in *-dus*, and yf þe participull fayly y schal take þis relatyff *qui, que, quod* and þe futer tens of þe same 210 verbe þat þe par(ti)cipull schold comme of. Exemplum: 'Y am to drede þe mayster', *Ego sum qui timebo magistrum*.

Tempus est ludendi diebus festiuis. What part of reson

---

[1] -t canc.   [2] vel addiscendum canc.   [3] -i- from a

INFORMACIO TEXT X

ludendi? The <fyrst>¹ gerundyff.² Why? For when y haue and Englissch of an infinityff mod sett after a nown generall as *hora, tempus, causa, propositum, desiderium* et similia, hitt schall be sett most comynly in þe gerundyff in *-di*, as *Tempus est ludendi, Veni*³ *causa legendi ad vesperas, Est hora pulsandi. Diebus festiuis*: what case? The ablatyff. Why? For when y haue a nown betokenyng tyme, price or spase 220
þat⁴ be neither door noþer sufferer of þe verbe wᵗowt a preposicion hit schall be sett in þe ablatyff case.

Magistro docente pueri vacant dissiplinis frutuosis.
Magistro: what case? Þe ablatyff case absolute. Why? For when y haue and Englyssch ⌈(of)⌉ a schurte hangyng resun⌉ of a nown and a particypull or els a⁵ pronown and a participull or ellys a partycipull of a verbe inpersonall ⌈sett⌉ by hymsylfe and no word in þe reson sett owt or understonde of þe wheche he may be gouer(n)d, hyt schall be sett in þe ablatyff case absolute and be⁶|expownd by *dum* or by *cum*. 230
Vnde versus:

    Non sine participe sextus rectore carebit:
    Me duce pergatur, existente teneatur
    Tunc intra clausam, Precianus testificatur.

How many⁷ maner of wysis may þe ablatyff case absolute be expownd? By *dum* or by *cum*. By *dum* as *Me vidente tu cecidisti*,⁸ id est *Dum ego video tu cecidisti*. By *cum* vt *Augusto* ⌈*impererator(e)*⌉ *Alexandria domita est*, id est *Cum Augustus erat imperator Alexandria*⁹ *domita est*. Vnde versus:

    Per *dum* uel per *cum* sexti resolucio detur, 240
    Huius namque rei Precianus testis habetur.

'What schalt þu doe when þu hast an Englysch to make in Latyn? Y schall reherse ⌈ons, ij or iij⌉' et cetera vsque ad 'a preposicion'.¹⁰ When ys thys rule trew? When my pryncypall verbe ys a verbe personall. Yff þi principall verbe ⌈be⌉ a verbe inpersonall what schalt þu do?¹¹ Y schall loke yf my Englyssh¹² haue eny nede of turnyng and begynne att þe verbe inpersonall. Whereby knowyst a verbe inpersonall? For hit hathe nether numburre nether person nether nominatyff case and commythe yn Englyssch wᵗ one of these iij signes 250
'hyt', 'me' or 'the'. Verbum dicitur inpersonal(e).¹³ Quare? Quia non habet suppositum rectitudinis a parte ante. How many maner of verbis inpersonall be there? II. Wheche ij? A verbe inpersonall of þe actiue voyce and verbe

---

¹ supyn *canc.*   ² and added *in margin of MS*
³ -*i*] *written over* y *by the rubricator*   ⁴ MS yt
⁵ els a] MS els *from a by a later hand*   ⁶ exp *canc.*
⁷ -y *from* er   ⁸ MS cecidiste   ⁹ est(?) *canc.*
¹⁰ usque ad 'a preposicion'.] *canc. and then restored*
¹¹ than ⌈I shale⌉ reherse ⌈me english⌉ *canc.*
¹² my Englyssh] *perhaps canc.*   ¹³ -e(?) *canc.*

INFORMACIO TEXT X

inpersonall of þe passiue voyce. How knowyst[1] | a verbe inpersonell of þe actiue voyce? For hyt endit in[2] -t lyke þe iij person, ⌜syngler number⌝ of a verbe actiue, vt *penitet* et cetera. How knowest a verbe inpersonall of þe passiue voyce? For hit endit in -r lyke þe iij person, syngler number of a verbe passiue as *amatur*, *amabatur*. Versus:[3] 260

    Impersonale fit in -t uel in -r speciale,
    Exemplum detur *tedet*, *miseret*, *perametur*.

A quibus verbis discendunt verba inpersonalia? Dicendum quod a verbis actiuis et neutris actionem significantibus. Vnde versus:

    Semper ab actiuis impersonale creatur,
    Vel neutris illis quibus accio significatur.

Numquam enim des(c)endunt ⌜impersonalia⌝ a verbis passiuis,[4] deponentibus siue communibus nec a neutris passionem significantibus. Vnde versus: 270

    A deponenti, communi uel pacienti
    Inpersonale numquam dicetur haberi.
    A neutris per que tibi passio significatur
    Impersonale numquam de iure creatur.

W^t what case wyll all verbis impersonall of þe actiue voyce be construyd w^t? Responsio: w^t a datiue case, owt-take xij, of þe whech xij v wyll be construyd w^t genityff and a accusatyff[5] ⌜as⌝ *penytet*, *tedet*, *miseret*, *pudet* and *piget*; and iiij w^t accusatyff case onely[6] ⌜as⌝ *iuuat*, *decet*, *dilectat*, *oportet*; and iij w^t a|genityff case and a 280 ablatyff[7] ⌜as⌝ *interest*, *refert* and *est* y-sett for *pertinet*.

Penitet ⌜*me*⌝ *tui*. *Me*: what case? The accusatyff case. Why? For these v verbis *penitet* et cetera[8] wyll be construyd w^t a genityff or and accusatyff: w^t accusatyff of þe thyng þat dothe þe dede of þe verbe and w^t a genityff of þe thyng þat þe dede of þe verbe ys do fore; and sumtyme w^t infenityff mode yn þe stede of and genytyff case, as *Penitet me peccare*. Vnde versus:

    Penitet et *tedet*, *miseret*, *pudet* et *piget*, ista
    Accusatiuos poscunt simul et genetiuos, 290
    Natura primum sed transci⌜ci⌝one secundum.

Libet michi comedere. *Michi*: what case? The datyff case. Why? For all verbis inpersonalis conteyned yn þes versus wyll be construyd w^t a datyff case, and all oþer of

---

[1] MS *adds* verbe of   [2] te *canc*.   [3] Semper ab actiuis impersonale creatur *canc*.   [4] siue *canc*.
[5] and thoe ben these *canc*.   [6] and thoe ben thes *canc*.
[7] and tho ben þes *canc*.   [8] in versibus *canc*.

INFORMACIO TEXT X

þe actyff voyce. Vnde versus:

Hec *libet* atque *licet*, *placet* et *liquet*, *accidit* atque
Congruit, *euenit* et *contingit* et *expedit*, ista
Cum reliquis paribus intersociato datiuis.

Iuuat[1] *me studium excercere*. *Me*: what case? The
accusatyff case. Why? For these verbis conteyned yn þis   *300*
versis wyll be construyd w^t and accusatyff case. Versus:

Quarto iunge *iuuat*, *decet* ac *dilectet*, *oportet*,
Et *latet* illorum numero vult associare.

How ys *iuuat* declined? *Iuuat*, *iuuabat*, *iuuit*, *iuuerat*,
iuuabit, *iuuare*. Why ys *iuuat* so|declynyd? For a verbe
inpersonell of þe actiue voyce in hys declynyng schall schue
the iij person of þe coniugacion þat he commyth owt of.
Forma: indicatiuo modo *iuuat*, preterito inperfecto *iuuebat*,
preterito perfecto *iuuit*, preterito plusquam ⌈perfecto⌉ *iuuerat*,
futuro *i*⌈*u*⌉*uabit*, et sic de ceteris modis. Vnicum   *310*
participium[2] traitur ab hoc verbo inpersonale presentis
temporis tantum, ut *iuuans*. How many participles of a verbes
inpersonalis of þe actiue voyce? One, of þe presentens, as[3]
of *penitet* comyth *penitens*, of *iuuat* comyth *iuuans*; owt-take
ii verbis impersonalis the wheche hathe ij participles, one of
the presentens a nother of þe[4] pretertens, as of *miseret* comyth
(*miserens*) an *misertum*, of *tedet* comyth *tedens* an *pertesum*.
Vnde versus:

Tedet pertesum flectet, *miseret*que *misertum*.
Actiue vocis reliquis non attribuatur   *320*
Preteritum tale, Precianus testificatur.

Hec est deferencia inter *iuuat* personale et *iuuat*
inpersonale, nam *iuuat* personale est verbum actiuum et idem
est quod *auxilior*, *iuuat* inpersonale est verbum nutrum et
idem est quod *dilectat*. Vnde versus:

Iuuo sit actiuum cum signat vt[5] *auxiliatur*,
Inpersonale signans *delectat* eritque.

Interest mea clerici iugitur studere. *Mea*: what case?
The ablatyff case. Why? For *interest*, *refert* and *est*
y-sett for *pertinet*[6] wyll be const⌈r⌉uyd w^t a genytyff case   *330*
of all partys casuall, owt-take of v pronowns primatiuis,
scilicet *mei*, *tui*, *sui*, *nostri* and *vestri*, instede of þe wheche
þe foreseyd verbis ben construyd w^t an ablatyff case, femynyne
gender, singuler number of there|possessyuis, scilicet *mea*,
tua, *sua*,[7] *nostra* and *vestra* in[8] þe wheche ys understond *re*
uel *vtilitate* for there[9] substantyuys.

---

[1] Delyty3th *added in margin opposite* Iuuat.   [2] trayto *canc.*
[3] a *canc.*   [4] presentens *canc.*   [5] MS et
[6] MS pertineth   [7] and *canc.*   [8] from to
[9] st *canc.*

INFORMACIO TEXT X

Refert, inter et *est* genetiuis iungere¹ prodest,
Et sexto proprie donant pronomina quina,
Nam *Refert nostra* dicas, *Refert* quoque *vestra*,
Sed possessiua demas pronomina quina.   340

Whyth what case wyl verbys impersonall of þe passiue voyce be construyd w^t? W^t and ablatyff or a datyff case, as *Dicitur a me* uel *mihi rex est Londoniis*.

Obuiabatur ⸢mihi⸣ a scolare bono socio. *Obuiabatur*:² what part of reson? A verbe inpersonall of þe passiue voyce.³ When y haue an Englyssch of a ⸢verbe⸣ passiue to be made by a verbe neuter where the passyffe faylyth y schall take þe verbe inpersonall of þe passyfe voyce suche mode and suche tens as þe passyfe semethe to be. Þe nominatyff case y schall turne into suche case as þe verbe wyll haue after hym. *Bono*   350 *socio*: what case? Þe ablatyff case. Why? For whan ij wordys come togeder (in) a reson þat longith to j thyng they schall be sett both in lyke case.

How declynest þu a verbe inpersonall of þe passife voyce? *Amatur, amabatur, amatum est* vel *fuit, amatum erat* vel *fuerat, amabitur, amari* et cetera. Forme hym: indicatiuo modo tempore presenti⁴ *amatur*, preterito inperfecto *amabatur*, preterito perfecto *amatum est* vel *fuit*, preterito plusquamperfecto *amatum erat* vel *fuerat*, futuro|*amabitur*; imperatiuo modo *ametur*, futuro *amator tu* vel *ille*; optatiuo modo *utinam*   360 *amaretur*, preterito perfecto et plusquamperfecto *utinam amatum esset* vel *fuisset*, futuro *utinam ametur*; coniunctiuo modo *cum ametur*, preterito inperfecto *cum amaretur*, preterito perfecto *cum amatum sit* vel *fuer(i)t*, preterito plusquamperfecto *cum amatum esset* vel *fuisset*, futuro *cum amatum (erit)* vel *fuerit*; infinitiuo modo *amari*, preteriti perfecto et plusquamperfecto *amatum esse* vel *amatum fuisse*,⁵ futuro *amatum iri*. Vnicum participium traitur⁶ ab hoc verbo impersonali preteriti temporis tantum, ut *amatum*, et declinatur nominatiuo *hoc amatum*, accusatiuo *hoc amatum*, ablatiuo *ab hoc amato*.   370

⸢Impersonali dat de se participale
Tresque habet casus, primum, quartum quoque sextum.
Ac illud numero priuatur iure secundo
Et per se positum sextum facit omne solutum.⸣

'The mayster betyth me': *Vapulo a magistro*. Why makyst þu in þis maner a wyse? For when y haue a Latyn to be made by any of these verbis *exulo, vapulo, veneo, fio* and *liceo*, þat þat dothe þe dede schall be sett yn þe ablatyff case w^t a prepocicion and þat þat sufferyth schall be þe nominatyff case. Exemplum: 'The kyng schall exyle trayturis', *A rege*   380 *exulabunt traditores*. And yf the pryncipall be a verbe inpersonall that⁷ þat sufferþ schal be suche case as þe verbe

---

¹ MS iungers(?)   ² MS Abuiabatur   ³ why ys thys englyssch made by a verbe inpersonall *canc*.   ⁴ MS *adds* tempore
⁵ -se *from* ce   ⁶ -i- *from* y   ⁷ MS *adds* þe

INFORMACIO TEXT X

wyll haue after hym. Exemplum: ''Hit⟩ befallyth the kyng
to exyle many men', *Interest a rege exulare multorum hominum*.
Regula habita materia componenda per aliquid istorum verborum
exulo, vapulo, vene⟨o⟩, fio, nubo et *licio*: res agens debet
poni¹ in ablatiuo casu cum preposicione, et res paciens erit
nominatiui casus nisi principale verbum sit impersonale tunc
enim res paciens erit talis² casus qualem illud verbum
inpersonale exigit post se, ut *Interest a rege exulare* 390
multorum hominum.

'My broþer hathe weddyd a wyfe': *Fratri meo nupsit vxor*.
Why ys thys made yn thys maner of wyse? For whan y haue and
Englyssch to be made by thys verbe *nubo*, -*bis*, þat þat doþe
þe dede of þe verbe schall be sett yn þe datyue case and þat
þat sufferyth schall be þe nominatyff case, as 'Y schall wedde
þe meyrys dowȝter of thys towne', *Mihi nubet filia maioris
istius ville*. And yf my principall verbe be a verbe
inpersonall þat þat suffereth schall be suche case as þe
verbe wyll haue after hym, as *Interest vxoris nubere fratri* 400
meo. Regula habita materia componenda per hoc verbum *nubo*,
-*bis*: res³ agens⁴ ⟨ponetur in⟩ datiuo casu⁵ et res paciens
⟨ponetur in⟩ nominatiuo casu⁶ ⟨nisi⟩ principale verbum sit
verbum impersonale, tunc res paciens⁷ ⟨ponetur in⟩ tali⁸
casu⁸ qualem verbum inpersonale exigit post se, vt *Interest
vxoris nubere fratri meo*.

Dedici gramaticam Eboraci et dioleticam Oxonie. *Eboraci*:
what case? Þe genytyff case. Why? For euery proper name
⟨sympyl⟩ of towne, place or cetey sett after a verbe,
participull, gerundiff or supyn betokenyng abydyng yn a p⟨l⟩ace 410
or at a place yf hyt be of þe fyrst declynson or þe second
and þe syngler number hit schall be sett in þe genytyff case
abuerbially, as *Fui Oxonie ⟨et Eboraci⟩*; and yf þe propur
name be of þe iij declynson or ellis þe plurell numbur of what
declynson þat euer hyt be hit schal⁹ be sett in þe ablatyff
case aduerbially wᵗout a prepocicion, as *Fui Londonijs ⟨et
Babulone⟩*.¹⁰ But yf suche a nown propur be vndeclyned hit
schall be sett in þe ablatyff case or þe genityff case
yndeferently like and aduerbe, as *Rex est Sarum bone ciuitatis*
vel *bona|ciuitate*.¹¹ 420

Rex vadit Londonias. *Londonias*: watt case? Þe¹²
accusatyff case. Why so? For when I haufe a propyr
name of towne, cyte or plase i-sett after a partycipyll,
gerundyff or supyn þat betokenethe mevynng to a plase
wathesoeuer declynyson hyte be or number hyt schall be sett
yn þe accusatyffe case aduerbialy wᵗowt a preposicion, as

¹ -i *from* y   ² -i *from* e   ³ *from* rex
⁴ debet esse *canc*.   ⁵ -s *canc*.   ⁶ -s *canc*; Sed si *canc*.
⁷ erit *canc*   ⁸ -s *canc*.   ⁹ MS schat
¹⁰ *late addition in margin*
¹¹ *fol.54ʳ⁻ᵛ is written in the second hand who was probably respons-
ible for many of the changes to the text on the previous folios*.
¹² no *canc*.

120

INFORMACIO TEXT X

Rex vadit Londonias.

Rex venit Londonijs. Londonijs: what case? Þe
ablatyf case. Why? For when y hawe a propyr nowne of[1]
tow(n)e, cyte or plas betokenyng mevyng[2] fro[3] a plas, by a   430
place, hyt schall be set in þe ablatyffe case adverbeally
w^{t}owt a preposission, as Rex venit Londonijs.

Regula: omne proprium nomen ville,[4] loci vel ciuitatis
non compositum constructum cum verbo, participio, gerundiuo
vel supino prime vel secunde declinacionis et singularis
numeri significante moram in loco in genetiuo casu
aduerbialiter posito est sumendum absque preposicione et
regimine, vt Rex moratur Oxonie et Eboraci. Si enim illud[5]
nomen proprium fuerit[6] terc(i)e declinacionis vel pluralis
numeri[7] vel cuiuscumque declinacionis aut numeri fuerit in   440
ablatiuo casu absque preposicione est sumendum. Secunda
regula est hec: omne proprium nomen ville vel ceuitatis non
compositum constructum cum verbo, participio, gerundiuo et
supino significante mocionem[8] ad locum cuiuscumque[9]
declinationis aut numeri fuerit in accusatiuo casu
aduerbialiter est sumendum absque preposicione et sine
regimine, ut Vado Romam. Tercia regula est hec: omne
proprium nomen ville vel loce vel ciuitatis non compositum
constructum cum verbo, participio, gerundiuo et supino
significante mocionem de loco uel per locum cuiusque   450
declinacionis[10] aut numeri fuerit in ablatiuo casu
aduerbialiter est sumendum, vt Rex venit Londoniis. Que
sunt illa nomina que excipiuntur ab istis regulis predictis?
Nomina composita, vt Bellus Mons,[11] Mons Accutus,[12] Mons[13]
Spesularus.[14] Nomina localia sanctorum, vt Sanctus Iacobus,|
Sanctus Albanus. Nomina patriarum, vt Ibernia, Cansea.[15]
Nomina regionum, vt Anglia, Fransea. Quomodo debent ista
poni? Cum preposicionibus explicitis, vt Vado a(d) Sanctum
Iacobum, Vado ad Canseam, Vado ad Franseam. Regula:
nomina patriarum seu sanctorum vna cum[16] nomenibus propri(i)s[17]   460
propria compositis aduerbialiter non debent sed eis addende sunt
preposiciones. Quot nomina appellatiua sequuntur regulas
propriorum nominum? IIII^{or}: rus, domus, humus et milicia. Domo
ponitur aduerbialiter.et non domu quia nullum proprium nomen est
quarte declinacionis.

Expliciunt Regule Latisandi, quod Slyngysby, teste Westam.

[1] now canc.   [2] for a canc.   [3] a canc.
[4] MS velle   [5] verbum canc.
[6] fu-] extra minim in MS   [7] num-] minim short in MS
[8] MS nocionem   [9] d canc.   [10] et canc.
[11] MS moñs   [12] mons canc.
[13] m-] extra minim in MS   [14] MS spesūlanus
[15] fransea canc.   [16] preposi canc.   [17] addende canc.

121

INFORMACIO TEXT Y

Y. Oxford, Bodleian Library, MS Rawl. D.328, fols.8^r-15^v and 73^v

'(T)he church is a p⌈l⌉ace which Cristen men ben much
holdun to luff.' Which is thi principall verbe in this
reson? 'Isse'. When this verbe *sum, es, fui* is thi
principall verbe how schalt þu witt which is thi nominatife
case? By this Engligh worde 'Who or what is?' as 'The church
is'. What case is 'the church'? Nominatife case. What
manere of speche is 'the which'? A noun relatife. What hath
a relatif? An ante(ce)dent. Whereby knowest an ancedent?
For it goth afore a relatife and is rehersed of the relatif.
How knowest a relatife? For it maketh mencion of a thinge   10
seide bifore. What case, what gender, what noumber schall
thi relatife be? Such case, such gender, such noumber as
his ancedent scholde be if it stode ther as the relatife
standith and the relatife wer put away.

Aliter sic. What case schall the relatife be when ther
comys eny nominatife case bitwix the relatife and the verbe?
Then schall the relatife be such case as the verbe will haue
after hym; and when ther comes no nominatif case betwix the
relatife and the verbe then schall the relatife be nominatife
case to the verbe. And if the verbe|be a verbe inpersonell   20
then the relatife schall be such case as the verbe inpersonell
will haue after hym. Isse that soth allway? Ye, but if
the verbe inpersonell haue his casuell wordis after hym, then
schall þe relatif be such case as the infinitife mode will
haue after hym.

How schall þu say in Latyn the Engligh aforeseide?
Ecclesia est locus quem Christiani multum tenentur diligere.
Quem: what gender? Masculyn gender. Whi so? For to
my next ancedent my relatife schall be referred but if the
sentence lett it, as in this Latyn: *Canis tuus momordit me*   30
quem ego occidam. This relatif *quem* acordith w^t the fyrst
ancedent in gender and nought w^t the latter bycause of the
sentence.

Ibo ad locum qui vel *quod est nouum castrum.* What gendirs
ben *qui* vel *quod*? Masculyn gender and neuter gender. Whi
so? For when I haue a relatife sett betuen tuo nouns
substa(n)tiues of diueres gender longyng both to one thinge it
may acord w^t ether sobstantife in gender. Versus:

    Quando relatiuum gen(er)um casus variorum
    Inter se claudunt qui rem spectant ad eandem,| 40
    Per genus hoc poterit vtrilibet associari:
    Est pia st(i)rps Iesse quem Cristum credimus esse.

Vtinam essa(m) episcopus qui vocor Iohannes sub spe releuandi
paupertatem amicorum meorum. Episcopus: what case?
Nominatife case. Whi so? For *sum, es, fui* is a verbe
copulatife and will cuppill lyke case. What maner of verbis
haue strenght to cuppill like case? Verbis substantifes and
verbes vocatifes. How many verbis substantifes ben there?

122

INFORMACIO TEXT Y

Thre. Which iij? *Sum, fio* and *existo*. Vnde versus:

> Ars substantiua tria dic tantummodo verba: 50
> *Sum* simul *existo, fio,* nil amplius addo.

How many verbes vocatifes ben there? V. Which v? Al þo þat ben contend in thies[1] verses:

> Quinque vocatiua dicas tantummodo verba:
> *Nominor, appellor* sic *nuncupor* et *voco, dicor.*

What maner of verbis haue strenght to cuppill leke case out-take verbes substantifes and verbes vocatifes? Verbes passifes: *Ordinor accolitus, Teneor sapiens;* and verbis as they were passifes, as *Vapulo ignarus;* and verbis betokynyng mevenge of body, as *Curro celere*;[2] and verbis þat betokyn rest, 60 vt *Sedeo tristis,* or mevyn of saule, vt *Meditor|sapiens;* and verbis that betokyn semynge, vt *Appareo*[3] *bonus, Imino celsus* cum similibus.

Istud doleum est plenum vini vel *vino* vel *vacuum vini* vel *vino.* What case *vini* vel *vino*? Genitif case and ablatife case. Whi so? For all nouns adiectifes betokyning fullnes or emptynes will constrew w^t genitif case and ablatife case. Vnde versus:

> Que plenum signant et que vacuata figurant
> Iunguntur sextis, vt scribitur, et genitiuis. 70
> Exemplum querens istos versus reteneto:
> *Vini* vel *vino duo dolia*[4] *plena videto*
> Dicere vel *vacua vini, vino*que studeto.

Abstineo me irarum et desino viciorum. Irarum and *viciorum*: what case? Genitife case. Whi so? For thies tuo verbes *abstineo* and *desino* will constrew w^t genitife case, accusatif case and ablatif case. W^t a genitif case ex vi transciscionis personalis, w^t an accusatif case ex vi transciscionis, w^t an ablatif case ex vi verbi mediante preposicione. 80

> *Abstineo* quartum, sextum petit et genitiuum:
> *A vini, vino, vinum* simul *abstineo me.*
> *Desino* do genitis, cum preposita quoque sextis:
> *Desinat irarum* vel *ab iris quisque suarum.* |

Dominor huius ville vel *huic ville cuius incolarum, incolis* vel *incolas miserebor.* What case *ville*? Genitife case and datife case. Whi so? For *dominor, -aris* will constrew with genitife case and datife case ex vi transciscionis personalis. *Incolarum, incholis* vel *incholas*: what case? Genitif, datif and accusatif case. Whi so? For this verbe 90 *miserior, -reris* will constrew w^t genitif and datife case ex

---

[1] MS thics   [2] MS celare   [3] MS Appargo
[4] MS dolio

INFORMACIO TEXT Y

vi transciscionis personalis and w^t accusatif case ex vi transcisc(i)o(n)is. Vnde versus:

>Do *dominor* ternis *misereri* siue secundis,
>Et sibi vult iungi quartum casum *misereri*:
>*Nostri* vel *nobis* vel *nos Ihesu misereri*.

Ricardus et Willelmus indigent diuine gracie, diuinam graciam vel *diuina gracia*. What case ben *gracie, graciam* vel *gracia*? Genitife, accusatif and ablatife. Whi so? For thies ij verbes *egeo, -es* and *indigeo, -es* will constrew w^t genitife case, accusatif and ablatif. Vnde versus: 100

>Des quartis, sextis *eget, indiget* et genitiuis:
>*Indigeo rem, re,* coniunge *rei, michi care,*
>*In quem respicias,* hoc asseret ipse Papias.

Indigent: what noumber? Plurell noumber. Whi so? For ij nominatife case singler with *et* coniunccion betwene[1] will| haue a verbe plurell, and ij substantifes singlere w^t *et* coniunccion bitwene will haue an adiectife plurell, and ij antecedentis singler w^t *et* coniunccion betwene will haue a relatife plurell. 110

Obuiemus regi et regine venientibus Oxonie qui sunt dignissime creaturarum. Regi et regine: what case? Datif case. Whi so? For all the verbis that ben contenyd in thies versis will gouerne after hem datife case.

>*Obuio, parco, placet, noceo, respondeo, seruit,*
>*Precipit, opponit* coniungimus ista datiuis,
>*Supplicat, arridet, faueo, vaco, proficit, heret;*
>*Subuenit* addatur, *succurrit, propiciatur,*
>*Congruo, conpacior, confert, succedit, adulor,*
>*Incidit, imponit, conuicior, improperabit,*[2] 120
>*Sufficit, aspirat, obtempero, gratulor, astat,*
>*Imminet, equiualet, alludit, obedit* et *obstat,*
>*Occurrit, restat* et *cedo,* quando locum dat,
>*Incideor, fido, pateo, minor* et *valedico,*
>*Dirogo, condoleo, preiudico, detraho, differt,*
>*Suppetit* his iungas. Que *sum* componit, eis das.
>Hec et quamplura ternis coniungere cura.

Postulo Deum graciam bene viuendi qui doceor gramaticam.|
Gramaticam: what case? Accusatif case. Whi so? For all the verbis that ben contenyd in thies versis þat folow will gouerne after hem dowble accusatif case betokynnyng diueres thingis, and there passyves will constrew w^t the lattere accusatif case by the same strenght. Vnde versus: 130

---

[1] -w- *from* e [2] MS impropiciabit

124

INFORMACIO TEXT Y

*Postulo, posco, peto, docio, rogo, flagito, zelo,
Exuo* cum *vestit, monet, induo, calcio, singo*:
Accusatiuos geminos hec verba requirunt,
Passiuis quorum coniugitur vnus eorum.
Istis[1] iungantur hec omnia que similantur,
Que poscunt, zelant ornant(que) rogantque,[2] magistrant.

Vtor rubio capicio. Capicio: what case? Ablatif case.   *140*
Whi so? For all the verbes that ben contenyd in thies verses
folowinge will gouerne after hem ablatife case ex vi
transciscionis. Vnde versus:

Vescitur et *fruitur, caret, utitur* atque *potitur*:
Hec ablatiuos transiscione[3] regunt.
Hijs iungas *fungor*, et *deficio* sociatur.

Michi Roberto fracto capud medicina proficiet. Capud:
what case? Accusatif case. Whi so? For when I haue a
noun adiectife, verbe neuter or passyfe or eny of|here
participuls, gerundifes or suppyns betokynnynge all comyng   *150*
in a reson bifore a worde that betokynneth partie of all it
schall be sett in the accusatife case and gouernede by the
strenght of this figure, synotoche. Exemplum de nomine
adiectiuo: *Sum albus faciem*. Exemplum de verbo neutro,
vt *Doleo capud*. Exemplum de participio, vt *Sum fracturus
capud*. Exemplum de gerundiuo, vt *Habeo voluntatem frangendi
tuum capud*. Vnde versus:

Accusatiuos per synotocheum sibi iunctos
Adiectiua regunt, passiua(que) verbaque neutra,
Cum partis[4] toti tribuantur proprietates,   *160*
Aut e conuerso. Mox hic exempla teneto:
Albus sum faciem, Doleo capud, Conputor[5] *aurem*.
Participans iunges, vt *Femina commpta capillos*;
Hijsque gerundiua coniungas, atque suppina.

How knowest a verbe inpersonell? For it hath nother
noumber ne person ne nomin(a)tife case and is declined in the
voice of the thrid person, singler noumber, and comes in
Ingligh w^t one of this ij signes 'it' or 'me'. How many
maner of verbes inpersonels ben ther? Two. Which ij?
One of the actife voice and anothere of the passyfe voyce.   *170*
How knowest a verbe inper|sonell of the actife voice? By
myn E(n)gligh and by my Latyn. How by thyn Engligh? For
when myn Engligh begynnes w^t 'itt' as 'it forthink', 'it
rewes', then my Latyn schall end in *-t* as *penitet, tedet*.
How schalt þu fynde oute thy verbe inpersonell of the actife
voice? After the thrid person, singluer number of a verbe
of þe actife voice, as *iuuat, dilectat*. How knowest a verbe
inpersonell of þe passyfe voice? By myn Engligh, which schall
begyn w^t 'me' as 'me loues', 'me teches', and my Latyn schall
end in *-r* as *amatur, docetur*.   *180*

[1] MS istec   [2] MS regantque   [3] -is- from -ss-
[4] MS partes   [5] MS oonputor

INFORMACIO TEXT Y

A quibus verbis discendunt inpersonalia? A verbis actiuis
et neutris accionem significantibus. Vnde versus:

> Semper ab actiuis impersonale creatur
> Vel neutris illis quibus accio significatur.

Et sciendum est quod a verbis neutris passionem significantibus
nec passiuis, deponentibus et communibus non discendunt
impersonalia. Versus:

> A deponenti, communi vel pacienti
> Impersonale numquam debemus habere.

W^t what case wyl alle verbes inpersonels of þe actyf voyce   190
constrew? Wyth datyf case, except xiij of þe|which v
constrew w^t genitif case and accusatif case which bene thies:
penitet, tedet, miseret, pudet and *piget*, and v w^t accusatif
case only which ben thies: *iuuat, decet, dilectat, oportet*
and *latet*; and thre w^t genitif case and ablatif case þe which
ben thies: *interest, refert* and *est* put for *pertinet* wil
constrew with genitif case and ablatife case.

Penitet me tui. Me: what case? Accusatif case. Why so?
For thies v verbis inpersonels *penitet, tedet* et cetera will
constrew w^t genitif case and accusatif case; w^t an accusatif   200
case of that thinge þat dose þe dede of the verbe, w^t a
genitif case of that þe dede of þe verbe is don fore.
Vnde versus:

> *Penitet* et *tedet, miseret, pudet* et *piget*, ista
> Accusatiuos poscunt simul et genitiuos,
> Natura primum sed transc(i)scione secundum.

Libet michi commedere. Michi: what case? Datif case.
Whi so? For all the verbes inpersonels contenyd in thies
versis will constrew w^t datif case.

> Hoc *libet* atque *licet, placet* et *liquet, accidit* inde,   210
> *Congruit, euenit* et *contingit* et *expedit* adde,|
> *Pertinet, incumbit, vacat* et *cedit*, quoque *prestat*
> Cum reliquis paribus potes associare datiuis.

Iuuat me studium ex(er)cere. Me: what case? Accusatif
case. Whi so? For all the verbis inpersonels contenyd in
thies versis will constrew w^t accusatif case.

> Quarto iunge *iuuat, decet, dilectat, oportet*,
> Et *latet* illorum numero[1] vult associari:
> Me *iuuat esse ducem, Monachum iuuat esse priorem*,
> *Me de velle tuo, te deque meo*[2] *latet, Hugo*.   220

Interest mea Iohannis respondere magistro. Iohannis:
what case? Genitif case. Whi so? For thies thre verbes

---

[1] MS nunero   [2] te deque meo] MS tu tere que

INFORMACIO TEXT Y

inpersonel*s* *interest, refert* and *est* put for *pertinet* will constrew w^t a genitife case of all[1] casuelles except v pronouns primitiffes, þat is to say *mei, tui, sui, nostri* and *vestri*, in the stede of which schall be takyn here possessiffes in the ablatife case, femynin gender and singler noumber, þat is to say *mea, tua, sua, nostra* and *vestra*; and this noun gentile *cugia*; and there schall be vndirstond for here substantife *re* vel *vtilitate*. Vnde versus: 230

Inter,[2] *refert*,[3] *est* genitiuis iungere prodest,
Et sextum proprie donant pronomina quinque,
Nam *Refert nostra* dicas, *Refert* quoque *vestra*.

How many endingis ben ther of gerundifes? Thre. Which iij? *-Di, -do, -dum*. Whereby knowest when the gerundifes in -di schall com in spech? When I haue a worde leke to an infinitife mode|comyng after *tempus* and *est* or after a noun substantife I schall haue a gerundife in *-di*. Exemplum: 'Masse endid it is time to breke oure fast', *Missa*[4] *finita tempus est soluendi ieiunium nostrum*. I schall haue a 240 gerundife in *-di* after a noun substantife as thus:[5] 'The pope hath powere to assoyle Cristen folke belevynge in Crist of her synnes', *Papa habet potestatem absoluendi Christianos credentes in Deum de peccatis suis*.

Whereby knowest when a gerundife in *-do* schall com in speche?[6] It schall com in speche in two maner of wyses. Which ij? When this Englygh 'in' cometh byfore a worde lyke to a participle of þe present tens w^{t}out a s(u)bstantife sett to hym I schall haue a gerundife in *-do* w^t this preposicion *in*, as thus: 'In fightyng many men ben wounded, many men ben 250 maymed and many ben slayn', *In dimicando quamplurimi homines sunt mutulati, quamplurimi*[7] *vulnerati et quamplurimi occisi*. *In discendo*[8] *adquiram gramaticam*. Whereby knowest a gerundife in *-do* in the secund manere? When the Englygh of a participle of þe present tens comyth after a noun substantife I schall chese wheþ(er) I will haue a gerundife in *-do* or a participle of þe present tens, as thus: 'The maister is besy in the scole informyng his discipuls', *Magister*[9] *est assiduus*[10] *in scola informando* vel *informans suos discipulos*.

When schall I haue a gerundif in *-dum*? A gerundife in 260 *-dum* may come in speche in ij maner wise. In which ij maner? W^t *ad* preposicion and (w^t)oute *ad* preposicion. When schall I haue a gerundife in *-dum* w^t *ad* preposicion?| When an Englygh of an infinitife modo comes in a resun and tellys the cause of the reson I schall haue a gerundife in *-dum* w^t *ad* preposicion, as thus: 'Men gone to batayle to fight w^t here enmys', *Viri vadunt ad bellum ad dimicandum cum inimicis suis*. When schall I haue a gerundif in *-dum* w^{t}oute *ad* preposicion?

[1] casel *canc*.   [2] MS interest   [3] MS *adds* et
[4] MS Misse   [5] Teh *canc*.   [6] MS place
[7] MS quamphurimi   [8] MS discend'   [9] MS Magñ
[10] MS assidiuis

INFORMACIO TEXT Y

When þe Engligh of an infinitife mode comes after *sum, es, fui* and *sum, es, fui* haue no nominatife case byfore hym I schall   270
haue a gerundife in *-dum* w^{t}oute *ad* preposicion, as thus: 'It is to w^{t}stonde oure enmys purposyng to distrye oure reume', *Resistendum est inimicis nostris proponentibus distruere regnum nostrum.*

Intendo ire oppositum scolaribus meis quos bene respondentes sum imtime dilecturus. Ire: what mode? Infinitife mode. Why so? For when ij verbes come togedere w^{t}oute a coniunccion or a relatife betuen hem þe lattere schall be infinitife mode. *Oppositum*: what manere[1] of spech? Þe first suppyn. Whi so? For whan I haue a worde leke to an infinitife mode or to a   280
participle of þe future tens folowyng a verbe that betokynneth bodely mefynge to a place I schall haue þe first suppyn, as *Vado lectum libros   Vado*[2] *doctum a magistro.*

How many endingis ben there of suppyns? II. Which ij? *Tum* and *-tu*, as *amatum, amatu.*[3] Whereby knowest þe lattere suppyn? When I haue a verbe lyke to a participle of the present tens or of þe preterit w^t þe signe of a preposicion byfore hym after verbe or participle betokynnyng mevynge fro eny thinge done I schall haue the lattere suppyn. Vnde versus:|

  Post motus verbum bene pones utrumque suppinum:
  Ad loca vult primum, de vult signare secundum,   291
  Vt *Vado lectum, dormitum* siue *comm⸢e⸣stum*,
  Vt *Venio lectu, dormitu* siue *comm⸢e⸣stu*.
  Ast infinitum si[4] non signet tibi motum,
  Vt *Cupio legere, Volo ludere, Curo docere.*

Magistro docente pueri proficiunt. Magistro: what case? Ablatife case absolute. Whi so? For when I haue a noun, a pronoun or a participle in a schort hangyng reson and no worde sett afore ne vndirstand that they may be gouerned of it schall be sett in þe ablatife case absolute. Exemplum: 'One latyn   300
taught anothere is to be taught', *Vna latinitate docta alia est docenda*, or elles thus: 'The sonn rysyng I com to scole', *Sole oriente veni scolas.* How many maners may the ablatife case absolute be expounde? By two. Which ij? By *dum* and by *cum*; (by *dum*) as thus: *Me*[5] *vidente tu cecidisti*, (id est *Dum ille vidit tu cecidisti*); by *cum*, as *Augusto imperatore Alixandria deuicta (est)*, is est *Cum*[6] *Augustus erat imperator Alixandria erat deuicta.* Vnde versus:

  Per *dum* vel per *cum* sexti resolucio detur,
  Huius namque rei Precianus testis habetur.   310

How knowest a verbe inpersonell? For it hath nethere noumber ne person ne nominatife case and is declinedem in þe voice of þe thrid person, singlere noumber, and comyth in Engligh w^t one of thies ij signes 'it' or 'me'. How many manere of

---

[1] MS marier
[2] MS vatum
[3] MS amatum
[4] on *canc.*
[5] *dubious reading*
[6] MS dum

INFORMACIO TEXT Y

verbes inpersonels ben there? II. Which two? One of þe
actife voice and anothere of the passyfe voice. How knowest
a verbe in|personell of the actife voice? By myn Engligh
and by my Latyn. How by thyn Engligh? For myn Engligh
schall begynne w^t 'itt' as 'it forthinketh', 'it reweth',
and my Latyn schall endem in -t as *penitet, tedet*. How   320
schall thow fynde oute thy verbe inpersonell of the actife
voice? After the thrid person, singler noumber of a verbe
of the actife voice, as *iuuat, dilectat, oportet*. How
knowest a verbe inpersonell of the passife voice? By myn[1]
Engligh and by my (Latyn). How by thyn Engligh? For myn
Engligh schall begyn w^t 'me' as 'me louys', 'me redis', 'me
techis'. How by thy Latyn? For my Latyn schall ende in
-r as *amatur, legitur, docetur*.

A quibus verbis discendunt inpersonalia? A verbis
actiuis et a verbis neutris accionem[2] significantibus.   330
Vnde versus:

> Semper ab actiuis inpersonale creatur
> Vel neutris illis quibus accio significatur.

Et sciendum est quod a verbis passiuis deponentibus et
comunibus non discendunt inpersonalia, nec a verbis neutris
passionem significantibus. Vnde versus:

> A deponenti, communi vel pacienti
> Inpersonale nunquam debemus habere.

How is this verbe inpersonell *iuuat* declined? Verbo
inpersonali, indicatiuo modo *iuuat*, preterito inperfecto   340
iuuabat, preterito perfecto *iuu(i)t*, preterito plusquamperfecto
iuuerat, futuro *iuuabit*; imperatiuo modo *iuuet*; optatiuo
modo *vtinam iuuaret*, preterito perfecto et plusquamperfecto
vtinam iuuisset, futuro *vtinam iuuet*; coniunctiuo modo *cum
iuuet*,|preterito inperfecto *cum iuuaret*, preterito perfecto
cum iuueret, preterito plusquamperfecto *cum iuuisset*, futuro
cum iuuerit; infinitiuo modo *iuuare*, preterito perfecto et
plusquamperfecto *iuuisse* futuro caret. Vnicum participium
trahitur[3] ab hoc verbo inpersonali[4] vt *iuuans*.

Que est differencia inter *iuuat* personale et *iuuat*   350
inpersonale? Dico quod *iuuat* personale est actiuum et idem
est quod *auxiliari, dilectari*, et *iuuat* inpersonale est
neutrum et idem est quod *dilectat*. Vnde versus:

> Est *iuuat* actiuum *dilectat* et *auxiliatur*,
> Inpersonale *iuuat* est *dilectat* vbique. |

The rest of fol.15^v is taken up with miscellaneous notes in
Latin in a second hand. The following paragraphs on fol.73^v
are in the second hand and may be seen as completing the text.

---

[1] MS nyn   [2] MS occionem   [3] MS trahrtur
[4] MS Inpersonalia

INFORMACIO TEXT Y

Nota¹ quod hoc verbum *decet* semper est inpersonale nisi quando adiungitur supposito ornamentum corporis signanti, vnde incongrue dicitur *Ego deceo² togam tolarem*, sed congrue dicitur *Me decet³ toga talaris*.

Interest mea clerici⁴ iugiter studere. Mea ys the   360
ablatiue case for these iij verbis *interest*, *refert* and *est*
y-sett for *(per)tinet* wyl construe wᵗ a genetif case off all
casuell wordys owte-take the v pronownys primitiuis, scilicet
mei, tui, sui, nostri and *vestri*, in the stede of whom they
wyll be construyd wᵗ an ablatiue case, femynyn gender and
singuler number of ther possatiuis, as in thys whys: *Interest
mea, tua, sua, nostra* et *vestra*, in the whych ys wnderstonde
a genitif case of ther primatiuis, scilicet *mei, tui, sui,
nostri* and *vestri* and these nownys *re* or *vtilitate* for ther
substantiuis, and thys nowne *cuius, -a, -um* folowyth the   370
samme rulle.

Vj tens byth furmyd of the pretertens only of the
indicatif mod, of the whych vj iij changeth *I* into *E*, the
whych byn these: the preterplusquamperfectens⁵ only of the
indycatyf mode, þe preter(per)fectens and futur tens off the
coniunctiue mode; and iij kepyth *I* styll þe whych ben these:
the preterplusquamperfectens of þe optatiue mode, and þe
preterplusquamperfectens of con(iunc)tiue mode, and þe
preterplusquamperfectens of infinitiue mode vt *amauissem,
-se, -ram, -ri(m), -ro*.   380

-Ram, -rim, -ro mutant *I*, *-sem, -sem, -se* retinent *I*.

Explicit totum

---

¹ MS Nata ² MS doceo ³ MS docet
⁴ -i *from* a ⁵ *and canc.*

TEXTS OF THE FORMULA

Z. **Cambridge, Corpus Christi College, MS 233, fols.164^r-169^v**

(F)ormula gramaticis hec copulata nouellis
Pr(i)ncipium facile¹ congruitatis habet.

Ego sum² creatura Dei. Þes verbe *sum* is þe singular number and þe frist persone. Whi so? For euery verbe schale acorde w^t þe nominatif case in ij. Whyche ij? Number and person.

Verbum supposito dic concordare duobus,
Persona,³ numero; sic tradit regula nobis.

Promus et pinserna debent aulam mundare. Þis verbe *debent* is þe plurell number. Why so? For ij nominatif casus ⎮singuler⎮ w^t an *et* coniuncion ⎮copulatife⎮ comyng betwene wyl haue a verbe plurell.   *10*

Dant tibi plurale verbum iunctum duo recti.

Pater meus et non mater mea est mortuus. Þis verþe *est* is þe singular number for⁴ when I haue a⁵ copulatife w^t a negatife comyng betwene þe nominatife case and þe verbe, þe adiectif scale acord w^{t6} þe first as it is shewid afore.

Si rectos binos tibi copula consosiabit
Affirmatiue, verbum plurale meabit.
Sique negatiue coniuncio consosietur   *20*
Verbum singulare tibi tunc de iure tenetur.

Bonus vir amat Deum⁷ super omnia. Þis adiectif⁸ *bonus* is þe singular number and þe nominatif case, maculin gender, for so is þe substantif *vir*, and euery adiectife schal (acord) w^t þe substantif⁹ in iij: case, gender and number.

Cum substantiuo tribus adiectiua¹⁰ locabis,
In casu, genere, numero simull assosiabis.⎮

Bonum est multum audire et modicum dicere. Þe adiectif *bonum* is þe neuter gender substantifly, for when I haue a adiectife i-set in a reson w^towt a substantif hit shal be in   *30*
þe neuter substantiuely.

¹ s *canc.*   ² creature D *canc.*   ³ MS persono
⁴ ij nominatif casus singular w^t a nom *canc.*
⁵ negatife *canc.*   ⁶ er *canc.* after w-   ⁷ se *canc.*
⁸ MS adiectis   ⁹ -is *canc.*   ¹⁰ MS adiectiuo

131

FORMULA TEXT Z

Mobile prolatum preter fixum sibi certum
In neutro genere fixe solet esse repertum.

Magister et ostiarius sunt assidui in scola. Þis adiectif *assidui* is þe plurell number for ij substantif singular w^t an *et* coniuncium copulatife comyng betwen wil haue a adiectif plurel.

Substantiua duo si singula sint tibi iuncta,
Tunc adiectiuum semper plurale requirunt.

Puer qui[1] *iugiter laborat cito addiscit gramaticam.* Þis relatif *qui* is þe masculyn gender and þe singular number and 40
þe iij person, for soo is þe antesedent *puer*, for euery relatife schal acorde w^t þe antecedent in gender, number and person.

Antecedente tribus hijs coniunge relatum,
Persona, numero, sit genus atque datum.

Ioh(ann)es et Robertus qui bene addiscent a magistro diligentur. Þis relatife *qui* is þe plurell number, for ij anticedens singular[2] w^t an *et* coniuncioun ⌈copulatif⌉ comyng betwen[3] wil haue a relatif plurel.

Post duo nomina singula des plurale relatum.

Socius meus quem magister verberat est valde insolens. 50
Þis relatif *quem* is þe accusatife case, for when þer comyth a nominatife case betwen þe relatife and verbe[4] þe relatife schal be such case as þe verbe wil haue after him, and þer be non nominatif case betwen þe relatif and þe verbe þe relatif schall be nominatif case to þe verbe.

Si rectus mediat inter verbum et relatum[5]|
Casu quem post se vult verbum pone relatum;
Si nil sit medium tunc recto pone relatum.

Pater meus est vna creaturarum Dei. Þis nown partitif[6] *vna* is þe femyn gender, for euery nown partitif and distributitife 60
schal acorde in gender (w^t) þe genitif case þat folowit plurell number and yf þey be of on significacion, and he schal acorde in case w^t þe substantif þat goith afore.

Concordans genere fore plurale genitiuo
Vult par(ti)tiuum semper, velud *vna sororum*.
Est vnus florum rosa dicat quisque virorum.

Deus est optima rerum. Þis superlatif degre *optima* is þe femyn gender, for euery superlatife degre schal acorde (in gender) w^t þe genitif case plurel number a⌈nd⌉ yf þe be of on kynde, and w^t þe[7] substantife set before in case and number; 70
and yf þi be not of on kynde þe superlatif degre schal acorde

---

[1] -i *from* e   [2] *et canc.*   [3] te *canc. after* be-
[4] MS *adds and* þerfor   [5] MS relatiuum   [6] -it- *from* -if-
[7] w^t þe] *repeated*

FORMULA TEXT Z

in case, gender and number w^t þe substantife before, as
Iohannes est stultissimus aucarum vel *inter aucas*.

Omne superlatum partitiue recitatum[1]
Semper vult genere genitiuis par retinere,
Vt pateat verum sic: *Est Deus optima rerum*.
Immo superlatum propria vi quando negatur
Per genus hoc fixo[2] precedenti similatur.

    Vinum est forcior potus quam seruisia et *magis tenuis*.
Þis ij wordys *magis tenuis* be set in þe sted of þe comparatife   80
degre of þis nown *hic hec tenuis*[3] et *hoc tenue*, (f)or euery
nown of þe positife degre hauuyng a vowel afore *-vs* as|
pius, and afore *-is* as *tenuis* lackyth þe compartife degre,
wherof is tak of þe positif degre w^t þis adverbe *magis*.

    Que per *-ius*[4] vel *-eus*,[5] *-vis* aut *-v(u)s*, *-or* caruere,
Per *magis* et primum quod comparat instituere.

    Manus mea est magna cum manus fratris mei est maior.
These five nownis *bonus, -a, -um*; *malus, -a, -um*; *paruus, -a,
-um*; *multus, -a, -um*; *magnus, -a, -um* formyth þe comparatif
degre and þe superlatife owt of rewlle, and þerfor we sey   90
magnus, maior, maximus.

    Res bona, res melior, res optima; *res mala, peior,
Pessima*; *res magna, res maior, maxima rerum*;
Parua, minor, minema dic; *multus*,[6] *plurimus* addes.
Plur(i)mus et *multus*[6] sic comparat abque secundo.

    Soror mea est pulcherima creaturarum.[7] Þis superlatif
deg⌈r⌉e *pulcerima* is formyd of þe nominatif case singular
number,[8] for when my nown of positif degre endyth in *R* letter
þe superlatif degre schal be formyd of þe nominatif case be
puttyng to a *-rimus*, as *pulcher, pulcerimus*, owt-tak þes in þis   100
verse.

    Cum rectus tenet *-r* poteris *-rimus* addere semper;
Nuperus atque *vetus, maturus*,[9] *detero* iunges.
In *-rimus* atque *-timus dexter*ve *sinister* habetur,
Et *memor* excipitur,[10] *memorissimus* hunc reperitur.

    Ricardus est humilimus omnium sociorum meorum. Þis
superlatif degre *humilimus* ys formid owt of *rewll*, and þes
v nownis *agilis, gracilis, facilis* and *similis* and *humilis*,
þe wich v be formyde of þe nominatif case be puttyng awey *-is*
and set þer-to a *-limus*, as *agilis*, put awey *-is* and put þer-to   110
a *-limus* and þ⌈en⌉ it wol be *agillimus*. |

    Dant tibi quinque *-limus* que signant nomina *f-a-g-u-s*;

[1] MS resuscitatum   [2] MS fixum   [3] vel canc.
[4] i- from e   [5] MS [e]us   [6] MS mult*is*
[7] MS creaturaturum   [8] fur canc.   [9] MS maturis
[10] MS accipitur

FORMULA TEXT Z

Hec *agilis, gracilis, humilis, facilis, similis*que
Et sua composita, que duplice (sunt) *L* habenda.

Socie mi doce me regulas meas. Thys word *mi* is þe vocatif case of *meus, -a, -um.* How many pronowns[1] conteynyth þe vocatif case? IIII. Wich iiij? *Tu, meus, noster* and[2] *nostras.*

    Quatuor exceptis pronomina nulla vocabis;
    Tu, meus, et *noster,*[3] *nostras*: hec sola vocantur.   *120*

Ego et frater meus ibimus[4] *iantatum.* Þis verbe *ibimus* ys þe frist persone for þe frist person is more worþer þan þe secunde and þe thyrd.

    Prima duas alias recipit sed non vici versa:
    Tu fraterque datis vt honore suscipiatis.

    Iohannes lesit socium suum pro quo a magistro vapulabit.
Þis word *Iohannes* is þe iij person, for euery nown and euery pronown and euery participul is þe iij person, owt-tak *ego, nos, tu, vos* w^t þer oblyks and euery vocatif case.

    Terne persone generaliter omnis habetur   *130*
    Rectus, sed demas pronomina iiij^{or} inde,
    Sunt *ego, nos* prime, *tu, vos* quoque nempe secunde.

    Frater meus et soror mea sunt assidui in domo patris mei.
Þis adiectif *assidui* is þe maculyn gender, for þe maculyn gender ys more wortheer þan þe femen and þe neuter ys more worthyer þan þe maculyn or þe femyn.

    Mas. sibi femenium, sed fe. non consipit vllum;
    Neutrum fe. sibi mas. si bene consipias.

    Istud dolium est plenum vini vel *vino.*[5] What case?
Þe genitife case and þe ablatyfe, for euery nown þat betokenyth   *140*
fulnes or emtynese wil constru w^t a genitif case and ablatife case.|

    Que plenum signant vel que vacuata figurant,
    Hec ablatiuis poteris dare vel genitiuis:
    Vini vel *vino duo dolia plena videto.*

    Obuiemus regi et regine. Þis word *regi* is þe datyf case, for al þes verbis þat be conteynyde in þis verse wil constru w$^{(t)}$ a datif case.

    Obuio, parco, placet, noceo, respondeo, seruet,
    Presipit, opponit coniungimus iste datiuis,   *150*
    Supp(l)icat, intersum, fauet, heret (et) inuidet, illis

---

[1] MS *adds* ys   [2] vester *canc.*
[3] et *noster*] MS noster et   [4] ua *canc.*
[5] waht *canc.*

FORMULA TEXT Z

Subuenit addatur, succurrit,¹ propiciatur.

Vtor rubio capicio. Capicio,² what case? Þe ablatif case, for al þes verbes þat be conteynyde in þis wil constru wᵗ a ablatif case.

Vescitur et fruitur, caret, vtitur atque potitur:
Hec ablatiuos transicione regunt.
Fungor iungatur, et dificio sociatur.

Dominor huius ville abstinens irarum. Huius ville, what case? Þe genitiue case, for al þe verbys þat be conteynyd in   160
þis versis wil constru wᵗ a genitiue case.

Abstineo, dominor, misereris cum genitiuis
Iunges: Abstineo panis; Miserere dolentis;
Dominor et wille bonus heres³ iure parentis.

Irarum, what case? Þe genitiue case. Why so? For euery participul, gerundif and suppyn wyl constru wᵗ sich case as þe verbe þat he comyth of.

Iudex quoscumque serie casus imitatur,
Illos tocius verbi flexus comitatur.⁴
Iunge gerundiua cum parti(ci)pante, supina.   170

Ricardus et Robertus indigent diuine gracie vel diuina gracia. What case diuine gracie vel diuina gracia? Þe genitiue and þe ablatife. Why so? For all þe(s) verbis wil constru wᵗ a genitiue case and a ablatif case.|

Des ablatiuis eget, indiget ac genitiuis,
Vt noscas verum sic: Indigeo quoque rerum;
Indigeo bobus ad rura colenda duobus.

Postulo te graciam⁵ qui doceor g⟨r⟩amaticam. Graciam, what case? Þe accusatif case, for all þes verbis þat be conteynyde in⁶ þes versis wil constru wᵗ a dobil accusatif case,   180
and þe passyuis of þem wyll constru wᵗ on accusatif case.

Postulo, posco, peto, doceo, rogo, flagito, celo,
Exuo cum vestit, monet, induo, calceo, singo:
Accusatiuos geminos hec verba requirunt,
Et cum passiuis postremus iungitur illi.

How many endyngis of gerundiuis ben þer? III. Whych iij? -Di, -do and -dum. When schal I haue a gerundife in -di in comyn spech? When þe Englich of a infinitif mode comyng after eny of þes nowns tempus, causa, desiderium, voluntas et sich oþer lyk, or after a nown substantife. Exemplum: Missa   190
finita tempus est soluendi⁷ ieiunium. Item: Papa habet

¹ pp canc.   ² MS capicis   ³ MS adds de
⁴ MS comutatur   ⁵ MS gramaticam   ⁶ in canc.
⁷ MS fouendi

135

FORMULA TEXT Z

potestatem so(l)uendi Christianos.

When schal I haue a gerundiue in *-do* in comen spech?
In ij maner of wys. On ys when þis Englich 'in' cometh
byfore þe Englich of a partisipul of þe presentens wᵗowt a
substantife to hym, þan schal I haue a gerundiue in *-do* ⁽wᵗ
thys preposicion *in*⁾¹. Exemplum: *In dimicando multi homines
sunt vulnerati.* The secunde maner ys when þe Englich of a
participul of þe presentens comyng after a substantif, þan I
maye chese wheþer þat I wolle haue a participull of þe   200
presentens or a gerundyue in *-do*. Exemplum: *Magister est
assiduus in scola informando vel informans suos scolares.*

When schall I haue a gerundiue in *-dum*? In to maner|
of whyse. The furst maner of whyse is (when) I haue a
Englich¹ of a infinitif mode þat comyth after a resen and
tellyth þe cause of þe reson, þan schal I haue a gerundif in
-dum wᵗ a preposicion ⁽*ad*⁾¹. Exemplum:² *Viri vadunt ad
bellum ad dimicandum.* The secunde maner of³ wyse is when I
haue a Englich of a infinitife mode comyng after þis verbe
sum, es, fui wᵗowt eny nominatif case to hym, þen schal I   210
haue a gerundif in *-dum* wᵗowt a prepos(ic)ion. Exemplum:
*Resistendum est inimicis*⁴ *nostris pugnantibus contra*⁵ *nos.*

Intendo ire oppositum scolaribus. Þis word *oppositum*
is þe frist suppyn, for when I haue a Englich of a infinitif
mode comyng after a verbe betokenyng to a place eny þyng to be
don it schall be set in þe first suppyn. *Venio lectu libros.*
Þis word *lectu* is þe latur suppyn, for when I haue an Englich⁶
of infinitife comyng after a verbe betokenyng meuyng fro a
place it schal be sett in þe later suppyn.

    Post motus verbum primum coniunge supinum,   220
    Vt *Vado lectum,*⁷ *senatum siue comestum*;
    Deque loco⁸ signans postremum iunge⁹ suppinum;
    Infinitiuum si non signet tibi motum;
    Vt *Venio lectu, senatu siue*¹⁰ *comestu,*
    Vt *Cupio legere, Volo ludere, Curo docere.*

And when I haue a Englich of a infinitif mode þat schuld be
set in þe¹¹ f(i)rst supyn, where þe supyn|faylyth I schal
take þis nown *locus* wᵗ þis preposicion *ad* and þat futur tens
of þe same verbe þat þe suppyn sch⁽u⁾ld cum of wᵗ þis aduerbe
vbi.¹² Exemplum: *Vado*¹³ *ad locum vbi addiscam gramaticam.*   230
And when þe Englisch of þe infinitife mode þat scul be set in
þe later supyn comyng in a reson, where þe supyn fallyth I
schal take þis nown *locus* wᵗ þis preposicion *a* and þe pretertens
of þe same verbe þat þe suppyn schuld cum of wᵗ þis aduerbe
vbi. Exemplum: *Veni a loco vbi addiscam gramaticam.* And

---

¹ n- *canc.*   ² vin *canc.*   ³ wh *canc.*
⁴ MS inimicis *from* inimicis   ⁵ MS con < > constra
⁶ an Englich] MS a nenglich   ⁷ *repeated*
⁸ MS loca   ⁹ MS iungitur   ¹⁰ cup *canc.*
¹¹ finitife *canc.*   ¹² -i *from* e   ¹³ MS vodo

FORMULA TEXT Z

yf þer[1] comyth a propar name of a place I schal haue þe propar name w^t þis aduerbe *vbi* and þe pretertens. Exemplum: *Veni Exonia vbi addidici gramaticam.*

Ego sum dilecturus socium. Þis worde *dilecturus* ys a participul of þe futur tens in *-rus*, for when I[2] haue a Englich 240 lik to a infinitife betokenyng 'to do' followyng þis verbe *sum, es, fui* it schal be set in[3] a participul of þe futur tens in *-rus*, as *Ego sum amaturus*; and yf þe Englich of þe infinitife mode betokyn 'to suffur' it shal be set[4] in a participul in *-dus*, as *Ego sum amandus.*

Magistro docente pueri proficiunt. Þis word *magistro* ys þe ablatif case absolute, for when I haue a schort hangyng reson of a nown and a participull or a pronown and a participul w^{t}owt eny worde set owt of þe whych he may be gouerynde it schalle be set (in) þe ablatif case absolute, as *Me sedente* 250 *tu curris.*

Placet mihi quod nos ibimus lusum. Þis worde[5] *placet* ys a verbe inpersonal, for a verbe inpersonall hath|no number nor person and he is declynyde in þe wyse of þe iij person singular number and he comyth after on of þes synys 'it' or 'me', as 'it delytit' or 'me redith'.

How many verbis inpersonall be þer?[6] II. Wych ij? A verbe impersonal of þe actife vose and verbe impersonal of þe passiue vose. How know yow a verbe impersonall of þe actiue? For he endyth in *-et*[7] as *penitet, tedet*. How know ye a verbe 260 impersonall of þe passiue vose? For he endyth in[8] *-r* as *statur, curritur*. W^t what case wil al verbis impersonal constru w^t of þe actiue vose? W^t to a datiue case, exceptis xiij of þe whych v will constru w^t a accusatif case and a genitife case, and þey be þis *penitet, tedet, miseret, pudet* and *piget*; and v w^t a accusatife case, and þey be þes *iuuat, decet, delectat, oportet* and *latet*; and iij w^t a genitif case al only, and þey be þes *interest, refert* et *est* i-set for *pertinet.*

Penitet me mali regimine. Me is þe accusatif case, 270 for þes v verbis *penitet, tedet, miseret, pudet* and *piget* w(i)l constru w^t accusatif case of þe þyng þat doþe þe dede of þe verbe. *Regiminis*, what case? Þe geni(ti)f case. Why so? For þes v verbis will construe w^t a genitiue case of þe þyng þat þe dede of þe verbe is don for.

Penitet (et) *tedet, miseret, pudet* et *piget*, ista
Accusatiuos poscunt simul et genitiuos,
Natura primum sed transicione secundum.[9]

[1] be *canc*.
[2] when I] *repeated*
[3] þe ablatiui case *canc*.
[4] be *canc*.
[5] w *canc*.
[6] iij *canc*.
[7] MS te
[8] er(?) *canc*.
[9] MS secunde

FORMULA TEXT Z

Thes iij verbis *penitet, pudet* and *piget* makyde in þe
pretertens *penituit, puduit*[1] et *piguit*, and þes ij verbis   280
tedet|and *miseret* makyth *pertesum* and *misertum*.

   Peni(tu)it, puduit,[2] *piguit* sic preteritis dant,
   Set *tedet, miseret* dant *pertesum*que *misertum*.

   Decet scolares[3] *honestos esse.* Þis worde *scolares* ys þe
accusatif case, for þes verbis *decet, iuuat, delectat,*[4] *oportet*
and *latet* will constru w^t a accusatif case al only.

   Quarto iunge *iuuat, decet* ac *dilectat, oportet,*
   Et *latet* illorum numero vult associari.

   Interest mea clerici iugiter studere. Mea ys þe ablatif
case, for þes iij verbis *interest, refert* and *est* i-set (for)   290
pertinet wil constru w^t a genitiui case of al caswell wordis,
owt-tak v pronownis primatiuis, scilicet *mei, tui, sui, nostri*
and *vestri*, in þe stede of whom þi wil constru w^{t5} a ablatif
case, femyn gender, singular number, as on þis wyse: *interest
mea, tua, sua, nostra* and *vestra*, in þe wich is vnderstonde þe
genitiue case of þer primitiuis, scilicet *mei, tui, sui,*[6] *nostri*
and *vestri*; and *re* vel *vtilitate* be onderstond for þer
substantiuis.

   Inter.,[7] *refert,*[8] *est* genitiuis iungere prode(s)t,
   Set sexto proprie iungas pronomina quinque,   300
   Nam *refert nostra* dicas, *ref$^($e$^)$rt* quoque *vestra*.

   Obuiatur mihi a scolare bono socio. Obuiatur, what
parte of reson? A verbe impersonal. Why is þis made by a
verbe impersonal? For when I haue a Englich of a verbe neuter
lic to a passiue, wher þe passiue faylit I schal tak þis verbe
impersonal of lic tens and mode as þe passiue semyt to be, and
þat at semit to be þe nominatif case schal be sich case as
verbe wil haue after hym. *Bono socio*, what case? Þe ablatif
case. Why so? For al þat longyth to on þing schal be put
in on case.   310

   How schal I sey in Laten, 'Þe master betit me'? Be þis
verbe *vapulo: Ego vapulo a magistro*. Why so? For when I
haue an Englich of a actif þat schuld be made be a verbe neuter-
passiue þat worde þat sem(i)t to be þe nominatif case schal be
turnyde into þe ablatif case w^t a|preposicion, or ellys into
þe datiue case[9] when I haue þis verbe *nubo, -is,* 'to be weddyd';
þat at semit to be þe accusatif schal be þe nominatif case.
Exemplum de[10] *nubo*: 'Þe schalt wede[11] my sister', *Soror mea
nubet tibi*. Al þes verbis þat be conteynyde in þis verse be
verbe neuturpassiuis.   320

[1] MS piduit   [2] MS piduit; MS adds et   [3] MS scolaret
[4] MS delatat   [5] MS adds þe   [6] nu canc.
[7] MS interest   [8] MS adds et   [9] MS adds but
[10] -e from u   [11] s canc.

138

FORMULA TEXT Z

Exulo, vapulo, veneo,[1] *fio, nubo licet*que[2]
Sensum passiue sub voce gerunt aliena.

How ys a verbe inpersonal declinyde? A verbe inpersonal
is declinid in þe vose of þe iij person singular number in
euery mode, and yf he[3] be of þe actiue vose þus[4] he is declinid:
penitet, penitebat, -nituit,[5] *-tuerat, -tebit, -tere*; and yf
he be of þe passiue voce he is decl(i)nyd þus:[6] *obuiatur,
-abatur, -atum est* vel *fuit, -atum erat* vel *fuerat,
obuiabitur,*[7] *obuiari.*

How many participulys longith to a verbe impersonal of
þe passiue voyse? On. Wich on? A participul of þe
presentens al only, as of þis verbe *opponitur,*[8] *oponibatur,*[9]
nominatiuo[10] *hoc oppositum,* accusatiuo *hoc oppositum,* ablatiuo
ab ⌈hoc⌉ *opposito.*

How many tensis be formyde of þe preterperfitens[11] of þe[12]
indicatif mode? VI. Wich vj? Þe preterpluperfitens of
þe indicatif mode, þe preterpluperfitens of þe optatif mode,
þe preterperfitens and þe preterpluperfitens and þe futer tens of
þe coniuntife mode, ⌈and⌉ þe preterpluperfitens of þe infinitif
mode. III changth *I* into *E* and þe (be) þe preterpluperfitens of
indicatif mode, þe preterperfitens of þe[13] coniuntif mode and
futer tens of þe same[14] mode; and iij hold *I* styl and þi be þes,
þe preterplufitens of þe op⌈ta⌉tif mode, þe preterplufitens of
þe coniuntif mode, and þe preterpluperfitens of þe infinitif
mode.

-Ram, -rim, -ro mutant *I*; *-sem, -sem*[15] *-se* retinent *I*.

330

340

---

[1] MS venio [2] MS licioque [3] MS þi
[4] MS þis [5] te *canc.* [6] MS þis
[7] MS abuiabitur [8] MS oppositur *with* -r *from* m
[9] MS aponibatur [10] no *canc. after* -na- [11] of *canc.*
[12] inj *canc.* [13] þe *canc.* [14] MS sane
[15] sem *canc.*

FORMULA TEXT AA

AA. London, British Library, MS Add. 37075, fols.30^v-37^r and 41^r

Formela grammaticis hec compilata nouellis
Principium facile congr(u)itatis habet.

Ego sum creatura Dei. Þis verbe *sum* ys þe singular
nomber and þe fyrst person, for so is the nominatyve case
ego, and euery verbe shall acord w^t the nominatyve case in
nombyr and person.

Verbum subposito dic concordare duobus,
Persona, numero; sic tradit regula nobis.

Promus et pincerna[1] *debent aulam mundare.* This verbe
debent ys the plurell nombyr, for ij nominatyve case singular   10
w^t an *et* coniunccion copulatyve commyng betwen[2] will haue a
verbe plurell.

Dant tibi plurale verbum iuncti duo recti.

Pater meus[3] *et non mater mea est mortuus.* This verbe *est*
ys the singuler nombyr, for when a copulatyve cum w^t a negatyve|
commyth betwen ij nominatyve case singuler, the verbe and the
adiectyve foloyng shall acorde w^t the fyrst nominatywe case.
Versus:

    Si rectos binos tibi copula consociabit
    Affirmatiue, verbum plurale meabit;   20
    Sique negatiue coniunccio consocietur
    Verbum singulare tibi tunc de iure tenetur.

[*Bonus vir amat Deum.* This adiectyve case for so ys þe
substan<tiue> *vir*, and euery adiectyve schall acord w^t þe
substantive in case, gendir and nomb<er>]

Bonus vir amat Deum super omnia. This adiectiue *bonus*
ys þe nominatiue case, masculin gender and singular number,
for so ys þe[4] substantiue *vir*, for euery adiectiue schall
acord w^t þe substantiue in case, gender and number. Versus:

    Cum substantiuo tribus ad(i)ectiua locabis: 30
    In casu, genere; numerum simull[5] associabis.

Bonum est multum audire et modicum dicere. This
adiectiue *bonum* ys the neuter gender substantiuili sett, for
whan I haue an adiectiue sett w^{t}wout a serten substantiue yt
schall be put in the neuter gender substantili. Versus:

    Mobile prolatum preter fixum sibi certum
    In neutris genere fixe solet esse repertum.

Magister et hostiarius sunt ⸢*assidui*⸣ *in scola.* This

---

[1] *r canc. after* pin-   [2] -w- *from* y
[3] MS meu̧g; est vna *canc.*[4] no *canc.*   [5] MS sumull

FORMULA TEXT AA

adiectiue *assidui* ys the plurell number, for ij substantiue
singuler w[t] a coniuncion copulatiue comyng betwen will haue a   40
adiectiue plurell.

       Substa(n)tiua duo si singula sint tibi iun(c)ta,
       Tunc adiectiuum semper plurale requirunt.|

Puer qui iugiter laborat addiscet cito grammaticam. This
relatiue *qui* ys þe masculin gender and the singuler number and
the third person, for so ys the antesedens *puer*; for euery
relatiue schall acord w[t] hys anticedent in gendir, number and
person.

       Antecedenti tribus hijs coniunge relatum:
       Persona, numero; sit genus hijsque datum.   50

*Ihoannes et Robartus qui bene adiscunt diligentur a
magistro.*[1] This relatiue *qui* ys the plurell number, for ij
anticedens singuler w[t] an *et* coniuncion copulatiue cum betwene
will haue a relatiue plurell.

       Post duo nomina singula des plurale relatum.

Socius meus quem magister varberat[2] *est valde insolens.*[3]
Þis relatiue *quem* ys the accistyve case, for when I haue a[4]
nominati case commy(n)g bytwen the relatyve and the verbe, than
þe relative schall be such case as the verbe wyll have after
hym; and yf þer com no nominative case he shall be the   60
nominatyve case to the verbe. Versus:

       Si rectus mediat inter verbumque[5] relatum,
       Casu quem post se vult verbum pone relatum;
       Si nil sit medium, tunc recto pone relatum.

Pater meus est vna creaturarum. Thys nown partityve
vna ys the femynyn gendyr, for euery nown partityve[6]
partityvely set or dystributyve schall acorde|in gendir w[t]
the genitive case plurell yf they be won kynd, and he schall
acord in case and nombyr w[t] the substantive that goth byfore.
Versus: 70

       Concordans genere fore plurali genitiuo
       Vult partitiuum semper, velut *vna sororum*:[7]
       Est vnus florum rosa dicat quisque virorum.

Deus est optima rerum. Thys superlatyve degre *optima*
ys the femynyn gendyr, for euery superlative degre schall
acord in gendir w[t] þe genitive case plurell yf they be of won
kynd, and w[t] þe substantive sett before[8] in nombyr and case;
and yf they be nott of won kynd the superlative schall acord

---

[1] sunt amandi *canc.*   [2] et *canc.*   [3] *repeated*
[4] i *canc.*   [5] pone *canc. after* verbum
[6] schall *canc.*   [7] *This line precedes the previous line in
MS, but is signalled to present place.*   [7] of won kynd and *canc.*

FORMULA TEXT AA

w^t the substantive byfore in case, gendir and nombyr, as
Iohannes est stultissimus aucarum vel *inter aucas.* Versus: 80

Omne superlatum partitiue recitatum
Semper vult genere genitiuo par retineri,
Vt pateat verum sic, *Est Deus optima rerum.*
Imo^1 superlatum propria vi quando negatur
Per genus hoc fyxo precedenti similatur.

Vinum est forcior potus quam ceruisia et *magis tenuis.*
These ij wordis *magis* and *tenuis* be sett in the stede of þe
comparative degre of þis nown *hic et hec tenuis* et *hoc tenue*
for euery nown of the posatyve degre havyng|a uowell^2 afore
-vs as *pius, -a, -um,* afore *-is* as *hic et hec tenuis* et *hoc* 90
tenue, lakyd the comparatyve degre, in the stede whereof we
take þe posytyve degre w^t þis aduerbe *magis.* Versus:

Que per *-eus* vel *-ius, -vis* aut *-vus, or* caruere,
Per *magis* et primum quod comparat instituere.

Manus mea est magna tamen manus fratris mei est maior.
These v nownus *bonus, -a, -num, malus, -a, -um, magnus, -a, -um,*
paruus, -a, -uum, multus, -a, -tum formyth the comparatyve and
the superlative out of rewle, and therefor we sey *magnus, maior,*
max(i)mus.^{3} Versus:

Res bona, res melior, res optima; res mala, peior, 100
Pessima; res magna, res maior, maxima rerum.
Parua, minor, minima dic, multus, plurimus addens.
Plurimus et multus sic comparat absque secundo.

Soror mea est pulcherima creaturarum. Thys superlatyve
degre *pulcherima* is formyd of the nominatyve case singuler nombyr,
for when any nown of þe posityve degre endyt in *R* letter the
superlatyve degre schall be formyd of the nominatyve case by
puttyng to *-rimus,* as *pulcher,* put to *-rimus,* it is *pulcherimus.*
Versus:

Cum rectus tenet *-r* poteris *-rimus* addere semper; 110
Nuperus^4 atque vetus, maturus, detero iunges.
In *-rimus* atque *-timus dexterve sinister* habentur,
Et *memor* exci(pi)tur, *me(mo)rissimus* hinc reperitur.|

If the posityue degre end in *-vs* the superlative ys formyd
of the genityve case, as genitiuo *iusti,* put to *S* and *-simus,*
it ys *iustissimus*; and yf it be of thryd declynson the
superlatyve is formyd of the genityve case by puttyng to
-simus,^{5} as genitiuo *fortis,* put to *-simus,* yt ys *fortissimus.*

*-Vs*que secunda tenens superantem de genitiuo
Sic format: iunges *S* atque *-simus* superaddens; 120
In terns fo$^{(r)}$mo *-simus* addens cum genitiuo.

^{1} MS Imio ^{2} uo- from w ^{3} -x- from g
^{4} tenet *canc.* ^{5} it is fortissimus *canc.*

142

FORMULA TEXT AA

Ihoannes est humilimus omnium sociorum meorum. This superlatyve degre *humillimus* is formyd oute of reule, for these v nownus *agilis, gracilis, humilis, facilis* and *similis* formyth the superlatyve degre of the nominatyve case singulere by puttyng awey -*is* and settyng to -*limus*, as putt awey -*is* and sett to -*limus*, it is *agillimus*. Versus:

Dant tibi quinque -*limus* que signa(n)t nomine *f-a-g-u-s*:
Hec *agilis, gracilis, humilis, facilis, similis*que
Et sua composita que duplice sunt *ll* habenda.   130

Socie mi doce me regulas meas. This word *mi* ys the vocatyve case of *meus, -a, -um*. How many prononus haue the vocatyve case? IIII. Whych iiij? *Tu, meus, noster* and *nostras.* |

Quatuor exceptis pronomina nulla vocabis;
Tu, meus et[1] *noster, nostras*: hec sola vocantur.

Ego et frater meus ibimus iantatum. Thys verbe *ibimus* is þe fyrst persone, for the fyrst persone ys more than the secund[2] or the thryd. Versus:

Prima duas alias recipit sed non vice versa: 140
Tu fraterque datis vt honorem suscipiatis.

Iohannes lesit socium suum pro quo a magistro vapulabit. This word *Iohannes* ys the thrid persone, for every nown and euery pronown ys the thrid persone, owte-take *ego, nos, tu* and *vos* w[t] thyr obliques, and euery vocatyve case. Versus:

Terne persone generaliter omnis habetur
Rectus, sed demas pronomina quattuor inde:
Sunt *ego, nos* prime, *tu, vos* quoque nempe secunde.

Frater meus et soror mea sunt assidui in domo patris mei. Thys adiectyve *assidui* ys the masculyn gender, for the masculyn   150 gendyr is more worthy than the femynyn, and the neuter is more worthy than the masculyn and the femynyn. Versus:

Mas. sibi femineum sed fe. non concipit vllum.
Neutrum fe. sibi mas. si bene concipias.

Istud dolium est plenum vini vel *vino. Vini* vel *vino*,[3] what case? The genityve case and the ablatiue, for all wordes| that betoken fullnes or emtynes will construe w[t] genityve case and ablatyve. Versus:

Que plenum signant vel que vacuata figurant,
Hec ablatiuis poteris dare vel genitiuis: 160
Vini vel *vino duo dolia plena videto.*

Vtor rub⌈i⌉o capicio. Capicio, what case? The ablatyve

---

[1] *et from and*   [2] MS secun*dis*   [3] MS vi*n*io

FORMULA TEXT AA

case, for all the verbys that be conteynyd in this verse will construe with ablatyve case. Versus:

Vescitur et *fruitur*, *caret*, *vtitur* atque *potitur*:
Hec ablatiuos transicione regunt.
Fungor iungatur et *deficio* sociatur.

Obuiemus regi et *regi(n)e*.[1] This word *regi* is the datyve case, for all þe verbis þat be conteyned in these verse will constru w^t datyve case. Versus: 170

Obuio, *parco*, *placet*, *noceo*, *respondeo*, *seruit*,
Precipit, *opponit*, concludit, iunge datiuis.
Supplicat, *imponit*, *fauet*, *heret* et *inuidet*, illis
Subuenit addatur, *succurrit*, *propiciatur*.

How many endyngis of gerundyvus be ther? III. Which iij? -*Di*, -*do* and -*dum*. Whan schall I haue a gerundyve in -*di*? Whan I haue the Englysh of the infinityve mode commyng after *tempus*, *causa* or *est* or a nown substantyve I shall haue a gerundyve in -*di*. Exemplum: *Missa finita tempus est soluendi ieiunium*. Item: *Papa habet potestatem absoluendi*   180
Christianos. Whan schall I haue a gerundyve in -*do*? In ij maner wyse.| Won ys whan this Englisch 'in' commyth byfor the English of a participull of the present tens w^{t}oute a substantyve to hym, than schall I haue a gerundyue in -*do*. Exemplum: *In dimicando multi homines sunt vulnerati*. The secund maner ys whan the English of a participull of the present tens commyth byfore a substantyve, than may (I) chese whedir I will haue a participull of the present tens or a^2 gerundyve in -*do*. Exemplum: *Magister est assiduus in scola informando*   190
vel *informans suos scolares*. Whan schall I haue a gerundive in -*dum*? In ij maner wyse. Þe fyrst ys: whan I haue þe English of þe infinityve mode þat commyth in a reson and tellith the cause of the reson I shall haue a gerundyve in -*dum* w^t a preposicion. Exemplum: *Viri vadunt ad bellum ad dimicandum*. The second maner ys: whan the English of þe infinitive mode commyth after *est* w^{t}owte a nominative case to hym I schall haue a gerundyve in -*dum*. Exemplum: *Resistendum est inimicis nostris pugnantibus contra nos*.

Intendo ire oppositum scolaribus. This word *oppo(si)tum* ys þe first supyn, for whan^3 I haue þe English of the infinitive   200
mode comyn after a verbe betokenyng mevyng to a place it schall be sett in þe fyrst supyn. *Venio lectu libros*. Þis word *lectu* ys the latter supyn, for whan I haue þe English of the infinitive mode commyng after a verbe betokenyng mevyng from ⌜a⌝ place it shall be sett in the latter supyn. Versus:

Post motus verbum primum coniunge supinum.
Vt *Vado lectum, cenatum* siue^4 *comestum*.
Deque loco signans postremum iunge supinum,

---

[1] MS regiem from regiam with correction not completed.
[2] MS adds in   [3] -n from d   [4] supinum canc.

FORMULA TEXT AA

Vt *Venio lectu, cenatu* siue *comestu*.
Infinitiuum si non signet tibi motum, 210
Vt *Cupio legere, Volo ludere, Curo docere*. |

And whan I haue þe English of þe infinitiue mode þat shuld be sett in the fyrst supyn, wher þe supyn fayleth I shall take þis nown *locus* w^t þis preposicion *ad* and the futer tens of the verbe þat þe supyn scholl com of w^t þis aduerbe *vbi*. Exemplum: *Vado ad locum vbi addiscam gramaticam*. And whan the English of the infinityve mode þat shuld be sett in þe latter supyn commyth in a reso<n>, wher þe supyn faylyth I schall take þis now(n) *locus* w^t þis preposicion *a* and the pretertens of the verbe þat þe supyn shuld com of w^t this aduerbe *vbi*. Exemplum: 220 *Veni a loco vbi addidici grammaticam*.[1] And yf ther com a propyr name of[2] a place I schall take þe propyr name w^t þis aduerbe *vbi*. Exemplum: *Veni Oxonia vbi addidici grammaticam*.

Ego sum dilecturus socium meum. This word *dilecturus* is a participull of the future tens in *-rus*, for whan I haue an English of the infinitive mode betokeny(n)g 'to do' folowyng þis verbe *sum, es, fui* it shall be a participull of the fyrst futur in *-rus*, as *Ego sum amaturus*; and yf the English of the infinityve mode betoken 'to suffyr' it shall be þe latter future in *-dus*, as *Ego sum amandus*. 230

Magistro docente pueri proficiunt. Þis word *magistro* is þe ablatyve case absolute, for whan I haue a reson of nown and participull or pronoun and participull w^{t}oute any worde set ow3te wherof he may be gouernyd, yt shall be sett in the ablatyve case absolute, as *Me sedente tu curris*.

Placet mihi bene quod[3] *nos transibimus lusum*. This word *placet* ys a verbe impersonall. How knos ye a verbe imp(ers)onall? For he haþe no nombyr nor persone (nor) nominatyve case and ys declyned in the voyce of the thryd persone, singuler nombyr and commyth w^t won of these ij signes 240 'it' or 'me', as 'it deliteth' or 'me redith'.

How many maner of verbis impersonall|be ther? II. Which ij? A verbe impersonall of the actyve voyce, a verbe impersonall of the passyve voyce. How knos ye a verbe impersonall of þe actyve voyce? For he endyth in *-t* as *penitet, tedet*. How knos ye a verbe impersonall of þe passyve voice? For he endyth in *-r*, as *statur, curritur*. W^t waht case will all verbis impersonall construe of þe actyve voyce? W^t the datyve case, excepte xiij of þe which v will construe w^t accusatyve and genityve, and they be thes: *penitet, tedet,* 250 *miseret, pudet* and *piget*; v will construe w^t accusatyve case only and they be these: *decet, iuuat, delectat, oportet* and *latet*; and iij w^t genityve case only and they be these: *refert, interest* and *est* sett for *pertinet*.

---

[1] ma *canc.* after -ma-   [2] a propyr name of] *repeated*
[3] MS q3

145

FORMULA TEXT AA

Penitet me mei mali regiminis. Me ys þe accusatyve case, for these v verbis *penitet, tedet, m(i)seret, pudet* and *piget* wyll construe w^t the accusatyve case of the thyng þat doth þe dede of þe verbe. *Regiminis* ys the genityve case, for these v verbis will construe w^t the genityve case of the thyng that the dede of the verbe doon for. Versus: 260

> *Penitet et tedet, miseret, pudet et piget*, ista
> Accusatiuos poscunt simul et genitiuos,
> Natura primum sed transicione secundum.

The iij verbis *penitet, pudet* and *piget* make the pretertens *penituit, puduit,* and *piguit*; and these ij verbis *tedet* and *miseret* make *pertesum* and *misertum.* Versus:

> *Penituit, puduit, piguit* sic preteritis dant,
> Sed *tedet, miseret* dant *pertesum*que *misertum.*[1] |

Decet scolares honestos esse. Thys word *scolares* is the accusa\<tyve\> case, for these v verbis *iuuat, decet, delectat,* 270
oportet and *latet* will construe w^t the accusatyve case. Versus:

> Quarto iunge *iuuat, decet* ac *delectat, oportet,*
> Et *latet* illorum numero vult associari.

Interest mea clerici iugiter studere. Mea ys the ablatyve case, for iij verbis *interest, refert* and *est* sett for *pertinet* will construe w^t the genityve case of all casualli wordis outake v pronou(n)s primitivus: *mei, tui, sui, nostri* and *vestri*, in stede whereof we schall take the ablative femynyn gendur of theyr possessyvus, in the which ys vnderstond the genitive case of ther primitivus, as *mei, tui, sui, nostri, vestri*, and *re* or 280
vtilitate be ther substan\<ti\>vus. Versu\<s\>:

> *Inter., refert, est* genitiuis iungere prodest;
> Sed sexto proprie iungas pronomina quinque,
> Nam *Refert nostra* dicas, *Refert* quoque *vestra*.

Obuiabatur mihi a scolare bono socio. Obuiabatur, what parte of reson? A verbe impersonall. Why ys thys mayde by a verbe impersonall? For when I haue the English of a verbe neuter like to a verbe passyve, wher the passyve fayleth I shall take þe verbe impersonall of like tens and mode as the passyve semyth to be and that that semyth to be nominatyve 290
case shall be such case as the verbe will haue after hym. *Bono socio*, what case? Ablatyve case. Why so? For all that longyth to won thyng shall be won case. |

How shall I say in Laten 'The master betyth me'? By this verbe *vapulo: Vapulo a magistro.* Why so? For whan I haue the English of an actyve that shuld be a verbe neuter-passyve, that word that semyth to be the nominatyve

---

[1] *This line precedes the previous line in MS, but is signalled to the present place.*

FORMULA TEXT AA

case shall be tornyd into þe ablatyve case, or ellis into þe
datyve case by thys verbe *nubo*, and that þat semyth to be
accusative case shall be the nominatyve case. Exemplum de   300
nubo: *Soror mea nubet tibi*. And all the verbis that be
conteyned in this verse be verbe neuter-passyvus. Versus:

    Exulo, vapulo, veneo, fio, nubo licet(que)
    Sensum passiui sub voce gerunt aliena.

    How ys a verbe impersonall declyned? In the voyce of
the thryd persone singuler nombyr in euery mode and tens, as
penitet, penitebat, penituit, peniturat, penitebit, penitere.
Yf it be of the passyve voyce as *obuiatur, obuiabar, obuiatum
est* vel *fuit, obuiatum erat* vel *fuerat, obuiabitur, obuiari*.
How many participullus com of a verbe impersonall of the passyve 310
voyce? A participull of the pretertens wonly, as of thys
verbe[1] *opponitur* commyth nominatiuo *hoc*[2] *oppositum*, accusatiuo
hoc oppositum, ablatiuo *ab hoc opposito*, and he hath no mo
case. Versus:

    Inpersonale de se dat participale|
    [Tres quod habet casus primum, quartum quoque sextum.

    VI tens be formyd of the preterperfyt tens of the indicative
mode, of the which iij chaunged *I* into *E* and they be these, the
preterpluperfyt tens of the indicatyve mode, the preterperfyt
tens and the future tens of the coniuntyve mode, as *amaueram*, 320
amau(e)rim, amauero; and iij kepe *I* styll and they be these,
the preterpluperfyt tens of the opta(t)yve mode, the
preterpluperfyt tens of the coniuntyve mode, and the
preterpluperfyt tens of the infinityve mode, as *vtinam
amauissem, cum amauissem* and *amauisse*. Versus:

    -*Ram*, -*rim*, -*ro* mutant *I*, -*sem*, -*sem*, -*se* retinent *I*.

    Explicit.][3]

    'Tres quod habet casus 'primum', quartum quoque sextum.

    VI tens be formyd of þe preterperfyt tens of the indicative
mode of the whych iij change *I* into *E* and they be these, the[4]   330
preterpluperfyt tens of the indicatyue mode, the preterperfyt
tens and the future tens of the coniunctyve mode, as *amaueram*,
amauerim, amauero; and iij kepe *I* styll and they be these,
the preterpluperfyttens of the optatyve mode, the preterpluperfyt
tens of the coniu(n)ct<yve> mode, and the preterpluperfyt tens
of the infenityve mode, as[5] *vtinam amauissem, cum amauisse(m)*
and *amauisse*. Versus:

    -*Ram*, -*rim*, -*ro* mutant *I*; -*sem*, -*sem*, -*se* retinent *I*.
    Explicit.'

[1] *opponitur canc.*   [2] *repeated*   [3] *Paragraph on fol.41*[r]
cancelled and re-written on fol.37[r] *in another hand.*
[4] *preterperfyt canc.*   [5] *vlt(?) canc.*

147

FORMULA TEXT BB

BB. London, British Library, MS Harley 1002, fols.1r-12r

Formula gramaticis hec compilata nouellis
Principium facile[1] congruitatis habet.

Ego sum creatura Dei. This verbe *sum* <i>s the syngler nombyr and[2] the fyrst person, for so is his nominatyfe case *ego*; and every verbe schall accord with his nominatyf case in ij, in nombyr and yn person.

Verbum supposito[3] dic concordare duobus,
Persona, numero; sic tradit regula nobis.

Promus et pincerna debent aulam[4] mundare. This verbe *debent* is the plurell nombyr, for ij nominatyf casys syngler w^t a coniunction copulatyf commyng bitwene woll haue a verbe plurell.   10

Dant tibi plurale verbum iuncti duo recti.

Iohannes cum fratre suo sunt docti scolares. This verbe *sunt* is the plurell nombyr, for a nominatif case singler w^t an ablatif hauyng afore him this preposicion *cum* woll haue a verbe plurell.

Per *cum* sed nunquam per *vel* conceptio fiet.

Ad forum videndum populus currunt. This verbe *currunt* is the plurell nombyr, for a nowne collectyf yn the nominatyf case syngler may haue a verbe plurell, and all nownes conteyned in thies[5] versis folowyng be nownes collectifis.   20

Sunt collectiua *populis, gens, plebs* quoque *turba,*
Turma, phalanx, legio. cuneus sociare memento.

Pater meus et non mater mea est mortuus. This verbe *est* is the syngler nombyr and the iij^d person, for so is his nominatyf case *pater*. For whan I haue a copulatyf commyng w^t a negatyf bitwene ij nominatyf cases singler,[6] then þe verbe,| the adiectyf or the relatif folowyng shall accord w^t the affirmatif as hit is rehercid before.   30

Si rectos binos tibi copula consociabit
Affirmatiue, verbum plurale meabit;
Sique negatiue coniunctio consocietur
Verbum singulare tibi tunc de iure tenetur.

Bonus vir amat Deum super omnia. This adiectif *bonus* is the nominatyf case, masculyn gendyr and the syngler nombyr, for so is his substantyf *vir*; and every adiectyf shall accord w^t his substantyf in gendyr, nombyr and parson.

---

[1] *written over an erased* hec   [2] MS *adds a stroke before* a-
[3] cum <recto> *written above* supposito   [4] MS aulam
[5] v *canc.*   [6] MS *adds* ÷

FORMULA TEXT BB

Cum substantiuis tribus adiectiua locabis:
In casu, genere, numerum simul associabis.   40

Bonum est multum audire et parum dicere. This adiectyf *bonum* is the neuter gendyr substantyfly, for whan I haue an adiectyf sett in a reson w^{t}oute a substantyf to him, hit shal be sett in the neuter gendyr substantyfly:

Mobile prolatum preter fixum sibi certum
In neutro genere fixum solet esse repertum.

Magister et hostiarius sunt assidui in scola. This adiectyf *assidui* is the plurell nombyr, for ij substantyfes syngler w^t a coniunction copulatyf commyng bitwene woll haue an[1] adiectif plurell.   50

Substantiua duo si singula sint tibi iuncta,
Tunc adie(c)tiuum semper plurale requirunt.

Iohannes tu vel uxor tua que est pulcra placuit michi. This relatyf *que* is the femyn gendyr and the syngler nombyr, for whan I haue ij antecedentis|syngler commyng togedyr w^t one of thes coniuntionis[2] '*Et vel, sed, quam, nec, sicut*' and '*nisi*', then the relatyf w^t the verbe folowyng shall accord w^t the later; and þe same strengh hathe somtyme this coniunction *et* as in this ensample: *Pater meus et mater mea est alba.*

Zeuma fit in verbo si plurima clauderis vno: 60
Ympnus Christe tibi, tibi laus, tibi gloria detur.
Vox que subsequitur reddatur proximiori,
Et *vel, sed, quam, nec, sicut, nisi* zeuma notant hec.

Pueri qui assidue laborant pro disciplina habenda cito sunt sapientes. Thys relatyf *qui* is the masculyn gendyr, plurell nombyr and the iij^d person, for so is his antecedent *pueri*; and every relatyf shall accord w^t his antecedent in iij, in gendyr, nombyr and person.

Antecedenti tribus hijs coniunge relatum:
Persona, numero, sit genus hijsque datum.   70

Iohannes et Robertus qui bene addiscunt diligentur a magistro. This relatif *qui* is the plurell nombyr, for ij antecedentis syngler w^t a coniunction copulatif commyng bitwene woll haue a relatif plurell.

Post duo nomina sing(u)la des plurale relatum.

Socius meus quem magister verberauit est valde insolens. This relatyf *quem* is the accusatif case, for when þer commyth a nominatyf case bitwene the relatif and the verbe, then the relatif shal be suche case as the verbe woll haue aftre him; and if ther com no nominatyf case bitwene the relatyf and the   80

---

[1] -n *from* m   [2] n(?) *canc. after* -io-

FORMULA TEXT BB

verbe, then the relatyfe shall be the nomynatyf case to the verbe.|

Si rectus mediat inter verbumque relatum,
Casu quem post se vult verbum pone relatum;
Si nil sit medium tunc recto pone relatum.
Nomina que querunt dictis normam subierunt.

Ibo ad locum qui vel *quod est castrum.* This relatyfe *qui* vel *quod* is the masculyn gendyr and the neuter, for when I haue a relatyf sett bitwene ij nownes substantyfes of dyuers gendyrs perteynyng bothe to one thing hit may accord w^t the fyrst yn gendyr and w^t the later bothe. 90

Quando relat(iu)um generum casus variorum
Inter se claudunt qui rem spectant ad eandem,
Per genus hoc poterit vtrilibet associari:
Est pia stirps Iesse quem Christum dicimus esse.

Ego sum ille qui scripsi vel *qui scripsit in cancellaria domini regis, ideo tu es homo qui scripturam meam vitio dare non debet.* This verbe *scripsi* vel *scripsit* is the fyrst person and the iij^d, for when þis relatyfe *qui, que, quod* folow^t a pronowne of the iij^d person hit may be the iij^d parson or suche parson as is the worde that goith before the pronowne. This 100 verbe *debet* is the iij^d parson, for when the relatif *qui, que, quod* folow^t a nowne of the iij^d parson hit shal be only the iij^d parson.

Quando relatiuum post pronomen recitabis
Persone duplicis sibi verbum consociabis:
Hic *Sum qui scripsi* vel *qui scripsit* bene dixi.

Ecclesia est locus quem Christiani multum visitant. This relatyf *quem* is the masculyn gendyr,| for to the next antecedent shall the relatif be referryd but if the sentence lett hit, as yn this Latyn: *Canis tuus occidit ouem meam quem ego* 110 *interficiam.* This relatif *quem* accordith w^t the fyrst antecedent and not w^t the later bicause the sentence lettith it.

Anglica gens est fortis qui bellicis rebus multum valent. This relatyf *qui* is the plurell nombir, for so is his antecedent *homines* that is vndrestand in *gens*.

Non des ad vocem quandoque relata sed ad rem
Nominis: *Est bona gens, Deus est protector eorum.*
Adiectiua modo poni reperimus eodem:
Pars hominum validi montes et menia scandunt.

Pater meus est vna creaturarum. This nowne partityf *vna* 120 is the femyn gendyr, for every nowne partitif or distributyf shall accord w^t the genytif case that folow^t ⌈yn gendyr⌉¹ yf thay be of one kynd, and if thei be nott he shall accord w^t the substantyf þat goith before.

¹ *added in margin by another hand*

FORMULA TEXT BB

Concordans genere fore plurali genitiuo
Vult partitiuum semper, velut *vna sororum*:
Est vnus florum rosa dicat quisque virorum.

Duo vestrum parum discipline habent saltem ille qui tercius puerorum sedet. This word *vestrum* is the genytyf case, for *duo* is a nowne partytif and may gouern a genytif case bi strength of particion. How many partis of reson may gouern a genytyf case aftre them bi strength of particion? All that bith conteyned in thies versis:

 Cum partitiuis numerum seriemque locabis,
 Vt patet exemplo: *Neuter, duo, quartus eorum*.
 Cum partitiuis pones aduerbia que dant
 Tempora, quanta, loca, duplicesque gradus quibus addes.
 Cum partitiuis pronomina terna locabis, |
 Vt *Volucrum gemit hec, canit ista, tacens manet illa*.

Deus optima rerum laude dignissima creaturarum salamone non excepto, qui erat audacissimus belluarum vel inter belluas. This superlatyf degre *optima* is the femynin gendyr, for every superlatyf degre shall accord in gendyr with the genytyf case that folowith yf the thinges compared be of one kynd; and if thei be not hit shall accord w^t the substantyf that goith before. Exemplum: *Iohannes est stultissimus aucarum vel inter aucas*.

 Omne superlatum partitiue recitatum
 Semper vult genere genitiuo par retinere,
 Vt pateat verum sic, *Est Deus optima rerum*.
 Immo superlatum propria vi quando negatur
 Per genus hoc fixo precedenti famulatur.

Laude is the ablatyf case and is gouerned of this[1] uorde *dignissima* bi strength of the sygnyficacion of his posityf. The positife degre may gouern no case[2] bi the strength of his degr<e>, but bi the vertue of his signyfycacion he may be construed w^t al cases out-take a nominatif case and a vocatyf case. Be it noted that the superlatyf degre may be construed w^t a genytyf case syngler after him (in) iij maner of wises. Fyrst when a nowne collectyf folow^t hym, as *Salomon fuit doctissimus populi*; the second wise by strength of his posityf, as *Iohannes est doctissimus gramatice huius ville*; the iij^{de} maner wise bi this figure metonomia, vt *Pater meus est doctissimus huius ville*, id est *hominum contentorum in hac villa*. | Also the comparatyf and the superlatyfe degre may gouerne al suche casea after them as her positif may while thei be one parti of reson.

 Quam vult structuram gradus offerri sibi primus,
 Illam naturam vult quisque secundus et imus,
 Quod sapias verum dum parte manent in eadem.
 Tu prope siste^3 *forum* recto sermone feretur,

---

[1] of this]repeated   [2] but *canc*.   [3] MS sisto

FORMULA TEXT BB

Sta propiusque thorum nulla racione tuetur.

Ego sum animal racionale et mortale. What case is *animal*? The nominatif case, for *sum, es, fui* is a verbe substantife and woll copill like case; and all verbis conteyned in thies versis folowyng bithe verbys substantifis.

Sum substantiuum proprie tibi dicitur vnum,
Sto, sisto, maneo quasisubstantiua vocantur,
Et que consimule sensum retinere probantur;
Ast adiectiua tibi cetera verba notantur.   *180*

Ego sedeo tristis qui vocor Iohannes. This word *tristis* is the nominatyf case, for all verbis that betoken mevyng, rest or semyng, and all verbis neutro-passyfys and passifis, hathe strengh to copill like cases.

Copula redditur hijs quibus apparentia detur,
Motus siue quies sub eadem lege regetur.
Neutro-passiua sic passio queque locetur
Apparet, graditur, sto, reddor, vapulo, fio.

Iohannes, what case? The nominatyf case, for *vocor, -aris* is a verbe vocatyf and woll copill like case; and all verbis þat *190*
be conteyned in thies versis folowyng be verbis vocatyfis.

Quinque vocatiua dicas tantummodo verba.
Nominor, appellor, sic *nuncupor*, addito *dicor*
Et *vocor*: hec simules semper poscunt sibi casus.

Iohannes non laudo te; quamuis sis doctus, osi esses virtuosus. This verbe *sis* is the coniunctif mode, for all wordis conteyned in this versis folowyng wol serue to the conyunctyf mode.

Si, quamuis, quamquam, tam(et)si, licet atque *priusquam,
Antequam, an, donec, vt, postquam* siue *quousque*,   *200*
Cum, nisi, quin,[1] *acsi, quo* coniungunt tibi recte.
Indicat et *quando, dum*, sicut cetera plura.

Esses is the optatyf mode, for all wordis conteyned in þis verse folowyng woll serue to the optatif mode.

Des optatiuis *vtinam, ne, quatinus, osi.*

Ego nobilis viri filius spretus sum iniuste de te.
Nobilis viri is the genytif case, for 'of' after a nown substantif, verbe substantif, nowne partitif or distributyf, the comparatif degre or the superlatif degre, is signe of the genytif case. What case is *te*? The ablatif case, for 'of'   *210*
after a propre name, nown adiectif, verbe, participull, gerundif or supyn is syne of the ablatif case w^t a preposicion.

---

[1] c *canc.*

FORMULA TEXT BB

Post proprium nomen, post mobile, post quoque verbum
Postque gerundiuum post participansque supinum
Si veniat sensus genitiui, iungito sexto.
Cum reliquis sextum non iungas sed genitiuum.

Dominor huius ville abstinens irarum. *Huius ville* is the genytyf case, for all verbis that bith conteyned in þis versis folowyng wol be construed w^t a genytyf case.

Abstineo, dominor, miserere cum genitiuo 220
Iunges: *Abstineo panis, Misere dolentis,*
Dominor et ville bonus heres iure parentis.

Irarum is the genytif case, for participuls, gerundifis and| supyns woll gouern suche case as the verbis þat they commyth of.

Iudex quoscumque serie casus imitatur,
Illos totius verbi flexus comitatur.
Iunge gerundiua cum participante, supina.

Robertus eget diuine gracie, diuinam graciam vel *diuina gracia.* What case is *diuine gracie, -am graciam* vel *diuina gracia*? The genytif, the accusatif and the ablatif, for this 230
ij verbis *egeo, -es* and *indigeo, -es* wol be construed w^t a genytif case, accusatif case and an ablatif case.

Des quartis, sextis *eget, indiget,* et genitiuis,
Vt noscas verum *Res indigeo* quoque *rerum;*
Indigeo rem, re, dic *Egeoque rei.*

Istud doleum est plenum vini vel *vino. Vini* vel *vino* is the genytif case and the ablatif, for all wordes that betoken fulnesse or emptynesse, worthinesse or vnworthinesse, wol be construed w^t a genytif case and an ablatif case.

Que plenum signant vel que vacuata figurant, 240
Hec ablatiuis poteris dare vel genitiuis:
Vini vel *vino duo dolea plena videto.*
Dignus et *indignus* similis[1] structura reposcit.

Obuiemus regi redeunti ad ciuitatem. This word *regi* is the datif case, for all verbis in thes verses folowyng wol be construed w^t a datif case.

Obuio, parco, placet, noceo, respondeo, seruit,
Precipit, opponit coniungimus ista datiuis.
Supplicat,[2] ⌈*arridet*⌉,[3] *fauet, heret* et *invidet,* illis
Subuenit addatur, *succurrit, propiciatur,* 250
Et multo plura quam sunt hic noscere cura.|

Mos est mihi cure. Michi[4] is the datif case and *cure* is the datyf case, for this verbe *sum, es, fui* wol be constred

---

[1] MS simulus [2] intersum canc.
[3] added in margin by another hand [4] -i canc.

FORMULA TEXT BB

w^t a dobill datif case.

Sum persepe duos regit adquirendo datiuos:
Hec michi sunt lucro, vobis sunt cetera dampno.

Iohannes fractus manicam erubescit versare inter proceres.
This word *manicam* is the accusatif case, for whan this syne
'the' commyth before any part of the body and folow^t a nown
adiectif, verbe neuter or passif or any of thair participuls,   260
the same part of the body shal be sett yn the accusatif case
bi this figure sinotiges.

Adiectiua regunt passiuaque verbaque neutra
Accusatiuos, per sinotigen sibi iunctos,
Cum partis toti tribuuntur proprietates.
Aut e conuerso mox hinc exempla videto:
Alba comas dolet Anna caput, crus frangitur illa.
Participans iunges, vt *Femina compta capillos.*

Peto Deum veniam omnium peccatorum meorum. What case is
Deum? The accusatif case. What case is *veniam*? The   270
accusatif case, for the verbis in thes versis folowyng wol be
construed w^t ij accusatif cases and the passifis of þem w^t one,
that is the later.

*Postulo, posco, peto, doceo, rogo, flagito, celo,
Exuo* cum *vestit, monet, induo, calceo, cingo,
Accusatiuos geminos hec verba requirunt
Et cum passiuis postremus iungitur horum.*

Ecce hominem qui spretor[1] *Dei ad interiora*[2] *confidit in arcu
et sagittis*[3] *sua.* This word *hominem* is the accusatif case, for
all aduerbis conteyned in this lesson of the 'Donett', 'Da   280
demonstrandi, et cetera', wol be construed w^t a nominatif case
and an accusatif by vndrestandyng of a verbe, as *Ecce hominem*,
here|is vndirstand *vide* vel *percipe*; *Ecce homo*, here is
vndirstond *stat* vel *currit* or other like.

Ecce vir, Ecce virum dices, intellige verbum
A quo tam rectus quam quartus sit tibi rectus.

Vtor rubio capicio. Capicio is the ablatif case, for all
verbis conteyned in thes versis folowyng woll be construed w^t
an ablatif case.

Vescitur et *fruitur, caret, vtitur* atque *potitur,*   290
Hec ablatiuos transicione regunt;
Fungor iungatur quod eodem more gubernat.

Here is difference bitwene *fruor, -ris, pocior, -ris* vel *-iris,
vtor, -ris* and *fungor, -ris.*

Diuinis fruimur exoptatisque potimur,

[1] MS (?) sprete   [2] MS (?) intorio   [3] MS sagittus

FORMULA TEXT BB

Vtimur vtilibus, fungimur officijs.

Currit in campum Iohannes in quo pueri ludunt. This word *campum* is the accusatif case, for 'yn' w^t 'to' is sine of þe accusatif case and 'yn' w^{t}out 'to' is syne of þe ablatif case.

'Into' vult quartum, sine 'to' vult ponere sextum.   *300*
In campo curro si sis, bene dicis, in illo;
Si sis^1 exterius in campum sit tibi cursus.

Latrones spoliauerunt me auro et argento. *Auro* is the ablatif case, for this ij verbis *priuo, -as* and *spolio, -as* wol be construed w^t an accusatif case betokennyng him that þe good is taken fro and w^t an ablatif case betokenyng the good whiche is taken away. *Gramatica est difficilis scitu.* This word *scitu* is the latre supyn, for whan I haue an Englissh of þe ynfynytif mode commyng after a nown adiectif endyng in *-ilis* or in *-bilis* hit schal be sett in the later supyn.   *310*

Ista virga est precise tribus pedibus longa nec vno pollice longior.| *Vno pollice* is the ablatif case, for euery comparatif degre betokennyng excedyng may gouern an ablatif case betokenyng the excesse.

Est ablatiuus demonstrans quantus habetur
Excessus, regit hunc excessum diccio signans:
Hoc lignum digitis est maius quatuor illis.

Tribus pedibus is the ablatif case, for euery adiectif betokenyng mesure may gouern an ablatif case.

Mobile mensuram designans addito sexto: *320*
Lignum sex pedibus longum latumque duobus.

Die sabbati emi michi togam forcipibus aptatam ex panno albo. What case is *die sabbati*? The ablatyf case, for all that betoken lengh, mesure, mater, price, tyme or space shal be sett yn the ablatif case.

Verbum materiam, causam, spacium preciumve
Aut tempus signans ablatiuos regit horum
Que predicta notant, vt *Frenum fabrica here;*
Ista pudore tacet; Stadijs sex distat ab vrbe;
Nocte morans tota; Panem nummis tribus emi.   *330*
Cedo te baculo, sic instrumenta notato.

Ego mallem vinum ceruisia. This word *ceruisia* is the ablatif case, for euery verbe hauyng in hymself a comparatif degre may gouern an ablatif case, and such be thies folowyng:

Prefero cum presto, malo coniungito sexto
In se quando gradum includunt comparatiuum:
Malo merum selia, panem quoque prefero petra.

^{1} MS *adds* et

FORMULA TEXT BB

Preualet addatur, *preponderat* associatur,
Et quamuis tale quod comparat associabis.

Magistro docente pueri proficiunt et vacant discipline sue. 340
Magistro is the ablatif case absolute, for|whan I haue a short
hangyng reson of a nown and a participle or a pronown and a
participle and no word sett forth nor undirstond in the reson
wherof he may be gouerned, hit shal be sett yn the ablatif case
absolute w^{t}out any preposicion. How many maner of wise may
the ablatif case absolute be expound? II maner of wise, bi
dum and bi *cum*. Bi *dum* as *Me sedente tu stetisti*, id est, *Dum
ego sedi tu stetisti*; bi *cum* as *Augusto imperatore Alexandria
domita est*, id est, *Cum Augustus erat imperator Alexandria
domita est*. 350

Per *dum* vel per *cum* sexto resolucio detur,
Huius namque rei Precianus testis habetur.

How many maner of wise may[1] a participle be sett in the ablatif
case absolute w^{t}oute any nown or pronown to him? II maner of
wise. First a participle of a verbe ynpersonell of the
passif voice, as *Michi opposito fratri tuo opponetur*; the
second wise the participle of a verbe of except action as
Pluuiam pluente non exeam hostium.

*Sanctum est diligere omnes sed sum maxime dilecturus eos
qui michi prosunt.* What partie of reson is *dilecturus*? A 360
participull of the furst future, for whan I haue an Englissh
of the infynytif mode commyng after this verbe *sum*, *es*, *fui*,
if it be of the actif voice I shall haue a participle of the
furst future, and if it be of the passif voice I shall haue a
participle of the later future in *-dus*. Exemplum: *Ego sum
amandus a magistro*. And if the nominatif case goyng before
this verbe *sum*, *es*, *fui* be the neuter gendyr substantyfly than
I shall take the ynfynytif mode and not the participle, as thus:
Durum est contra stimulum calcitrare.|

In *-rus* participans post *sum* da si 'to' sequatur; 370
In *-dus* participans post *sum* si 'to be' sequatur.

And when the participle faylith I shall take this relatif *qui*,
que, *quod* and a like tens of the verbe that the participle shuld
com of. Exemplum: 'I am to forsake my synnes whiche I haue
offendid God yn', *Sum qui respuam peccata mea quibus Deum offendi*.

Si sit participans fallens velut arte probatur,
Tempus persimule verbi tunc proficiatur,
Vt *Sum qui viuam* dicetur, *Sumque studebo*.
Et sic participii defectum rite replebo.

And if the Englissh of a participle that lackyth shuld be 380
sett in the ablatif case absolute then I shall take a
circumlocucion w^t a conuenyent significacion. Exemplum:

---

[1] the ablatif case absolute *canc*.

FORMULA TEXT BB

'This lesson i-studid[1] I am to studi a nother.' *Ista leccione per studium capta sum qui studebo aliam.*

Iohannes lesit socium[2] suum pro quo a magistro vapulabit. This word *Iohannes* is the iij^d person,[3] for euery nown and euery pronown and euery participle is the iij^d person, owt-take *ego* and *nos*, *tu* and *vos* w^t thaire obliquis and all vocatif cases.

Terne persone generaliter omnis habetur
Rectus, sed demas pronomina quatuor inde,   390
Sunt *ego*, *nos* prime, *tu*, *vos* quoque nempe secunde.

Ego et frater meus ibimus iantatum. This word *ibimus* is the[4] first person, for the first person is worthier then the second or the iij^d and conceyvith thaym bothe.

Prima duas alias recipit sed non vice versa:
Tu fraterque datis et honorem suscipiatis.

Frater meus et soror mea sunt assidui in domo patris mei. This adiectyf *assidui* is the masculyn gendyr, for the masculyn gendyr is more worthi the femynin or the neuter.

Mas. sibi femineum sed non fe. concipit illum.   400
Neutrum fe. sibi mas. si bene concipias.

How many endyngys of gerundifis be ther? III: -*di*, -*do* and -*dum*. How many endyngis of supyns be ther? II: -*tum* and -*tu*, as *doctum*, *doctu*, or -*sum* and -*su*, as *visum*, *visu*.

-*Tum*, -*tu* mas. quarte, -*di*, -*do*, -*dum* neutra secunde;
-*Tum*, -*tu* motiuis, -*do*, -*dum* da prepositiuis,
Cuncta gerundiua dicas fore singula neutra,
Que genito, quarto, sexto tantummodo flecto.

Whan shall I haue a gerundif in -*di* in comyn speche?
When I haue an Englissh of the infynitif mode commyng after   410
a nown substantif, as þis: *hora, causa, voluntas, tempus, desiderium* and other like, than shall I haue a gerundif in -*di*.
Exemplum: *Missa finita tempus est dissoluendi ieiunium nostrum. Papa habet potestatem absoluendi Christianos.*

Gracia, pax, tempus, coniungimus ista *voluntas.*
Rite gerundiuum casus poscunt genitiui.

Whan shall I haue a gerundif in -*do* in comyn speche?
II maner of wise. Furst whan this Englissh 'yn' or 'of' commyth before a participle of the presentens, than shall I haue a gerundif in -*do* w^t this preposicion *in*. Exemplum: 420
'Yn fightyng meny men bith wounded'. *In dimicando multi homines sunt vulnerati.* The second maner of wise whan the

---

[1] MS i'studid *(apostrophe in MS)*   [2] soi *canc.*
[3] outtake Ego and nos *canc*; the 3 person added in margin by another hand   [4] iij^d *canc.*

FORMULA TEXT BB

Englissh of a participull of the presentens folow^t a nown
adiectif, than may I chese whe þer I woll haue a gerundif in
-do or a participull of the precentence. Exemplum: *Magister
est assiduus in scola informans* vel *informando scolares suos.*

When schall I haue a gerundif in -*dum*? II maner of wise.
Fyrst when the Englissh of the infinitif mode commyth yn a reson
and tellith the cause of the reson, then I|haue a gerundif
in -*dum* w^t this preposicion *ad*. Exemplum: *Viri vadunt ad*   430
bellum ad dimicandum. Te second wise whan the Englissh of the
ynfynytif mode commyth after this verbe *sum*, *es*, *fui* and no
nominatif case to hym, then shall I haue a gerundif in -*dum*.
Exemplum: *Resistendum est inimicis nostris pugnantibus contra nos.*

Frigidus in campus cantando rumpitur anguis. This word
cantando is of the passif significacion for al gerundifis
commyng of verbis betokenyng doyng bith of þe actif voice and
the passif significacion.

 Actum siue pati signare gerundia possunt
 Si tamen a verbis veniant signantibus actum: 440
 Hec delectatur inspectando quasi pulcra.

Intendo ire oppositum scolaribus. This word *oppositum*
is the first supyn, for whan I haue an Englissh of the
ynfynytif mode commyng after a verbe betokenyng mevyng to a
place where anything is done or to be done it shal be sett in
the fyrst supyn. Exemplum: *Vado lectum libros. Venio lectu
libros.* This word *lectu* is the later supyn, for whan I haue
an Englissh of the ynfynytif mode commyng after a verbe
betokenyng mevyng from a place than shall I haue the later supyn.

 Post motus verbum bene pones vtrumque supinum,   450
 Vt *Vado lectum, dormitum* siue *comestum*;
 Deque loco signans postremum iunge supinum,
 Vt *Venio lectu, dormitu* siue *comestu.*
 Ast infinitum si non signet tibi motum,
 Vt *Cupio legere, Volo ludere, Spero docere.*

And whan I haue an Englissh of þe ynfinytif mode þat shuld be
sett yn the furst supyn, where þe supyn faileth I shal take
þis nown *locus* w^t this preposicion *ad* and þe future tens of
the verbe that þe supyn shuld com of. Exemplum: 'I go to
lerne gramer', *Vado ad locum vbi addiscam gramaticam.*| And when 460
I haue an Englissh of the ynfynytif mode that shuld be sett in
the later supyn, where the supyn fayleth I shall take this nown
locus w^t þis preposicion *a* and the future tens of the verbe þat
the supyn shuld com of w^t this aduerbe *vbi*. Exemplum: 'I com
from lernyng gramer', *Venio a loco vbi addidici gramaticam.*

Placet michi quod ibimus lusum. This word *placet* is a
verbe ympersonell of the actif voice, for he hath neyther
nombyr ne parson nor no nomynatif case and is declyned in the
voice of the iij^d person and singler nombyr and commeth w^t
one of thes ij synes 'it' or 'me', as 'it plesith', 'me louyth'. 470

FORMULA TEXT BB

How many verbis ynpersonellis be ther? II. Which ij?
A verbe ynpersonell of the actif voice and a verbe ynpersonell
of the passif voice. How knos a verbe ynpersonell of the actif
voice? For he is declyned in the iij^d person singler nombyr,
every word and euery tens like to a verbe actif, and this is he
declyned: *iuuat, -bat, -iuuit, -rat, -bit, -are, -di, -do,
-dum*, supinis caret, *iuuans*. Whi is *iuuat* so declyned? For
he bigynnyth at the present tence, singler nombyr and the iij^d
parson, then to þe preterynperfit tence, and to þe preterperfit
tence, and to þe preterpluperfit tence, and to þe future tens,   480
then to the infynytif mode, and then to the gerundifis, and to
þe participull of þe presentence. How is *iuuat* formed?
Indicatiuo modo *iuuat*, preterito inperfecto *-abat*, preterito
perfecto *iuuit*, preterito plusquamperfecto *iuuerat*, futuro *-bit*;
imperatiuo modo *iuuet*, futuro *iuuato*; optatiuo modo *vtinam
-aret*, preterito perfecto et plusquamperfecto *vtinam iuuisset*,
futuro *vtinam iuuet*, coniunctiuo modo *cum sic*, preterito
inperfecto *cum -aret*, preterito^1 perfecto *cum iuuerit*, preterito
plusquamperfecto *cum iuuisset*, futuro *cum iuuerit*; infinitiuo
modo *-are*; gerundia vel participalia verba sunt hec *-di, -do,* 490
-dum; supinis caret. Vnicum participium trahitur ab hoc
verbo inpersonali presentis temporis, tantum *iuuans*. |

How many participuls commyth of a verbe ynpersonell of
the actyf voyce? One, of the present tens only, as of
penitet commyth *penitens*, out-take ij verbis ynpersonellis,
scilicet *tedet* and *miseret*, of whom commyth ij participuls,
as of *tedet* commyth *tedens* and *pertesum* and of *miseret* commyth
miserens and *misertum*.

Tedet pertesum flectat, *miseretque misertum*.
Actiue vocis reliquis non attribuatur   500
Preteritum tale, Precianus testificatur.

W^t what case woll all verbys ynpersonellis of the actif
voice be construed? W^t a datif case, out-take xiij of the
whiche v wol be construed w^t an accusatif case and a genytif
case, scilicet *penitet, tedet, miseret, pudet* and *piget*; and
v wol be construed w^t an accusatif case, scilicet *decet, dilectat,
oportet, iuuat*^{2} and *latet*; and iij with a genytif case and an
ablatif case, scilicet *interest, refert* and *est* sett for *pertinet*.

Penitet me tui mali regiminis. Me is the accusatif case,
for this v verbis *penitet, tedet, miseret, pudet* and *piget* wol 510
be construed w^t an accusatif case of the thing that doith the
dede of the verbe. *Mali regiminis* is the genytif case, for it
is the thyng that the dede of the verbe is done for.

Penitet et *tedet, miseret, pudet* et *piget*, ista
Accusatiuos poscunt simul et genetiuos,
Natura primum sed transicione secundum.

This iij verbis *penitet, pudet* and *piget* makith *penituit,*

^{1} plusquam *canc.* ^{2} de *canc.*

159

FORMULA TEXT BB

puduit and *piguit*,¹ but *tedet* and *miseret* makith *pertesum* and *misertum* yn the preterperfitens.

Penituit, puduit, piguit sic preteritis dant,   520
Sed tedet, miseret dant pertesumque misertum.

Decet scolares esse honestos. This word *scolares* is the accusatif case, for this v verbis *iuuat, decet, dilectat,| oportet* and *latet* wol be construed w^t an accussatif case.

Quarto iunge iuuat, decet ac dilectat, oportet,
Et latet illorum numero vult associari.

Here is difference whan *iuuat* is a verbe personell and when he is a verbe ynpersonell.

Est iuuat actiuum dilectat et auxiliatur,
Inpersonale iuuat est dilectat vbique.   530

Interest mea clerici iugiter studere. Mea is the ablatif case, for thes iij verbis *interest, refert* and *est* sett for *pertinet* wol be construyd w^t a genytif case of all casuali wordis, out-take v pronownys prymytifis, scilicet *mei, tui, sui, nostri* and *vestri*, in stede of whom I shall take the ablatif case syngler nombyr² and femynin gendyr of ther possessifis, scilicet *mea, tua, sua, nostra* and *vestra*, and thes ij wordis *re* vel *vtilitate* shal be vndrestand for thayr substantifis.

Inter.,³ refert,⁴ est genitiuis iungere prodest,
Sed sexto proprie iungas pronomina quinque,   540
Nam refert nostra dicas, refert quoque vestra.

Clerici: what case? The genitif case, for yn euery nown possessif⁵ or pronown possessif is vndrestond the genytif case of his primatyf, to the whiche the adiectif or the relatif folowyng shal be referrid, as *Virga magistralis docentis nos gramaticam intulit nobis timorem magnum.*

In possessiuo possessor clausus habetur
Rite relatiuum cui⁶ per normam varietur,
Ast adiectiua tibi qualificare videntur,
Vt Mea defuncti da molliter ossa cubare.   550

How knos a verbe ynpersonell of the passif voice? For he endith in *-r*, as *statur*, and this is he declyned: *obuiatur, -batur, -atum est* vel *fuit, -atum erat* vel *fuerat, -bitur, -ari, -di, -do, -dum*, supinis caret, *obuiatum*. How is he formyd?| Indicatiuo modo *obuiatur*, preterito inperfecto *obuiabatur*,⁷ preterito perfecto *-atum est* vel *fuit*, preterito plusquamperfecto *-atum erat* vel *fuerat*, futuro *obuiabitur*; imperatiuo modo *obuietur*, futuro *obuiator*, optatiuo modo *vtinam -aretur*, preterito perfecto et plusquamperfecto *vtinam -atum*

¹ and pig *canc.*   ² -r from i   ³ MS interest
⁴ MS *adds* et   ⁵ is *canc.*   ⁶ -a *canc.*   ⁷ MS obuiabitur

FORMULA TEXT BB

esset vel *fuisset*, futuro *vtinam obuietur*; coniu(n)ctiuo modo   560
cum sic, preterito inperfecto *cum -aretur*, preterito perfecto
cum -atum sit vel *fuerit*, preterito plusquamperfecto *cum -atum
esset* vel *fuisset*, futuro *cum -atum erit* vel *fuerit*; infinitiuo
modo *obuiari* et cetera. How many participuls commyth of a
verbe ynpersonell of þe passif voice? One, of the pretertens
only, as of *opponitur* commyth nominatiuo *hoc oppositum*,[1]
accusatiuo *hoc oppositum*, ablatiuo *ab hoc opposito*.

    Obuiatur michi a scolari bono socio. What part of reson
is *obuiatur*? A verbe ynpersonell of the passif voice like mode
and like tens that the passif semyth to be. For whan I haue an   570
Englissh of a verbe passif that shuld com of a verbe neuter of
whom none commyth, than I shall take a verbe ynpersonell of like
mode and like tens that the passif semyth to be and that that
semyth to be the nominatif case shal be such case as the verbe
ynpersonell woll haue after him.

    Verbum passiue si non vsu retinetur
    Inpersonale sensum spoliare videtur,
    Vt *michi seruitur* per *seruior* hoc reperitur.

Bono socio, what case? The ablatif case, for so is the word
that he longith to, *scolari*, and all that longith to one thing   580
shal be putt ynto one case.

    Ad precedentem vocem si vox referatur,
    Prime naturam vox illa sequens imitatur.

Of what verbis commyth verbis ynpersonellis? Of verbis[2]
actifis and neuters betokenyng doyng.

    Semper ab actiuis inpersonale creatur|
    Vel neutris illis quibus actio significatur.

    How shall I say in Latyn 'The master betyth me'? Bi this
verbe *vapulo*, as *Ego vapulo a magistro*, for whan I haue an
Englissh to be made yn Latyn by a verbe neuter-passif, that   590
whiche semyth to be the[3] accusatif case shal be the nomynatif
case to the verbe, and that whiche semith to be the nominatif
case shal be the ablatif case w^t a preposicion, or ellis the
datif case w^t this verbe *nubo, -bis*. Exemplum: 'Þu shalt
wed my suster', *Soror mea tibi nubet*.

    Neutris[4] passiuis paciens vnit sibi rectum,
    Ponitur in sexto sed agens cum prepositiuo;
    Nubo valet sed agens coniungere iure datiuo.

All verbis in this versis folowyng bith verbis neutro-passifis:

    *Exulo, vapulo, veneo, fio, nubo, licet*que[5]   600

---

[1] h *canc.*   [2] whereof com̄eth verbis Impersonellis
added in margin by another hand   [3] nominatif case *canc.*
[4] Nu *canc.* before Neutris   [5] MS liceoque

FORMULA TEXT BB

Sensum passiui sub voce gerunt aliena.

How many tens be formyd of the preterperfit tens of the yndicatif mode? VI. Which vj? The preterpluperfitens of same mode, the preterperfitt and the preterpluperfit tens of the optatif mode, the preterperfit tens and the preterpluperfit tens and the future tens of the coniunctif mode, and the[1] preterperfit tens and the preterpluperfit tens of the ynfynytif mode. How many changith *I* into *E* and how many kepith *I* still? III changith *I* into *E* and iij kepith *I* still. Which iij changith *I* into *E*? The preterpluperfit   610 tens of the indicatif mode, as *amaui*, change *I* into *E* and put to *-ram* and it wol be *amaueram*; the preterperfit tens of the coniunctif mode, as *amaui*, chang *I* into *E* and put to *-rim* and it wol be *amauerim*; and the future tens of the[2] same coniunctif mode, as *amaui*, change *I* into *E* and put to *-ro* and it wol be *amauero*.| Whiche iij kepith *I* still? The preterperfitt and preterpluperfit tens of the optatif mode and the preterpluperfit tens of the coniunnctif mode, as *amaui* put to *S* and *-sem* and it wol be *amauissem*; and the preterperfitt and[3] preterpluperfit tens of the ynfynytif mode, as *amaui*, put   620 to *S* and *-se* and it wol be *amauisse*.

-Ram, *-rim*, *-ro* mutant *I*, *-sem*, *-sem*, *-se* retinent *I*.

Whan I haue an Englissh of a propyr name of a town, citie or place sympull not compound commyng after a verbe betokenyng duellyng yn a place or beyng at a place, if it be the furst declenson or[4] the second and the singler nombyr it shal be sett yn the genytif case aduerbially w^toute a preposicion, but if it be the third declenson and the syngler nombyr or the plurell nombyr whatsoeuyr declenson it be, hit shal be sett in the ablatif case aduerbially w^tout a preposicion. Exemplum: *Ego*   630 *moror Eboraci qui quondam moratus sum Oxonie*. And thes iiij nownes *rus*, *domus*, *humus* and *milicia* folow^t the same rule. And if the propyr name be vndeclyned hit may be sett yn the genytif case or yn the ablatif case yndifferently. Exemplum: *Rex est Sarum bone ciuitatis* vel *bona ciuitate*.

Nomina que propria sunt prime siue secunde
Inque loco si sint signantia singula tantum
In genitis pones; sed sextis absque regente
Nomina que terne sunt aut pluralia prime.

Rex vadit Eboracum. What case is *Eboracum*? The accusatif   640 case, for whan I haue a propir name of a town, citie or place sympull not compound commyng after a verbe participull, gerundif or supyn betokenyng mevyng or steryng to a place of whatsoeuyr declenson or nombyr it be,| hit shal be sett in the accusatif case aduerbially w^tout a preposicion, and thes iiij nownes *rus*, *domus*, et cetera vt supra. *Rex venit Londonijs*. What case is *Londonijs*? The ablatif case, for whan I haue a

[1] prer *canc.*   [2] st(?) *canc.*   [3] prepli *canc.*
[4] from and

FORMULA TEXT BB

propyr name of a town, cite or place simpull not compound
commyng after a verbe, gerundif or supyn betokenyng mevyng or
steryng from a place, bi a place or thorgh a place, whatsoeuyr   650
declenson or nombyr it be, hit shal be sett in the ablatif case
aduerbially w^{t}oute a preposicion, and thes iiij nownes *rus*,
domus, *humus* et *milicia* folow^t þe same rule.

> Nomina que propria designant ad loca semper[1]
> Accusatiuis bene pones absque regente;
> Deque loco fruimur ablatiuis repete te:[2]
> *Londonijs vixi*, simul *Oxonie*[3] bene dixi,
> Atque *Beuerlaco Romam vult pergere draco*;
> *Milicie rure*que *domi residebis humi*que.

Explicit

---

[1] MS *adds* In genitis pones sed *which should be canc*.
[2] repete te] MS repetente   [3] -e *from* o

FORMULA TEXT CC

CC. Oxford, Bodleian Library, MS Rawl. D.328, fols.76ʳ-79ᵛ and 83ᵛ-89ʳ

Formula gramaticis hec compulata nouellis
Principium facile congruitatis habet.

Ego sum creatura Dei. Thys verbe *sum* is þe singuler number and þe firste person, for so is his nominatiue case *ego*, and þe verbe shall haue number and person of þe¹ nominatiue case. Vnde versus:

    Verbum supposito dic concordare duobus:
    Persona, numero; sic tradit regula nobis.

Promus et pincerna debent aulam mundare. Þis verbe *debent* is þe plu⸀r⸀ell number, for ij nominatiue case   *10* singuler wᵗ and *et* coniuncion copulatiue wyll haue a verbe plurell. Vnde ver<sus>:

    Dant tibi plurale verbum iun(c)ti duo recti.

Pater meus et non mea mater est mortuus. This verbe *est* ys þe singuler number, for when y haue a copulatyff wᵗ an negatiue comyth betwen ij nominatiue case singler, þe verbe and þe adiectiue schall acorde wᵗ þe first nominatiue case² as hit ys schayd before; and yff þer come an *et* before þe firste nominatiue case and a noþer betwne than þe verbe schall be singuler number as ⸀Et⸀ *Iohannes et Robertus currit.*   *20* Vnde versus:

    Si rectos binos³ tibi copula consociabit
    Afirmatiue, verbum plurale meabit.
    Sique⁴ negatiue coniuncio consocietur
    Verbum singulare tibi tunc de iure tenetur.
    Et Petrus et Thomas currit ⸀sic⸀ rite profatur.|

Bonus vir amat Deum super omnia. Thys adiectiue *bonus* ys þe masculyn gender and singulere⁵ number and þe nominatiue case, for so ys þe substantiue *vir*, and euery adiectiue schall acorde wᵗ his substantiue in case, gender and number. Vnde   *30* versus:

    Cum substantiuis tribus adiectiua locabis,
    In casu, genere, numerum simul associabis.

V(i)num est bonus potus. What case, gender and number ys þe adiectiue *bonus*? Nominatiue case, synguler number and masculyn gender. Why so? For so ys þe substantiue. Which ys þat? *Potus.* Why ra<d>er acordyth þis adiectiue *bonus* wyth *potus* then wyth *vinum*? For by my rule whan an adiectiue þat ys not a participull ys set betwene ij substantiuis of

---

¹ firste *canc.*   ² MS *adds and* a noþer betwene
³ -o- *from* e   ⁴ -que] MS q3 *from* que
⁵ v *canc.*

164

FORMULA TEXT CC

dyuerse gender pertenyng to þe same þyng þe adiectiue schall 40
acorde yn case, gender and number whyth þe later substantiue,
vt *Homo est racionabile animal*; and yf he be a participyll
adiectiue hit schall acorde w[t] þat first substantiue þat
goyth before: *Deus factus est refugium pauperibus*. Vnde
versus:

    Inter fixa duo si mobile nomen habetur
    Fixo quod sequitur semper conforme tenetur,
    Sicut *Bos animal album* non *albus* habetur;
    Si sit participans precedenti famuletur:
    Est[1] *aqua facta merum* exemplum stare notetur.| 50

Opinio tamen quorumdam quod quando adiectiuum pono inter duo
substantiua diuersorum generum quorum primum[2] significat materiam
et secundum materiatum tunc illud adiectiuum conformabit in
genere diccioni significanti materiatum et non diccioni
significant(i) materiam, qu(i)a materiatum est dign(i)us sua
materia. Vnde versus:

    Dic[3] linpham vinum subtilius esse paratum:
    Materiam[4] quoniam superabit materiatum.

    Bonum est multum audire et modicum dicere. Þe adiectiue
bonum ys þe neuter gender substantiuele, fore[5] when a adiectiue 60
ys y-set yn a reson w[t]out eny substantiue to hym he schall be
set yn neuter gender leke a substantiue.

    Mobile prolatum preter fixum sibi certum
    In neutro genere sic tripliciter var⌈i⌉abit.

Qu⌈o⌉t[6] modis potest nomen positum in neutro genere
substantiuate resolui?[7] Tribus[8] modis. Quibus? Primo
modo per hoc nomen *res*: *Bonum est*, id est *bona res*; et
secundo modo per hoc nomen *pars, partis*, vt *Habeo modicum vini*,
id est *modicum partem vini*; tercio modo per nomen abstractum
vt *Desc(e)ndamus in planum*, id est *in planicie*. Vnde versus: 70

    Nam substantiue[9] tibi quamuis mobile stabit
    In neutro genere sic tripliciter variabit.
    Multum: *pars multa*, veluti Petrus memorab<it>;
    Planum: *planicies*; *album*: *res alba* vocatur.

Quocienscumque adiectiuum vel relatiuum ponitur in neut<ro>|
genere substantiuate[10] tunc assumere sibi poterit substantiuum
(c)uiuscumque gen(er)is, vt *Vir est bonum*, *Mulier est bonum*,
Video mulierem quod tu amas, *Video magistrum quod tu vides*.
Vnde loquitur in Theodolo, vnde versus:

    Dulce viro mulier pratis virentibus imber. 80

[1] MS Eest   [2] MS primam   [3] linfa *canc.*
[4] g *canc.*   [5] substantiuele, fore]MS substantiue before
[6] MS Ou⌈o⌉t   [7] MS resoluī   [8] MS 3dis
[9] MS substantiui(?)   [10] MS substantiuato

165

FORMULA TEXT CC

Magister et hostiarius sunt assiduj in scola. Þis adiectiue *assiduj* ys þe plurell number, for ij substantiuis singler w^t an *et* coniuncioon betwene wyll haue and adiectiue plurell. Vnde versus:

Substantiua duo si singula sint tibi iuncta
Tunc adiectiuum semper plurale requirunt.

Puer qui iugiter[1] *laborat addiscet cito gramaticam.* Þis relatiue *qui* ys þe singuler number and þe iij^{de} person for so ys þe antecedens *puer*, for euery relatiue schall acorde w^t his antecedens in gender, number and person. Vnde versus: 90

Antecedenti tribus hiis coniunge relatum.
Persona, numero; sic genus hiisque datum.

Iohannes et Robar(t) ⸢us⸣ *qui bene addiscunt a magistro diligentur.* Þis relatiue *qui* ys þe plurell number, for ij antecedens singuler w^t an *et* coniunccion copulatiue comyng betw⸢e⸣ne wyll haue a relatiue plurell. Vnde versus:

Post duo nomina singula des plurale relatum.|

Socius meus quem magister verberat est valde insolens. Þis relatiue *quem* ys þe accusatiue case, for whan a nominatiue case comyth be(t)wene þe relatiue and þe verbe then þe relatiue   100
schall be such[2] case as þe verbe wyll haue after hym and yf þer cum none þe relatiue schall be nominatiue case to þe verbe. Vnde versus:

Si rectus mediat inter verbumque relatum
Casu quem post se vult verbum pone relatum;
Si nil sit medium tunc recto pone relatum.

And all nownys interrogatiuis kepith þe sam⸢e⸣ rule. Wh<ic>h be nownys interrogatiuis? All þat bith yn these verse. Vnde versus:[3]

Quis, qualis, quantis, cuius, ⸢*cuias*⸣, *quotus* et *quot*,   110
Adde *quotennis, vter*: sunt quesatiua tibi tot.

Ecclesia que vel qui est locus sanctus bene frequentatur a populo Christiano.[4] What gender ys þe relatiue *que* vel *qui*? Masculyn and þe femynin gender. Why so? For when þe relatiue *qui, que, quod* ys referryd to ij antecedens of diuerse gender pertinyng to þe same þyng þe relatiue may acorde in gender w^t bothe antecedens. Vnde versus:

Quando relatiuum[5] generum casus variorum
Inter se claudunt qui rem spectant ad eandem,
Per genus hoc poterit vtrilibet associare: 120

---

[1] MS iugitur   [2] MS suth   [3] *These and some of the subsequent verses have English glosses in the hand of the text.*   [4] MS xpūno   [5] generum *canc.*

FORMULA TEXT CC

Est pia stirps Iesse quem Cristum dicimus esse
Dicas ad lumen, qui vel quod Christus¹ habetur. |

And euery relatiue schall acorde wᵗ þe nex antecedens but
yf þe sentens let hit, vt *Canis tu⌈u⌉s occi<di>t ouem meam
quem ego occidam*; and yf hit be oþerwyse þe sentens wol not
be trw. Oþerwyse yn Latyn: ad proximum antecedens fiet
relatio. Quando relatiuum referretur ad nomen collectiuum
vel collectiue positum potest referre ad vocem vel ad
intellectum; ad vocem vt *Ista est pulcra societas que*² *bene
addiscit*, ad intellectum vt *Ista est pulcra societas qui bene*   130
addiscunt. Vnde versus:

   Non des ad vocem quandoque³ relata sed ad rem
   Nominis: *Est bona gens, Deus est protector eorum*.
   Adiectiua modo poni reperimus eodem:
   Pars hominum validi turres et menia scandunt.

Que sunt nomina collectiua? Dico quod ista que secuntur in
hijs versibus, cum simil(i)bus. Vnde versus:

   Sunt collectiua *populus, gens, plebs* quoque *triba*,
   Turma, phalanx, legio, cuneus sociare memento
   Et multa plura que sunt: hec noscere cura.   140

   Ego sum ille qui amo vel *qui ama<t> morcellum beni cibi
et haustum ceruisie desicate*. What person ys þe verbe *amo*
and *amat*. Þe i person and þe iij person. Why so? For
when þe relatiue *qui, que, quod* ys referrid to a pronowne of
diuerse person þe verbe þat foluyth þe relatiue may acord wᵗ
boþe pronownys. Vnde versus: |

   Quando relatiuum *qui* pronomine recitabit
   Persone duplicis sibi verbum consociabit:
   Hiis *Sum qui scripsi*⁴ vel *scripcit*⁴ bene dixi.

*Mulier que*⁵ *dampnauit saluauit* sic exponitur. *Mulier*, id est.   150
Maria, saluauit nos quo (*mulier*), id est Eua, dampnauit nos,
et hec est relacio simplex, pro quo nota quod⁶ duplex est
relacio, scilicet⁷ relacio simplex et relacio personalis.
Relacio simplex est relacio quando relatiuum et suum antecedens
supponunt pro eodem re in specie et non in numero, vt
Mulier que dampnauit saluauit. Relacio personalis est quando
relatiuum et suum antecedens suppo(n)unt per eodem modo
in numero et specie;⁸ vel relacio secundum rem et secundum
vocem.

   Quando duo verba diuersi re⌈g⌉iminis concurrit in oracione,   160
si precedat relatiuum tunc relatiuum⁹ cum priore verbo dic
concordare vt in hcc exemplo, *Ego sum clericus cui magister*

---

¹ quod Christus] MS quodx̄ p̄c   ² MS qui
³ MS qm̄₃   ⁴ MS scirp-   ⁵ MS qui
⁶ q- *from* d   ⁷ *repeated*   ⁸ MS relacio
⁹ MS verbum

FORMULA TEXT CC

apponet et examinabit, quem magister examinabit et apponet;
si duo[1] huius modi verba venia(n)t sine precedenti, posteriore
verbo fiet regimen vt *Gaudio et diligo precenciam vestram*, vt
Diligo et gaudio presenc<i>a vestra.[2] Quando relatiuum
refertur ad sensum tocius oracionis et non ad diccionem
oratione tunc relatiuum debet poni in neutro genere vt *B<ene>
addisco quod placet magistro.*[3]

Pater meus est vna creaturarum. Thys nowne partitiue   170
vna ys þe femynin gender, for euery nowne partitiue y-put or
dystributiue schall acorde yn gender|w^t þe genitiue case
þat foluyt yf þay ben of oune significacion, and he schall
acorde yn case and number w^t þe substantiue þat goyt before.
Vnde versus:

Concordans genere fore plurale genitiuo
Vult partitiuum semper, velud *Vna sororum;*
Est *vnus florum rosa* dicat quisque virorum.

Que sunt nomina partatiua siue distributiua? Patent per
(h)os versus: 180

Omnis[4] et *vnus, vter, alius, nullus* quoque *neuter,
Quisquis, quicumque,* sic *quilibet, alter, vterque,*
Ac *vnusquisque, quidam quicunque*ve, *quisque*
Sunt partitiua vel distribuentia[5] dicta.
Ordinis hijs iunge numeralia nomina queque.

Deus est optima rerum. Þis superlatiue degre *optima* ys
þe femynin gender, for euery superlatiue schall acord yn
gender w^t þe genitiue case þat foluyth yf þay be of on kynd
(and) w^t þe substantiue þat goyt before yn number and case; and
they be not of on kynd þe superlatiue schall acorde w^t þe   190
substantiue þat goyt before yn case, gender and number, as
Iohannes est stultissimus aucarum vel *inter aucas.*

Omne superlatum partitiue resitatum
Semper uult genere genetiui pa<r> retinere,
Vt pateat verum sic: *Est Deus optima rerum.*
Immo superlatum propria vi quando negatur
Per genus hoc fixo precidenti famulatur.

Why may hit not be sayd *Hoc est sapientissimus aucarum?*
⌈For *homo* and *auca* acordith⌉ not in kynd and therfore þe
superlatiue degre schall not acord in gender w^t þe genitiue   200
case þat folowith.

Explyciunt Concordancie. |

A version of the *Comparacio* follows at this point on fols.
80^r to 83^r, and this is given separately as text R.

---

[1] MS uð   [2] MS vestram   [3] MS m̄r̄
[4] MS omnes   [5] *from* distributiua

168

FORMULA TEXT CC

Istud dolium est plenum[1] *v(i)ni* vel *-no*. *V(i)ni* vel *-no*: what case? Genitiue case and ablatiue case. Why so? For euery worde þat betokenyth fulnysse or awntessnesse whil be constr⸢u⸣yd w^t a genitiue case and an ablatiue case.[2]

Que plenum signant vel que[3] *vacuata figurant*
Hec ablatiuis poteris dare vel genetiuis:
Vini vel *vino duo dolia plena videto.*
Dignus et *indignus, reus* ac *immunus, exsors,*   210
Expers et *diues, pauper* vel *egenus,*[4] *opimus,*
Infelex, felex et *inops doctus*que, *peritus.*
Ignarus, sapiens, fertulis ac *opilentus:*[5]
Istac cum paribus genito,[6] *sexto sociabis.*

Nota quod si sensus genitiui casus veniat post aliquid contentorum in versibus ponatur[7] in ablatiuo casu.

Post proprium nomen, post mobile, post quoque verbum,
Postque gerundiuum, post participansque supinum
Si veniat sensus genitiui iungito sexto;
Cum reliquis sextum non iungas sed genitiuum.   220

Frater meus et soror mea sunt assidui in domo patris mei.[8] Þis adiectiue *assidui* ys the masculyn gender, for þe masculyn gender[9] ys more worthe þan þe femynin[10] and þe neuter ys more worþy than þe masculyn or þe femynin.

Mas.[11] *sibi femineum sed fe. non concepit vllum,*
Neutrum fe. sibi mas. si bene concipias.

Obuiemus regi et regine. This word *regi* ys þe datiue case, for all verbis þat bith[12] yn thes versis wil be construed w^t[13] datiue case.|

Obuio, parco, placet, nocio, respondeo, seruit,
Precipit, opponit, coniungimus ista datiuis;   231
Supplicat, intersum, fauet, heret, mundet,[14] illis
Subuenit addatur, *succurrat, propiciatur.*

Vtor[15] *rubio capicio*. (*Capicio*) ys þe ablatiue case, for ⸢hale⸣ þes verbis þat ben contayned yn those verse will be construid w^t an ablatiue case.

Vescitur et *fruitur, caret, vtitur* atque *potitur*:
Hec ablatiuos transicione regunt;
Fungor iungatur et deficio sociatur.

---

[1] vini *canc.*   [2] s verb þat betoke⸢net⸣ fulnys or entenys wyl be constru<> w^t a genitiui case *and* a ablatiui casus *canc.*
[3] *from* qu   [4] e *canc.*   [5] -us *from is*
[6] *from* genitiuo; iungito *canc.*   [7] MS ponotur
[8] MS meis   [9] for þe *canc.*   [10] vnde versus *canc.*
[11] *glossed* id est mas. genus   [12] MS hith
[13] adiec *canc.*   [14] -n- *from* m   [15] MS vter

FORMULA TEXT CC

Que est differentia inter[1] *vtor, -eris; vescor, -ceris;* 240
fruor, -eris; fungor, -ris; poteor, -teris vel *-tiris?*

Diuinis fruimur, exoptatisque potimur,[2]
Vtimur[2] vtilibus, fungimur[2] officio,[3]
Vescimur ac escis sic potu delicijsque.

Ista verba que continentur in hijs versibus construuntur
cum genitiuo et accusatiuo et ablatiuo. Versus:

Participo, miror, eget, indiget atque *recordor*
Et *memini, dignor, obliuiscor, reminiscor*
Nempe regunt genitum, iiii^{tum}, sextum quoque casum.

Postulo te graciam qui doceor gramaticam. Graciam: 250
what case? Accusatiue case. Why so? For al þe verbis
þat bith contaynyd yn these verse wyll construe w^t dobyll
accusatiue case betekenyng dyverse[4] thy⌐n⌐gis. *Gramaticam:* what
case? Accusatiue[5] case. Why so? For all þe passyuys
comyng of þe actiue (when) þe actiue wyll construe w^t dobyll
accusatiue case the passyuys of them whyl construe w^t þe later
accusatiue case.[6] |

Postulo, posco, pedo, doceo, rogo, flageto, celo,
Exu(.)o cum *vestit, monet, induo, calcio, singo:*
Accusatiuos[7] geminos hec verba requirunt; 260
Et cum passiuis postremus iungitur horum.

Dominor huius ville abstinens irarum. Huius ville:
what case? Genitiuo case. Why so? For thes iij verbis
dominor, -ris; miserior, -ris and *abstenio, -es* wyll construe
w^t a genitiue case and sumtyme w^t a datiuo case, vnde versus:

Abstenio, dominor, miserere cum genitiuis:
Dominor et ville bonus heres iure parentis;[8]
Iunges *Abstenio panis, Miserere dolentis.*

Irarum: what case? Genitiue case. Why so? For euery
gerundif, participill and suppyn[9] shall construe w^t such 270
case as þe verbe þat he comyth of. Vnde versus:

Omne gerundiuum sic[10] participansque suppinum:[11]
Casus illa petunt quos sua verba regunt.

Michi Roberto fracto caput medicina proficiat. Caput:
what case? Accusatiue case. Why so? For when y haue a[12]
nowne adiectiue, verbe neuter or passiue or eny of here
participill comyth before a nowne yn a reson betekenyng party
of þe hole þat worde þat betekenyng party of þe hole schall

---

[1] MS anter   [2] -ur *from* us   [3] -io *from* oc(?)
[4] wyll construe *canc.*   [5] a stroke *canc.*   [6] Postulo posco
peto doceo rogo flagito celo *canc.*   [7] a letter *canc. after* Acc-
[8] MS parentes   [9] -up *from* ub   [10] MS c̄s
[11] *from* supīn   [12] w *canc.*

FORMULA TEXT CC

be set yn þe accusatiue case and be gouernyd[1] by þis figure sinodege. Exemplum de verbo vt *Doleo ⸢ca⸣put*; exemplum de verbo passiuo vt *Frangor ⸢ca⸣put*; exemplum de participio vt *Sum fractus caput*. Vnde versus:

    Adiectiua regunt passiua(que) verbaque neutra
    Accusatiuos per sinodegen sibi iun(c)tos:
    Alba comasque[2] *caput doleo*, sic *Conputor*[3] *aurem*.
    Participans iunges sic: *Femina comta capill<os>*.

    How many endyngis of gerundiuys bet þer? III: *-di, -do, -dum*. When schall y haue a gerundyf yn *-di* yn comyn speche? When þe Englys of þe infenitiue mode comyth after *tempus, causa* or *est* or after a nown substantif hit schall be set yn þe gerundyf yn *-di*. Exemplum: *Missa*[4] *finita tempus est soluendi ieiunium*. Alium exemplum: *Papa habet potestatem soluendi Christianos*. When schall y haue gerundif yn *-do* yn comyn spech? Yn ij maner wyse. When þe Englys 'in' comyth before a participill of þe presentens wᵗout a substantyf y-set to hym þen schall y haue a gerundyf yn *-do*. Exemplum: *In dimicando multi omines sunt*[5] *vulnerati*. The ij maner wyse ys when þe Englys of þe participill of þe presentens comyth after a substantyf. Þen may y chese wheþer[6] y schall haue a participill of þe precentens or a gerundyf yn *-do*. Exemplum: *Magister est assiduus in scola informando* vel *informans suo(s) paruos*. When schall y hau<e> a gerundyf yn *-dum*? Yn ij maner of wyse. Þe fyrst ys when þe Englys of infinitiuo mode[7] comyth after a worde and tellyt þe cause of þe reson þat goyt before; then y schall haue a gerundyf yn *-dum* wᵗ a preposicion. Exemplum: *Viri vadunt ad bellum ad dimicandum*. The ij maner wyse ys when þe Englys of infinitiuo m<ode>|comyth after þis verbe *sum, es, fuj* wᵗowt eny nominatiue case to hym; then schall y haue a gerundyf yn *-dum* wᵗowt a preposicion. Exemplum: *Resistendum est inimicis nostris pugnanti⸢bus⸣ contra nos*.

    Intendo ire appos⸢i⸣tum scolaribus. Thys worde *appositum* ys þe fyrst suppin, for when y haue an Englys of yn infinitiuo mode comyng after a verbe betokenyng mevyng to a place, betokenyng anything to be done, hit schall be put yn þe fyrst suppyn. *Venio lectu libro*. Þis worde *lectu* ys þe later suppin, for when y haue an Englys of infinitiuo mode comyng after a verbe betokenyng mevyng fro any place anythyng to be don hit schall be set yn þe later suppin.

    Post motus verbum primum coniunge suppinum
    Vt *Vado lectum, cenatum* siue *commestum*;
    Deque loco signans postremum iunge suppinum
    Vt *Venio lectu, senatu* siue *commestu*.
    Infinitiuum si non signat tibi motum
    Vt *Cupio legere, Volo ludere, Curo docere*.

[1] -ny- *from* yn
[2] MS *comes* que
[3] MS jᵤpiter
[4] -i- *from* a
[5] vu *canc*.
[6] MS where
[7] MS *adds* þat

FORMULA TEXT CC

And when y haue and Englys of þe infinitiuo[1] mode þat schall be set yn þe fyrst suppin where þat þe suppin faylyth y shal<l> take þis nown *locus* w^t ys preposicion *ad* and þe futur tens of þe same verbe þat þe suppine schold come of w^t þis aduerbe *vbi*. Exemplum: *Vado ad locum vbi addiscam gramaticam*;[2] and when y haue and Englis of þe infinitiue mode þat schall be set in þe later suppin where þe suppin faylyth[3] y schall tak<e> þis nowne *locus* w^t ys preposicion *a* and þe preterperfectens of þe same verbe þat þe suppin schuld come of w^t ys aduerbe *vbi*. Exemplum: *Veni a loco vbi addidici gramaticam*. | And yf þer come a proper name of a place y shal<l> haue þe proper name w^t ys aduerbe *vbi* and þe preterten<s>. Exemplum: *Veni a loco vbi addidici gramaticam*. 330

Ego sum dilecturus socium meum. Dilecturus ys a participill of þe fyrst futer in *-rus*. For when schall y 340 haue a participill yn *-rus*? When þe Englys of þe infinitiuo mode comyth after þis verbe *sum, es, fui* betokenyng 'to do' þen hit schall be set yn þe fyrst futer in *-rus*; or when y haue and Englys 'to' w^{t}owt 'be' comyng after þis verbe *sum, es, fui* w^{t}owt a neuter substantyf þen schall y haue a participill in *-rus*, vt *Ego sum amatur<us> socium meum*. And yf þe Englys of þe infinitiue mode come after þis verbe *sum, es, fui* and betokenyth to suffer hit schall be set yn þe later futer in *-dus*; or when 'to' and[4] 'be' comyth after þis verbe *sum, es, fui* y schall haue a participill yndyng yn *-dus*, vt 350 *Ego sum amandus*.

Magistro docente p⌈u⌉eri proficiunt. *Magistro* ys þe ablatiue case absolute,[5] for when y haue a schort reson of a nown and a participill or a pronown and a participill and no worde y-set owt whereof he may be geuerynd, hit schall be set yn þe ablatiue case absolute, as *Me*[6] *secenti tu curris*. How many maner a wise schall þe ablatiue case absolute be | exponyd? By ij maner a wise. Whiche ij? By *cum* or *dum*; (by *dum*) vt *Me vidente cecidisti*, id est *Dum vidio cecidisti*; by *cum* vt *Augusto imperatore Alexandria domita est*, id est 360 *Cum August<us> (erat imperator, Alexandria domita est)*.

Per *cum* vel per *dum* sexti resolucio[7] detur, Huius namque rei Precianus testis habetur.

Placet mihi bene quod nos transibimus lasum. Thys word *placet* ys a verbe inperso⌈n⌉ell. How knost þu a verbe inpersonell? For he hat no number uþer[8] person and ys declyn yn þe vose of þe thyr person, sinler numb<er>, and commyt w^t on of þes ij synys 'hyt' or 'me', as 'hyt delytyt' oþer 'me redyt'. How ma⌈n⌉y maner verbys ynpersonall ben þer? II. Wych ij? A verbe inpersonall of þe actiwoce 370 and a verbe inpersonall of þe passiwoce. ⌈How knowst a

[1] i *canc. after* -t- [2] -i- *from* a [3] MS saylyth
[4] MS or [5] MS *also* lute
[6] MS *adds* fecend *not canc.* [7] -u- *from* c
[8] s *canc.*

172

FORMULA TEXT CC

verbe inpersonall[1] actiwose? For yt endit in[2] -t (as tetet,)
penitet.¹ How knowst þu a verbe inpersonall of þe passiwoyse?
For <yt> endit in -r as statur, curritur. Wyt what case wyll
all verbys inpersonall of þe actiff woyse be construyd? W^t
þe datiui case, exsepte xiii of þe wych v wyll construj w^t
þe accusatiui cese and þe genitiue case and þay beth þese:
penitet, and tedet, miseret, pudet and piget; and v w^t þe
accusatiue case only and þay byth þese: iuuat,[3] decet,
delectat, oportet and latet; and iij w^t þe genity<ue>   380
(case and þe ablatiue case and þay byth þese: interest,
refert, and est sett for pertinet).|

    Penitet me mali regiminis. Me is[4] þe accusatiue case,
for these v verbis penitet, tedet, miseret, pudet and piget
wyll construe w^t an accusatiue case of þe[5] thyng þat doith þe
dede of þe verbe. Thys word regiminis ys þe genitiue case,
for these verbis wyll construe w^t þe genitiue case of that
þyng þat þe dede of the verbe ys done (for).

    Penitet et tedet, miseret, pudet et piget, ista
    Accusatiuos poscunt simul et genitiuos,   390
    Natura primum sed transi(ci)one secundum.

Thys iij verbis penitet, pudet and piget makyth þe pretertens
penituit, puduit[6] and piguit; and þes ij verbis tedet and
miseret makyth pertesum and misertum. Vnde versus:

    Penituit, puduit,[6] piguit sic preteritis dant,
    Sed tedet et miseret dant pertesumque misertum.

    Licet mihi comedere. (Mihi): what case? Datiue case.
Why so? For all þes verbis þat byth contaynyd in these
verses wyll construe w^t a datiue case.

    Hec libet atque licet, placet et liq(u)et, accidet atque 400
    Congruit, euenit (et) contingit (et) expedit, ista[7]
    Cum re(li)quis paribus intersociato datiuis.

    Decet scolares esse honestos. Þis worde scolares ys þe[8]
accusatiue case, for these v verbis decet, iuuat, dilectat,
oportet[9] and latet wyll construe w^t a accusatiue case.|

    Quarto[10] iunge iuuat, decet ac dilectat, oportet,
    Et latet illorum numero vult associari.

    Hec est differencia inter iuuat actiuum et iuuat inpersonale.
Iuuat[11] actiuum est idem quod auxiliatur, et iuuat inpersonale
est verbum neutrum, est idem quod dileciat.   410

---

[1] s canc. after in-   [2] yt endit in] MS ys englys
[3] MS Iuitet   [4] me canc.   [5] -e from -t(?)
[6] MS piduit   [7] from atque   [8] MS þis
[9] MS oportes   [10] at head of folio wyl be construe w^t and
accusatiue only hyt hys but sagyn off a pyma not canc.
[11] personale added and then canc.

173

FORMULA TEXT CC

Iuuo sit actiuum cum signat ut *auxiliatur*,
Inpersonale signans *dilectat* eritque.

Quando hoc verbum *oportet* venit in oracione sine infinitiuo
modo sequente tunc in vi⌈c⌉e eius fungendum est adiectiuo quod
discend(i)t ab hoc verbo *oportet* cum hoc verbo *sum*, *es*, *fuj*,
vt in ista locucione Anclicana: 'Ion behouit a new gowne
ayens þe fest of[1] Ester', *Iohanni noua toga est oportuna
erga festum pasche.*[2]

    Omnes[3] participes dic simplicis esse figure
    Aut decom⌈p⌉(o)site dicereue dubites,   *420*
    Excipe contractus, confractus et inde redactus:
    Componuntur que non sua verba secuntur.

    Semper ab actiuis inpersonale[4] creatur
    Vel neutris illis quibus[5] accio si⌈n⌉gnif(ic)atur.
    A deponenti, conmuni vel pacienti
    Inpersonale numquam debemus habere.

A quibus verbis descendunt verba (in)personalia? A verbis
acctiuis et a verbis acctiuum significan(ti)bus.|

    Inter.,[6] *refert*,[7] *est* genitiuis iungere prodest
    Set sexto proprie iungas pronomina quinque   *430*
    Nam *Refert*[8] *nostra* dicas, *Refert*[8] quoque *vestra*.

    Exulo, *vapulo*, *venio*, *fio*, *nubo licet*que[9]
    Sensum passiui sub voce gerunt aliena.
    Audio cum *solio*, *fio* cum *gaudio*, *fido*
    Quinque, puer, nu(m)ero neutro-passiua tibi do.
    Neutro-passiua dant participancia trina.

    -Sidero, *-leo*, *-fendo*, *-leo*, *-spicio* templa[10]
    *-Clino*que componenens: sic iam capiantur in vsu.

Nota quod quando latinitas est componenda per hoc verrbum
deficeo, *-is* illud quod apparet esse nominatiuus[11] casus ponetur *440*
in datiuo casu et illud quod apparet esse accusatiuus[12] casus
ponetur in nominatiuo casu vt in hoc exemplo: 'Y lacke a
boke', *Mihi deficit liber*.

Al proper namys of townys, vylagys or setys simpill and
not y-compownyd and þes iiij nownys appellatiuis *rus*, *domus*,[13]
humus and *milicia* y-put after verbis gerundiuis, suppinis or
participilis betokening mevyng to a place or at a place, then
hyt schall be put in þe accusatiue case w⌈t⌉oute[14] ony preposicion;
and yf þe betokenyng mewyng frow a place or by a place þen
schal be put in þe ablatiue case; and yf þe betokenyng bydyng *450*

---

[1] h canc.   [2] *The text is confused from this point
onwards.*   [3] MS Omnis   [4] MS inpersolale
[5] MS quibis   [6] MS interest   [7] MS refret; MS
adds et   [8] MS refret   [9] MS li⌈ci⌉oque   [10] sic MS   [11] MS nominatiui
[12] accusatiuo   [13] *a letter canc. after* d   [14] MS v⌈t⌉owte

FORMULA TEXT CC

in a place or at a place and þey be þe fryst declinson or þe secunde and singler number þey schald be pute in þc genitiue case; and yf þey be þe iij^{de} clinson or plurel number þen þey schald be put in þe ablatiue case w^toute[1] a preposicion adverbialiter and w^towte any gouernans.|

When y haue ij comparatiuis degreys and ij they(ng)s then myne Latyn schall be made by *in quanto* and *in tanto* as 'Þe meryer þat ȝe[2] be þe glader y am', *In quanto vos estis iocundior in tanto ego sum amenior*. When I haue on comparatiue degre and on positiue þan myne Latyn schall be   460 made by *eatenus* and *quatenus* as[3] 'I[4] fare þe[5] beter ȝe be mere and glad', *Eatenus melius valio quatenus vos estis illaris et iocundus*.

When y haue an Englysche of þe infinitiue mode comyng after a verbe betokenyng besechyng or prayyng hyt schall be set in a gerundiue in *-do* w^t[6] a preposicion, as 'Y beseche yow to dyne w^t me', *Supplico vobis de iantando mecum*.

Quatuor exceptis pronomina nulla vocabis:
Tu, meus, noster et *vester*, hec sola vocantur.
Cum natis *alius, vter, alter, sola, quis, vnus*,   470
Totus et *vllus*: habe pronomina ista secunde.
Pone vocatiuos[7] cum *totus, solus* et *vnus*,
Set non in reliquis quorum genitiuus in *-ivs*.
Terne persone geniraliter omnis habetur
Rectus, set demas pronomina iiij^{or} inde:
Sunt *ego, nos* prime, *tu* et *vos* sunt nempe secunde.

Largior, experior, veneror, moror, osculor, ortor,
Criminor, amplector tibi sunt communia, lector.
Stipulor, amplexor, interp(r)etor, hospitor adde,
Hij qui respiciunt autores talia dicunt.| 480

-Ens, -ans presentis semper dic temporis esse,
-Tus, -sus preteriti, *-rus, -dus* dic esse futuri.
-Ens, -ans, -rus et agunt, sed *-tus, -sus, -dus* paciuntur.
-Ens, -ans preterito *-dus* formes de genetiuo,
-Tus, -sus preteritum *-rus* fac formare supinum.
'Into' cum quarto, sine 'to' coniungito sexto.
In campo curro si sis, bene dices, in illo;
Si sis exterius *in campum* sit tibi cursus.

Explicit totum

Auram preualet argento. Þis whord *argento* ys þe ablatiue   490 case, for all þes werbis þat bit yn thes wers hathe[8] þe strynngkyth of þe comparatiue degre and other mo. Vnde versus:

Prefero cum *presto, malo*, coniungito sexto

[1] MS v^toute [2] MS he [3] þe *canc.*
[4] MS he [5] my *canc.* [6] owte *canc.*
[7] MS vocatiu*us* [8] t- *canc.*

175

FORMULA TEXT CC

In se quando gradum claudunt apte mediatum.
Malo merum celia, Panem quoque prefero petra.
Preualet addatur, *preponderat* associatur,
Et quoduis tale sic comparat addite quale.

Explicit totum

TEXT DD

DD. Cambridge, Gonville and Caius College, MS 417/447, fol.15^v

 Whan I haue þis Englysch 'at' comyng byfore a proper name
of a towne, vylage oþer syte noght componyd, yf þat þe proper
name by þe fyrste clynson oþer the secunde and synguler numbyr
hyt schall by sette yn þe genetyf case, and yf þat þe proper
name by þe thyrde clynson oþer plurell numbyr hyt schal by
sette yn þe ablatyf case w^{t}oute any preposicyon. 'To' a
place, what clynson, what numbyr þat euer hy by, hyt schal by
sette yn þe accusatyf case; 'by' and 'fraw' yn þe ablatyf case
w^{t}oute any preposicion; and also þis iiij nownys *rus*, *domus*,
humus and[1] *milicia* folowyth þis same rule.   10

  'To' poscit quartum, 'by' vel 'fro' dat tibi sextum,
  At terne sextum pluralis possit eundem,
  At genitum prime singularis siue secunde.

---

[1] h *canc.*

TEXT EE

EE. Cambridge, Trinity College, MS 0.5.4., fols.4^r and 6^v-7^v

In how many maners schalt thou bygynne to make Latyn?
By foure by ryghtfull order of construccyon. By a nominatyf
case or by summewhat y-set in the stede of the nominatyf case,
by the vocatyf case, by an ablatyf case absolute, or by a verbe
inpersonall. How[1] bygynnestowe by a nominatyf case? As
'The mayster syltyth in the scole', *Magister sedet in scola*.
How by summewhat sette in the stede of the nominatyf case?
As 'To dyne bytyme hyt schall conforte mannes herte', *Iantari
tempestiue confortabit humanum cor*. How by a vocatyf case?
As 'Willyam come hydere and haue a peny', *Willelme venias huc*   10
et habebis denarium. How by an ablatyf case absolute? As
'The mayster stondyng in the scole I am agast', *Magistro stante
in scola sum perteritus*. How by a verbe inpersonall? As
'Me syttyth in scole', *Sedetur in scola*.

In how many maners is the ryghtfull order of construccyon
y-lette? By fyve. By askyng, as 'Whom louest thou?',
Quem diligis tu? By relacion, as 'My lorde comyng to contre
hys bonde men gretlych dredyth', *Dominum meum venientem ad
istas partes sui serui vehementer formidant*. By negacyon, as
'No an I loue but God', *Neminem diligo preter Deum*. By   20
infinitacion, as 'Whomeuer thou louest hym folwe in goodnesse',
Quemcumque diligis illum sequaris in bono. By prolemps(is),
as 'Maystres disputyng in scole on is connyngg anothyr ys a
fole', *Magistrorum disputancium in scola vnus est sapiens alius
stultus*.

How many acordys hast thou in grammer? Foure. On
bytwene the nominatyf case and the verbe, the secunde bytwene
the adiectyf and the substantyf, the thrydde bytwene the
relatyf and the antecedent, the fourthe bytwene the noune
partytyf, the noune dystributyf, the noune of superlatyf degre,   30
and the genityf case that folweth.

In how many maners schall the nominatyf case and the
verbe acorde? In tweyne, in noumbre and persone, as 'My
felowe redyth hys bokes', *Socius meus legit suos libros*. In
how many thynggys may they be lette? By foure. By euocacion,
as 'I Wylyam am youre frende', *Ego Willelmus sum vester amicus*.
By apposicion, ⌈as 'The cyte of London is ful of merchendyse',
Ciuitas Londonie est plena mercibus. By concepcion,[1] as 'The
folk renneth swythe to churche', *Populus currunt festinantes ad
ecclesiam*. By colleccyon, as 'Ther gooth a grete company of   40
knyghtes wel aparelled out of Englonde into hethenes', *Vadunt
grandis turma militum bene apparati ab Anglia in paganam*.[2]

The secunde acord is bytwene the adiectyf and the substantyf.
In how many maners schul they acorde? In thre, in case, gender
and number. Ensaumple as 'Thys good man 3af me a faire
3yfte', *Iste bonus homo dedit michi pulchrum donum*. In how
many maners may they be lette? By foure. By particion, as

---

[1] H *canc. before* How   [2] -gan- *from* gin

178

TEXT EE

⌈'My brother⌉ is on of creatours', *Frater meus est vna
creaturarum*. By dystribucion, as¹ 'Nouthyr of thys² twey
stones is cristall', *Neuter istoram duorum lapidum est*   50
cristallum. By sylempsis, as 'Folk comyth hy3ynge to churche',
P(o)pulus veniunt festinantes ad ecclesiam. By defaute of
gender, as 'A grete stryf is of a poure kyngdam', *Magna lis
est de paupere regno*. Vnde versus:

  A substantiuo adiectiuum variatur
  Cum partitiuum distribitiuumve sequatur;
  Silempcis, generis defectio, quart⌈a⌉ notatur.

    The thrydde acorde in grammer is bytwene the relatyf and
the antecedent. In how many maners schull they acorde? In
thre, in gendre, in noumbre and person. As 'Thys breedc   60
the whych is made of whete is mewly', *Iste panis qui fit de
frumento est mussidus*. In how many maners ben they lette?
In thre. The fyrste by intransicion, as 'The metal the
whyche is a peny is dere', *Metallum qui est denarius est carum*.
In the secunde manere when myn antecedent bytokenyth party and
the noun that comyth aftur the relatyf bytokeneth the hole,
thenne my relatyf schal take hys gendre of the noun that goth
byfore and hys noumbre of the noun that cometh aftur.
Exemplum: 'Ich haue i-3eten today twey cantalles of breede
the which is an hole lofe', *Comedi hodie duo minicalia quod* 70
fuit panis integer. In the thrydde manere whenne myn
antecedent betokenith the kynde of thynge and the relatif
betokenyth³ the partye of the same thyng, thenne myn antecedent
schal be singuler and the relatyf plurel. Exemplum: 'What
thynge is foulere than a man the which the bytynge of flyes
sleeth?', *Quid est imbecillius homine quos muscarum morsus
necat*? And also whenne a noune collectyf is the antecedent
and feminine gendre and singuler noumbre my relatyf may be
masculyn gendre and plurell noumbre, as 'The folk of thys
toune the whyche knowyth not Godes lawe beth⁴ acursed', *Gens* 80
de hac villa qui nescit legem diuinam sunt maledicti.

    Which is the fourthe acorde in grammer? Bytwene the
noune partytyf and the genityf case that folwyth. In how
many manerys schull they acorde? In on, in gendyr onlych,
as 'My fadyr is on of creatures', *Pater meus est vna
creaturarum*. In how many maners is that acord i-let? In
on onlych, in discord of kynde, as whenne the noune partityf
bytokenyth a thyng of o kynde and that at semyth genityf case
bytokenyth anothyr kynde, thenne my noune partytyf schall
acorde in gendyr wyth the substantyf byfore and that at semeth 90
genityf case schall be tornyd into accusatyf case wyth an
inter preposicion, as 'I am on of asses the whyche my fadur
boughte in the feyre', *Ego sum vnus inter asinos quos pater
meus comparauit in nundinis*. In the same manere schall the
noune distributyf acorde wyth the genityf case that folweth,
as 'Nouther of these twey stones is margery ston', *Neuter*

¹ MS A- *from* a-   ² folk *canc*.   ³ the l *canc*.
⁴ *from* is

179

TEXT EE

istorum duorum lapidum est margarita. Also the superlatyf
degre schall acorde wyth the genityf case that folweth[1] in
gendere and they be on kynde, as 'My brothur is wysyst of
creatures', *Frater meus ⌈est⌉ sapientissima creaturarum.*   100
    In how many maners schall that acorde be lette? By
tweyne. On is if my superlatyf degre bytokenyth a thynge of
on kynde and myn genityf case a thyng of another kynde, as
'I am wysyst of gees', *Ego sum sapientissimus aucarum.* How
the secunde?[2] Whenne my superlatyf degre is construid wyth
a genityf case of a noun collectyf, as 'I am wysyst of thys
companye', *Ego sum sapientissimus istius comitiue.* But hyre
⌈k⌉now for a sertayn rewle that the superlatyf degre is nouȝt
holde to acorde wyth the genityf case that folweth but hyt so
be that thylke genityf case be plurel noumbre, and also thylke   110
thynge that bytokeneth that is to knowe by the genityf case
as by wey of kynde ⌈be on⌉ wyth that thyng that is bytokenyd
by the substantyf of the superlatyf degre, as 'I wysyst of
thys folk am fayrest of gees', *Ego sapientissimus istius gentis
sum pulcherimus aucarum.*⌉

    A version of the *Accedence* follows at this point on fols.4ᵛ-
6ᵛ, and this is given separately as text D.

    How many fygures of construccion haste? Fyue, videlicet
prolempcis, silempcis, zeuma, antitecis, sintecis.

    How knowyste prolempcis? A figure by the whych men
diuiden a noun that bytokenyth the hole by the singuler or by
the plurell, as 'Men syttyth in the scole summe on the benche   120
and summe on the erthe', *Homines sedent in scola quidam super*[3]
scamnum alii super terram. In how many maners may prolempcis
be made? By thre. By whych thre? By the nominatyf case
onlych, by obliques onlych, by the nominatyf case and by the
obliques. By the nominatyf case onlych, as 'Men comyth to
toune, on on[4] horse another on fote', *Homines veniunt ad villam
vnus eques alius pedes.* By the obliques onlych as whenne the
verbe is not i-put[5] to the noun that bytokenyth not the hole
nother to the noun that bytokenyth the hole, bote to another
noun as 'Weuers weuyng a newe cloth on atte the ryght syde and   130
anothyr atte the lyfte syde fayre is the crafte', *Textorum
texencium nouam telam vnius a dextro alterius a sinistro pulchra
est ars.* By the oblyques and by the nominatyf case whenne the
verbe is put to the noun that diuidyth the hole as 'Scolers
lernyng grammer on hath a good wyt anothyr euel', *Scolarium
adiscencium gramaticam vnus habet bonum ingenium alius malum.*
Her knowe for a certayn reule that an *et* coniunccion schall not
go bytwene the nounes that diuidyth the hole, wherefor hyt is
couenable i-seyd,[6] 'Twey maystres dysputyth on in grammer anothyr
in logyk', *Duo magistri disputant vnus in gramatica alter in*   140
logica, as 'Catholicon' preuyth in the fyrst parte of hys bok.

[1] A *canc.*   [2] au *canc.*   [3] terram *canc.*
[4] *from* an   [5] MS I- *from* y-   [6] sette *canc. after* i-

TEXT EE

What is silempcis? A figure by whych concepcion is mad.
How many maners schall concepcion be made? By foure, by
concepcion of person, concepcion of gendre, concepcion of
noumbre, and concepcion of case. How knowyst concepcion of
person? Whenne I haue twey nominatyf cases of diuerse person
joynyd togedyr wyth an *et* coniunccion in reward of a verbe
plurel, as 'I and thu rennyth', *Ego et tu currimus*. Whych
be the persones that conceyuyth and whych be conceyuyd? The
furst conceyuyth the secunde and the thrydde, as 'I and thu   150
and he rennyth', *Ego et tu et ille currimus*. The secund schal
conceyue the thrydde, as 'Thu and he were in the felde', *Tu
et ille fuistis in campo*. How knowest concepcion of gendre?
A joynyng togedre of the nounes substantyfys of diuerse gendre
in reward of an adiectyf plurell, as 'Willyam and Katerine and
the maunciple be syttyng atte mete', *Willelmus et Katerina et
mancipium sunt sedencia ad prandium*. Knowe thys for a certayn
reule that the neutre gendre schall conceyue the masculyn and
the femynyn; and hyt is open in the Latyn byfore the masculyn
schall conceyue the femynyn and nouʒt aʒenward, as 'Catholican' 160
and P.H. techeth. Whereuer is concepcion of person ther is
concepcion of noumbre but nouʒt aʒenward. The singuler schall
conceyue another singuler, as 'Men and an asse rennyth',
Homines et asinus currunt. Concepcion of case is whenne a
nominatyf case is joynyd wyth an ablatyf case and a preposicion
i-sette bytwene, as *Ego tecum currimus*. Knowe thu for a
certeyn reule that a man may sette a word that conceyuyth
byhynde or byfore at hys owne lykyng, saue in concepcion of
person the worde that conceyuyth schall go byfore and the word
that is conceyuyd schall come aftur, as *Ego et tu currimus*, for 170
this is the reule of 'Catholicon' et cetera.

Zeuma is a joynyng togedyr of twey nominatyf cases in
reward of a verbe so that the verbe acorde wyth that on
nominatyf case and nouʒt wyth that othyr, as *Ego lego et tu,
Sortes legit et Plato*. Here knowe that for a certayn reule
that the verbe and the relatyf and the adiectyf schall acord
wyth the nexte nominatyf case in construccion of zeuma, as
Vir et mulier est bona, Mulier et vir est bonus. In how many
maners schall zeuma be made? By syxe. By whych syxe? By
a coniunccion copulatyf as *Ego et socius meus legit*; by a   180
coniunccion aduersatyf vt *Vos estis mundi sed non omnes*; by
an aduerbe of lycclynes as *Tu respicis sicut latro*; by an
aduerbe of comparatyf degre as *Ego lego melius quam tu*; by
a coniunccion disiunctyf as *Ego vel tu es culpandus*; by thys
coniunccion *nec* as ⁽*Nec*⁾ *panis nec seruisia est in villa hodie
vendenda*.

How knowest antitecis? A settyng on case for anothyr,
as *Sermonem quem audistis non est meus*.

How knowest sintecis?[1] A general figure that hat thre
speciall figures vnder hym, that is to wete euocacion,   190
apposicion and synodochen. How knowest euocacion? A

---

[1] MS S- *from* s-

TEXT EE

settyng togedre of twey nominatyf case of diuerse person
wythoute a coniunccion i-sette bytwene, as *Ego Iohannes
sedeo in cathedra*. Wheche by the partyes that conceyuyth?
Pronounes of the furst person and the secunde, the verbe
substantyf and vocatyf.

How knoweste ap|posicion? A joynyng togedre of twey
nominatyf cases singulers wyth a verbe substantyf wythoute
an *et* coniunccion j-sette bytwene so that the nominatyf that
is more comyn schal go tofore and that at is lasse comyn schal   200
come aftur, as *Animal homo currit*. Her know for a certeyn
reule that a verbe and a noun adiectyf and a relatyf schull
acorde wyth the nominatyf case that goth byfore and not wyth
that at comyth aftur in apposicion, as 'The cyte of London
the wheche is full of merchaundyse is worthy to be preysyd',
Ciuitas Londonie que est plena mercibus est collaudanda.

How knowyst synodoche? A sygnyng of the party to al or
a signyng¹ of al to the party. In how many maners schal he
be made? By foure. By whyche foure? Whenne that at is
the hole is delyueryd in to the party wythoute gouernynge of   210
an accusatyf case, as 'Thys maide is clere the kynde', *Ista
virgo est clara genus*. How in the secunde manere? As whenne
that at is of the party is delyueryd to the hole wyth
gouernyng of the accusatyf case, as 'Thys man is whyte the
face', *Iste homo est albus faciem*. In the thrydde manere
is whenne that at is of the hole is delyueryd to the party
wythoute gouernyng of the accusatyf case, as 'A goode soule
is weddyd to my brother', *Bonus animus est nuptus fratri meo*.
In the furthe manere whenne that at is of party is delyueryd
into the hole wyth gouernyng of the accusatyf case, as 'Ion   220
is cryps the hede', *Iohannes est crippus caput*. Thys be the
principal reulys that Precian putteth in the furst bokis of
construccion.

In how many maners schal the nominatyf case be gouernyd
of a verbe? In on, by strengthe of person, as *Ego sum homo*:
ego is gouernyd of *sum* ex vi persone. Quare? ⌈Quia⌉ verbum
personale est et regit nominatiuum casum ei supponentem
personam. *Homo* regitur in the same manere of *sum* for that
is a certeyn reule of P.H., in 'Absoluta'²; est, 'A quocumque
regitur casuale precedens ab eodem regitur casuale subsequens   230
eadem vi dum tamen illi casus pertineant ad eandem rem'. Her
know a certeyn reule that a nominatyf case schal ⌈neuere⌉ be
gouerned by any othyr strengthe ⌈than⌉ of person, other ellys
by strengthe of intransicion, wherfor they be vnwyse that sey
that the nominatyf case is gouerned ex vi zeumatis vel ex vi
concepcionis and many other maneres, the whych opynyons be not
funded of non autoritez.

Tthe³ genityf case is gouerned in sixe maners of a noun.
By strengthe of ow(n)yng, as 'The lord of thys place is atte
London', *Dominus istius loci est Londonijs*: *loci* is gouerned   240

¹ to canc.   ² MS absolut⁹   ³ *sic* MS

of *dominus* ex vi possessionis vel possessoris. Quare? Quia
omnis diccio significans possessorem vel possessionem (potest
regere genitiuum casum ex vi possessoris uel possessionis).
In the secunde manere ex vi transsicionis personale, quia omne
nomen verbale terminans in *-tor* uel *-trix* et omne nomen
participale terminans in *-ens* uel *-ans* deriuata a verbis
actiuis et omne nomen adiectiuum equipollens eis in
significacione regere possunt genitiuum casum post se ex vi
transsicionis, as *Ego sum amator vini*: *vini* regitur de *amator*
ex vi transsicionis personalis, et cetera. In the thrydde   250
manere ex vi equiperancie, as *Ego sum similis tui*: *tui*
regitur de hoc nomine *similis* ex vi equiperancie, quia omne
nomen adiectiuum significans equiperanciam potest regere
genitiuum casum ex vi equiperancie, vt *similis*, *dissimilis*,
par, *impar*. In the fourthe manere ex vi particionis, vt,
Vnus istorum currit: *istorum* regitur de hoc nomine *vnus* ex
vi particionis. Quare? Quia omnis diccio partitiua vel
partitiue[1] posita regere potest post se genitiuum casum illam
particionem determinatam ex vi particionis. In the fyfthe
manere ex vi demonstracionis essencie, vt *Vir magne laudis*   260
currit: *laudis* regitur ex *vir* ex vi demonstracionis essencie,
quia omnis diccio significans[2] subiectum per modum dependencie
potest regere genitiuum casum uel ablatiuum ex vi demonstracionis
essencie. In the sixte manere ex vi superlatiui gradus, vt
Ipse est sapientissimus virorum: *virorum* regitur ex
sapientissimus ex vi superlatiui gradus quia omnis
superlatiuus gradus tam nominalis quam aduerbialis regere
potest genitiuum casum ex vi superlatiui gradus, vnde versus:

> Nomine fit sena geniti construccio plena:
> Pos., trans., equipera., parti., superla., demonstra..   270

In how many maneres schall the genityf case be gouerned
of the pronoun? Ex vi possessoris, vt *Suum est azinorum*
rudere: *azinorum* regitur ab hoc nomine *suum*, regula prius
ponitur. Alio modo ex vi demonstracionis essencie vt *Iste*
pulcher aspectus respondebit michi: *aspectus* regitur de *iste*
ex vi demonstracionis, vt prius dictum est. Ex vi particionis,
as *Volucrum ista canit illa gemit*: *volucrum* regitur de ⌈ly⌉
ista, regula prius ponitur. Vnde versus:

> Pronomen de vi vocis forma viduatur,
> Quam tamen adquirit cum monstrat uel referratur,   280
> Et per quisita genitiuus sepe regetur,
> Aut cum subiecti laus uel crimen[3] referetur,
> Et cum possessa particio siue notetur.

In how many maners schal the genityf case be gouernyd of
the verbe? By tweyne. On by strengthe of transicion. *Ego*
obliuiscor tui: *tui* regitur de *obliuiscor* ex vi transicionis,
quia omnia verba significancia memoriam uel obliuionem uel
absenciam et ista quinque verba impersonalia actiue vocis,
scilicet *penitet*, *tedet*, *miseret*, *pudet* et *piget*, regere

---

[1] MS partitis   [2] modum canc.   [3] from crimine

possunt genitiuum casum ex vi transicionis. Alio modo   290
regitur ex vi intransicionis quia *interest* et *refert* (et *est*)
posita pro *pertinet* regunt genitiuum casum omnium casualium a
parte ante ex vi intransicionis. Item aduerbium regit
genitiuum casum aliquando natura nominis, as *Vbicumque
locorum est dominus meus, ibi est bonus vir*: *locorum* regitur
de *vbicumque* ex vi particionis, regula prius ponitur.

The datyf case is gouerned in fyue maneres. Vno modo
ex vi equiperancie, vt *Ego sum similis tibi*: *tibi* regitur
de *similis* ex vi similitudinis uel ex vi equiperancie, et
cetera. Alio modo ex vi possessoris uel possessionis, as   300
Ego sum pater tibi: *tibi* regitur de *pater* quia omnis diccio
significans possessionem uel possessorem mediante verbo
substantiuo regere potest datiuum casum. Tercio modo regitur
datiuus casus ex vi intransicionis, vt *Placet michi ire domum*:
michi regitur de *placet* ex vi intransicionis, quia omnia verbum
impersonale actiue vocis potest regere eundem casum a parte
ante natura supposicionis quem regit verbum a quo descendit a
parte post per naturam transicionis. Quarto modo regitur
datiuus casus ex vi adquisicionis, as *Sum vtilis tibi*: *tibi*
regitur de *vtilis* ex vi adquisicionis, quia omnis diccio   310
adquisitiua uel adquisitiue posita potest regere datiuum casum
ex vi adquisicionis. Quinto modo ex vi contrarietatis, vt
Insurgo tibi: *tibi* regitur de *insurgo* ex vi contrarietatis,
quia omnis diccio significans contrarietatem potest regere
datiuum casum ex vi contrarietatis. Vnde versus:

    Equiperancia., pos., intran.,[1] adquisicio, contra.:
    Istis quinque modis regimen datur esse datiuis.

The accusatyf case is gouerned of the verbe (in) twey
maners. O manere ex vi transicionis, vt *Video te*: *te*
regitur de *video* ex vi transicionis. Quare? Quia verbum   320
transitiuum est et regere potest accusatiuum casum, et cetera.
Secundo modo ex vi intransicionis, vt *Magistrum legere libros
vtile est*: *magistrum* regitur a verbo *legere* ex vi
intransicionis, quia omne verbum infinitiui modi preter
infinitiuum modum verbi impersonalis, passiue vocis, potest
supponere accusatiuum a parte ante regere illum ex vi
intransicionis. Similiter verbum impersonale actiue vocis
construitur cum accusatiuo a parte regit illum ex vi
intransicionis, ut[2] *Miseret me tui*, *Te oportet ire domum*,
et sic de consimilibus. Accusatiuus casus regitur a nomine   330
tribus modis. Primo modo ex vi intransicionis, vt *Magistrum
legendum est libros*: *magistrum* regitur ab hoc nomine *le|gendum*
quia omne gerundiuum presupponens accusatiuum a parte ante
potest regere illum ex vi ⌈in⌉ transicionis vt modus infinitiuus.
Alio modo ex vi transicionis, vt *Veni causa amandi te*: *te*
regitur de *amandi*, regula ut in sexto. Tercio modo ex vi
synodoches. Qu<are>? Quia omnia nomina adiectiua verba
neutra et passiua possunt regere accusatiuum casum ex vi
synodoches, et cetera.

[1] MS adds simul   [2] *a minim stroke canc. before* u-

TEXT EE

The ablatyf case is gouernyd in sixe maners. Primo modo 340
ex vi comparatiui gradus, vt *Sum forcior te*: *te* regitur ab
hoc nomine *forcior* quia omnis comparatiuus gradus comparatiue
tentus regere potest post se ablatiuum casum. Alio modo ex
vi verbi mediante preposicione, vt *Doceor a magistro*:
magistro regitur de *doceor*, quia omne verbum et eius participium,
gerundium et suppinum regere possunt ablatiuum casum ex vi verbi
mediante preposicione expresse posita uel subintellecta. Tercio
modo ex vi passiue significacionis, vt *Sum fessus labore*:
labore regitur de *fessus*, quia omne nomen adiectiuum passiuam
habens[1] significacionem regere potest ablatiuum casum. Quarto 350
modo ex vi demonstracionis essencie: regula ista superius
est in genitiuo. Quinto modo ex vi excessus quantitatis,
vt *Ego sum altior te vno police*: *police* regitur ab hoc
nomine *altior* ex vi excessus quantitatis. Sexto modo et
vltimo ex vi intransicionis, vt *A me curritur in Bellum
Montem*: *me* regitur ab hoc verbo *curritur*, quia omne verbum
impersonale presupponens ablatiuum casum a parte ante per modum
supposicionis regere potest illum ablatiuum, vt dicit
'Catholican' in I parte, ex vi intransicionis, et cetera.

[1] in *canc*.

TEXT FF

FF. Dublin, Trinity College MS 430, pages 3-11

(W)hen thow hast an Englyss reason to be made yn Latyn thow shalte reherse hyt vntyll thow mayst sey yt perfytly, and thow shalte knowe the nomynatyue case for he answeryth to thys questyon 'Who or what?'; notw^{t}stondyng a verbe ympersonall do let yt for he hath nor number nor person nor nomynatyue case.

    Vult primus casus tibi respondere roganti,
    Sed rectum querunt impersonalia nullum.

The fyrst verbe shal be the pryncypall verbe excepte a relatyue or a conyunctyon or the ynfynytyue mode do let hyt. Thow shalte knowe a relatyue by thys synys 'that', 'whom', or 'the wyche', and a conyunctyon by thys synys 'yff', 'than', 'althcw', w^t many other[1] lyke. The ynfynytyue mode ys knowne by thys Ynglyss wordis 'to' of þe actyue voyce and 'to be' of the passyue voyce.   10

    Quod fertur prime tibi sit verbum capitale,
    Sed referens, mo., con. tantum sunt impedimenta.

The nowne that folowyth ⌜þe verbe⌝ shal be the accusatyue ⌜case⌝ for the more parte, excepte þe verbe do require another after hym.

    Quarto iungantur si nomina verba sequantur,   20
    Omnia diuersos signaque regentia casus.|

Too substantyuys or mo longyng both to on thyng, they shal be put yn on case. Vnde versus:

    Substantiua duo casu ponantur in vno
    Si spectent ad idem, sicut *Te diligo fratrem*.

Thys Ynglyss worde 'that' ys a conyunctyon when he cannot be takyn for thys Ynglyss worde 'the wyche', and ys a relatyue when he ys so takyn. Thys conyunctyon *quod* may be put owte of a reason, and then the nomynatyue case shal be the accusatyue and the verbe the ynfynytyue mode.   30

    Excludi sepe *quod* condecet a ratione.
    Infinitari verbum petit atque teneri
    In quarto rectus, velut *Estimo te fore gratum*.

Thys ys the rule of the relatyue. When ther cumyth nothyng betwene the relatyue and the verbe the relatyue shal be the nomynatyue case to the verbe; but yff ther cume a nomynatyue case betwene the relatyue and the verbe the relatyue shal be gouernyd of the verbe.

    Quando inter verbum mediat nichil atque relatum

---

[1] *The scribe uses a single abbreviation mark for ur and er, in both English and Latin.*

TEXT FF

Sit rectus verbo; secus atque regatur ab illo.   40

A verbe ympersonall do let the rule of the relatyue.

Norman non seruat impersonale relati:
Cui peccare licet peccat minus ut puta dices.

When a relatyue ys put betwene ii substantyuys of|dyuers genders longyng both to on thvng the relatyue may be referryd to both yn gender. Exemplum: *Ibo ad locum qui* vel *quod est castellum nouum*. But yff the latter substantyue be a nowne proper the relatyue shal be referryd only to hym. Exemplum: *Est locus in carcere quod Tullianum appellatur*.

    Cum generis varii ponatur clausa relati   50
    Inter que substant ad eandem rem quoque spectant,
    Vt decet vniri poterit tunc illud vtrique.
    Posterius proprium cum sit sibi iunge relatum.

The verbe shall agre w^t the fyrst person afore the second and w^t the second afore the thyrd, vt *Ego et ille disputamus*. In luke manner the adyectyue shal acord w^t the masculyn gender afore the femyn and w^t the femyn afore the neuter, vt *Pater et mater mei venerunt*.

    Tertia cedit enim prime simul atque secunde
    Persone; primo generi genus omne parebit.   60

Thys verbe *sum*, *fio* and *fore* hath power to copull case, and also thys v verbys vocatyuis *nominor*, *appellor*, *nuncupo<r>*, *dicor* and *vocor*, w^t many other verbys passyus and verbys þat sygnyfyth mouyng, restyng and semyng as *moueo*, *sedeo*, *appareo*, w^t many other lyke.

    Copulat hoc verbum *sum*, *fio*, iunge *fore*mque;|
    Nuncupor, *appellor* sic, *nominor* addito, *dicor*.
    Si bene connumeres *vocor* istis addito verbis,
    Et que passiuum retinent sic plurima sensum,
    Que motum signant sic *apparens*que quietem.   70

Thys verbe *sum* may be takyn for *habeo*, and that þat semyth to be the nomynatyue case shal be the datyue and that that semyth to be the accusatyue shal be the nomynatyue; and oftentymis thys verbe *sum* gouernyth a dobull datyue case.

    Pro *habeo sum* posito fit permutatio recti
    In ternum casum,[1] pro quarto ponito primum;
    Atque regit duplicem casum quandoque datiuum.

Euery partycypull, gerundyue and supyn wyl be construyd w^t þat case that the verbe ys of whom they cumyth.

    Participans simul atque gerundia siue supina   80

---

[1] post *canc*.

TEXT FF

Poscunt cum verbis casus, tu lector, eosdem.

When I haue a nowne substantyue or a pronowne substantyue or an adyectyue substantyuely put set yn a reson w^{t}owte ony gouernans yt shal be put yn the ablatyue[1] case absolut<e>.

Sextus nonnumquam permittitur absque regente.

The ablatyue case absolute ys resoluyd by *dum* or by *cum*.

Per *dum* vel per *cum* sexti resolucio fiat.|

The ablatyue case absolute cannot be put w^{t}owte a partycypull expressyd or vnderstond.

Sepe subauditur existens participale. 90

Nownys that betokenyth instrumente, yff yt be not the nomynatyue case to the verbe nor otherwyse gouernyd, they shal be put yn the ablatyue case w^{t}owte þis preposytyon *cum*.

Instrumenta quidem que signant nomina cuncta
In sexto poni dic sine preposito.

Nownys that betokenyth tyme, mesure or space, yff yt be not the nomynatyue case to the verbe nor otherwyse gouernyd, they shal be put yn the ablatyue case, and many tymis yn the accusatyue case.

Designans tempus vel mensuram spaciumve 100
Aptius in sexto sinautem ponito quarto.

A verbe ympersonall of the actyue voyce endyth yn -*t* and ys declynyd yn the thyrde person, synglar number, as *penitet*, -*bat*, -*tuit*, -*erat*, -*bit*, -*re*. A verbe ympersonall of the passyue voyce endyth yn -*r* and ys declynyd yn the thyrd person synglar, as *placetur*, -*batur*, -*citum est* vel *fuit*, -*citum erat* vel *fuerat*, -*bitur*, -*ri*.

-*R*, -*t* cuiusque impersonalis retinebit
Finis voce simul, persone flectito terne.|

Verbys that betokenyth bodely movyng as *eo*, *is* and *venio*, -*is* may haue the signyfycatyon of the passyue voyce yn the 111 preterperfectens of the indicatyue mode and all tensys that be formyd of hym.

The Ynglyss of the ynfynytyue mode cumyng after ony of thys nownys yn thys versys folowyng or ony other lyke shal be ᵐade by the gerundyue yn -*di*.

Copia, libertas, modus, otia, causa, voluntas,
Ius, tempus, venia, locus, finis arsque facultas:

[1] s canc.

TEXT FF

Ista gerundia -*di* poscunt cum talibus apte.

Thys Ynglyss worde 'muste', where yt semyth to be made   120
by thys verbe *opportet*,[1] yt may be put yn the gerundyue[2] yn
-*dum* w[t] thys verbe *est* set ympersonally, and than the worde
that semyth to be the nomynatyue case shal be the datyue.

The gerundyue yn -*di*, -*do* and -*dum* ys declynyd yn iii
casys synglar as the genytyue, the accusatyue and the ablatyue,
as genytiuo *legendi*, accusatiuo *legendum*, ablatiuo *legendo*.

Per genitum, quartum sextumque gerundia flecte.

The gerundyue yn -*dum* ys oftyntymis takyn for the gerundyue
yn -*do* w[t] thys preposytyon *inter*.

Sepe gerundia -*dum* pro -*do* ponuntur et *inter*   130
Preiungetur eis: *Bene cures inter agendum*. |

Thys nownys adyectyus yn thys versys folowyng wyll haue
the gerundyue yn -*dum* w[t] thys preposytyon *ad*[3]. Exemplum:
Ne vacuum me ad narrandum credas.

Commodus atque *bonus, tardus, rudus, vtilis, aptus,*
Ponensque *velox, doctus, vacuus* simul adde.

When the Ynglyss of the ynfynytyue mode cumyth after a
verbe, partycypull, gerundyue and supyn betokenyng movyng or
goyng to a place yt shal be put yn the fyrst supyn or yn the
gerundyu<e> yn -*dum* w[t] thys preposytyon *ad*, but yt ys moste   140
vsyd yn the fyrst supyn. Also yt may be put yn a partycypull
of the fyrst futur tens and sumtyme yn the conyunctyue mode
w[t] thys conyunctyon *vt*. When the Ynglyss of the ynfynytyue
mode[4] cumyth after a verbe, partycypull, gerundyue or supyn
betokenyng movyng or goyng fro a place yt shal not bc made by
the gerundyue yn -*do* nor by the latter supyn but by the nowne
verball or sum nowne yn the stede of a nowne verball w[t] a
preposytyon before hym.

When the Ynglyss of the ynfynytyue[5] mode cumyth after a
nowne adyectyue endyng yn -*ilis* or yn -*bilis* of þe neuter   150
gender comparatyue or superlatyue degre, or after ony of thys
nownys yn thys versys folowyng or ony other lyke, they shal be
made by the latter supyn.

Indignus, dignus, obscenus, fedus, acerbus.
Rarus, iocundus, obsurdus, turpe, salubre,
Mirandus, mirus, pulchrum sic *periculosus.* |

When I haue an Ynglyss to be made by ony of thys verbys
exulo, vapulo, veneo and *fio*, that that doth the dede of the
verbe shal be put yn the ablatyue case w[t] a preposytyon and

[1] MS apportet   [2] d *canc.*   [3] a stroke *canc.*
[4] m- *from* a   [5] of the ynfynytyue *canc.*

189

TEXT FF

that þat ys the sufferer shal be the nomynatyue case, excepte   160
the verbe be the ynfynytyuᴄ mode, than the sufferer shal be
the accusatyue case.

When I haue an Ynglyss to be made by[1] thys verbe *nubo*
the manne shal be put yn the datyue case and the woman yn the
nomynatyue case, excepte the verbe be the ynfynytyue mode,
than the woman shal be the accusatyue case.

A proper name of a towne, cyte or vyllage, yf yt be the
fyrst declynson or seconde, synglar number, betokenyng bydyng
at a place or yn a place, yt shal be put yn the genytyue case
aduerbyally; but yff the proper name be ony other declynson   170
than the fyrst or the second, or the plurell number, yt shal be
put yn the ablatyue case. Also when suche proper namis of
place cumyth after a worde that betokenyth mouyng or goyng to
a place yt shal be put yn the accusatyue case w^{t}owte a
preposytyon, fro a place or by a place yn the ablatyue case.
Thys ii nownys *rus* and *domus* folowyth the rule of proper namys
yn euery case saue that *rus* betokenyng bydyng yn a place or[2]
at a place ys put euer yn the datyue case. *Bellum*, *humus*
and *militia* do folow the rule of proper namys yn the genytyue
case only. Other namys of place,[3] whether they be|proper
or appellatyue, shal be vsyd w^t a preposytyon before them.   181

Finis istius libri, quod M.

---

[1] o *canc.*   [2] y *canc.*   [3] f *canc.*

TEXT GG

GG. Durham Cathedral, MS B.IV.19, fol.1^(r-v)

How mony case has yow? Sex. Whilk er þay? Þe nominat(if), geniti(f), datif, acusatif, vocatif, þe ablatif. Whareby knawis þow þi case? By þaire takyns. Whylk er þay? Þe nominatif 'þe mayster', genitif 'of þe mayster', datif 'to þe mayster', accusatif 'þe mayster', vocatif 'o þou maister', ablatif 'thowrgh þe mayster'. 'Off' aftir a verbe, afftir a participil, 'off' aftire a comparatif gre sal be ablatif case. 'Off' after a nown sal be genitif case.

How mony nowmers has þow? Twa. Whilk? Þe singulere and þe plurere. Þe singulere is þat þat spekis of a thyng be   10
itself, þe plurele is þat spekys of mony thyngys monyly.

How mony gendirse has þow? Fowre. Whylk? Þe masculyn, þe feminyn, þe neuter, þe commun of twa and þe commun of thre. Þe masculyn gender declines wyth *hic*, þe feminyn w^t *hec*, þe neutir w^t *hoc*, þe commun of twa w^t *hic* and *hec*, þe commyn of¹ thre w^t *hic* and *hec* and *hoc*.

Whilk is a nown and whilk a verbe? Þat is a nown þat declines w^t artikyls and case or w^t thre diueris endyngys in a case as *hic magister, hec musa, hoc scannum, hic et hec sacerdos, hic et hec et hoc felix*; w^t thre diuerse endyngys² in a case   20
as *legendus, -da, -dum*. Þat is a verbe þat betakyns doyng and suffirryng, þat is lykkynd tyl *amo, -as; amor, -aris; doceo, -ces; doceor, -ceris; lego, -gis; legor, -geris; audio, -dis; audior, -diris*.

How mony modys has þow? Fywe. Wilk? Þe indicatif, inperatif, optatif, coniunctif, þe infinitif. Þe indicatif mod is þat þat schewis þe sothe or þe false; þe inperatif þat commandis; þe optatif þat yernys; þe coniunctif þat settis togydyr and spekes in drede; þe infinitif þat has nowyr nowmer nor person as 'for to rede' or 'for to be redde',   30
'for to teche', 'for to be teched': all swylk sal be infinitif mode.

How mony persons has þcu? Sex. Whilk? Thre in þe singulere and thre in þe plurele, as 'I' and 'þow' and 'he' in þe singulere and 'we' and 'ȝe' and 'þay' in þe plurele.

How many tens has þou? Thre. Whylk thre? Þe present, þe pretert, þe futur. Þe present is þat þat spekys of þe time þat is now, þe preterd þat spekys of þe time þat es past, þe futur þat spekys of þe tyme þat is for to cum.

Whilk is a adiectiuf and whilk is a sustantif? Þat is a   40
adiectif þat declines w^t thre artikyls or w^t thre diuerse endyngys in a case, as *hic et hec et hoc felix* or *bonus, -na, -num; malus, -la, -lum*. Þat is a sustantiue þat declynes w^t a artikyl or |w^t twa w^twtyn any ma.

¹ tre *canc.*   ² as *canc.*

TEXT GG

When sal þe relatif be nominatif case? When þar commys
na nominatif case betwene þe relatif and þe verbe þen sal þe
relatif be nominatif case; and when þar commys a nominatif
case betwene þe relatif and þe verbe þen sal þe relatif be swylk
case as þe verbe wyl haf aftir hym.

Whylk is a comparatif gre? Þat þe nominatif case endys 50
in -or and ⸌in⸍ -vs, as *hic et hec melior* et *hoc melius, hic
et hec grauior* et *hoc grauius, hic et hec peior* et *hoc peius*.
To what case serues þe comparatif gre? Til ablatif case of þe
ta numere and þe othyr. Why? For ilk a comparatif gre
may gouerne þe ablatif case of þe ta numere and þe othyr
w^{t}outen preposicion betakynnand thyng to whayme comparacion
is made.

Hic et hec et hoc amans is a participil and askys swylk
case aftir hym as þe verbe þat he commys of, and þe verbe þat
he commys of askys accusatif case aftir hym. 60

When twa verbys commis togydyr w^{t}outen a coniunccion þe
latter sal be infinitif[1] mode. 'Gode thyng', 'euyl thyng' and
all swylk sal be neutre gendir substantiuate.

When we haf a reson w^{t}outen a verbe we sal sette it in
þe ablatif case absolute.

In preposicion serues til accusatif case when he betakyns
steryng fra a place til a nothyr, fra a gre til a nothir, fra a
state til a nothyr.

Þe worde sal be accusatif case þat betakyns party of body
command aftir a[2] noun adiectif, aftir a verbe neutre, aftir 70
verbe absolute, aftir a verbe passiue or any of þair participils.

Þe futir tens of optatif mode and þe present tens of þe
coniunctif mode er sette for þe imper(a)tif mode.

Twa nominatif case singuler makys a verbe plurele. Twa
substantif singuler makys a adiectif plurele.

All swylk wordys 'swld', 'cowde',[3] 'mwght', 'wald', 'ware'
sal be coniunctif mode preterneperfite tens. All nouns and
all pronouns and al participils and all casualis sal be þe
thyrd person outane *ego, tu, nos* and *vos* w^t þayr obliquis.

A comparatif gre may haf genitif case aftir hym when þe 80
nownn þat commys aftir has þis takynnyg: 'off'. A superlatif
gre sal haf genitif case plurele afftir hym or ellys a genitif
singuler off a nown collectiue. Þe superlatiue gre sal acord
in gendir w^t þe genitif case þat commys afftir if so be þat
þe genitif case be of þe same keynde, and þe genitif case may
be turned into þe nominatif case vt *Ego sum fortissimus hominum*,
id est, *Ego sum fortissimus homo*.

[1] i *canc. before* -fin-   [2] nune (?) *canc.*   [3] mo mw (?) *canc.*

TEXT HH

HH. London, British Library, MS Add. 19046, fols.49^r-63^r

Ego sum creatura Dei c⌈r⌉eatoris mei. What noumbre and person is the verbe sum? The syngler noumbre and the fyrst person, for so is þe nominatyfe case ego. In how meny schall þe nominatife case and þe verbe acorrde? In ij. In whych ij? In numbre and person. Say thys in Latyn. Nominatiuus supponens et suum verbum personale conuenient in numero et persona. Vnde versus:

    Verbum supposito fac concordare duobus:
    Persona, numero, ceu tradit regula nobis.

Why rather accordith this verbe sum rather w^t þe nominatyfe   10
case ego than w^t þe nominatyfe case creatura? For euery verbe personale schall accorde w^t þe nominatyfe case supponent þat goth befor hym and not w^t þe nominatyfe case apponent þat commyth aftir hym in þe reson. Say thys in Latyn. Omne verbum personale modi finiti conueniet in numero et persona cum nominatiuo supponente et non cum nominatiuo apponente. Vnde versus:

    Verbum supposito semper conforme tenetur
    Et non apposito, nil illi namque tenetur.

Allso hit is to be notyd þat ther be iij maner of   20
nominatyfe cases, that is to say þe nominatyfe case supponent, þe nominatyfe|case apponent, and þe nominatyfe case exponent. The nominatyfe case supponent commeth byfore þe verbe personall; þe nominatyfe case apponent commeth after þe verbe personall copulatyfe; the nominatyfe case exponent exponeth þe verbe impersonall, as opponitur: est opposicio fit. Say thys in[1] Latyn. Triplex est nominatiuus casus, scilicet supponens, apponens et exponens. Nominatiuus casus supponens supponit verbum personali precede(n)s ipsum in construccione; nominatiuus casus apponens sequitur verbum personale   30
copulatiuum; nominatiuus casus expone(n)s exponit verbum impersonale. Vnde versus:

    Triplex est rectus: supponens primus habetur.
    Aliter[2] et apponens, exponens consocietur.

What case ys creatoris mei in the Latyne byfore? The ienetyfe case, for casualle wordys þat perteynyth to oon thyng schall be set in leke case. Say thys in Latyn. Casualea ad idem pertinencia in simili casu sunt ponenda.

Ego et Iohannes discimus diligenter. What numbre is þe verbe dicimus? Þe plurell numbre, for ij nominatyfe case   40
syngler or moo w^t a coniunccyon copulatyfe bytwene wyll haue a verbe plurel, yf neither of theym be a negatyfe. Say thys in Latyn. Duo supposita vel plura singularia affirmatiue copulata requirunt verbum plurale, si neutrum illorum sunt

[1] 1 canc.   [2] MS allter

TEXT HH

negatiuum.|

Si rectos binos tibi copula consociabit
Affirmatiue, verbum plurale meabit.

Why is þe verbe *discimus* þe fyrst person? For so is þe
nominatife case *ego* þat conceyueth þe other nominatyfe case
Iohannes, for þe fyrst person conceyueth þe secounde and þe   50
iij^{de} and þe secounde conceyueth also þe iij^{de}, but þe iij^{de}
person conceyueth not ayenward neither¹ þe fyrst ne þe secounde.
Say thys in Latyn. Prima persona concipit secundam personam
et terciam, et secunda² persona² concipit eciam terciam
personam, sed non e converso. Vnde versus:

Prima duas alias recipit sed non vice versa,
Sic *Ego tuque damus, Ego tu fraterque rogamus.*
Conscipiens terne mediam dic,³ nec retrouerte,
Tu fraterque datis; hoc quisquis dicet aperte.

Pater meus et non mater mea mor⁽i⁾tur. What numbre is   60
þe verbe *moritur*? Þe syngler numbre, for ij nominatyfe cases
syngler or mo w^t a coniuncion⁴ copulatife negatife bytwene
wull haue a verbe syngler. Say thys in Latyn. Duo supposita
syngularia vel plura negatiue copulata requirunt verbum singulare.
Vnde versus:

Sique negatiua binos mediat tibi rectos,|
In primo numero recte tunc ponitur actus.

Ego est pronomen. what numbre and person is þe verbe *est*?
The syngler numbre and þe thyrd person, for soo ys þe nominatyfe
case *ego* stondyng materiali; and euery worde stondyng materialli   70
stondyth for noo syngnificacion but for þe word onli, and then
he stondyth in þe stede of a nowne substantyfe of þe neuter
gender syngler numbre in þe strengtht of þe⁵ thyrde person and
vndeclined. Say thys yn Latyn. Omnis diccio materialiter
posita stat pro sola voce et non significacione in vice nominis
substantyfe⁶ in neutro genere, singulari numero, tercia persona
et vndeclinabiliter.

Bonus vir amat Deum super omnia. What case, gendre and
numbre ys þe adiectiue *bonus*? Þe nominatyfe case, þe masculyn
gendre and þe syngler numbre, for so ys þe substantyfe *vir*.   80
Yn how many schall þe adiectyfe and þe substantyfe acorde?
Yn iij. Yn which iij? In case, gendre and numbre. Say
thys yn Latyn. Adiectiuum et suum substantiuum conuenient in
casu, genere et numero. Vnde versus:

Cum substantiuis tribus adiectiua locabis,
In casu, genere et numero simul associabis.

Incaustum et penna scholasticis sunt oportuna. What

¹ MS ne[y]rther   ² MS adds -m   ³ nē *canc.*
⁴ copu¹ *canc.*   ⁵ thyr *canc.*   ⁶ *sic* MS

194

TEXT HH

numbre is þe adiectyfe *oportuna*? The plurell numbre, for
ij substantyfys|syngler or mo w^t a coniuncion copulatyfe
betwene well haue a adiectife plurell yf nether of them be a   90
negatyfe. Say thys in Latyn. Duo substantyua singularia
vel plura affirmatyue copulata coniunccione copulatiua mediante
requirunt adiectiuum plurale. Vnde versus:

    Substantiua duo si singula sunt tibi iuncta
    Affirmatiue mobile plurale requirunt.

    Why is þe adiectyfe *oportuna* the neuter gender? For so
ys the substantyfe *incaustum*, and euer more þe adiectyfe schal
be suche gender as ys þe gender þat conseyuyth. And here ys
to be notyth þat þe masculyn gender conseyuyth þe femenyne and
þe¹ neutyre yn þyngys hauyng kynde or lyfe, as thus: *Vir*,   100
mulier et mancipium sunt albi; but þe nutyr gender concey(uy)th
þe masculyn and þe femynyn yn thyngys that haue no kynde ne
lyfe, as thus: *Paries, fenestra et hostium sunt aperta*. Say
thys in Latyn. Masculinum genus concipit femininum et neutrum
in rebus sexatis et animatis, vt *Puer, puella et mancipium sunt
occupati*; sed neutrum genus concipit masculinum et femininum
in rebus insexatis et inanimatis, vt *Paries, fenestra et hostium
sunt fracta*. Vnde versus:

    Fem(i)neum, neutrum mas. concipit mageque dignum
    Rebus sexatis, si sermo sit tibi factus;   110
    Sed si de rebus non sexatis tibi fiat,|
    Neutrum tunc sibi mas. bene concepit et femininum.

*Celum*² *est amenus locus*. Why ys þe adiectyfe *amenus* þe
masculyn gendre? For when an adiectyfe þat ys a nown ys putte
bytwene ij nownes substantyfes of dyuers genders perteynyng
bothe to oon thyng, then þe adiectyfe shall accorde in case,
gender and numbre with þe substantyfe that folowith, as thus:
Homo est racionale animal; but yf þe adiectyfe be a participull
then ytt schall accorde with þe substantyfe byfore, as thus:
Dominus est factus refugium pauperi. Say thys in Latyn.   120
Adiectiuum nominale positum inter duo substantyfa diuersorum
generum ad idem pertinencia conuenient cum substantiuo posteriori
in casu, genere et numero, vt *Bos est vtile aratro*, et non *vtilis*.
Sed adiectiuum participale positum inter duo substantiua³
diuersorum generum ad idem pertinancia conuenient⁴ cum substantiuo
priori in casu, genere et numero, vt *Hec lana est futura pannus*;
Aqua est facta vinum. Vnde versus:

    Inter fixa duo si mobile nomen habetur
    Fixo quod sequitur fieri conforme tenetur,
    Sic *Bos est animal album* non *albus* habetur.   130
    Si sit participans precedenti similetur:
    Est aqua facta merum sapiens ita quisque loquetur.
    Autor 'Catholicon' ssuper⁵ hoc testis retinetur.

---

¹ mascu *canc*.   ² Consonu *canc*. *before* Celum
³ priori *canc*.   ⁴ co *canc*.   ⁵ *sic* MS

TEXT HH

Vir locutus est bene. Why ys þe participle *locutus* þe
masculyn gendre? For eueri participle y-set in circumlocucion|
of a verbe personale of þe infinitife[1] mode schall accorde in
case, gender and numbre w^t þe substantyfe befor hym, as this:
Vir locutus est;[2] *Mulier loquuta est; Mancipium locutum est.*
But a participle set in circumlocucion of a verbe impersonale
or ellis of a verbe personale of þe infinityue mode schall   140
be set[3] invariabile in þe neuter gender, singler numbre, as
this: *Michi oppositum est a magistro; A muliere amatum est;
A multis obuiatum est; Desidero omnes sanctos et sanctas Dei
deprecatum esse Deum pro me.* Say thys in Latyn. Participium
positum in circumlocucione verbi personalis modi finiti conueniet
cum substantiuo precedenti in casu, genere et numero. Sed
participium positum in circumlocucione verbi impersonalis siue
verbi personalis modi infiniti potest esse invariabile in casu
et numero et in neutro genere tantum, vt patet in prioribus
exemplis. Vnde versus: 150

> Infinitiui circumloquium quoque verbi
> Impersonalis stabit cum stantibus ipsum;
> Sed personale circumloquium generali
> Mutat, namque: *Puta quondam testudo locuta.*

Consonum est oracioni. What gender ys thys adiectyfe
consonum? The nuter gender substantyfely, for when ther ys
and adiectyf y-putt yn a reson wythowte a substantyfe then schall
þe adectyfe be set yn þe neuter gender substantyfeli. Say
thys in Latyn. Adiectiuum in voce et significacione positum
in oracione sine substantiuo explicito|vel subintellecto   160
debet poni in neutro genere substantiuato, vt *Bonum est,
Malum est.* Vnde versus:

> Mobile prolatum[4] preter fixum sibi sertum,
> In neutro[5] genere fixum solet esse repertum.

Vir qui laborat manducet. What gender, numbre and person
ys þe relatyfe *qui*? Þe masculyn gender, syngler numbre and þe
iij^d person, for so ys þe antecedens *vir*. In how meny schall
þe relatyfe and þe antecedens accorde? In iij. In which iij?
In gender, numbre and person. Say thys in Latyn. Relatiuum
et suum antecedens conuenient in genere, numero et persona.   170
Vnde versus:

> Antecedenti tribus hijs coniunge relatum:
> Persona, numero, sit[6] genus hijsque datum.

Panis et ceruisi⌈a⌉ *qui sunt in villa venales sunt*[7]
oportuni. Why ys þe relatyfe *qui* þe[8] plurell numbre? For
ij antecedens syngler or moo w^t a coniuncyon copulatyfe bytwene
wull haue a relatiuefe plurell yf nether of them be a negatyfe.
Say thys in Latyn. Duo antecedencia syngularia vel plura
affirmative copulata requirunt relatiuum plurale. Vnde versus:

---

[1] mode *canc.*   [2] b *canc.*   [3] -t *from* d
[4] MS perlatum   [5] gener<a> *canc.* [6] MS *sic*
[7] oportun<(?)>t *canc.*   [8] l *canc.*

TEXT HH

Singula si iungas duo precedencia vere   180
Tuncque relatium debet plurale manere.

Socius meus quem semper dilexi grauiter infirmatur. What
case ys þe relatife *quem*? Þe accusatife case, for when ther
commeth a nominatyfe case bitwene þe relatyfe and þe verbe
then þe relatyfe|schall be such case as þe verbe wulle haue
after hym, and þat ys most comenly þe accusatyfe case. But
and ther comme no nominatyfe case bytwene þe relatyfe and þe
verbe then þe relatyfe schall be þe nominatyfe case to þe verbe.
Say thys in Latyn. Quando rectus casus mediat inter relatium
et verbum tunc relatium erit talis casus qualem verbum exigit   190
post se. Set si¹ non mediat rectus casus inter relatium et
verbum tunc relatium erit nominatius casus verbo personali.
Allso all nownes interrogatiuis folowyth þe same rule. Omnia
nomina interrogatiua eandem regulam sequuntur. Vnde versus:

  Si rectus² mediat inter verbumque relatum
  Casu quem verbum vult post se³ pone relatum;
  Si nil sit mediatum pro recto pone relatum.
  De personali tamen hoc intelligi dici.
  Nomina que querunt dictam normam subierunt.

And thes be þe nownes interrogatyfes þat be conteynyd yn thes   200
versus folowyng. Vnde versus:

  Quis, qualis, quantus, cuius, cuias, quotus et *quot*;
  Hijs *vter* addatur, sunt quesitiua tibi tot.

Ecclesia que vel *qui est locus sacratus bene frequenta(tu)r
a populo Cristiano.* What gender ys þe relatyfe *que* vcl *qui*?
The femynyn|and þe masculyne, for when þys relatyfe *qui*, *que*,
quod ys putte bytwene too nownes substantyfes of dyuers gendres
perteynyng boþe to oon thyng than the relatyfe may accorde wᵗ
boþe substantyfes yn gender. Say thys in Latyn. Quando hoc
relatium *qui, que, quod* ponitur inter duo substantiua diuersorum 210
generum ad idem pertinencia potest tam vni quam alteri in genere
confirmari. Vnde versus:

  Quando relatium generum casus variorum
  Inter se claudant que rem spectant ad eandem,
  Per genus hoc poterit vtrilibet associari:
  Est pia stirps Iesse quem Christum dicimus esse.

Schola est locus quem disc(ip)uli spernunt. Why ys þe
relatyfe *quem* the masculyne gender? For so ys þe antecedens
locus. Why rather accordyth the relatyfe wᵗ þe later
antecedens then wᵗ þe frist? For by þe rule the relatyfe   220
schall be referyd to þe nexte antecedens but yf þe sentense
lett hytt, as in thys Latyn: *Canis tuus occidit ouem meam quem
ego occidem si possum capere.* Yn thys Latyn þe relatyfe *quem*
schall accorde wᵗ the firste antecedens and nott wᵗ þe later
bycause of þe sentens. Say thys in Latyn. Ad proximum

¹ MS oī   ² MS rectos   ³ post se]MS posse

TEXT HH

antecedens semper fiet relacio nisi centencia impediat quia
tunc ad remocius antecedens fiet relacio. Vnde versus:

> Antecedenti propiori iunge relatum;
> Hoc dum permittat sensum fore notificatum.

Ista est pulcra commetiua quam vel *quos Deus saluet a malc.* 230
Whey ys þe relatyfe *quos* the plurel numbre? For so ys þe
antecedens y-vnderstond|yn þe nowne collectife *commetiua*.
Whych ys þat? *Homines*, for when a relatyfe ys referyd to a
nowne collectyfe then hyt maye accorde w^t þe thyng vnderstonde
in þe nowne collectyfe and nott w^t þe voy(c)e or nowne expressyd
and allso a nowne adiectyfe ys sumtyme referyd to the thyng
vnderstond and nott w^t þe voy(c)e exppreyssyd. Say thys in
Latyn. Quando relatiuum refertur ad nomen collectiuum tunc
potest relatiuum referri ad rem intellectum et non ad vocem
exppresam; et eciam adiectiuum aliqucm potest conuenire cum   240
re intellecta et non cum voce exppresa. Vnde versus:

> Non des ad vocem quandoque relata sed ad rem:
> Nominis:[1] *Est bona gens, Deus est protector eorum.*
> Adiectiua modo poni reperimus eodem:
> *Pars hominum validi turres et menia scandunt.*

Ego sum ille qui nolo vel *non vult fugere.* Why ys þe
verbe *nolo* vel *non vult* þe firste person and þe thyrde? For
when this relatyfe *qui, que, quod* is referryd to ij pronownes
of dyuers persones then þe relatyfe may accorde wyth[2] either
pronownes in person. But yf thys relatyfe *qui, que, quod* be   250
referryd to a pronown and a nown then þe relatyfe schall be
only þe thyrde person. Saye thys yn Latyn. Quando hoc
relatiuum *qui, que, quod* refertur ad pronomina diuersarum
personarum tunc verbum relatiui potest|conuenire in persona
cum vtroque pronomine, vt *Tu es ille qui seruis* uel *seruit Deo.*
Sed quando relatiuum refertur ad nomen tercie persone et ad
pronomen prime vel secunde persone tunc verbum relatiui erit
tantum tercie persone, vt *Ego sum homo qui patriam seruauit.*
Vnde versus:

> Quando relatiuum *qui* pronomen recitabit   260
> Persone duplicis, sibi verbum consociabit,
> Vt *Sum qui scripsi* vel *qui scripsit* bene dixi.
> Ad nomen quociens recitari qui videatur,
> Tercia tunc verbi tantum persona sequatur.
> Istac vera scias quia sic vult Petrus Alias.

*Magister non attente laborat circa suorum dissipulorum
instruccionem, propter quod criminandus est.* Why ys þe relatyfe
quod þe neuter gendre ⌈and þe singuler numbre⌉? For when thys
relatyfe *qui, que, quod* ys referryd to þe vnderstondyng of all
þe reson þat goeth before or to a worde stondyng materially or   270
to a infenetyfe mode taken for a nowne, then þe relatyfe schall
be þe neutre gender and þe singular numbre. Say thys in Latyn.

[1] MS Nomines   [2] then þe *canc*.

198

TEXT HH

Quando hoc relatiuu· *qui, que, quod* refertur ad sensum tocius
oracionis premisse vel ad diccionem materialiter positum vel
ad infenitiuum modum nominaliter sumptum, tunc relatiuum erit[1]
neutri generis et singularis numeri.⌐ Exemplum: *Primi discoli
auertuntur scolam propter quod sunt indocti.* Exemplum secundi:
Ego quod est pronomen est dissillabum. Exemplum tercij:
Tuum scire quod[2] *audio est laudandum,* et cetera. Vnde versus:

    Ad sensum sepe vel materiale relatum   280
    Inuenies: *Fugis aut piger es, mihi quod procul absit.*

Pater meus dedit mihi tria grossa quod est solidus. Why
ys þe relatyfe *quod* þe neutre gendre and þe singuler numbre?
For when thys relatyfe *qui, que, quod* is putt bytwene ij
nownes substanty of dyuerse gendres wherof oon bytokeneth
parties and that other bytokeneth þe hole then þe relatyfe
schall accorde in gendre[3] with þe substantyfe þat bytokeneth
þe ⌐parties⌐ ⌐and wyth þe substantyfe þat bytokeneth þe⌐ hole
in noumbre and person. Saye thys in Latyn. Quando hoc
relatiuum *qui, que, quod* ponitur inter duo substantiua quorum   290
prius significat partes et posterius significat totum tunc relatiuum
conveniet cum substantiuo significante partes in genere tantum et
cum substantiuo significante totum in numero et persona, vt *In*[4]
*eu⌐a⌐ngelio vna vidua paupercula misit in gazaphilacium duo
minuta quod est quadrans,* etcetera·

Pater meus est vna creaturarum. What case, gendre and
nowmbre is this nown[5] partetife *vna*? The|nominatyfe case,
þe femynin gendre and þe syngler noumbre, for euery nown
partetyfe sette partetyfly[6] schall accorde in case and noumbre
wyth þe substantyfe that gooth byfore and in gendre with þe   300
genetyfe case that folowith, yf they accorde in significacion.
Say thys in Latyn. *Omne nomen partitiue partitiue positum
siue distributiuum conueniet cum substantiuo precedenti in
casu et numero et cum genetiuo sequenti in genere tantum, si
conueniant in significacione.* Vnde bene dicitur: *Deus est
vna rerum,* sed male dicitur: *Deus est vna creaturarum.* Vnde
versus:

    Concordans generi ⌐fore[7]⌐ pluralis genetiui
    Vult partitiuum veluti *Lepus vna ferarum.*
    Est vnus florum rosa ⌐dicat⌐ *quisque virorum.*   310

Deus est optima rerum. What case, gendre and numbre
is the superlatyfe degre *optima*? The nominatyfe case, þe
femynin gendre and syngler noumbre, for euery superlatife
degre schall accorde in case and numbre with the substantife
that goeth byfore and in gendre only with the genetyfe case
þat folowith, ⌐yf⌐ thei accorde in significacion. Say thys
in Latyn. *Omnis superlatiuus gradus conueniet cum substantiuo
precedenti in casu et numero et cum genetiuo sequenti in genere|*

---

[1] n *canc. after* -i-   [2] audito *canc.*   [3] ˰wh *canc.*
[4] gazaphilacium duo minutam quod *canc.*   [5] ˰partife *canc.*
[6] ty *canc. after* par-   [7] MS flore

199

TEXT HH

tantum, si conueniant in significacione. Vnde versus:

> Omne superlatum genetiuo sit sociatum   320
> Atque suo genere conforme cupit retincre,
> Vt pateat verum sic: *Est Deus optima rerum*.

Vtinam essem episcopus qui vocor Iohannes. What case is *episcopus*? The nominatyfe case, for *sum*, *es*, *fui* is a verbe copulatyfe and may copull lyke cases. Saye thys in Latyn. *Sum*, *es*, *fui* est verbum copulatiuum copulans consimiles casus. Howe many verbes have strenght to copull like cases? Verbes substantyfes, verbes vocatyfes, and verbes hauyng[1] their strenght. Howe many verbes substantyfes be there? III. Which iij? *Sum*, *es*, *fui*; *fio*, *fis* and *existo*, *-tis*. Say this in Latyn.   330
Tria sunt verba substantiua, scilicet *sum*, *fio* et *existo*. Vnde versus:

> Ars substantiua tria dat tantummodo verba:
> *Sum* simul *existo*, *fio*, nil amplius addo.

Howe many verbes vocatyfes be there? V. Which v? *Nominor*, *-aris*; *appellor*, *-aris*; *nuncupor*, *-aris*; *vocor*, *-aris* and *dicor*, *-ceris*. Vnde versus:

> Quinque vocatiua dicas tantummodo verba:|
> *Nominor*, *appellor* sic *nuncupor*, addito *dicor*
> Et *vocor*; hec similes[2] semper poscunt sibi casus.   340

Istud doleum est plenum vel *vacuum vini* vel *vino*. What case ys *vini* vel *vino*? The genetyfe case and þe ablatyfe case, for all wordes þat betokenyth fulnes or amptines, worthynes or[3] vnworthynes, preysyng or blamyng maye construe w^t a genctyfe case and a ablatyfe case. Saye thys in Latyn. Omnis diccio significans plenitudinem vel vacuetatem, ⌈dignitatem vel in⌉-dignitatem, laudem vel vituperum potest construi cum genetiuo et ablatiuo casu ex vi significacionis passiue. Vnde versus:

> Que plenam signant vel que vacuata figurant
> Iunguntur sextis, vt scribitur, et genetiuis.[4]   350
> Exemplum querens istos versus retinere:
> *Vini* vel *vino* duo *dolea*[5] *plena videto*.
> Dignum vel laudem vel que contraria sunt hijs:
> *Sum dignus laudis* vel *laude ducere debes*.

Abstinio irarum et desino viciorum. What case ys *irarum* and *vic(i)orum*? The genetyfe case, for þes too verbes *abstinio*, *-es* et *desino*, *-is* maye gouern a genetyfe case and allso a ablatyfe case w^t a preposicion. Saye thys in Latyn. Ista[6] duo verba *abstineo*, *-es* et *desino*, *-is* regunt genetiuum casum et eciam ablatiuum casum|cum preposicione, et *abstineo*, *-es* aliquando exigit accusatiuum casum secundum Hugucionem.   361
Vnde versus:

---

[1] MS hauyng [2] MS siniles [3] MS on
[4] MS genetiɡ [5] MS doleo [6] est *canc.*

TEXT HH

Abst(i)neo quartum, sextum petit et genetiuum:
A vini, vino, vinum simul *abstineo*¹ *me.*
Desino do genetis cum preposita quoque sextis:
Desinit irarum vel *ab ira quisque suarum.*

Dominor huius ville vel *huic ville uius incolarum* vel
incolis ego miserebor. What case be þes wordes *incolarum*
vel *incolis*? The genetyfe case and þe datyfe case, for þes
ij verbes *dominor, -aris* and *miserior, -ris* maye governe a   370
genetyfe case and a datyfe case, and *miserior, -ris* maye
governe an accusatyfe case. Saye thys in Latyn. Ista duo
verba *dominor, -aris* et *miserior, -ris* possunt regere genetiuum,
datiuum et accusatiuum casum ex vi transicionis. Vnde versus:

> Do *dominor* ternis *miserere* siue secunde,
> Et sibi vult iungi quartum casum *miserere*:
> *Noster, nobis* vel *nos Ihesu miserere.*

Scholares indigent librorum vel *libris.* What case ys
librorum vel *libris*? The genetyfe case and the ablatyfe case,
for theis ij verbis *egeo, eges* and *indigeo, -es*² maye goverm   380
a genetyfe case and a ablatyfe case. Saye | this in Latyn.
Ista duo verba *egeo, -es* et *indigeo, -es* regunt genetyuum casum
et ablatyuum casum ex vi transsicionis. Vnde versus:

> Des ablatiuis³ *eget, indiget* et genetiuis,⁴
> Vt noscas verum dic *Indigeo quoque rerum,*
> *Indigeo bobus ad rura colenda duobus.*

Memento mortis, mortem vel *morte tua.* What case ys *mortis,*
mortem vel *morte tua*? Þe genetyfe, þe accusatyfe and þe
ablatyfe case, for all verbes perteynyng to remembrance, hauyng
in mynde or forgetyng may governe a genitife, a accusatife and   390
a ablatife case. Say thys in Latyn. Omnia verba pertinencia
ad memoriam, recordacionem vel obliuionem possunt regere
genitiuum, accusatiuum et ablatiuum casum ex vi transicionis.

> Verbum quodque⁵ notans obliuisci, memorari
> Quarto cum genito sextove petit associare:
> *Eius, eum* vel *eo mimini*⁶ ⌈*poteris*⌉ *resitare.*
> Vult genitum partum totum quartumque⁷ notare.

Also all the verbys þat be conteynyd yn thees verses
folowyng woll construe wᵗ a genetyfe case, a accusatyfe and a
ablatyfe ⌈case⌉. Say thys yn Latyn. Item omnia verba in   400
hijs versubus sequentibus contenta possunt regere genetiuum,
accusatiuum et ablatiuum casum ex ui transicionis. Vnde
versus:

> *Participo, miror, eget, indiget* atque *recordor*
> Et *memini, dignor, obliuiscor, r(e)miniscor:* |

---

¹ MS abstines   ² r canc.   ³ MS ablatig
⁴ MS genitig   ⁵ MS quod₃   ⁶ MS minimi
⁷ MS quartum qui

TEXT HH

Ista regunt genitum, iiij^{rtum}, sextum quoque casum.
Hijs *pocior* detur, Hugucio testis habetur.

Inimicus homo accusauit me iudici criminis vel *crimine cuius* vel *quo indigne vituperior.* What case ys *criminis* vel *crimine*? Þe genetyfe case and þe ablatyfe case, for all verbis   *410*
actyfes perteynyng to accusyn, dampnyng or reprevyng, blameng or monyschyn[1] may governe a accusatyfe case betokenyng the person þat the dede of the verbe passyth ynto, and w^t a genetyfe case and a ablatyfe case betokenyng the cryme or blame of þe person; and þe verbys passyfs of thees forsayd verbys actyfys may gouerne a genetyfe case and a ablatyfe case. Say thys in Latyn. Omnia verba pertinencia ad accusacionem, damnacionem, vituperacionem, reprehencionem, monicionem vel ad istorum contraria[2] possunt regere accusatiuum casum significantem rem in quam transit actus verbi, et genitiuum et ablatiuum significantes *420* causam vel materiam sue accionis; et verba passiua istorum actiuorum possunt regere genitiuum, accusatiuum et ablatiuum significantes causam vel materiam sue passionis ex vi transicionis. Vnde versus:

> Verbum damnare significans vel vituperare
> Aut accusare, reprehendere siue monere
> Quarto cum genito sextove petit associare.
> Actum qui recipit iiij^{to} dabis, sed genitiuo|
> Aut ablatiuo que causam terminant[3] actus:
> *Te furti damno* vel *furto* sic bene dico.   *430*
> Passiuum genitis vel sextis adiciatis:
> *Furti* vel *furto damnor* bene sic recitatis.
> Que contraria sunt iungi ceu laude sciatis.

Obuiemus episcopo Cantuarienci. What case ys *episcopo*?
Þe datyfe case, for all verbys þat byth conteynyd in thes verses folowyng may governe a datyfe case. Say thys in Latyn. Omnia verba in hijs versubus sequentibus[4] contenta possunt regere datiuum casum ex vi transicionis. Vnde versus:

> *Obuio, parco, placet, noceo, respondeo, seruet,*
> *Precipit, opponit,* concludo, iunge datiuis,   *440*
> *Supplicat, aridet, faueo, vaco, proficit, heret.*
> *Subuenit* addatur, *succurrit, propiciatur.*
> *Congruo, conpacior, confert, succedit, adulor,*
> *Incidit, inponit, conuicior, improperavit,*
> *Sufficit, aspirat, valedico, gratulor, astat,*
> *Emenit* ac *equipollet, alludit,*[5] *obedit* et *obstat.*
> *Occurrit, restat* et *cedo,* quando locum dat,
> *Incidior,*[6] *pateor, minor, est, obtempero,*[7] *fido,*|
> *Derogo, condoleo, preiudico, detraho, differt,*
> *Suppetit* hijs iungas. Que *sum* componit eis das.   *450*
> Hec et quamplura ternis coniungere cura.

---

[1] *hy canc. after monys-*   [2] *pti canc.*   [3] *sic* MS
[4] *conte canc.*   [5] *sic* MS   [6] *fido canc.*
[7] MS *obtempere*

TEXT HH

Pater meus em⁽ⁱ⁾t equum viginti solidorum vel *viginti solidis.* What case ys *viginti solidorum* vel *viginti solidis?* The genetyfe case and þe ablatife case, for all wordys perteynyng to price may gouerne a genetyfe case and a ablatyfe case betokenyng the pryce and allso a accusatyfe case betokenyng the thing y-bowght. Say thys in Latin. Omnia verba pertinencia ad precium possunt regere genitiuum et ablatiuum precium desygnantes et eciam accusatiuum significantem rem emptam. Vnde versus: 460

    Cum precij verbis in casubus verte sextis,
    Cum quibus etsi vis vti poteris genetiuis.
    Quanti vel *quanto constat res ista* petenti,
    Tanti vel *tanto* responde more dice(n)ti.
    Quanto querenti bene possis discere *tanti*;
    Vi norme talis[1] fallit sermo generalis,
    Quo casu queris hoc respondere teneris.|

Also thes verbe *valeo, -les* betokenyng price may gouerne a accusatyfe case as thys: *Hic equs valet viginti solidos,* and a genetyfe and an ablatyfe betokenyng incerteyn pryce as 470
thus: *Hec res valet tanti* vel *tanto, Quanti* vel *quanto possunt*[2] *vendi.* Say thys in Latyn. Hoc verbum *valeo, -les* potest regere accusatiuum casum denotantem certum precium, et genetiuum casum et ablatiuum denotantes incertum precium. Vnde versus:

    Designans *valeo* certum precium dabo quarto,
    Incertum signans genitiuo iungeve sexto.

Consulo tibi bonitatis tue vel *bonitate tua consulere magistrum tuum de hac re.* Why ys *bonitatis* vel *bonitate* the genetyfe case and the ablatyfe case? For when þis verbe *consulo, -is* betokenyth[3] 'to geue consell' hyt ys a verbe neuter 480
and may gouerne a genetyfe and a ablatyfe case, and when hyt betokenyth 'to aske counsoll' hyt ys a verbe actyfe and may gouerne a accusatyfe case. Say thys in Latyn. Quando hoc verbum *consulo, -is* significat dare consilium est verbum neutrum et potest regere genitiuum casum et ablatiuum casum, et|quando hoc verbum *consulo, -is* significat petere vel accipere consilium est verbum actiuum et potest regere accusatiuum casum. Vnde versus:

    Consulo consilium querens pariterque ministrans:
    Consulo te rogito, *Tibi consulo* consilium do. 490
    Est prius actiuum, sit postremus quoque neutrum.

Michi Iohanni dolenti caput qui es oportuna. Why ys *caput* the accusatyfe case? For when a nowne adiectife, verbe neuter or verbe passyfe or eny of ther participull commyth befor thys Englyssche 'the', and a nowne substantyfe betokenyng part of mannys body or ellis the hole body inmedyatly folowyth,

---

[1] -i- from e   [2] MS pussut
[3] other lyke to them then the englyssche of þe Infinityfe mode schal be a gerundife in di as thys Tempus est *canc.*

TEXT HH

then the nowne substantyfe schal be put in þe accusatyfe case
and be governe by thys fugure: sinatygen. Say thys in Latyn
Quando nomen adiectiuum, verbum neutrum ʿvelˈ passiuum vel
aliquod eorum participium precedet hoc Anglicum ' he', et   500
nomen substantiuum significa s partem corporis humani vel totum
corpus (sequitur), tunc illud nomen substantiuum ponetur in
accusatiuo casu et regitur ex vi sinotiges. Vnde versus:

  Adiectiua regunt passiuave verbaque neutra
  Accusatiuos per sinotigen sibi iunctos
  Cum partis toti tribuantur proprietates,
  Aut e conuerso. Mox hinc exempla videto:|
  Alba comas dolet Anna caput, crus frangitur illa.
  Participans iunges vt Femina compta capillos;
  Iunge gerundiua cum participante, suppina.   510

  Postulo Deum graciam bene addiscendi qui doceor[1] gramaticam.
Why ys graciam the accusatyfe case? For all þe verbys actyvys
that perteynyng to doctryn, prayyng or askyn or arayyngis of
manys body may governe ij accusatyfe cases, and þe passyfys of
þe forsayd actyvys may governe a accusatyfe case. Say thys
yn Latyn. Omnia verba pertinencia ad doctrinam, deprecacionem,
peticionem vel ad ornatum corporis possunt regere duplices
accusatiuos casus, et verba passiua istorum actiuorum possunt
regere vnum accusatiuum casum. Vnde versus:

  Corporis ornatum verbum quod significabit,   520
  Atque precationem sic doctrinamque notabit,[2]
  In duplicem iiij^{rtum} vehementi iure meabit,
  Quorum posterior cum passiuis bene stabit.
  Istis iungatur celo quod eis[3] sociatur.

What party of reson ys addicendi yn þe forsayd Latyn?
A nowne gerundyfe yn -di, for when a Englysche of þe infynityfe
mode commyth after eny of thees|wordys hora, tempus,
prepositum, causa, desiderium, gracia, voluntas or eny other
lyke to them þe Englyssche of þe infynitife mode schal be a
gerundyfe in -di as thys: Tempus est iantandi, Veni gracia   530
discendi ad vesperas, Est hora pulsandi. Say thys in Latyn.
Quando vox infinitiui modi sequitur aliquod[4] istorum nominum
hora, tempus, prepositum, causa, desiderium, gracia, voluntas
vel aliquod istorum simele tunc vox <infinitiui> modi ponetur
in gerundiuo m(o)di. Vnde versus:

  Gracia, pax, tempus, coniungemus ista voluntas,
  Rite gerundiua possunt casus genetiui:
  Est tempus flendi, Non est mihi causa dolendi.
  Que nunc narrandi non est locus Affricus inquit.

  How knos a gerundyfe in -do? A gerundyfe in -do may be   540
in speche iij maner of wysys. Fyrste when þe Englyssche
worde 'in' commyth befor a Englyssche of a partycyple of þe

[1] MS docēor   [2] nota- from mea   [3] simelatur canc.
[4] MS aliqū

TEXT HH

present tense w^tout a substantyfe[1] put to hym then schall hyt be set in a gerundyfe in -*do* w^t thys preposicion in as thys: 'In fyghttyng meny men be woundyd, meny be maymyd and meny be slayne'. Say[2] thys yn Latyn. Quando hoc Anglicum 'in' precedit Anglicum participij presentis temporis sine substantiuo sibi posito, tunc Anglicum participij ponetur in gerundiuo[3] in -*do* cum ista preposicione *in* vt sic: *In|dimicando multi homines sunt vulnerati*,[4] *multi mutilati et multi sunt occisi*.   550

   Intendo me ire oppositum scholaribus quos bene respondentes intime sum dilecturus. What party of reson ys *appositum*? The fyrste subpyne, for when an Englysch of þe infenetyfe mode folowyth a verbe betok(en)yng[5] meuyng or steryng to a plase[6] eny thyng to be done or sufferyd hyt schall be put in þe fyrst suppyng in -*um* as thys: 'I goe to rede bokys'; and when a Englysche of a participul of the presentens folowyth þe verbe betokeneng meuyng or steryng from a plase eny thyng to be done or sufferd hyt schal be putt in þe later subpyng as thus: 'I cum from reddyng bokys'. Say thys in Latyn. Quando vox   560 infenetiue modi sequitur verbum singnificans motum ad locum ponetur primo suppino vt sic: *Ego vado lectum libros*; et quando vox participie presentis temporis sequetur verbum significans motum de loco ponetur in vltimo suppino vt: *Ego vado lectu libros*. Vnde versus:

   Post motus verbum primum coniunge suppinum
   Vt *Vado lectum, senatum* siue *commestum*.
   Deque loco signans postremum[7] iunge suppinum
   Vt *Venio lectu, senatu* siue *commestu*.|
   Ast infenitum dum non signat tibi modum
   Vt *Cupio legere, Volo ludere, Cura docere*.   571

   Rex noster profectus est nuper Londoniis, Cantuariam; *regina vero manet Wyntonie*. What case ys *Wyntonie*? The genetyfe case, for whan a propir name of a place, towne or sety notte compownyd folowyth a verbe or partycypule, gerundyfe or suppine betokenyng or bidyng in a place or at a place, yf the nowne be the fyrste declenson or the cecunde and the syngler numbre hyt schal be put in the genityfe case aduerbeally as yn thys Latyn befor. But yff the nowne be of the iij^d declynson and the syngler number or ellis of the fyrste   580 declenson and the plurell numbre hyt schal be put yn the ablatyfe case as thus: *Ego fui Atheniis, Cartagene*, and thes iiij nowns *rus, domus, humus*,[8] and *milecia* folowyng the same rvle. Say thys in Latyn. Quando proprium nomen loci, ville vel ciuitatis simplex non compositum nec de sanctis dictum sequitur verbum participium, gerundiuum vel suppinum significans permanenciam in loco, si nomen fuerit primo declinacionis vel secunde et singularis numeri ponitur in genitiuo casu aduerbialiter et sine regimine.[9] Sed et nomen fuerit tercie declinacionis et singularis numeri siue prime delinacionis et   590

---

[1] per *canc*.
[2] t *canc*.
[3] u *canc. after* ge-
[4] y *canc. after* -t-
[5] tok *canc. after* be-
[6] ey *canc*.
[7] MS postrenum
[8] MS humlus
[9] fuerit *canc*.

205

TEXT HH

pluralis numeri ponitur in ablatiuo casu aduerbialiter et sine
regimine, et ista quatuor nomina appellatiua *rus*, *domus*, *humus*
et *milicia* eandem regulam sequntur. Vnde¹ versus:|

    Nomina villana mora si presit genitis des
    Singula dum fuerint nec per ternam² variata.
    Terna si fuerint vel si pluralia dentur
    Aduerbij more sextorum sede sedebunt,
    Dum sint simplicia nec de sanctis recitata.
    Rus quoque *milicia*, *domus* ac *humus* ista sequuntur.

    What case ys *Cantuariam* in the forseid Latyn? Þe   600
accusatife case, for when a proper name of a plase, towne or
cyty not compownyd folowith a verbe, participull, gerundyfe or
suppine betokenyng mevyng to a plase³ hit schal be putt in the
accusatyfe case aduerbyaly as thus: *Ego intendo ire Londonias
et Eboracum.* Say thys in Latyn. Quando proprium nomen loci,
ville vel ciuitatis simplex non compositum sequitur verbum,
participium, gerundium vel suppinum significans motum a(d) locum
ponetur in accusatiuo casu aduerbialiter sine regimine; et⁴
ista quatuor nomina appellatiua *rus*, *domus*, *humus* et *milicia*
eandem regulam sequntur. Vnde versus: 610

    Villarum propria post motus ad loca dum sint
    Ponantur quartis velud hec adverbia stabunt,
    Dum sint simplicia nec de sanctis⁵ recitata.
    Rus quoque *milicia*, *domus* ac⁶ *humus* ista cequntur.

    What case ys *Londonijs* in the Latyn byfore sayd? The
ablatyfe case, for when I haue a propir name of a plase, towne
or cyty nott compownyd folowth a verbe, participle, gerundife
or suppyn betoken(i)ng mevyng|from a place or by a place hitt
schal be putt in þe ablatyfe case aduerbyally as thus: *Ego
veni nuper Cantuaria, Londonijs,* and thys iiij nownes appellatiuis 620
rus, domus, humus et *milicia* folowyth the same⁷ rwle. Say thys
in Latyn. Quando proprium nomen⁸ loci, ville vel ciuitatis
simplex non compositum sequitur verbum, participium,⁹ ierundiuum
vel suppinum significans mocionem loco vel per locum ponetur in
ablatiuo casu aduerbialiter et sine regimine; et ista iiijᵒʳ
nomina appelatiua *rus, domus, humus* et *milicia* eandem regulam
sequntur.

    Post motum de loco ville proprium dato sexto
    Aduerbi more sine prepositoque fruetur
    Simplex dum fudit nec de sanctis recitatum.   630
    Rus quoque *milicia, domus* ac *humus* ista sequntur.

    *Magister est faturus discipulis qui attendunt sine
discipline sed illi sunt grauiter castigandi qui ne coligunt
disciplinam.* What party of speche ys *faturus*? A partycipull
of the firste futer tens, for an Englysche of the infenityfe

¹ R *canc.*   ² MS tarnam   ³ t *canc.*
⁴ MS Est   ⁵ MS sanctes   ⁶ MS hac
⁷ rul *canc.*   ⁸ lo *canc.*   ⁹ -t(?) *canc.*

TEXT HH

mode of the actife voyce commeth nexte after thys verbe *sum*,
es, *fui*, hit schal be put in a participull of the futer tens
in -*rus*, and an Englice of the infinityfe mode of the passyfe
voyse commeth nex after *sum*, *es*, *fui*, hyt schal be put in a
participull of the futer tens in -*dus* as in thys Latyn byfore 640
apperith. Say thys in Latyn

The text breaks off at this point, and is not continued on
the verso of fol.63.

TEXT JJ

JJ. London, British Library, MS. Add. 37075, fol.72ʳ

For 'of' aftyr a nown substantyve, verbe substantyve, ys syne of the genityue case, and the ablatyue ⁽whan⁾ he betokenyth presyng or dyspresyng.

Valeo, *-es* wyll constrwe wᵗ accusatiue case when he betokenyth serteyn pryce, and wᵗ the genitiue and ablatiue when he betokynyth vnserteyn pryce.

All verbis þat betokenyth pryce wyll constrw wyth the genityue and þe ablatyue, owte-take *valeo, -es*.

All verbis that betokenyth mevyng or resstyng haue strenkyth wyth coplicase.[1]   *10*

All verbis that betokenyth remembryng or forgettyng wyll haue genitiue, accusatiue and ablatyve.

Ista leccio *Est facilis compositu*: what ⁽parte⁾ of[2] reson ys *compositu*? Þe later suppyn. Why so? For when I haue the[3] Englesch of þe infinityve mode commyng after a nown[4] e(n)dyng in *-ilis* or in *-bilis* yt shall be later suppyng.

All verbis þat betokenyth damnyng, accusyng or repreuyng shall be þe genityve and the ablatyve.

---

[1] *sic* MS.   [2] -c(?) *canc*.   [3] yn *canc*.
[4] In *canc*.

TEXT KK

KK. London, British Library, MS Arundel 249, fols.118^r-120^r

Howe many compoundis hath þis verbe *sum, es, fui*?

Sum cum bis septem componis vocibus istis
Ad, subter, de, potis, sub, in, inter, ob, ab, super, pre.
Exsum cum *prosum* sociantur, teste Perotto.
Que *sum* componit ut *sum* caruere supinis;
In *-rus* participans, sine *possum*, nata tenebunt.
Participans presens ex hijs tantum tria prebent
Hec: *absum, prosum,* coniungi vult quoque *possum*.

    Adsum, -es, Englyshed 'to be att', 'to be present' or 'to
be by', is construed w^t a datyue case or an ablatyue case w^t 10
þis preposicion *in*. 'I was present at þe sopper'. *Assui cene
vel in cena*.¹ Englyshed 'to helpe' or 'to fauour' is construede
w^t a datyue case. But somtyme is þer addid an ablatyue case
w^t a preposicion. But when he is Englyshed 'to come' he
requyreth no case of hymmselfe but symtymes in poetis he is
founde put for his prymatyue.

    Subtersum, -es, þe which is found but seldon, and *subsum*,
Englyshede 'to be vndre', be construed w^t a datyue case only.
Plinius: *Suberat abieginne trabes. Talpa subterest terre,
pisces subtersunt aque.*   20

    Desum, -es, Englyshede 'to lacke' or 'want', is construed
with a datyue case of þe lackar and w^t a nominatyue case of
þe thynge þat is lackyd, except þe infinityue mode lete it.
Seneca: *Felix est cui nihil deest. Ad bene beateque viuendum
dum nihil deesse memini.* 'Þese children lack² betynge.'
*Istis pueris d<e>sunt flagra. Deest mihi penna ad scribendum
qua scribam vel vt scrib.*

    Possum, -es, Englishede 'to may' or 'to can', gouerns
no case of hymmselfe but by vndrestondynge of another verbe.

    Intersum w^t all his significacyons is compound of *in*   30
and *sum, es, fui*, except he be put for *pertinet*, for than
he is compound of *in, re* and *est*. *Interfui officijs
matutinis*. Sumtyme he is Englyshed 'to be present' and þan
he gouerns after hym a datyue case. Sumtyme he is Englyshed
'to be betwen' or 'to be|different'. Þan he is construede w^t
an accusatyue case w^t *inter* or an ablatyue case w^t þis
preposicion *a* or *ab*. '<W>hat is betwen vs two?' *Quid
interest inter te et me?* '<I> am different from the'.
Intersum a te. '<S>apiens interest <a> stult<o> plurimum.'
Sumtyme he is put for *distat*, Anglice 'to be fro', and þan the   40
thynge þat betokyns distance shal be put in þe nominatyue case,
except þe infinityue mode lete it, and þe thyng þat þe distance

---

¹ *The unattributed Latin and English examples are in the margins
  of the MS. I have introduced them into the text at the
  appropriate points.*
² *MS lackis*

209

TEXT KK

is fro shal be put in þe ablatyue case w^t a preposicion, and
þat thynge þat þe distance is to in the accusatyue case w^t þis
preposicion *ad*. Sumtyme he is Englyshed 'to be for profytt',
'to longe to' or 'to perteyn to', and þan he is construed
(whether he be personall or impersonall)[1] w^t a genytyue case,
oute-take þe genytyue case of þes v pronowns *mei, tui, sui,
nostri* and *vestri*, in the stede of whom we shall take the
ablatyue case, the femynyn gendre singuler of þer possessyues.   *50*
Also we shal take þe ablatyue case of *cuius, -a, -um*, and in
þis significacyon he may be construed w^t a duble genytyue case,
or w^t a genytyue and an ablatyue when he hath *magni* and *parui*
joynede with hym. '<I>t is for the children profytt.'
Interest puerorum. 'It is for a yong manys profytt.'
Interest adolescentis. *Interest nostra ediscere composita
de sum et fui*. 'It makith no matter[2] to me.[3] *Parui mea
refert*. *Mala verba tua magni mea refert*.

    Obsum, -es, Englyshed 'to hurt', is construede w^t a
datyue case.   *60*

    Absum, -es, Englyshed 'to be away' or 'absent' and 'to
be distant', in all significacions is construed with an
ablatyue case w^t a preposicion. *Tu abfuisti a precibus.
Afficior dolore <t>e abfuisse a societate tam diu*.

    Prosum, -es, 'to profett', 'to availe' or 'to do good',
is construed with a datyve case. *Hec precepta non
proderunt tibi nisi ediscas eas memoriter*.

    Supersum, Englished 'to be last', 'to remayn' or 'to
lyffe', is construed w^t a datyue case, and sumtyme in þes
significacions he is put absolutly also. 'Is þer eny drynk   *70*
in þe pott?' *Superestne aliquid potus in amphora?* 'What
more?' *Quid superest? Estne pater tibi superens?*[4]
Sumtyme he is Englyshed 'to be habundant' and in þat
significacion he is put in the ablatyue case w^tout a
preposicion. Also he hath many mo significacions.|

    Presum, -es, Englyshede 'to haue preemynence' or 'to
bere a rule', is construede w^t a datyue case. 'A man hath
th<e> rule of all oth<er> bestys.' *Homo preest omni<bus>
ceteris animantibus. Non solum interfui sed eciam prefui*.
But *presens* when he is a participle he is Englyshed 'to be   *80*
present'. Also *presens* hath many mo significacions.

    And after Pyrott here may be addide þese ij compoundis
exsum, Anglice 'to be oute', and *prosum*, 'to be greatly'.
Perottus: *Mulier virgo existo*.

                        Finis

---

[1] *The parentheses are in the MS*.   [2] MS *natter*
[3] MS *the*   [4] MS *superstes*

TEXT KK

Affero, ⌈*attuli, allatum*,⌉[1] Englished 'to brynge' or
'to fache', is construed with an accusatiue case and a datyue;
and sumtyme in þe stede of þe datyue case he will haue an
accusatiue case w^t þis preposicion *ad*. 'Brynge my book to
me.' *Affer librum mihi* v<el> *ad me*. 90

Aufero, 'to take' or 'bere away' or 'to stele', is
construed w^t an accusatiue case or a datyue, or ellys an
accusatyue case and an ablatyue with a preposicion. *Vnus
abstulit birretum mihi* vel *a me*.

Antefero, Englished as *prefero*, Anglice 'to preferr' or
'to sett more by', be construed w^t an accusatyue case and a
datyue case. Also *prefero* joyned w^t *me, te, se, nos* or *vos*,
Anglice 'shewe'. 'Þu semyth a sade man.' *Pre te fers
grauitatem. Pre te fero humanitatem facultatibus*.

Circumfero, ⌈*circumlatum*,⌉ Englishede 'to be aboute' or 100
'to sprede aboute' is construed with an accusatyue case.
Quis circumtulit hanc famam de te? 'Who brought vpe þis
fame vpon þe?'

Confero, Englished 'to gyve', is construed w^t an accusatiue
and a datyue; and comynly in þe stede of þe datyue case he
wyll haue an accusatiue w^t þis preposicion *in*, *Contuli in te
multa beneficia. Contulit in te beneficia*. Englished 'to
compare' is construed w^t an accusatiue and a datyue, or ellys
an accusatiue case and an ablatyue w^t þis preposicion *cum*.
Virgilius non est conferendus cum Homero. Englyshede 'to aske', 110
or 'to comyn withall', is construed w^t an accusatyue case
and an ablatyue case w^t þis preposicion *cum*, sumtyme w^t an
accusatiue case w^t þis preposicion *inter*, and oftyn tymes
þe accusatiue case is not expressed but vnderstond. 'I
command þis matter to the.' *Confero hanc rem tecum*.
Englyshed 'to be good' or 'holsome for' is construed w^t a
datyue case joyned w^t eny of þese accusatiue cases *me, te,
se, nos* or *vos*. *Hec rudimenta conferunt uobis*. Englishede
'to goo also' joynede w^t a thynge þat hath no lyffe he may
haue after hym an accusatiue case w^t *ad* or *in*, joynede|w^t
a thynge þat hath lyffe he hath an accusatiue case w^t *ad* only. 121
Conferamus nos ad edem, ad magistrum. *Confero* takyn for
ascribo, 'to putt to' or 'vpon', is construed w^t a duble
accusatiue, howbeit þe latter hath þis preposicion *in* before.
*Confers culpam in me. Multa probra contulit in me. Defer
hec feucula intro a mensa*.

Defero, ⌈*delatum*⌉, 'to bere' or 'to brynge', is construed
w^t a duble accusatiue, allbeit þe latter hath þis preposicion
ad or *in* before hym. Englyshede 'to accuse' is construede w^t
w^t an accusatiue case and a datyue case, or ellys w^t a duble 130
accusatiue case of þe which the latter wyll haue þis preposicion
ad before hym. *Quis detulit te ad magistrum?*

---

[1] Added beside the main text, as in other cases below.

TEXT KK

Differo, [*dilatum*], Englished 'to differ', is construde w^t an accusatiue case w^t *inter*, sumtyme an ablatyue case w^t a preposicion. *Neuter eorum duorum differt ab altro.* Englishede 'to prolonge', 'to scater abrode', 'to name abrode' or 'to breke asondre' is construed w^t an accusatiue case. *Differs me diatim de die in diem.* 'Þu dryvest me <...> fro day to <day>.'

Infero, Englished 'to brynge in', 'to bere in' or 'to fach in', 'to put in', 'to conclude' as in dispicions, also put for þis verbe *facio*, is construede w^t an accusatiue and sumtyme w^t a datyue; also sumtyme w^t an accusatiue w^t þis preposicion *in*; also joyned w^t *me, te, se, nos* or *vos* is Englished 'to goo' or 'to cum in'. <*I*>*nfer te huc.* <*I*>*nferamus nos intro.* 'Lete vs goo in.'   140

Effero, Englished 'to brynge' or 'bere forth', 'to fach forth', 'to prayse', 'to exalte', is construede w^t an accusatiue. Englished 'to translate on language into another' is construed w^t an accusatiue and an ablatyue w^t a preposicion. Sumtyme he may haue a seconde accusatiue case w^t a preposicion.   150

Offero, Englished 'to offre' or 'to profer' is construed w^t an accusatiue and a datyue. 'He proferd me money.' *Vbtulit mihi pecunias.* Ioynede w^t *me, te, se, nos* or *vos* is Englishede 'to mete' and is construede w^t a datyue case. 'I mete the.' *Offero me tibi.* 'Who mett the?' *Quis obtulit se tibi?* 'Lete vs mete them.' *Offeramus nos illis.*

Prefero, Englishede 'to suffre greatly' or 'to sett more by', is construede w^t an accusatiue. *Preferis*[1] *me. Pater prefert me ceteris liberis. Prefero neutrum altro.* Englished 'to bere' is construed w^t a duble accusatiue, but þe latter is vsed w^t þis preposicion *ad*.   160

Profero, Englished 'to shewe' or 'to brynge forth', 'to prolonge', 'to put of', 'to differ', is construede w^t an accusatiue case. *Profer secreta cordis tui.*

Refero, Englished 'to tell', is construed w^t an accusatiue and a datyue. *Venio ad referendum* vel *relatum* vel *ut referam nuncias.* 'We haue worde.' *Relatum est nobis.* 'What did he tell þe?' *Quid retulit tibi?*| Englishede 'to put in ornament' is construed w^t a duble accusatiue. But þe most part *refero* in þe stede of þe fyrste accusatiue wyll haue a duble case w^t þis preposicion *ad*. 'Lete us put <þis> matter in hym.' *Referamus ad* <*illem*> *de hac re.* Englyshede 'to brynge agayn' is construed w^t an accusatiue and a datyue, and sumtyme in þe stede of þe datyue he wyll haue an accusatiue w^t þis preposicion *ad* joyned w^t þis word *gracia* or *par*. Englished 'to quyte' is construed w^t a datyue. Sumtyme he is put for *distat*, Anglice 'to be different', and þan comynly he is put absolutly. *Refero* also joynede w^t *me, te, se, nos* or *vos*, Englished 'to gyve' or 'to cum agayne'. *Refert* is   170

[1] MS Prefereris

TEXT KK

put for *pertinet*, 'to care' or 'to reke', and is construed 180
w^t a genytyue case of all casuall wordys and w^t an ablatyue of
þes v pronowns possessyves *meus*, *tuus*, *suus*, *noster* and *vester*
and of þis nown possesyue *cuius*, *-a*, *-um*.

    Suffero, 'to suffre', is construede with an accusatyue case.

    Transfero, Englishede 'to translate on langage into a
noþer', is construede w^t an accusatiue case and an ablatyue
w^t a preposicion, sumtyme w^t an accusatiue w^t þis preposicion
in. Sumtyme he is takyn for *ascribo*, Anglice 'to putt to' or
'to putt vpon', and is construed w^t a duble accusatiue of þe   190
which the latter wyll haue on of þes preposicions *ad* or *in*.
Englished 'to bere ouer' is construed with a duble accusatiue
case but þe latter is vsed w^t a preposicion.

    Postfero, 'to sett lesse by', is construed w^t an accusatiue
and a datyue case.

Finis. ⌜**Finis. Finis. Finis.**⌝¹

---

¹ *In paler ink.*

TEXT LL

LL. London, British Library, MS Harley 1742, fols.1^r-11^r

Hov mani maner of|wayes schall thou begynne to make
Laten and constru? V maner off wayes. The fyrst att the
vocatyue case: *Francijse inuigilate huic abstracto*. The
secunde at the nomenatyue case w^t hys verbe, vt *Franciscus
formosus est pusus*. The thred att the infenytyue mode or
els sumwhat sett in the sted off the nomenatyue case, vt
Mane surgere prestat sanitatem corporis. The forte at the
werbe inpersonnall, vt *Piget me tui*. The fyfte at the
ablatyue case absolute: *Francisco ludente preceptor intrauit
ludum litterarum*.   10

How schalt thou doo when thou hast a Englys to make in
Laten? I must reherse my Englys tyll I haue yt perfitely be
hart, and see how many verbys be in that reson, and yff ther
be but one he hys the pryncypale verbe. Than I must put
before hym thys question, 'Whoo or what?', and that worde
that anssorthe to thys quesstion schall be the nomenatyue case
or the vocatyue to the|werbe, as 'The master teche thys worde':
'teche' ys the werbe.' 'Who or what techeth?' 'The master'.
Thys word 'master' her answeryth to thys questyon and therfor
yt schall be the nominatyue case to the verbe, vt *Preceptor* 20
docet. In lyke maner yt ys off the vocatyue case, vt
Francisce ama[1] *dissiplinam*. Iff hony thyng cum
after the werbe I must put before verbe thys question
'Whom or what?', and the word that answerth to
thys question 'Whom or what?' schall be most comonly þe
accusatyue case, as 'The master teche'. 'Whom or what dothe
he teche?' 'Me'. Thys worde 'me' answherth to thys
question, 'Whom or what?', and therfor yt schall be the
accusatyue case to the verbe, vt *Preceptor docet Franciscum*:
'The master t(e)hche Francis.' But and yff the worde that   30
folluth the verbe may conuenyenly answher|to thys question,
'Whom or what?', yt schall be put in the ablatyue case w^t one
off thes preposicions *a, ab, abs, de, e, ex*, as, 'Francyss ys
bete off the master', *Franciscus a preceptore vapulatur*.

How knouest thou the principall verbe in a reson when
thou hast many verbys in yt? Euermore my fyrst verbe schall
be my principall verbe except he cum ny after ony off thes
sygnys: 'that', 'whom' or 'the wyche', or ony off thes:
'but', 'whan', 'after that', 'before that', 'alltho', 'sinthe',
'except' or other like.[2]   40

Concordis of gramer|

Hov many concordis of gramer be ther? III. Wyche iij?
Þe fryst, þe secunde and the iij^{de}. The fyrst betwyn þe
nomenatyue case and the verbe, the secunde betwyn the adiectyue
and the substantyue, the iij^{de} betwyn þe relatyue and þe
antecedent. Yt hath be sayd þat ther wher ij more, but lernyd
men reducyd them to þe secunde, as *Rosa est pulcherimus florum*

[1] MS amat   [2] MS *adds* or

214

TEXT LL

wher ys vnderstond þe substantyue *flos*; *Alter istorum currit*
wher ys vnderstond *vir*, *puer* or sum other like.|

In hou many schall þe nomenatiue or þe vocatiue case and
hys verbe personall agre? In ij, in number and person, as   51
Ego amoo, *Francisce ama*. To nomenatiue case si(n)guler w^t a
coniuccion copalatyue comyng betwyn wull haue a uerbe plurell,
as *Iohannes et Franciscus obnixe student*.[1] Whan a nomenatyue
case singuler cum w^t a ablatyue case hauyng thy preposicion
cum cummyng betwyn then wyll haue a verbe plurell, as
Franciscus cum Roberto carcita(n)tur. Also a nowne off
multytude as *turba*, a nowne off colectyue as *populus*, *plebs*,
gens w^t many other wyll haue a verbe plurall, as *Turba*
flauerant vestimenta sua in vias. Whan I haue ij nomenatyue   60
case one of the fyrst person and a nother off þe secunde or
off þe thred, þe verbe schall acorde w^t þe nomenatyue case
off the fyrst persen,|as *Ego et tu preclari ingenio sumus*,
Vir et ego dissputamus. Whan I haue a nomenati(u)e case off
þe secunde person and a nother off þe thred, þe verbe sch(a)ll
acorde w^t þe nomenative case of þe secunde person and not w^t
þe iij^{de}, as *Tu et frater tuus boni discipuli*[2] *estis*. Whan
ij verbis cum together w^{t}owt a relatiue or a coniunccion, þe
later off them schall be put in þe infenytyue mode, as *Volo*
amare.   70

The secunde concorde

In how many schall þe adiectiue and þe substantiue acorde?
In iij, in case, gendyr and nombyr, as *Vir doctus legit*. How
schalt thow knowe þe substantiue to þe adiectiue whan thow hast
a nowne or a pronowne adiectiue? I schal put thys question
'Wo or what?' after hym, and þat word þat anssorth to thys
schall be þe substantiue to þe adiectiue, as 'My boke', 'My
what?' 'My boke'. But|iff þe adiectyue be a partycypyll
þe question schall be put before, as 'Growyng t⌈h⌉res', 'Who
or what growyng?', 'Thres'. To substantyuys singuler w^t a   80
coniunction copulatyue commyng betwyn them wyll haue a
adiectyue plurall, as *Franciscus et Ricardus sunt*[3] *boni*.
Also one substantyue singuler w^t an ablatyue case hauyng
thys preposicion *cum* cummyng betwyn them wyll haue a
adiecty(u)e plurall, as *Franciscus*[4] *cum Ricardo sunt laudandi*.
Whan I haue ij substantyuys, one off þe masculyne gendyr and
a nother off þe femynyne gendyr or off þe neuter, þe adiectyue
schall agre w^t þe substantyue off þe masculyne gendyr, as *Ego*
et soror mea sumus nitidi. Whan a verbe cum betwyn to
nomenatyue casys off dyuers nombyrs pert⌈e⌉ynyng bothe to one   90
thyng the verbe schall agre w^t eyther off them. Whan I haue
ij substantyuis one off þe femynyne gendyr|...

A folio is missing at this point.

... Whan ther cum a nomenatyue case betwyn the relatyue and

---

[1] *obnixe student*] MS obnixei studunt(?) [2] MS disci[l]plini
[3] *a stroke canc.* [4] MS Franciscijs

215

TEXT LL

the verbe the relatyue schal be scoche case as the verbe wyll
haue after hym, as *Franciscus quem preceptor amat scribit*.
Whan ther cum nothyng betwyn the relatyue and the verbe the
relatyue schall be the nomenatyue case to the verbe. But yf
the verbe þat cummythe next the relatyue be a verbe inpersonall,
than the relatyue scha⌈1⌉ be soche case as the verbe inpersonall
wyll haue after hym.   100

Whan thys worde 'that' may be turnid into thys Inglysche
'whiche' it ys a relatiue: yf yt betokyn schoyng by *ille, illa,
illud* or sum other pronownys demonstratyus; whan it betokyn a
thyng as wyll to be done by *vt*; and if yt be a thyng schoyng
the case by *quod* or *quia* or sum or¹ casuell con(i)unccion.²|
Thys coniu(n)ccyun *quod* in Latyn makyng schal be excludyd
and the worde that semyth to be the nomenatyue case schal be
the accusatiue case and the verbe schal be þe infenytyue mode
of the same tense as yt scholde haue byn yf it had be made
be thys coniu(n)ccyon *quod*.   110

To antecedentis synguler w^t an *et* coniunccion copulatyue
commyng bytwyn wyll a relatyue plurall, as *Franciscus et
Ricardus quos ego docui non studiose discu(n)t*.

Whan I haue a relatyue cummyng betwyn ij substantyuis of
diuerys gendyrs longyng both to one thyng, yf the substantyue
that foluyth be a nowne appellatyue than the relatyue schall
acorde wythe eyther of them in gender indeferently, as *Eo³
Cantabrigiam qui* vel *que est locus studendi*. But yf the
substantyue þat folowthe be a proper the relatyue schall acorde
in gendyr wythe the later, as *Hic locus in carcere*⁴ *quod*   120
Tullianum appellatur.|

The construccion of þe genetyue case

Similis et *dissimilis* when they betokyn lykenes in
condicion be construyd w^t a genetyue case, ortherwyes wythe⁵
an ablatyue, as *Franciscus similis est matris*. *Diues,
inops* and sochę other wordis as betokyn ryches or pouerte wyll
be construyd w^t a genetyue case; also *plenus* and *refertus* be
of the same strenthe. *Dignus* and *indignus* sumtyme be construyd
wythe a genetyue case, as *Franciscus sex plagarum est dignus*.

Thys nowne *sertus*⁶ and *incertus, certior,*⁷ *securus, solitus,* 130
dubius w^t many other be construyd w^t a genetyue case, as
Franciscus huius rei est certus.

Nownys distributiuis as *quisquis, nullus, nemo*, nowns
interrogatiuis as *quis, quisnam, quot*, nownis infenetyuis as
quicumque,⁸|*quisquis*, nownys partytyuis as *vnus, alius, quid,*

---

¹ *a stroke canc.*   ² MS adds at foot of page Coniunccions
   copulatyuis disiu(n)ctyuis dubitatyuis and interrogatyuis wyll
   copyll like case gender numbyr mode and tense
³ *a canc.*   ⁴ *quod canc.*   ⁵ MS adds w^t
⁶ *-us from is*   ⁷ MS cercior   ⁸ quinq *canc.*

216

TEXT LL

quidam w^t other ben construyd w^t a genatyue case: *Francisse quis illorum*,[1] *inter illos* vel *ex illis hoc tibi annunciauit.*

Aduerbys of quantyte, tyme and space may be construyd w^t a genatyue case, as *Satis sapiencie est Francisco.*

The construccion of þe datyue case   140

Thes nownys *gratus, ingratus, credulus, vtilis, facilis, fidelis, molestus, difficilis, ineptus, aptus, charus,* (...)[2], *obnoxius* w^t many other wyl be construyd w^t a datyue case: *Franciscus molestus est mihi.*

In euery nowne and pronowne possescyue ys vnderstonde the datyue case of hys primatyue: *Franciscus (...)*[3] *sibi ingenium.*[4]

The construccion of þe ablatyue case

All nownys that betokyn fulnes or emtynes, ryches or pouerte be construyd w^t an ablatyue case: *Ollula est vacua potu.* | 150

Thys nowne *opus*[5] for 'nede' ys construyd w^t an ablatyue case, and he ys sumtyme vsyd wythe thys verbe *habe(o), -es,* but he ys most comonly vsyd w^t thys verbe *sum, es, fui: Francisce est mihi opus*[5] *libro.*

Thes nownys *preditus, lassus, grauis, orbus, onustus, horidus, potens, eger, tradus* w^t many other wyll be construyd wythe an ablatyue case: *Franciscus est libro preditus.*

Dignus and *indignus* wyl be construyd w^t an ablatyue case, and sumtyme in the sted of the casuell worde they wol haue   160
an infenytyue mode: *Franciscus seuis est dignus plagis*; by the infenytyue mode thus: *Sum dignus amare* vel *amore.*

Nownys that betokyn tyme, meser or space, yf they be not the nomenatyue case to the verbe nor otherwyes gouerned, the schall be put into the ablatyue case and sumtyme in the accusatyue case: *Franciscus tota*[6] *die* vel *totam litteris incumbit.* |

Affter the comparatyue degre the worde that betokyn the excesse wyl be construyd w^t an ablatyue case w^{t}owt a preposicion and sumtyme w^t a nomenatyue case w^t thys   170
coniunccion *quam: Franciscus est altior te* uel *quam tu pede.* The comparatyue, superlatyue and supreme Latyne degre wyl be construyd w^t seche case as þe posatyue: *Franciscus est preceptor charior ceteris condiscipulis.*

Whan I haue a nowne substantyue or a pronowne substantyue

---

[1] ind *canc.*   [2] *space one word long*   [3] *space one word long*
[4] -i *canc.*   [5] *sic* MS   [6] de *canc.*

TEXT LL

cummyng w^t a partycypyll wheras ys no worde expressyd nor vnderstond wherof he may be gouernd, yt schall be put in the ablatyue case absolute, as *Francisco ludente preceptor beat*.

A werbe foluyng ther aduerbys *postquam*, *dum*, *quando* w^t other lyke, also whan a verbe gothe before thes coniunccions *nisi*, *quamquam*, *quamuis*, *licet*, *tametsi*, thes aduerbys and coniunccions schall be excludyd and the verbe put into a partycypyll w^t an ablatyue case: *Francisce confectis negotijs huc redito*. 180

The construccyon of verbys|

Thys verbe *sum*, *es*, *fui* and verbys passyuis as *eligor*, *declaror*, *vocor*, also verbys that betokyn bodely mouyng, goyng or restyng as *do*, *curro*, *sedeo*, *appareo*, also *forem*, *exto*, *existo* wyl copul lyke case, specyaly wher the worde goo before the verbe and the worde that commythe after the verbe long bothe to on thyng. 190

Thys verbe *sum*, *es*, *fui* goueren a genatyue case of the possessor, as *Domini est terra*, but yf yt betokyn laud or schame he schal goueren a genatyue case or an ablatyue case indeferently: *Franciscus est clarus ingenio*. Also sumtyme he wol haue a dobyll datyue case.

Obliuiscor, *admoneo*, *reminiscor*, *miserior*, *egeo*, *indigeo*, *memini*, *recordor*, *satago* wyl be construyd w^t a genatyue case: *Franciscus oblitus est sui irascor*.

The construccion of þe datyue case 200

Miserior, *-eris* sumtyme wyl be construd w^t a datyue case: *Franciscus misertus est michi*. *Benedico*, 'to say wyll by' or 'to say wyll of' and maledico,[1] 'to say ill by' or 'to say ill of' ys construyd w^t a datyue case, as *Preceptor mihi benedixit*.| Whanne this Inglys 'for' may be chongyd into this word 'to' it ys allway the signe of the datyue case, as *Lac est bonum Francisco*. *Benedico*, 'to blysse', and *maledico*, 'to curse', wyll be construid w^t a datyue case, as *Genitor michi benedixit*. Werbys that betoken 'to agre' as *congruo*, 'to runne' as *occurro*, 'to cummande'[2] ⌈as⌉ *iubeo*, 'to helpe' as *subuenio*, 'to appley' 210 as *incumbo*, 'to serue' as *seruio*[3] 'to counsell' as *suadeo*, 'to please' as[4] *placeo*, 'to dysplese' as *displiceo*, 'to fauer' as *faueo*, 'to hurt' as *noceo*, 'to obey' as *pareo*, 'to resist' as *resisto*, wyll be construid w^t a datyue case, as *Franciscus incumbat libro*. All werbis that betokyn accelent[5] gouerne a datyue case, also *dominor*, *-naris* and *imperteor*,[6] *-eris* haue sumtyme that same strenthe, as *Franciscus multis terris dominabitur*. *Inpono*, 'to dysseyue', is construid w^t a datyue case. *Consulo*, a verbe neuter 'to gyffe counsell', 'to prouide' or 'to helpe', is construid w^t a datyue case, as 220

[1] -i- from y
[2] MS cummamde
[3] MS seiuio
[4] s canc.
[5] sic MS
[6] MS imperceor

TEXT LL

Consulo tibi.|

Sum, es, fui is put oftentymis for *habeo, -es,* and that worde that semith to be the¹ nomenatyue case shall be put into the datyue case and that worde that semith to be the accusatyue case schall be the nomenatyue case except the infenytyue mode let it, as *Francisce est mihi namque domi pater.*

The construccion of the accusatyue case

Obliuiscor, admoneo, reminiscor, egeo, indigeo, memini and *recordor, misereor, -eris*² be construid w^t an accusatyue case: *Non meam recordor lecturam.* *Leuo* and *iuuo* w^t all ther   230
compunndis, also *moderor, comitror, adulor,* also *offendo, ledo, dominor, impertior,*³ also verbis that betokyn fere or drede, and thes verbis *intelligo, sentio,* will be construid w^t an accusatiue case after them, as *Franciscus te sentit.*

Thes verbis *postulo, posco, peto, rogo* w^t many other wyll be construid w^t a dobyll accusatiue case, as *Francisce postulato preceptorem veniam.* Also|all werbis that betokyn demandyng or axing will haue an accusatyue case of the thyng that is axid, as *Postulo veniam.* *Celo* will haue a dobill accusatiue case.   240

Thes verbis *priuo, fraudo* w^t other like will haue after them an accusatyue case of the thyng that is rowyd or takyn away, as *Franciscus priuauit cultellum.* *Consulo,* a verbe actyue 'to axe counsell', is construid w^t an accusatiue case of the thyng that the counsell is axid of, as *Consulo tibi hanc rem.* Thes verbis *exuo, calceo, cingo,* requere⁴ after them an accusatiue⁵ of the body, as *Cingo me gladio.* Also *gaudeo, letor, tristor* will be construid w^t an accusatiue case w^t thys preposicion *ob* or *propter,* as *Gratulor tuam humanitatem.*

The construccion of the ablatiue case   250

Admoneo, reminiscor, obliuiscor, recordor, memini w^t many other, also the werbis *priuo, fraudo, adnuo, precipio, demo,* will be construid w^t an ablatiue case. *Consulo,* 'to axe counsell', ys of the same strenthe.|

Thes verbis *emo, vendo, loco, conduco* and all verbis that may haue price after them will be construid w^t a ablatiue case of the price, whether the price be serten or unserten, as *Tu eam viginti (...)*⁶ *emisti.*

All verbis that betokyn reprouing or condemnyng the word that betokyn the peyne schall be put in the ablatiue case and   260
sumtyme in the genetyue case, as *Accusare hunc potes furti* vel *furto.* Also the compoundis of the werbis *pleo, farcio,*⁷

---

¹ *a stroke canc.* ² MS *aris* ³ MS *impercior*
⁴ *or perhaps* regnere *and so also elsewhere below* ⁵ *after them canc.*
⁶ *space one word long* ⁷ MS fertio *with* -o *from* a

219

TEXT LL

compleo, infercio[1] will be construid w^t an ablatyue case or an accusatyue case, as *Refersi*[2] *apothecam vino. Decisto, cesso* will haue an ablatyue case w^t a preposicion; also thes verbis *vescor, fungor, careo, vtor, pocior, delector, fruor* and all verbis that betokyn abundans will be construid w^t an ablatyue case; as *Cessa a ludo*.

Thes verbis *exuo, calceo, induo, cingo* requere after them an ablatyue case of the thyng that is wornud, as *Cingo me* 270 *zonula. Abstineo, es* will haue an accusatyue case of the thyng|that we do obsteyne and an ablatyue case of the thyng that we do absteyne form, as *Omni lacticinio me abstineo*. Also verbis that betokyn 'to fede', as *pasco*, be of the same strenthe, as *Pasco gregem harba*.

The construccion of the verbis inpersonallis

Thes verbis inpersonallis *est, refert* and *interest* put for *pertinet* be construid w^t a genetyue case of all casuell wordis, owte-take thes v pronownis *ego, nos, tu* et *vos* et *sui*, in the sted of whom we must take the ablatyue case of ther 280 possessiuis. Also this verbe *est* will be construid w^t a nomenatyue case of the neuter gender of thes v pronownis *meum, tuum, suum (nostrum* and *vestrum)*.

Thes verbis *accidit, placet, licet, libet, obtigit, congruit, euenit, contingit, prestat, constat* wyll haue a datyue case: *Non libet michi studere. Iuuat,*[3] *decet, delectat, oportet* and *latet* will haue an (a)ccusatyue case before them in the sted of the nominatiue[4] case, and an infenytyue mode after them: *Iuuat me legere*.

Thes verbis *penitet, tedet, miseret, pudet, piget* will 290 haue an accusatyue case before them in the sted|

Folio missing.

When too verbis cum together w^t a coniu(n)ccion copulatyue I schall exclude the coniu(n)ccion copulatyue and put one of the verbis into a participill, as *Domum me conferens senaturus sum*.

Telos huius libri.

---

[1] MS Infertio [2] MS referti [3] MS Iuıat
[4] MS notioue

NOTES TO THE TEXTS

The following notes attempt to elucidate the grammatical teaching of the texts , identify sources where possible, and point out the characteristics of each text. Further characterisations of the texts, and information on their background and provenance, is given in my Catalogue. The major difficulty in the annotation of these texts has been the overlap of material between them, which is very great. I have attempted to cross-reference the notes on a few major points of interest or difficulty, but in many cases only the first occurrence of a particular subject is annotated. The notes to the **first text of each group therefore contain material relevant to the similar** following texts, and should be consulted as necessary. To facilitate this, and to provide a conspectus of the contents of the major texts, the following tables give the common material of the Accedence, Comparacio, Informacio and Formula with the line references for each text.

NOTES TO THE TEXTS

THE ACCEDENCE TEXTS

	A	B	C	D	E	F	G	H	J	K	L	M
Parts of speech	1	1	1	1	1	1				1	1	1
Noun												
definition	11	10	11	8	11	11				12	27	12
*adjectives	12	11	12	11	14	14		22		14	29	20
accidents	20	24		17		12					39	35
quality	21	35		19								45
comparison	27		27	23		24				27	41	
gender	38		46	74		32		6		43		
number	52		69	95		46		1		22+54		
figure				98								
case	55		73	104		50	1			59		
declensions	78	39	95	168		64	53		1	75		
Pronoun												
definition	120	71	198	198		80				90		
*derivatives	124	77	202	202		86				95		
accidents	132	73		219		81						
quality	133			221								
gender	138			226								
number				228								
figure				229								
person		141	105	217	231		94			36+84		
case				240								
declensions		147	122	227	241		101			100	47	
*of asking				257								
Verb												
definition	165	152	356	291		123				114		
accidents	167	154		294		125						
mood/quality	169	178	394	296		127	22			142		
conjugation	183	198	437	315		138				130		
voice/gender	198	156	358	326		146				116		
number				432	348		159					
figure					350							
tense		214	210	419	352		163	12		154		
person				434	379		176					
declensions				474								
Adverb												
definition	226			482	381		180			165		
accidents	228				383		181					
signification					384							

NOTES TO THE TEXTS

	A	B	C	D	E	F	G	H	J	K	L	M
comparison			483	386		183						
figure				392								
*formation	230			430								
*place names				396								
Participle												
definition	239		492	440		186				168		
accidents	241			442								
gender	243			444								
case				444								
tense	245		495	449		189	41			173		
*formation	253			479		204				179		
signification	284		509	472								
number												
figure												
*endings	299											
Conjunction												
definition	304		571	491		216				200		
accidents	305			494		217						
power	307		573	495		219						
figure				518								
order				513								
Preposition												
definition	310		590	520		227				203		
accidents	312			521		228						
case	313	238	591	523		230						
Interjection												
definition	324	261	612	530		238				207		
accidents	326	263		532								
signification	328	264	613	533		238						
*Concord		331	278	617		241	32					

*The itemisation of contents follows that of the Ars Minor, except for the asterisked items which represent additions. Note that this table, unlike those which follow, includes material specific to one text as well as material held in common.

NOTES TO THE TEXTS

THE COMPARACIO TEXTS

	N	O	P	Q	R	S
Introduction: what is a comparison?	1	1	1	1		16
the three degrees	10	13	15	9	1	1
The positive: identification	9	15	17	11	3	4
formation	15	18	27			28
construction		19	119	17		
The comparative: identification		21	21			7
formation		25	30		5	31
– from genitive		36	32		11	
– from dative		49	39		17	
– irregular		53	43		33+61	
gender		74			91	
syllables		86			83	
construction		98	125	18		
The superlative: identification		102	25	14		11
formation		105	62		101	
– from nominative		108	64		105	
– from genitive		112	86		126	
– from gen./dat.		120	107		148	
– bonus etc.		117	92		135	
– dexter etc.		128	71+96		116	
– agĭlĭs etc.		143	77		157	
construction		151	144	21		
Adverbs with adjectival comparison	92				171	

224

NOTES TO THE TEXTS

THE INFORMACIO TEXTS

	T	U	V	W	X	Y
Introduction to constructions						
ways of beginning a sentence	1	1	1	1		
active, passive & impersonal verbs	16	16	21		1	
active construction; relatives	32	33	37	19	20	1
relatives with nouns of diff. gender	63	66			45	34
Constructions of the finite verb						
verbs with the nominative	72	75		42	63	43
(adjectives of fulness & emptiness)	93	97		⎱	102	64
verbs with the genitive	101	105		61	⎱ 89	74
genitive & dative	107	110		⎰	⎰	85
gen., acc. & abl.	115	119			111	97
genitive & ablative					119	
dative	129	134		85	131	111
double accusative	145	150		100	147	128
ablative	158	164		108	160	140
Constructions of the infinite verb						
gerunds	165	171		115	213	234
supines	204	210		145	171	275
participles	251	257			203	
the ablative absolute	259	264		165	223	296
('sinodoche' – acc. of respect)	275	281		177		147
The impersonal verb						
introduction	293	297		191	242	165*
constructions with the genitive	328	334		205	282	198
dative	337	343			292	207
accusative	344	350			299	214
declension of the active verb	353	359		⎱ 223	304	339
participles	371	376		⎰	313	
verbs both personal & impersonal	380	385			322	350
constr. with abl. of pronouns	386	391		210	328	221*
passive impersonals (obviatur)	397	402		231	341	
neuter-passives (vapulo, nubo)	408	412		241	375	
declension of the passive verb	421	425		257	354	
Formation of tenses	436	440				372

*These passages are repeated at Y311 and Y360 respectively.

NOTES TO THE TEXTS

THE FORMULA TEXTS

	Z	AA	BB	CC
Concord: nominative and the verb	1	1	1	1
multiple subjects and plural verb	9	9	9	9
– and negated copulative verbs	14	14	25	14
adjectives and substantives	22	23	35	27
adjectives set substantively	28	32	41	59
adjectives and multiple substs.	34	38	47	81
relative and antecedent	39	44	64	86
relative and multiple antecedents	45	51	71	93
the case of the relative	50	56	76	98
partitive & distributive nouns	59	65	120	170
superlatives	67	74	140	186
Comparison: tenuis, pius etc.	79	86		
irregular comparison	87	95		
pulcher etc.	96	104		
agilis etc.	106	122		
Pronouns used in the vocative	115	131		
Concepcion: of person	121	137	392	
on the person of nouns	126	142	384	
of case	133	149	397	221
Adjectives of fulness and emptiness	139	155	236	203
Finite verbs: with the dative	146	168	244	227
ablative	153	162	287	234
genitive	159			262
gen. & abl.	171			
double acc.	178		269	250
The infinite verb: gerunds	186	175	402	287
supines	213	199	442	312
participles	239	224	359	339
ablative absolute	246	231	340	352
Impersonal verbs: introduction	252	236	466*	364
with acc. & gen.	270	255	510	383
participles	279	264	493	392
with accusative	284	269	522	403
with abl. pronouns	289	274	531	
passives	302	285	568	
neuter-passives	311	294	588	
declension	323	305		

NOTES TO THE TEXTS

	Z	AA	BB	CC
passive participles	330	310		
Formation of tenses	335	317	602	

*BB466f. and BB493f. are repeated at AA502 and AA517 respectively.

NOTES TO TEXT A

Notes to text A

2   The order of the parts of speech here, which is the order in which they are treated in the body of the text, is that of Donatus. The classification of the parts of speech which follows in lines 3-10 is not, however, from Donatus, but reflects Priscian's analysis of the parts of speech into the two broad categories of declinables and indeclinables (Keil iii, 24).

5   Note that verbs are said in Middle English to decline, although their groupings are referred to as conjugations (see below, lines 183f).

11 The texts show considerable variation from Donatus and between themselves in their definitions of the parts of speech, using phrases and ideas from Priscian (probably indirectly) and medieval grammarians, who often cite the definitions of both Donatus and Priscian and adjudicate between them (so Thomas of Hanney in his Memoriale iuniorum, for which see my Catalogue pp. 37-8). Donatus defines the noun as 'pars orationis cum casu corpus aut rem proprie communiterve significans' (Keil iv, 355), Priscian as 'pars orationis quae unicuique subiectorum corporum seu rerum communem vel propriam qualitatem distribuit' (Keil ii, 56-7). Neither of these definitions is that of the present text, which is not satisfactory since it does not cover abstract nouns.

12 In the Ars Minor Donatus classifies adjectives as nouns of gender 'omne', which is reflected in the present text's comyn of iij gendyrs (lines 45f). Lines 12-19 are an addition to Donatus and represent a step towards the treatment of adjectives as an independent part of speech by introducing the basic distinction between adjective and substantive as the first level of analysis.

15 Hic, hec, hoc are referred to as articles in discussing Latin in this and other English texts, reflecting general medieval practice (cf. Doctrinale 523, 546). Donatus in the Ars Maior calls these pronouns articles when they are joined to nouns 'ut hic huius huic hunc o ab hoc, et pluraliter hi horum his hos o ab his', i.e. in formal declensions (Keil iv, 381), while not allowing them status as a part of speech as in Greek (Keil iv, 372). Other grammarians disagreed with this on the grounds that all words must be taken as one of the eight parts of speech without exception (cf. Probus, Keil iv, 133).

NOTES TO TEXT A

19 The reference is to such declensions as bonus, bona, bonum and tener, tenera, tenerum / niger, nigra, nigrum, i.e. adjectives of the first and second declensions. Those of the third declension are not covered here.

21 Qualite has different implications for the different parts of speech. In dealing with nouns it covers proper and common denotation, in dealing with pronouns defined or undefined person, and in dealing with verbs mood and aspect. Figur generally refers to whether a word is simple or compound.

23 The use of hys Englysch where 'the noun' would be more correct is symptomatic of the way in which these texts take the English equivalent of the Latin as their starting point in analysing it.

24 on thynge translates Donatus accurately, but it would be better expanded to 'a thing which is unique by its nature', although this is still not a completely adequate definition. Priscian develops the definition further in his section on the noun (Keil ii, 58-9).

25 kyndly means 'by its nature'.

26 With the examples compare the medieval addition 'communiter vt vrbs, flumen' at this point in Donatus (as in Worcester Cathedral MS F123).

27 This paragraph is not in Donatus, who has instead a section on which nouns take comparison and what cases they take.

40 the dubyn: neither Priscian or Donatus have a 'dubius' gender as such, although in his Ars grammatica Donatus does give a list of nouns 'incerti generis' (Keil iv, 375). The Doctrinale and Graecismus do not set up a separate gender of this sort either. The carrier of the tradition seems to be John of Garland's Compendium grammatice - see the verses cited at C60-2. Thomas of Hanney, writing circa 1313, makes out a case for regarding these words as of common gender in the Latin of his day (Bod. Lib. MS Bodl. 643, fol. 167v).

40 How knos þu... The text does not, of course, represent a way of knowing the gender of a noun as found in a piece of Latin, but of knowing the rules governing the various genders. The teaching of this part of the paragraph (lines 40-52) does not appear in Donatus in this form.

53 Lines 53-5 are the first of a number of paragraphs added

NOTES TO TEXT A

to Donatus which use English words and examples to drive home the writer's point (cf. lines 58-77, 171-182, 216-225, 249-283). Donatus at this point has simply 'singularis, ut hic magister' (Keil iv, 355). Note also that the equivalence assumed in this section between singular number of reference and the grammatical singular is not total: collective nouns are an obvious exception.

56 Donatus' section on 'figura' (simple and compound nouns) is omitted here.

58 Lines 58-77 are not found in Donatus.

58 he comys byfor þe verbe: this is, of course, by no means always true in Latin. The reference is to the simple examples used in the schoolroom and, perhaps, to English usage.

59 serten person and certayn nowmbyr: subjects agree in person and number with their verbs.

60 Wo or wat? elicits the subject of a verb, but this does not cover the appositional use of the nominative, for instance.

61 'of' aftyr a nowne substantiue: in classical usage some constructions of this sort could be translating an ablative of quality, e.g. 'a man of supreme audacity', vir summa audacia.

61 verbe substantiue: the verb 'to be' and its equivalents. The example at D122 is Thys man is of fayre berynge (genitive of quality).

62 partitiue or distributyue: for example, 'one of the lions', 'each of the tigers'.

66 w^{t}out a preposicion: i.e. without a **second preposition** preceding 'to'.

67 casuell: 'declinable'

68 comys next after: the reference is to English rather than Latin.

68 gerundyue usually means 'gerund' (the verbal noun, as amandum, '(the) loving', ars amandi, 'the art of loving'). What we call the gerundive (the verbal adjective, as amandus, 'fit to be loved') is usually called the 'future participle in -dus' or the passive future participle in these texts.

72 'Of' aftyr a nowne adiectiue... The construction with an

NOTES TO TEXT A

adjective is presumably 'free of ...', and while that with a verb could be 'deprived of' or 'descended of', the example at D161 (We be louyd of the maystre) suggests the agent construction with ab and the ablative. It should be noted, however, that 'full of' (plenus), 'accused of' (reus), 'convicted of' (convictus), 'acquitted of' (absolutus), 'gained possession of' (potiti sunt) and 'reminded of' (admonitus) would all take genitives. Cf. CC215f.

73 'throgh' and 'w^t': the ablative of instrument

'fro': i.e. ab with the ablative

'w^{t}out': i.e. sine with the ablative

'then' and 'by': e.g. 'Nothing is greater than love', and 'Smaller by half'.

75 The distinction is between the place where something is or happens, expressed by the ablative, and the place to which someone or something is going, expressed by the accusative.

78 Lines 78-119 are not in Keil's Latin text but are based on a new section found in the text of Donatus used in late medieval England, which begins, "Que est agnicio prime declinacionis?" and distinguishes five declensions as here, where Donatus only distinguished three.

82 -e is written for classical -ae, as is usual in medieval texts.

þe accusatiue neuter as þe nominatiue: compare the last line of the paragraph. For first declension neuters, by which are meant such words as pascha, iota, see C121-5.

83 -am: the references to nominatives and ablatives in -am are to Hebrew words borrowed into Latin, such as Abraham (cf. Doctrinale 30).

84 -as: Greek words such as Aeneas.

87 -abus: found in words such as deabus, filiabus, dominabus, animabus, where it is important to maintain the distinction from the cognate masculine forms.

94 -ius: words such as Claudius, Vergilius, filius, genius take vocatives in -i, and the proper names naturally lack a plural. The common nouns do not, however, have their plural in -i as the text seems to suggest, but in -ii, although the omission of the -i- from the

NOTES TO TEXT A

following endings implies perhaps that we should assume its presence in all of them as part of the stem.

101 -ĭm: the early Latin form for the accusative singular of ĭ- stem nouns. So also the ablative singular in -ĭ and genitive plural in -ĭum.

113 The -vbus of the text is an error for -ĭbus.

120 The definition here is based on that given by Priscian: 'Pronomen est pars orationis quae pro nomine proprio uniuscuiusque accipitur personasque finitas recipit' (Keil ii, 577), rather than that given by Donatus: 'Pars orationis quae pro nomine posita tantundem paene significat personamque interdum recipit' (Keil iv, 357). For a mon may depend on a misreading 'pro homine' in one of the texts, or might be a misunderstanding of Priscian's 'pro nomine proprio uniuscuiusque'. Texts B, D and K also use Priscian's definition. See also my Catalogue, p.50.

121 resayuys certayn person and certen nowmbyr: i.e. is declined for both person and number (but cf. also the note to F81).

122 This list of pronouns and the subsequent division into primitives and derivatives are from Priscian (Keil ii, 577). Donatus' list includes quĭs and gives some composite pronouns (egomet etc.), but omits nostras, vestras and suĭ.

123 suĭ: the reflexive pronoun commonly found in the ablative as se.

hĭjs: i.e. ĭs. Cf. C108 and C205.

124 nostras and vestras: meaning 'of our people' and 'of your people'.

132 In pronouns 'quality' covers definite and indefinite reference, while 'figure' deals with whether the pronoun is simple or compound.

133 The text omits Donatus' sections on number, figure and case.

143 Lines 143-6 are not Donatus' method of distinguishing the persons.

147 The section beginning here replaces Donatus' simple listings of the declensions.

150 -ĭs: mĭs, sĭs, tĭs are early Latin forms, mentioned by

NOTES TO TEXT A

both Donatus and Priscian.

153 ĭn -ĭus and ĭn -ĭus: either because -ĭus is the ending for all three genders, or because the -ĭ- may be long or short.

-c: i.e. the forms from hĭc. Some texts may read -e here. This is a possible early Latin form for the feminine dative singular of these words.

165 The definition is near to that given by Priscian: 'Verbum est pars orationis cum temporibus et modis, sine casu: agendi vel patiendi significativum' (Keil ii, 369). Priscian covers the verb 'to be' in the passage following his definition.

168 VI: an error for VII. Donatus' list is that of the present text but with 'qualitas' covering both mood and form (i.e. aspect, omitted by the English text) instead of mod. 'Gender' in verbs is what we would call voice. Figure covers the distinction between simple and compound verbs.

171 Donatus adds the imperative as a mood; Priscian has the list as here. Lines 171-182 are not from Donatus.

175 'Wold': i.e. in constructions such as '(God) would that ...', 'Would (to) God that ...'. Schuld is not, however, to be found in constructions of this sort.

178 wosumevyr may be an error for wensoevyr. If it is not an error then it would seem to represent quicumque, but this is neither a conjunction, nor is it usually used with the indicative in direct speech. A misread abbreviated quamquam might be the cause of the confusion.

evyr must also be referred to 'whenever'.

181 wen ij verbus comyn togedyr. The example at D313-4 is 'I here the mayster teche scolers', Audio magistrum docere scolares.

183 Donatus only has three conjugations, but Priscian and the medieval text of Donatus give four as here. Donatus gives more information on the formation of tenses than does the Accedence, (although it is treated more fully in the English treatises on syntax).

199 neuter: i.e. intransitive, including the quasi-passives, called neuter-passives in these texts (cf. note to W248-256).

comyn: i.e. passive in form but both active and passive

NOTES TO TEXT A

in meaning (cf. D337f.).

205 uerbe comyn: the definitions of common and deponent verbs, which are not based on Donatus, appear to have been reversed in the present text (cf. text F for instance), even though the definition here mistakenly given for the deponent is strictly speaking more accurate than the 'correct' one, since the gerundive of a deponent verb is passive in meaning. The definitions of deponent verbs in these texts in general do not attempt to deal with the complexities of the matter: the present and future participles, future infinitive, supine and gerund of deponent verbs, for instance, are generally active in form as well as meaning.

curo: i.e. curro.

211 These verses are from the Doctrinale, lines 980-2.

213 Donatus' sections on number and figure are omitted at this point.

214 Donatus gives three 'tempora' (present, preterite and future), but goes on to give five 'tempora in declensione verborum' as here.

216 Lines 216-225 are not based on Donatus.

218 þe tym þat ys lytyll agon: this follows neither Donatus nor Priscian, and is not strictly accurate. The imperfect refers to uncompleted action in the past (cf. the definitions given by B and D making it speak of what is not fully gone or past).

221 comys w^t syne 'haue': this is again inaccurate. The Latin perfect covers the aorist or historic 'I asked' as well as the perfect or primary 'I have asked'.

225 Donatus' section on person is omitted at this point.

226 The definition combines that of Donatus ('Pars orationis quae adiecta verbo significationem eius explanat atque inplet', Keil iv, 362) with that of Priscian ('Adverbium est pars orationis indeclinabilis, cuius significatio verbis adicitur', Keil iii, 60).

230 Lines 230-8 replace Donatus' sections on signification (i.e. the classification of adverbs into those of time, place etc.), comparison, figure (simple and compound formation) and adverbs of place. The English section does not cover the few adverbs whose form is the accusative singular neuter of the related adjective.

NOTES TO TEXT A

239 The definition is neither that of Donatus nor that of Priscian. (Cf. the similar definition at D440f.) Significacion refers to voice in participles, fygur to whether they are simple or compound.

245 Donatus' section on case is omitted.

249 Lines 249-283 are an addition to Donatus.

261 'i-louyt': the i- prefix is not part of the present writer's dialect. D, a more southerly text, does use the prefix and also uses it as a sign of the past participle at D461.

262 latyr supyn: i.e. the form in -tu (dative).

266 The distinction between lecturus and legendus is not given in this form by Donatus, who also treats them as active and passive future participles. The two forms can be construed to give future reference ('about to read', 'fit to be read'), but actually describe a present state.

284 This paragraph is based on Donatus' section on signification.

299 Lines 299-303 replace Donatus' listed declensions. The verses can be compared with Doctrinale 1356f., but are not the same.

304 The definition follows the first part of Priscian's: 'Pars orationis indeclinabilis, coniunctiva aliarum partium orationis, quibus consignificat, vim vel ordinationem demonstrans' (Keil iii, 93). Powere refers to the species of conjunction (see below), figur to whether they are simple or compound, ordyr to whether they are pre- or post-positioned.

308 The 'powers' are from Donatus (Priscian listing seventeen instead of five). Copulatyuis are conjunctions such as et, -que, with the sense of 'and'; disiunctiuis are those such as aut, -ve with the sense of 'or'; explatyuis are so called because they fill out the sense of the clause they introduce, either purely for ornament (quidem) or with adversative (tamen) or expositive (videlicet) force; casuels such as si show that the clause they introduce contains the cause of the action or state of the following clause; racionels such as ita introduce a clause which represents an inference from another clause, or (like quia) introduce the clause from which the inference is made. The distinction between the last two

NOTES TO TEXT A

groups is neither easy nor sharp. Sergius' Explanationum in artem Donati libri contain a useful commentary on Donatus' distinctions (Keil iv, 576). Thomas of Hanney also comments (MS Bodl. 643, ff.219r-220v), and the explanations at D497-515 are helpful.

309 Nothing is said in this English text about figure or order.

310 The definition here follows that of Priscian: 'Est igitur praepositio pars orationis indeclinabilis, quae praeponitur aliis partibus vel appositione vel compositione' (Keil iii, 24). See my Catalogue p.50 and Study p.38.

312 apposicion refers to when the preposition stands as a separate word, composicion to when it is compounded with another word.

316 þis leson of þe 'Donet': 'Da preposiciones ...': the text here presupposes the availability of the Ars minor in the schoolroom. The Latin text cited is found at Keil iv, 365-6.

324 The definition of the interjection is not based on Donatus but is similar to the second part of Priscian's comment on this part of speech: 'Interiectio tamen non solum quem dicunt Graeci σχετλιασμον significat, sed etiam voces, quae cuiuscumque passionis animi pulsu per exclamationem intericiuntur' (Keil iii, 90).

331 This final paragraph is not from Donatus and is an English version of part of John Leylond's De concordantiis gramatice (for which see my Catalogue pp.42-3).

Notes to text B

1 maners of speche: this phrase, also found at M1, may have arisen as a result of such usages as How many maner partyes of resun bu ther? (D1).

10 The definition of a noun offered here is very weak.

13 For he may be vnderstond by hymselfe: this method of distinguishing between substantives and adjectives is also found in texts C, E, F, L and M.

25 The section on the conjugation of accido is not in A. Note that accidunt is picked out from Nomini quot accidunt?, Donatus' Latin equivalent to the beginning of this paragraph. This suggests that the Latin and English

NOTES TO TEXT B

texts would both be available in the schoolroom. The technique of picking out a word and asking grammatical questions about it in this manner is that of the Dominus: que pars? and many other elementary texts of this period, including others in this present collection.

49 declinentur: the jussive subjunctive indicates a command to the reader to decline the listed nouns. Set in its classroom context this shows that the text was not simply followed through from beginning to end but would have been elaborated upon with practical exercises.

71 The definition of the pronoun follows that given by Priscian: 'Pronomen est pars orationis quae pro nomine proprio uniuscuiusque accipitur personasque finitas recipit' (Keil ii, 577), but where Priscian presumably means 'for the proper name of some particular person or thing', the present writer's propur noun misconstrues the sense by restricting the pronoun to personal reference.

77 The sections on demonstratives and relatives, on the vocative, and on possessives, are in neither A nor the Ars minor. There is no treatment here, however, of quality, gender, number, figure or case.

111 The third person is handled rather more subtly than in A.

116 Doctrinale 1088-92, with an additional third line.

132 Doctrinale 60-1, with variations.

154 No reference is made to the verb 'to be' and its equivalents.

156 This additional section also takes no account of the verb 'to be'.

175 For the treatment of deponent verbs, see the note to A205. It is not clear to me what purpose the reference to the first and second persons here is intended to serve. The point being made at C377 may be intended, but the verbs chosen (for, aro) would not be classed as deponent today.

187 'ʒɒuʒte': i.e. 'though'.

230 amauero is classed as future subjunctive rather than future perfect indicative, following the Ars minor.

242 Doctrinale 1529-30 with a new first line. quartum = accusative, sextum = ablative, following Donatus' order of listing the cases (nominative, genitive, dative,

NOTES TO TEXT B

accusative, vocative, ablative).

245 Donatus' treatment of super is phrased differently: 'Vbi locum significat, magis accusativo casui servit quam ablativo; ubi mentionem alicuius facimus, ablativo tantum, ut multa super Priamo rogitans.'

255 sepem means 'hedge' not 'fold'.

278 recto: i.e. 'to the nominative'.

283 mobile: 'adjective'; fyxo: 'to the substantive'.

289 relatum = relatiuum, the shortened form being used to fit the metre (cf. superlatum, C642).

Notes to text C

1 Reson in the sense of a statement was probably carried over from the French raison in the fourteenth century, and the present use may be an extension of that sense, although it is tempting to see a misreading 'partes rationis' for 'partes orationis' underlying it.

12 By omitting 'the name thereof' (cf. A12) before a noun this definition is made even weaker. E and F have the same omission.

27 The sections on accidents and quality are omitted.

38 The text here expands on Donatus by dealing with the cases taken by comparatives and superlatives.

41 lyke case: i.e. to the noun with which the comparison is being made.

45 Graecismus XXV.15

60 John of Garland, Compendium gramatice, MS Bruges 546, fol. 125v; also in Thomas of Hanney, Memoriale iuniorum, Bodl. Lib. MS Auct.F.3.9, p.232. For discussion of the 'dubyn gender' see the notes to A38 and D86f..

84 Da preposiciones ...: i.e. the Ars minor (Keil iv, 365).

87 'beforn' and 'aftyr': these are not in A's list (A73f.). 'Beforn' presumably refers to prae and pro with the ablative. Unless 'aftyr' is a reference to the ablative absolute construction denoting previous action it is an error, perhaps based on such a phrase as F62: 'þan' and 'by' aftyr a comparatyff degree. K73 shows the sort of scribal slip which could underlie the misreading.

NOTES TO TEXT C

89 See the note to A72 on these constructions. Aftyr a propyr name probably refers to the ablative of quality, e.g. vir summa audacia, 'a man of supreme audacity'.

108 -horum: i.e. -orum. Cf. hijs for is at A123 and C205 below.

121 The addition refers to the accusative feminine plural, which was omitted earlier by mistake.

124 pascha, polenta, mammona and manna are listed as first declension neuters in the Doctrinale 543ff. Only the first and last of these words are given as neuter in Lewis and Short.

126 The section on the second declension is omitted in error.

198 This definition begins by following Donatus, but goes on to list the fifteen pronouns following Priscian. Text F has the same approach.

205 hijs: i.e. is.

215 Doctrinale 434-5.

225 Doctrinale 1088-9.

234 The MS reading -e is discussed in the note to A153.

257 For mis and similar forms see the note to A150.

295 qui in the ablative singuler is a pre-classical form, cited by Donatus.

296 qua in the nominative and accusative neuter plural is also a pre-classical form.

358 The section on the accidents of the verb is omitted.

378 These verbs would not now be regarded as deponent.

386 Doctrinale 980-2.

396 lees could be an error for fals.

406 'mote' can be used optatively in 'might that...' constructions (see OED 'may' v.[1] II.8.c) but 'at my wille' is not used in this sense, to my knowledge, although there is obviously a general sense of desire.

407 opti: shortened forms like this are commonly used in the Latin verses to preserve the metre.

413 quousque is an adverb in classical Latin; quoad would be the conjunction.

448 The reference to enormal or irregular verbs is not in

239

NOTES TO TEXT C

Donatus.

462 cisto: i.e. sisto.

481 There is no section on figure in the verb.

483 The section on the comparison of adverbs is not taken from the Ars Minor.

491 No treatment of signification or figure, or list of the accidents of the adverb, is offered.

492 The definition is essentially that given by Donatus. No direct list of accidents is given, and gender, case, number and figure are not treated.

498 '-and': the northern participial ending. This would not be the form local to St. Alban's where this text was probably in use.

500 scort is an interesting description of preterite participles.

571 The definition is based on that in the Ars Minor: 'Pars orationis adnectens ordinansque sententiam'. The 'Da ...' instructions refer to Donatus' lists, which are quoted later in the paragraph. The various categories of conjunction are explained in the note to A308.

590 Set beforn oþer partys of reson follows both Priscian and Donatus, but seruyth to certeyn case follows neither (cf. D521).

594 The reference is again to the Ars Minor.

602 Doctrinale 1529-30, with a new third line.

612 The second half of the definition is from Donatus, but it lyth among oþer partys of reson is new.

Notes to text D

8   The definition given here of a noun is more sophisticated than is usual for these texts, but still makes no attempt to approach the problems of this style of definition which had been discussed by the speculative grammarians for some time. Michel of Marbais in the late thirteenth century can take as his basis for discussion, 'Duo sunt modi essentiales ipsius nominis, sicut dicunt nostri doctores gramatice, scilicet modus significandi substantie ... et modus significandi qualitatis' (Thurot, p.160), but he quickly goes on to

NOTES TO TEXT D

modify this position, in his case substituting the idea
of permanence for substance and determinedness for
quality, in order to allow a distinction between nouns
as the signifiers of stability and verbs as the
signifiers of becoming, reflecting the philosophical
framework of his time. (For discussion of this point in
the context of the speculative text most widely used in
England, see pp.50f. of the useful Introduction to G.L.
Bursill-Hall's edition of Thomas of Erfurt, Grammatica
Speculativa (London, 1972).)

21 appellatyf: from Donatus' 'appellativum'.

23 The section on comparison is fuller than is usual for the
Accedence texts, but is not to be regarded as a text of
the Comparacio.

26 echyng can be used with the sense of 'suffix' (MED
'eking' 1c), but a more general sense of 'augmentation'
applying to the meaning rather than the form of the word
perhaps fits this passage better.

56 dexter et sinister: These two words normally make the
irregular superlatives dextimus and sinistimus. Priscian
(Keil ii.95) does not suggest that the -errimus forms are
to be used. The English treatises normally follow this
rule, but at 0137 both sets of forms are given, and here
the -errimus forms are added.

memor does not follow niger because it has a consonant
stem in -r rather than a vocalic stem in -ro, -ri as
found in niger, tener etc.. It therefore follows the
standard rule for forming its superlative rather than
the rule just given.

59 The first line is Doctrinale 477. The second is an
additional line found in some Doctrinale texts, and is
from John of Garland's Synonyma. (See Reichling's note
on this line in his edition of the Doctrinale.)

64 maturus: Priscian explains the occurrence of these
exceptional forms by positing ante-classical variants
or pre-cursors of the positives, viz. matur and veter
(Keil ii, 95-7). Lewis and Short record super as an
early collateral form of superus.

66 To the list, which is derived from Priscian (Keil ii, 96),
can be added the negatives difficilis and dissimilis.

67 cessus: presumably the preterite participle of cedo,
although I can make no sense of the addition.

NOTES TO TEXT D

72 Doctrinale 480-1. f-a-g-u-s is an acronym of the -ili stem adjectives, humilis dropping its initial letter.

81 dubye gendre: See note to A38.

86 The verses are also found in John of Garland's Compendium gramatice (Bruges MS 546 fol. 125v) and Thomas of Hanney's Memoriale iuniorum (Bodl. Lib. MS Auct. F.3.9 p.232). cortex, silex, finis and dies are in Donatus' list of nouns of uncertain gender as between masculine and feminine (Ars grammatica, Keil iv, 375). Priscian places all the nouns mentioned in the verses in this category (margo, silex, cortex, panthera, damma, finis Keil ii, 141; dies Keil ii, 158; clunis Keil ii, 160).

91 Doctrinale 545-7 labels damma and panthera epicene, and the newe grammer of line 94 presumably refers to this.

98 Donatus only gives simple and compound. Decompound is from Priscian's discussion of 'figura' (Keil ii, 177f.) where 'decomposita' are established as a third category. Magnanimitas is used as an example by Priscian.

109 The examples here and elsewhere in D are not found in the other texts. The whole treatment of case is clearer, more careful and more comprehensive than is usual in the ME grammars.

127 emtynesse or fullenesse: i.e. egeo, indigeo, impleo, plenus. An ablative can also often be used. See the note to line 166 below.

128 byggyng: 'buying' rather than 'begging'. The genitive of value is used where no definite price is expressed.

vndernymynge: 'reprimanding'. Here the genitive is of the fault or crime with verbs of accusing, condemning, convicting or acquitting.

137 byddyng, hotyng or comaundyng: i.e. the dative of the indirect object.

138 lycclynesse ... vneuenesse: the dative of the indirect object is used with adjectives implying nearness, fitness or likeness.

138 profyt or vnprofyt: the dative of advantage.

145 Sum amans ... Vado amatum ... : These look like literal translations of 'I am loving', 'I am going to love'.

148 The accusative of respect. For whether the English

NOTES TO TEXT D

examples represent actual usage, see the Introduction to the present volume.

154 Most of these constructions are exemplified in the notes to A72ff.. 'Vnder' and 'for', which do not occur there, refer to sub(ter) when denoting rest under, and the ablative of price.

165 Vescitur et fruitur: The verses are found in full at T162-4.

166 fulness ... vndernymyng: cf. lines 127-8 above where the same qualities are given as expressed by the genitive. The ablatives of separation and association are used with verbs and adjectives denoting deprivation and fulness respectively; the ablative of price denotes particular price rather than general value; and verbs of accusing etc. which take a genitive of the charge take an ablative of the penalty.

273 Cuius declined as an interrogative adjective is pre-classical. The preceding example does not in fact decline cuius to agree with armilausa.

278 dedlych: i.e. 'mortal'. The equivalent Latin word has dropped out of the example.

287 Quotus is the interrogative ordinal pronoun, meaning 'Which in order of number?'. The second example given shows its extended use: literally, 'Which in order of number was the bishop when he came to town? He was the twentieth etc.', and hence, 'How many accompanied the bishop ...'.

306 wyth an et coniunccion: This is misleading: a subordinating conjunction is required rather than et. Wyth could be an error for wythout.

309 quosque: i.e. quousque.

318 The purpose of the exception is to point out that dare, and those of its compounds that are first declension, have a short vowel in the stem.

330 resonable would be naturally taken to mean 'rational' here and in the following lines, but while this fits these specific examples, it does not give the required general sense. There may be some confusion with the use of 'reasonable' to mean 'that may be reasonably used' (OED A4b).

337 curro is active intransitive, vapulo quasi-passive;

NOTES TO TEXT D

they would be called neuter and neuter-passive respectively in the terminology of the ME grammars. (Cf. my note to W248f.)

342 Doctrinale 980-2.

352 In the distinction between the three times of the verb and the five times of conjugation there is a hint of distinction between time and tense.

396 This section is not taken from the Ars minor. Similar passages are found in other texts (e.g. BB623f., CC444f., DD).

398 This is the rule of the locative case, expressing place where.

405 The locative case is not used with plural or third declension town names, which take the usual ablative of place where. The preposition in would not normally be omitted in classical prose.

412 The accusative of place whither.

417 The ablative of place whence.

422 Domus, rus, humus and militia all have a true locative case, similar in form to the genitive singular.

424 Compounded place-names do not in fact follow rus but take a preposition with place whither and place whence. Although the rule as formulated here is misleading, the examples are correct.

440 This definition, which is from neither Priscian nor Donatus, has some similarities to that at A239f..

479 party of the 'Donet' seems to be used here as equivalent to 'part of the verb's conjugation'.

490 As usual, nothing is said on number and figure in the participle.

491 The definition is not from Priscian or Donatus. The exposition of the various categories of conjunctions which follows is unusually full. The note to A308 refers to them.

510 cheson: i.e. 'the cause'.

520 Again, the definition is from neither Priscian nor Donatus.

534 to gooderhele: a very late example. See OED 'goderheal'.

NOTES TO TEXT E

Notes to text E
11 On the definition of the noun, see the note to C12.

Notes to text F
11 On the definition of the noun, see the note to C12.
45 There is no treatment of figure.
49 This is not adequate grammatically: collective nouns and plural place-names are obvious exceptions.
81 The sumtyme reflects Donatus' 'personamque interdum recipit' rather than Priscian's 'personasque finitas recipit', although Priscian's 'pro nomine proprio' underlies the first part of the definition here. The writer presumably has the distinction between definite and indefinite pronouns in mind, rather than the fact that they all inflect for person. See also the notes to A120-1 and B71 (on propir nown as a misleading translation of Priscian).
122 There is no treatment of quality, gender, figure, number or case in the pronoun.
133 joynyth mode to mode, tens to tens: this is rather confused – a conjunction is a joining agent, the verb of conjunctive mood is joined to a verb of some other mood (so D306). The reference to tense may reflect the sequence of tenses which differentiates that of the main clause from that of a subordinate clause, but this is not a usual part of elementary grammar at this period, and the writer is probably looking back to his definition of the verb as declyned w^t mode and tens at line 123.
160 The reference is to a typical Ars minor conjugation in which the singular forms are given, and then, after 'et pluraliter', the corresponding plural forms. The Latin text is clearly being used, in part at least, alongside the English. Cf. also the notes to lines 216 and 310 below.
176 The treatment of person also relies on a knowledge of Donatus' form of conjugation.
179 There is no treatment of figure in the verb.
185 There is no treatment of signification or figure in the adverb.
215 There is no treatment of order, case, signification,

NOTES TO TEXT F

number or figure in the participle, and no list of 'accidents' is given.

216 The definition is based on Priscian (Keil iii, 93), but the references which follow are to Donatus.

226 There is no treatment of figure or order in the conjunction.

227 Priscian's definition is used, as in A and K. Cf. the note to A310-12. The references which follow are again to the text of the Ars minor.

238 The same definition is found at A324.

Notes to text G

7 foydnesse: i.e. 'voidness, emptiness'. Cf. note to D127.

'Of' efter þis verbe of sum, es, fui: the genitive of quality ('he is of noble countenance') or the partitive genitive with the word on which the genitive depends omitted ('he is (one) of our party') could be intended, but there are other similar constructions where the ablative would be used.

8 The ablatives without preposition with verbs of deprivation, fulness and possession, and the genitives used with verbs of accusing, gaining possession and reminding, are exceptions to this ill-framed rule.

18 alþer-varnyst a-go: varnyst is the superlative of fern adv. (OED), and means 'furthest'. alþer or aldyr is probably the genitive plural of 'all'. The whole phrase then means 'furthest past of all'.

28 be c: an error of dictation for be 'si'.

30 Cf. A181, D311 for more careful statements of this rule.

32 Five concords are usually given, as for example at F241f..

44 þat ende: this and the þat schall in line 46 seem to be parallel forms of þat schal ende (line 42), perhaps the result of trying to keep pace with dictation.

50 The text here begins to repeat itself (cf. line 41).

Notes to text H

1 The text enigmatically begins and ends incomplete on the verso of a leaf which is blank on its recto - perhaps a

NOTES TO TEXT H

cancel rejected from another book because the recto was accidentally left blank.

2 English is treated more directly as the basis of grammatical classification in this text than in the others.

30 The 'correction' of vtile to vtilius is mistaken.

Notes to text J

13 and has the force of 'if' here.

Notes to text K

14 This text omits the lists of 'accidents' of each part of speech.

22 In treating comparison and person in the noun only English forms are referred to.

36 This section is normally given under the pronoun.

53 pascer: i.e. passer.

54 This section repeats lines 22-26.

63 Cf. the notes to A60f. on these constructions.

67 wyttoty remewyng: 'without removing', i.e. 'to' with the indirect object, not motion 'to'.

84 A partial repeat of lines 36-42.

89 There is no treatment of quality or figure in the noun.

91 propur name: cf. the note to B71.

113 Cugeas: i.e. cuias.

There is no treatment of quality, gender, number or case in the pronoun.

115 and coniugacion: in neither Donatus (who gives time and person) or Priscian (who gives time and mood).

145 sowyt: i.e. 'showeth'.

157 These definitions are bare tautologies.

164 There is no treatment of number, figure, or person in the verb.

167 There is no treatment of signification, comparison or figure in the adverb.

NOTES TO TEXT K

173 There is no treatment of gender, case, signification, number or figure in the participle.
201 or dyscowpulyth: an expansion on Priscian and Donatus. Cf. C572.
202 There is no treatment of power, figure or order in the conjunction.
204 be-endyth: i.e. in post-position (as -ve, -que, autem).
206 There is no treatment of case with prepositions.

Notes to text L

27 Despite the disorganisation of this text, this is one of the more satisfactory definitions of the noun. It makes nouns the names of things and not things themselves, and covers emotions and abstract concepts, as well as physical objects.

Notes to text M

13 This definition is unlike those of the other Accedence texts, and is rather a crude attempt to approach the problem of non-sensible objects.

37 This section has a parallel at B25-34. The section on quality which follows is also closely related to that given in B (35-8).

Notes to text N

2 in a certen accedens: i.e. 'employing the grammatical forms we are about to discuss'. Q and S omit the phrase, but a lyknes of diueris thyngus alone is not specific enough a reference to identify grammatical comparison.

3 qualite or quantite: cf. Donatus' Ars grammatica (Keil iv. 374 lines 17-18): "conparantur autem nomina quae aut qualitatem significant aut quantitatem." In purely practical terms, the introduction of the adjectives as a class makes this specification otiose.

4 that may be made more or lasse wyt a good sentens: cf. Doctrinale 460-1: "Est adiectivis graduum collatio talis, / Dum valet augeri sua proprietas minuive", actually quoted by text O.

NOTES TO TEXT N

6   This definition depends on the theory of accidents as developed by the speculative grammarians, but does not approach the crux of the problem for the modistae which was, in this field, the distinction between real and intentional accidents (cf. Pinborg, p.300 lines 20-31).

16 Note that there is no reference to Latin at all in this short text. Only the existence of its companion pieces prevents us from claiming it as a direct treatment of English grammar.

Notes to text O

5   Doctrinale 460-1. The short chapter III of the Doctrinale (lines 458-498) is cited extensively in the Comparacio texts, and was clearly an important underlying source.

20 i.e. the positive adjective construes according to the usual rules, whereas the comparative and superlative take special constructions. Cf. P119-124.

22 The variation in spelling of the English comparative ending is typical of these texts.

27 Doctrinale 463-8, followed by four supplementary verses referring to John of Genoa's Catholicon.

32 Nouns in -ficus make their comparison as if from a positive in -ficens. It is not clear to me why amicus, which compares normally, should be part of this list.

40 This passage on the pronunciation of doctior is not found elsewhere in the ME treatises.

54 The first party of þis rule: i.e. of comparatives formed from the genitive.

55 sinisterior: irregular because sinister has a genitive sinistri. The exception is noted at Doctrinale 467.

60 Not from the Doctrinale, which has different verses covering this point (line 490).

61 primum: i.e. the positive degree.

67 Doctrinale 486-9.

72 iuuenis is noted at Doctrinale 487.

73 tenuis is noted at Doctrinale 491.

74 polys and nequam are noted at Doctrinale 468.

81 This section is not found in the other texts of the

NOTES TO TEXT O

Comparacio. The verses are also found in John of Garland, Compendium gramatice (MS Bruges 546, fol. 97r) although it is unlikely that the present author found them there.

85 Ianuensis: i.e. John of Genoa.

88 gradus medij: i.e. the comparative grade.

89 The first three verses = Doctrinale 492-4. The final line and the line preceding it are found in John of Garland, Compendium gramatice (MS Bruges 546, fol. 97r).

92 The adjectives mentioned in this section, especially in ante- and post-classical usage, carry two senses. Taking proximus as an example (this is the only one of the list noted as having a double sense by Priscian (Keil ii, 97)), it can either be a full superlative meaning maxime prope, or it can have a positive grade sense of propinquus, and then receive a further comparison. This example is explained at R144-8.

100 sextum: i.e. ablative. See note to B242.

124 Doctrinale 475-6, 478-9. The omitted line has the sense of the present line 139.

131 maturimus: the r is not doubled although the rule just enunciated, and usage, require it.

135 dexter and sinister: see the note to D56.

140 eis does not scan. See the note to R112.

148 Doctrinale 480-1. The middle line and the second half of the last line are new.

154 The examples given here resemble those used in the treatises on syntax.

Notes to text P

21 Text O divided its material under the three grades of comparison. Texts P, Q and S put all the information on identification together, then that on formation, and then that on construction.

51 comparant: the metre requires a singular here. Cf. lines 57 and 104.

54 Doctrinale 486-8 with a new last line.

82 The verses added to those from the Doctrinale at O148-50 here stand in a new context.

NOTES TO TEXT P

99 Doctrinale 475-6, 486-8, and three further verses.

102 Pessimus: an error for pessima.

108 w^{t}outyn endyng in -r: i.e. the positives, not the superlatives.

113 The first two verses are Doctrinale 478-9. The third follows them in some Doctrinale texts. The last three verses are based on Doctrinale 480-1 with a new middle and last half line, as at 0148-50.

123 sinotheges: i.e. 'synecdoche'. Synecdoche is a figure of rhetoric in which the part stands for the whole. Donatus, in his Ars grammatica (Keil iv.400), gives synecdoche as 'significatio pleni intellectus capax, cum plus minusve pronuntiat', and Doctrinale 2517-8 reads, 'si partem sumas pro toto vel vice versa, synodochen facies'. But at Doctrinale 1235-7, in the section dealing with the constructions of the accusative case, Alexander writes, 'saepe, quod est partis, toti datur et regit illam. est ibi synodoche: quando faciem nigra dentes albet; nuda pedes; mulier redimita capillos.' This is the accusatif ex vi sinotheges, so called because what is true of a part of the body is predicated of the whole before being qualified by the accusative of the part concerned. Modern grammars refer to this usage as the accusative of respect. (Priscian deals with this at Keil iii, 220-1, without mentioning synecdoche.)

134 I have not found these verses in the works of John of Garland, but they do occur in Thomas of Hanney's Memoriale iuniorum (Bodl. Lib. MS Auct. F.3.9, p.217). The verses do not make easy sense, but a possible meaning is on the lines of, "Whatever nature of case one grade of comparison will have set to it, the other two will also enjoy".

161 This section on the formation of adverbs is not found elsewhere in these texts.

178 i.e. of the comparative adjective.

182 i.e. of the superlative adjective.

Notes to text Q

18 kynde: i.e. 'degree' here.

28 Graecismus XXV.15.

NOTES TO TEXT Q

29 This section is not found in the other texts in this form. Without further instructions and qualifications it would be quite inadequate.

Notes to text R

25 of both said: i.e. as given in both the preceding sections.

26 Doctrinale 463-7 with two extra verses.

30 susterior: this, which is the apparent reading of the MS, is an error for sinisterior. The line as given here does not scan; the form at line 59 is to be preferred.

31 amicus: See the note to O32. The words are discussed in lines 47-60 below (a section not found in the other texts), where the 'correction' to amicior in line 55 highlights the awkwardness of this example.

48 murificus: i.e. mirificus.

55 Some such phrase as ending in -icus is needed after declinson to save this rule.

89 The source of these verses is as at 088-91. Hec in line 3 of the verses is an addition which breaks the metre.

99 senex can be used of either a man or a woman, but is always grammatically masculine.

102 The syntax here is confused. Possibly the scribe began by writing When ... positif? in the same form as later sections, and then only partially emended his mistake. Whereof ... is required.

112 The verses are also found at 0139-43.

113 detero: this is the verb meaning 'to impair', given by Priscian (Keil ii, 84) as the origin of deterior. Scanned as a dactyl (acceptable in Late Latin) it fits the metre, while the eis substituted at 0140 does not and is probably an attempt to get round what seemed a nonsense word.

120 dexterimus (and 123 dexter, dexterimus): these should read deterimus and detero, deterimus (see above). Dexter clearly does not fit the sense of the passage.

122 materimus: i.e. maturimus.

138 murificus, minificus: i.e. mirificus, munificus.

NOTES TO TEXT R

144 This section is not found elsewhere. Cf. the note to 092.

147 0120-7 forms these superlatives from the genitive, but the effect is the same.

164 The source of the verses is as at 0148.

166 This section is not found elsewhere. The verses are also found in John of Garland's Compendium gramatice (MS Bruges 547, fol. 97^r).

173 The rule makes better sense if positiue and superlatiue are interchanged.

180 This last section is not found elsewhere.

190 The superlative of nuper is the adverbial nuperrime and so is not relevant to the present list which is of positive adverbs which are used for the positives of adjectival comparatives and superlatives. Several of the other adverbs also have a separate adverbial comparison (e.g. post, posterius, postremo).

190 citra: a superlative citimus is also found.

191 osis: i.e. ὠκύς, only used in Greek. The superlative ocissimus is also found in Latin.

Notes to text S

This short text does not call for separate comment.

Notes to text T

1 This first section, which outlines five forms of construction, also circulated in a Latin form (in which only four forms of construction are given: see my Catalogue, p.46). As a guide to what words properly begin a Latin sentence it is of limited value, but it does introduce the main ways in which the subject of the sentence is expressed. The accusative and infinitive construction is not covered, but this was rarely used in the Late Middle Ages.

2 construe: here 'construct'.

26 This is hardly true outside school-room examples.

41 ys rehersid of: i.e. 'is repeated (understood) in'.

50 This assumes that all subjects will be expressed, and is

NOTES TO TEXT T

therefore (perhaps deliberately) oversimplified.
- 59 sentens: 'sense' is meant here.
- 62 enchosyn: 'cause'.
- 68 Doctrinale 1442-5.
- 80 Graecismus XXVI.111-2.
- 84 Graecismus XXVI.114-5.
- 85 This section gives a pragmatic listing of verbs which may be found with a following nominative; the constructions involved are, however, very different, as the following notes show.
- 87 verbus passiuis: i.e. factitive verbs (of making, saying, thinking, choosing, showing), which are copulative (take a complement rather than an object) in the passive.
- 88 verbus as þei were passiuis: i.e. quasi-passives, which have an active form but a passive meaning. These are not, properly speaking, copulative. As with the intransitive verbs listed next, the nominative adjective following the verb is not a complement but is in apposition to the understood subject of the verb.
- 89 stuping: in the wider sense (cf. Latin inclino) of any bodily suffering of an action. Cf X85.
- 92 Immineo: i.e. emineo.
- 101 This usage was not current in prose, but was used by poets (especially Horace, whose example Abstineo irarum is) in imitation of Greek usage.
- 104 ex vi transicionis personalis: 'by the force of transitivity in personal verbs'; i.e. this is the case they normally take as transitive personal verbs. The classification of syntactical rules using ex vi ... terminology was developed by John of Genoa (cf. my Catalogue, p.35) and remained popular until the sixteenth century.
- 113 iiij^{tum} casum: i.e. the accusative. As U114 makes clear (see the note to that line) the reference is to the impersonal construction miseret me etc..
- 124 Papias: the reference is to the Italian grammarian, author of the Vocabularium. I can, however, find no treatment of this subject in that work.
- 133 seruit: in the sense 'preserve for me'.

NOTES TO TEXT T

135 uaco: in the sense 'have leisure for'.

141 quando locum dat: i.e. 'when it has the sense of "give place to"'.

142 preiudico: in the post-classical sense of 'be prejudicial to'.

154 Doctrinale 1265-7, with a new last line. The verbs are all of entreating or clothing.

154 peto: the double accusative construction is ante- and post-classical, with the sense of 'entreat'.

155 monet: takes a second accusative of a neuter pronoun occasionally.

159 Utor rubeo capicio: i.e. 'I use a red vest'.

163 transicione regunt: 'take as their object in transitive construction'.

165 gerundiuis: i.e. 'gerunds'. See the note to A68, and my Catalogue, p.72.

173 confitentes: the correct reading is confidentes.

176 w^{t}oute a substantif sett to hym: i.e. where the '-ing' word is not an adjective qualifying a noun.

180 in discendo gramaticam sapienciam: in this tag the **verb** governing sapienciam is omitted.

187 (in)formans: the scribe's error comes from reading informando as in formando.

194 resun: i.e. 'clause'.

220 lyke to a participull of the presentens: the English construction which is in the writer's mind is presumably 'I come from reading books', with 'reading' labelled as being 'like a present participle'. This could be read as a comparison with the Latin participle - in which case 'reading' is a present participle in the writer's estimation - or as a comparison with the English participle, in which case 'reading' is formally similar to it, but is not one. A case could be made for analysing 'reading' as either a participle or a gerund, in fact. At line 240 below (where the underlying English is 'I have come from learning grammar') the **'-ing' word is labelled as 'lyke to an infinitif mode'.** Although the infinitive has something in common with these usages, this is most likely a mistaken carry-over from the treatment of the construction 'I am going to learn to

NOTES TO TEXT T

read'. This error is found in most of the ME grammars at this point and demonstrates the coherence of their tradition. See also the Introduction, p.xxii.

220 before: an error for 'after'.

231 where þe furst suppin falyth: not all verbs have supines.

240 See the note to line 220.

256 þe particípull of the futur tens yndyng in -dus: i.e. the gerundive; see the note to A68. This terminology is found in Priscian and most subsequent grammarians before the Renaissance.

273 Priscian (Keil iii, 215) deals with ablative absolutes and their expansion, but does not mention cum.

274 The verse adds three more ways of 'resolving' the ablative absolute.

275 sinodoche: the accusative of respect is meant. See the note to P123.

293 The question of how far the English examples given in this section reflect actual usage is discussed in the Introduction.

326 when þey bene sette for pertinet: 'when they are used with the sense of pertinet'. This actually only applies to est when it means 'belongs to' (cf. U333). These words take the ablative of certain personal pronouns – see lines 386-96 below.

334 The verses are found at Doctrinale 1257-9 and Graecismus XVI.31sqq.. They circulated widely.

340 These verbs taking the dative differ from those at lines 133-144 in that these are all used impersonally.

341 expedit: 'it is advantageous (to me)'.

342 vacat: 'there is time for', 'it is permitted'.

342 cedit: 'it happens'.

342 prestat: i.e. praestat, 'it is better'.

349 Monachum decet: U355 reads iuvat here, and is probably to be preferred.

351 These two lines may be a quotation, or the second line could be a re-working of the first. The lines mean, 'It is not clear to me, Hugo, what your will is, nor mine to you; it is not clear to me what your will is,

NOTES TO TEXT T

most beautiful girl'.

353 How is iuuat declind?: i.e. 'How does one recite the declension of iuvat?'.

356 ioyn: U360f. has a less corrupt version of this passage, mentioning all the various parts of the verb in order, and reads then at this point.

359 'Quod est impersonale actiue vocis?': this refers to an elementary Latin treatise on impersonal verbs which must have been available in the schoolroom.

376 pertesum: taedet is generally used in the present, pertaedet in the past. Lewis and Short do record one instance of the uncompounded form taesum.

379 Precianus testificetur: presumably Keil ii, 560, 'impersonalia deficiunt in supinis et participiis, quae ex supinis nascuntur'.

389 est sett for pertinet: see the note to line 326.

389 casuels partes: i.e. 'parts of speech inflected for case'.

396 re or vtilitate: this refers to constructions such as haec tua re feceris: 'You will do this to your advantage'.

400 when y have a verbe in Englysh neuter lyke to a passif where the passyue faylyth: this is clumsily put. The required sense, as comparison with X346 and W234 shows, is: 'When I have to use an intransitive verb which has no passive forms to express the sense of a passive construction in English ...'. As phrased, the text confuses the English and Latin and also suggests that the quasi-passive neuter verbs such as exsulo (cf. notes to A199 and W248-56) are being referred to, which is not the case.

411 verbe neuter-passif: verbs like exsulo now usually called quasi-passives. They have active forms but passive meanings (respectively, to be banished, beaten, sold, made, married and valued). Neutropassiva in Latin refers to the semi-deponent verbs like audeo (cf. lines 418-20). W249 labels verbs like exsulo neutra-passiva which helps to resolve the potential confusion.

416 The verses are from the Doctrinale 978-9 with some alteration. The Doctrinale lists only the first four verbs. In order to accommodate nubo and liceo alterations had to be made, and this is done in various ways by the texts - contrast the wording at U420: ... fio licet

NOTES TO TEXT T

quoque nubo'.

416 licet in this sense is not to be confused with its impersonal usage.

418 verba neutropassiva: semi-deponent verbs which have only **active forms** in the present but only passive forms in the preterite.

419 Doctrinale 976-7.

436 T and BB have an extended form of this section, as opposed to B, D, U, Y, Z and AA. The shorter version has as the second group of three verses the pluperfect optative, the pluperfect subjunctive and the pluperfect infinitive. The longer version adds in the perfect optative and perfect infinitive.

456 On the verse 'Rosa flos florum ...' see my Catalogue, p.8.

Notes to text U

This text is very closely related to T, and of the points of divergence only a few call for notice.

89 This extra line is not found in T.

93 No reference is made to verbs of bodily motion.

96 Aperio: i.e. appareo.

110 incolorum: for incolarum.

114 and wyth the accusatiue ex vi transicionis: i.e. with an accusative of what would be the subject in a personal construction.

130 The clause about the plural adjective is omitted in T.

134 qui sunt digniscimi creaturarum: not in T.

146 This line seems corrupt. Cf T141 and the note on cedo in that line. Sedit must be for cedit.

162 Lines 162-3 are found in neither T nor the Doctrinale.

173 in comyn speche: this could just be taken at its face value (although it is hard to see to what common speech it would apply), but it is more likely to be a corruption of comyn(g) in speche - cf. line 182 and the note to line 220 below.

178 after a nowne substantyue: omitted by T.

NOTES TO TEXT U

184 par(ti)cipull of the precentens: T176 has worde that yndyth yn '-yng'. W124 and Y248 follow U.

190 fer: not in T. See the note to W128.

195 informannte: this should be informans. T's second illustration of this point is missing here.

220 in comyn speche: cf. T215 comyng in spech.

226 vado: T's venio here is less ambiguous.

233 Lines 233-6 have no parallel in T.

247 infenetyue mode: see the note to T220.

296 This line replaces three different lines in T.

306 T's 'hit noeys' is omitted here. T, however, adds pudet and piget to the list of Latin examples and so also breaks the equivalence between the two lists.

322 These verses differ from those at T318-9.

328 w^t the accusatyue case: 'and the genitive' is omitted by mistake.

357 de teque: T351 te deque is to be preferred.

359 U's text in this passage is to be preferred to that of T. See the note to T356.

425 in the schewyng maner: not in T. This is a rare attempt in these texts to use a vernacular expression to translate Latin grammatical terminology, rather than a calque.

440 See the note to T436.

458 Note the varying title of this piece. Cf. my Catalogue, p.9.

Notes to text V

2 In iiij: cf. W2 but contrast T2, where five are given. In fact the same manners of construction are given in both cases, but nominatyf or somwhat sette in þe stede of þe nominatyf is taken as two separate cases by T. Cf. the verses at line 18 below.

9 The examples given differ from those in T.

11 The omission of non here is confusing.

15 Hyt heuyethe my soule my lyf: this impersonal

NOTES TO TEXT V

construction is not recorded elsewhere in ME to my knowledge, and is probably a calque on the Latin. These constructions are discussed further in the introduction to this volume.

16 belouythe: for beleuythe.
18 The verses are not in T.

Notes to text W

19 The text seems to be referring to the example, 'The church is a place which ...', without, however, giving it. The section beginning 'what shall you do ...' is also omitted.
46 Graecismus XXVI.111-2.
50 Graecismus XXVI.114-5.
55 sterynk: 'steering' seems to be meant (cf. W149, X176).
58 These verses are not found in the other texts of the Informacio.
61 This section casts together four Latins found in T. Longer Latins covering several points are a feature of, for example, Leylond's Tractus. See my Catalogue, p.43.
63 iconomis: i.e. oeconomis, 'householders'; not used in the other texts.
75 themenes: i.e. 'emptiness'.
94 expirat: cf. T139 aspirat which is preferable. Expirat is not used with the dative.

maledico: T139 has valedico. Both words can take the dative.

regracior: this is not Latin. T139 has gratulor.

exstat is not used with the dative; T's astat is better.

These errors may be caused by dictation. This text is highly abbreviated and may represent lecture notes, possibly taken from Leylond's own teaching. The next two notes also deal with probable dictation errors.

95 sedit: i.e. cedit.
105 singo: i.e. cingo.
114 This line is not in T.

NOTES TO TEXT W

123 confitentes: for confidentes as at T173.

124 See the note to T184.

128 a participull or ... an adiectyf: T183 has a substantyf. U190's fer after is intended to indicate that it is not the immediately preceding word that is in question, as W seems to suppose.

143 The verses are not in the other Informacio texts.

165 The section on participles is omitted.

186 The verses vary slightly from those at T287.

195 'me redes': this is dubiously a genuine ME construction. See the Introduction.

207 Doctrinale 1257-9; Graecismus XVI.31sqq., etc..

210 The sections on impersonal verbs construed with the dative and the accusative and on verbs which can be both personal and impersonal are omitted.

220 Graecismus XXVI.8-10. Although the MS text here is that usually found in these treatises (cf. Y231, Z299, BB539, CC429) I have emended it to agree with that of AA282 for the sake of the metre.

223 The sections on the conjugation of impersonal verbs and on their participles are run together here.

234 The analysis here is more careful than that at T400 in distinguishing the English and Latin constructions.

238 p(er)fit: If the conjectured expansion is right, the text has perhaps an error for 'impersonal' (cf. U408).

247 me: not in the Latin, and awkward in the English.

251 Doctrinale 978-9.

253 neutro-passiva: the text here distinguishes carefully between neutra-passiva or quasi-passives (exsulo) which are active in form and passive in meaning, and neutro-passiva or semi-deponents which have active forms in the present and passive forms in the past.

255 Doctrinale 976-7.

Notes to text X

1 This text omits the preliminary discussion on the ways in which constructions in Latin can begin.

NOTES TO TEXT X

15 'whom' is not given in the other Informacio texts.

22 verbe personall: T and U have 'sum, es fui' at this point. Their reading is more particularly applicable to the example which follows, but X's reading has a more general validity.

25 Why so? ... : This question and its abbreviated reply are not in the other Informacio texts. X adds in a number of extra Responsiones; the abbreviation here is testimony to the well-known nature of the response to one of the most elementary questions. (For the abbreviation cf. line 173.)

33 William Slyngysby, the corrector (see my Catalogue, p.288), has here mistakenly deleted personall. These mistaken 'corrections' are a feature of this text.

49 The cancellation is unnecessary.

50 Doctrinale 1442-5.

54 Ego sum ille ... : this Latin example was widely used by grammarians of all levels in the middle ages. Texts AA, CC and HH also use it.

62 Petrus Helias: as often in late medieval texts, the reference is not to Petrus Helias but to the Absoluta of Petrus Hispanus. The relevant passage of the Absoluta is found on fol. 206^v of Merton College, Oxford, MS 301 (and is printed in my Catalogue, pp.32-3).

66 The addition here may be faintly subpunctuated.

68 strenkth: i.e. the same strength or pattern of construction as the verbs just listed.

71 The verses are not in the other Informacio texts.

77 Graecismus XXVI.114-5.

79 semper poscunt casus: is the corrector's replacement for the cancelled phrase given in the footnote.

85 strength or soffer is written above the lined through meuyngge.

89 Two sections, on verbs with the genitive and on verbs with the genitive and dative, are run together here.

93 The verses are not found in the other Informacio texts.

99 The verses are not found in the other Informacio texts.

104 antyng: i.e. 'wanting'.

NOTES TO TEXT X

105 amtynesse: i.e. 'emptiness'.

108 The verses are not found in the other Informacio texts.

116 These verses vary from those at T122.

119 This section on verbs taking the genitive and ablative is not found in the other Informacio texts. It confuses two distinct groups of verbs. The first, verbs of remembering, reminding and forgetting, take either an accusative or a genitive of what is remembered etc., although recordor is more often found with de and the ablative (with an accusative of the person reminded). The second group, verbs of accusing, condemning and blaming, are construed with an accusative of the person but with either a genitive or, less commonly, an ablative with or without de. The genitive is often of the charge, the ablative of the penalty, although this rule does not hold for all cases. Only the second group can be reasonably said to construe as a rule with either the genitive or the ablative.

129 On verbs of price see the note to D166.

136 erit: sc. haeret.

139 incidet: sc. insidet.

140 obtempero: T139 has valedico. There are other slight differences between the verses in the two texts.

153 and: this attempted emendation spoils the sense of the passage. The texts of T and U show that the cancellation of verbis in the preceding line was also mistaken, although it should follow rather than precede the þe.

156 Doctrinale 1265-7.

159 The reading here is preferable to that at T157.

166 This small section is not found in the other Informacio texts.

173 et cetera: cf. the note to line 25.

199 infinityff mode: this is confused; see the note to T220.

213 Most of the material on gerunds is omitted.

215 noun generall: a nomen generale in Priscian and the grammatical tradition generally is 'quod in diversas species potest dividi, ut animal, arbor' (Keil ii, 61). I have not found the words used elsewhere in the present sense.

NOTES TO TEXT X

225 schurte hangyng resun: this phrase is used in the Formula texts (e.g. Z247) and also at Y298 within the Informacio texts. hangyng means 'not grammatically dependent on another part of the sentence'.

232 The verses are not found elsewhere in the Informacio texts. Their sense - which demands the presence of a participle, explicit or implicit, in the absolute clause - does not completely accord with Priscian's comments at Keil iii, 215.

242 There is no treatment of the accusative of respect.

242 The writer quotes himself at this point. He is more conscious than most of the writers of the ME treatises of the structure and form of his work.

246 This point of technique - re-arranging the English construction for literal translation - is not mentioned elsewhere in these texts.

251 'the': this is an addition to the text as found in the other manuscripts, as is the following Latin. It is not clear to me what English construction the writer has in mind.

261 The verses are not in the other Informacio texts.

375 The treatment of vapulo and nubo is particularly full in this text.

407 This final section is not found in the other Informacio texts but does occur elsewhere. See the note to D396.

Notes to text Y

1 Both the opening sections on construction given by T are omitted here.

39 Doctrinale 1442-5.

50 Graecismus XXVI.111-2.

54 Graecismus XXVI.114-5.

62 Imino: sc. emineo.

78 The categorisation of the construction of the accusative and ablative cases is not found in the other texts. It makes clear that the ablative case is used with a preposition and that the person restraining himself is in the accusative.

NOTES TO TEXT Y

81   The verses are not found in the other Informacio texts.

92   accusatif case ex vi transicionis: again the additional terminology helps to make the construction clear by specifying that the accusative is that used for the 'subject' of the impersonal verb.

133 Doctrinale 1265-7, with extra verses.

231 Graecismus XXVII, 8-10.

248 lyke to a participle of þe present tens: the '-ing' form in In fightyng would normally be classified as a gerund rather than a participle. See the note to T184.

280 a participle of þe future tens: this might refer to a continuative infinitive ('I am going to be reading') or more probably - since the gerundive is called a passive future participle in these texts and has the sense 'to be --' - to the passive infinitive ('I am going to be taught').

286 The text here provides a more careful and convincing analysis of the construction than is usual at this point (see the note to T220).

296 There is no treatment of the Latin participles in this text.

298 schort hangyng reson: see the note to X225.

311 Lines 311-338 repeat lines 165-197. Cf. the note to line 360.

350 There is no treatment of impersonal participles.

356 This note is not found in the other Informacio texts.

360 Lines 360-371 repeat lines 221-233.

372 There is no treatment of the declension of passive impersonal verbs.

Notes to text Z

1   gramaticis nouellis: the verse claims that this text is a compilation from the 'new grammars', which in this context most probably refers to the English treatises on grammar as promulgated by John Leylond and his successors. The Informacio is the largest single source: most of lines 139-346 are drawn from it. For the theory that this compilation is the work of Leylond's pupils - John Cobbow in particular - see my Catalogue,

NOTES TO TEXT Z

p. 10.

3 The first section of the Formula, up to line 78, deals with concord.

7 supposito: 'the subject'.

11 copulatife: i.e. meaning 'and' rather than 'or' (disjunctive).

18 rectos: 'nominatives'. The nominative is casus rectus, the rest of the cases casus obliqui.

29 substantifly: not just 'set as a noun', since this would include e.g. sapiens, 'a wise (man)', but set as a noun which does not have personal reference.

31 mobile: 'adjective', a nomen mobile as opposed to a substantive or nomen fixum; hence also fixum: 'substantive'.

43 relatum: this abbreviated form of relatiuum is often used to help the verses fit the metre. The scribes occasionally write the word in full when the metre demands the shortened form (e.g. line 56); in this and similar cases I mend the verses.

60 partitif and distributitife: see the note to A62.

62 and yf þey be of on significacion: EE93 gives an example of this exception: Ego sum unus inter asinos, which is not, however, helpful, since ego and asinus are not obviously of different genders. The parallel example at Z73 below exemplifies the point more clearly – a fanciful comparison is present in both constructions, whose two elements are not in fact part of the same class and so retain their own gender ex vi propria (cf. line 77).

64 The syntax of these verses is, as often, indirect and contorted, both to fit the metre and also perhaps to make them more memorable! Unravelled, the first line and a half becomes partitiuum vult semper futurum esse concordans genere (cum) plurale genitiuo, 'The partitive noun will always be going to be in concord in its gender with the genitive plural'.

74 superlatum: i.e. superlatiuum; cf. the note to line 43 above.

79 The Formula now passes on to deal with the comparative. The rules and verses are often close to the Comparacio (e.g. with lines 79-95 compare O54-70) but are cast in

NOTES TO TEXT Z

the form of the Informacio sections of an example, a prose explanation, and a rule in verse.

92 Doctrinale 486-9.

102 These verses are also in the Comparacio. On detero see the note to R112.

112 Doctrinale 480-1 expanded.

119 Doctrinale 434-5.

121 The Formula now has a brief discussion of concepcion or syllepsis, the name given to constructions where a word of one person, case, number or gender agrees with a group of other words, only one of which is its own person, case, number or gender. The present rules are concerned to establish what inflection should be given to the single word: e.g. when a verb has a compound subject, the elements of which are of different persons, as ego et tu et ille ibimus, the first person is preferred to (is more worþer þan) the second and third. See EE142f. for a fuller presentation of the rules than is given here.

125 This line illustrates the point made in the preceding text that a compound subject of second and third person takes a second person verb.

130 Doctrinale 1088-9 with a new third line. This section of the text does not deal with concepcion, but the verses from the Doctrinale adjoin the part of that work which deals with it.

139 From here to its end, the Formula is based on the Informacio, beginning with its sections on the use of cases. There are many changes of detail.

164 wille: i.e. ville.

171 The corresponding section of the Informacio has these verbs also taking the accusative (T117). See the note to T113.

188 in comyn spech: see the note to U173.

189 The list of possible expansions of the gerund is fuller than that given in the Informacio.

195 partisipul: see the note to U184.

218 infinitife: see the note to T220.

231 infinitife: see the note to T220, as above.

NOTES TO TEXT Z

247 schort hangyng reson: see the note to X225.

252 Cf. T294ff. The Informacio passage is given a new Latin to introduce it, so that it conforms to the usual pattern.

276 Doctrinale 1257-9; Graecismus XVI.31f.

297 re vel vtilitate: see the note to T396.

299 Graecismus XXVII.8-10.

303 Englich of a verbe neuter: see the note to T400.

321 Doctrinale 978-9.

336 VI: only five tenses are in fact given; the perfect conjunctive is omitted by mistake.

Notes to text AA

Text AA is closely related to Z and does not call for separate annotation.

Notes to text BB

Text BB appears to be the result of conflating the Formula with further material from the Informacio. See my Catalogue pp.83-4. The section on comparison is omitted, and that on concepcio comes rather earlier than in Z.

14 This section and the next are not in Z.

18 Doctrinale 1103.

23 Graecismus XXV.15.

53 This section and the two which follow are not in Z, but are found together in the Informacio text X34-62.

91 Doctrinale 1442-5.

113 This section is not in Z.

116 Doctrinale 1485-8.

128 This section is not in Z.

130 bi strengh of particion: this is translating ex vi particionis. This and other similar phrases (lines 153-4, 357) show the use of Latin material in the revision of the English grammars. See note to T104.

153 Lines 153-235 are not in Z. Some of the material here is derived from the Informacio.

NOTES TO TEXT BB

154 in strengh of the sygnyficacion of his posityf: this translates ex vi significacionis positiui sui. The sense is that dignissima takes a genitive because its positive digna takes one.

181 On the use of these verbe with the nominative, see the note to T88.

192 Graecismus XXVI.114-5.

217 Cf. A61 etc.

252 This and the next section are not in Z.

254 dobill datif case: mihi is a dative of reference, expressing the person for whose advantage or disadvantage something is done or in reference to whom something happens; cure is a predicative dative, used with an explicit or understood dative of reference for a noun or adjective in the predicate after sum and certain other verbs which would otherwise be in the nominative or accusative.

262 sinotiges: see the note to P123.

274 Doctrinale 1265-7.

281 'Da demonstrandi': Keil iv, 362 line 25. Words like ecce are taken as adverbs by Priscian (Keil iii, 21) and the medieval tradition, although they would now be analysed as interjections, and an accusative following them as an accusative of exclamation.
This section is not in Z.

293 Lines 293-339 are not in Z.

300 Doctrinale 1529-30 with a new first line.

315 Doctrinale 1294-5 with an extra line.

326 Doctrinale 1302-6 with an extra line.

357 except action: translating excepte actionis. The reference is to verbs of weather where no human agency is involved. This part of this section is not in Z. The following two sections are also expanded with new material.

389 Doctrinale 1088-9 with an extra line.

395 Doctrinale 1098-9.

435 This section is not in Z.

448 ynfynytif mode: see the note to T220.

NOTES TO TEXT BB

466 Lines 466-492 and 493-501 are repeated at lines 502-9 and 517-21, in part, respectively.

527 This short section is reintroduced from the Informacio.

539 Graecismus XXVII.8-10.

542 This section is not in Z. The following section is also not in Z, but is found in the Informacio tradition

558 obuiator: the third person imperative is referred to as of the future tense in these lists (cf. T424) since 'Let him be ...' has future reference.

584 This short section is not in Z, but cf. X263f..

600 Doctrinale 978-9.

623 This is not in Z, but sections on the adverbial use of place names are added to texts of all the groups. See the note on D396.

Notes to text CC

Text CC, like BB, is an expanded and rearranged text of the Formula. Its structure is discussed in my Catalogue, p.85. It incorporates a text of the Comparacio which is given separately as text R.

34 Lines 34-58 are not in text Z.

51 This is the first of a number of passages in Latin which are introduced into this text of the Formula, and which often carry its discussion beyond the usual limits of these texts. This particular passage introduces a note of controversy rare in the English treatises.

57 linpham: sc. lympham, 'water'.

65 Lines 65-80 are not in Z, and are again a more sophisticated discussion than usual for which Latin is used.

79 This citation from the Ecloga Theodoli is very unusual for the English texts, which do not usually give examples from the authors.

107 Lines 107-169 are not in Z, but draw in part on Informacio material.

110 Doctrinale 1417 with an additional line.

118 Doctrinale 1442-5 with an additional line.

NOTES TO TEXT CC

132 Doctrinale 1485-8.

138 Graecismus XXV.15 with extra material.

141 This paragraph can be compared with BB95f. and X54f. to show the variation commonly found between the texts in treating standard material.

150 Lines 150-9 are probably derived from the Catholicon chapter xxxi (University College, Oxford MS129 fol.16vb) to which they are textually close. This sort of direct dependence is unusual in the English texts. The point about the example given is that although a woman achieved our damnation and also our salvation, it was not the same woman and so there is no one-to-one equivalence between 'woman' and 'who'.

163 apponet: sc. opponet, 'oppose in disputation'.

179 Lines 179-185 are not in Z.

205 awntessnesse: 'emptiness'.

215 Lines 215-20 are not in Z. Cf. A72f.

240 Lines 240-261 are not in Z. Although part in Latin, the material is elementary, and paralleled in the Accedence and Informacio.

258 Doctrinale 1265-7 with an additional line.

274 Lines 274-286 are again not in Z but are from the Informacio, cf. T276f.

317 an Englys of infinitiuo modo: cf. the note to T220.

370 actiwose ... passiwoce: 'active voice ... passive voice'. These unusual forms may have their origin in dictation error, although the present writer uses the full phrase as well and shows a competence which would make him unlikely to commit such errors himself.

397 Lines 397-402 are not in Z but cf. T337f.

408 For lines 408-412 which are not in Z, cf. T380f.

413 From this point on the text becomes confused. Among a miscellany of paragraphs and verses a section on place names used adverbially is found as in BB.

429 Graecismus XXVII.8-10.

432 Doctrinale 978-9 with extra material.

437 Doctrinale 976-7.

NOTES TO TEXT CC

474 Lines 474-5 = Doctrinale 1088-9.
477 Doctrinale 980-2 with an extra line.
486 Lines 487-8 = Doctrinale 1529-30.

Notes to text DD

This single paragraph is a straightforward treatment of the use of place names in adverbial constructions. Using the English prepositions as a key to the constructions produces a more readily understandable text than, for instance, BB444f.

Notes to text EE

On the general structure of this comprehensive and relatively advanced text see my Catalogue pp.87-9. Text D of the Accedence is taken from this treatise.

15 It is immediately apparent from this section that the writer of this treatise is extending the range of the English grammars in subject matter (by introducing exceptions to the rules of construction), in examples (this text provides the fullest exemplification of those known to me), and in technical vocabulary (introducing infinitacion for example).

17 relacion: i.e. the use of a relative construction.

19 negacyon: i.e. the use of a negative construction.

21 infinitacion: i.e. the use of an indefinite construction.

22 prolempsis: sc. 'prolepsis', the construction where something given in general terms is then dealt with part by part.

35 euocacion: i.e. the specification of the referent of a first or second person pronoun, usually by a proper name, which produces an apparent lack of concord between the proper name and the verb.

37 apposicion: not the appositional genitive, since Londinie is the usual feminine nominative plural form of this place name. Note that the same example is used at line 206 where these figures are re-stated.

38 concepcion: see the note to Z121.

40 colleccyon: i.e. the use of a collective noun, with a plural verb in this instance.

NOTES TO TEXT EE

47 particion: the use of a partitive construction.

49 dystribucion: the use of a distributive construction.

51 sylempsis: sc. 'syllepsis', a construction where two words which agree in sense do not agree gramatically.

52 defaute of gender: some adjectives do not differentiate the genders in all cases. Pauper is used as an example of an adjective which uses the same form for the ablative singular of all three cases in Priscian (Keil ii, 343).

63 intransicion: when the relative clause uses a copulative verb the relative may agree with the complement in the relative clause in number and gender rather than with its antecedent in the main clause.

107 This does not contradict what has gone before but restates it in general form: the superlative only necessarily agrees with the following genitive if the genitive is plural and refers to a category of which the superlative's referent is a member.

116 fygures of construccion: the writer of this text claims in lines 221-3 that this section is derived from Priscian. There is in fact little in Priscian to compare with it (what there is is at Keil iii, 183), but the writer rather draws on that part of the Catholicon's treatment of alleotheca which is allegedly drawn from Priscian, although it is considerably simplified in the text before us. The fourth variety of 'concepcion' given here (of cases) is for instance a peculiarity of the Catholicon. A sample passage from the Catholicon for comparison with EE136-141 is given in my Catalogue on p.36, where the passage in which the Catholicon claims to be drawing on Priscian is also given.

Permissible figures of speech form a complex and very varied area of the study of language in the Middle Ages. James J. Murphy, Rhetoric in the Middle Ages (Berkeley 1974), especially chapter four, gives some introduction to it, but two points in particular are important in understanding the treatment before us. First, of the three categories of permissible figures - metaplasms (word distortions), schemes (syntactical distortions or patternings) and tropes (which have an element of semantic distortion) - it is the second category of schemes which concerns us here. Secondly,

NOTES TO TEXT EE

the writer confines himself to points of construction which are raised in grammatical treatises, and does not venture into the realms of rhetoric (although, of course, there is no easy distinction between the two areas). Also, to repeat, the treatment here is very simplified by comparison with the tradition as a whole, although there is nothing else to approach it in our elementary English texts.

118 prolempcis: cf. line 22, and note.

124 obliques: 'cases other than the nominative'; this is the only passage in the English texts to us the word.

136 The writer of EE often only mentions his debt to the Catholicon where that work is controversial, as at this point. The passage from the Catholicon is printed on p. 36 of my Catalogue. (University College, Oxford MS 129, fol. 58va.)

142 silempcis: cf. line 51, and note, and also the note to Z121.

160 The reference is to chapter cxl of the Catholicon. There was some controversy about this point in the medieval grammarians.

171 The source passage is found in University College, Oxford MS 129 fol. 58ra.

172 zeuma: in general, zeugma is the addition of a second, less appropriate, subject to a construction, so that one verb is governed by two nouns, but only one of them fits normally with it. In the present limited grammatical application, zeugma can be hard to distinguish from syllepsis, but where syllepsis is concerned with the way one of the subjects takes precedence over the other, zeugma is concerned with the way the second subject is added to the construction.

187 antitecis: note that here 'antithesis' is used to refer neither to substitution of one letter for another (as found in Donatus and Alexander de Villa Dei and widely elsewhere), nor in the common modern sense of a balanced and contrasted construction, but to mean the use of one case where another would be expected. This sort of flexibility in terminology is fairly common with the figures of speech.

189 sintecis: this rather unusual schematic category is intended to cover constructions where two nouns are set

NOTES TO TEXT EE

next to each other.

191 euocacion: cf. line 35, and note.

197 apposicion: cf. line 37, and note.

207 synodoche: see the note to P123.

224 Grammarians of the late Middle Ages expanded considerably on the analysis of the regímena of the cases according to various principles of construction expressed as vis ... which is found in the Catholicon. This section accordingly depends more on later tradition than on the Catholicon.

229 P.H.: this stands for Petrus Helias who was taken to be the author of the Absoluta, actually by Petrus Hispanus. (See my Catalogue, p.32.) The passage quoted is to be found on fol. 210v of Merton College, Oxford MS 301.

231 This reflects Thomas of Hanney's massive attack on the multiplication of vires in the construction of the nominative case (see my Catalogue pp. 38, 41), which is also reflected in John Leylond's de regimine casuum (see ibid.). ex vi zeumatis vel ex vi concepcionis would be attempts to see a separate principal of construction, other than the demand of a personal verb for a nominative subject, in the constructions labelled zeugma and syllepsis in the previous section.

234 strengthe of intransicion: = ex vi intransicionis; i.e. in an impersonal intransitive construction.

238 The schematic way in which the series of constructions are presented suggests a source not unlike Leylond's de regimine casuum with a highly controlled catalogue format, to which the present writer has characteristically added examples. Each point is presented as a miniature dialogue in Latin, and only a bare framework of Anglicisation is provided. Although the terminology is strange at first sight it is mostly both elementary and straightforward. It is presented as the operation of grammatical forces or rules, but is in reality a simple catalogue of constructions, most of which are treated in the other English texts.

277 ly: this word, presumably of French derivation, commonly introduces a word quoted as an example in the Latin grammars of this period.

331 magistrum: a dative of the agent would be more usual. The similarity in many functions between the gerund

NOTES TO TEXT EE

and the infinitive, which takes a subject accusative, is here urged on us.

359 The source passage is found in University College, Oxford MS 129 fol. 48vb (printed in my Catalogue, p. 36).

Notes to text FF

1 This sixteenth century text owes some of its phraseology and structure to the Informacio and Formula but cannot be regarded as a text of one of those treatises. The verses are by and large new, possibly written by the composer of this text.

14 The ground covered in the preceding paragraph gives a good idea of its summary nature and paucity of examples. Note also the consistent use of English words as keys to Latin constructions.

28 There is an indication here of a return to classical usage of the accusative and infinitive construction in indirect speech, although its use seems to be permissive rather than prescriptive.

86 Once again, the summary nature of this text is very apparent.

120 This is a good simple rule for the gerundive of obligation.

121 gerundyue: this does refer to the gerundive, not the gerund, another sign of the late date of the text, although the gerund is still called by this name as well being called the nowne verball.

144 The construction with the supine in -u is dropped in favour of classical practice, but (and this should be regarded as a conservative feature in keeping with the text as a whole) the text still refers to an English infinitive at this point, when one would not in fact be used.

163 This explanation also is particularly clear.

Notes to text GG

4 For an early text, possibly written before 1400, this shows a striking transference of the Latin categories to English examples, but this is partly accounted for

NOTES TO TEXT GG

by the compression of the text, which is little more than an aide-memoire.

11   mony thyngys monyly: not otiose; collective nouns speak of many things singly.

27   A more thoroughgoing attempt is made here than in many later texts to speak of the moods in native English terms.

53   þe ta numere and þe othyr: i.e. 'either number'.

62   The reference is to the substantival use of adjectives.

Notes to text HH

1   This text opens with same passage as the Formula and shares other passages, as well as a similar overall structure, with it. There is, however, about twice as much new material as old, and I regard it as a new treatise. The teaching of the text is careful without achieving sophistication.

5   Say thys in Latyn: A particular feature of this text is that its discussions of each point are followed by their Latin equivalent, in phraseology reminiscent of the such standard works as the Catholicon, Thomas of Hanney's Memoriale iuniorum or Leylond's Latin treatises. Such Latin versions are given for paragraphs which occur only in English elsewhere, and we may assume that some at least of them are the work of the present writer.

27   Triplex est ...: cf. the treatment of the nominative in Leylond's de regimine casuum and the similar treatise in Corpus Christi College, Cambridge MS 233 fols. 20v-34v, both of which are drawing on the Catholicon.

70   materiali: 'as an example'.

96   Cf. the note to EE160. The 'concepcion' of the neuter case was a topic of debate among the late medieval grammarians, and this text gives quite a full account of one position which was taken.

135   circumlocucion: this is treated more fully than usual.

230   This section gives a more detailed treatment of the concord between the relative and a collective antecedent than is usually found.

NOTES TO TEXT HH

265 Petrus Alias: sc. Petrus Helias. He is also cited as an authority on this point at X62. As usual Petrus Hispanus in the Absoluta is probably the actual source, and the relevant passage from Merton College, Oxford MS 301, fol. 206v is printed on pp. 32-3 of my Catalogue. (Note that the reference to FF265 there is a misprint for HH265.)

333 Graecismus XXVI.111-2.

338 Graecismus XXVI.114-5 with an extra verse.

361 Hugucionem: the reference is to the Derivationes magnae of Hugutio of Pisa. Like the Catholicon this work was written in Northern Italy in the thirteenth century, but it was less widely used by elementary grammarians in England in the fifteenth century. Earlier English grammarians such as Richard of Hambury and John of Cornwall cite Hugutio but not John of Genoa, and the popularity of the latter's work may be due to its very extensive use by John Leylond. (See R.W. Hunt, 'Oxford Grammar Masters in the Middle Ages', Oxford Studies presented to Daniel Callus, OHS new series xvi, pp. 184-6.) There is a further reference to Hugutio at line 407.

498 sinatygen: see the note to P123.

Notes to text JJ

This collection of short notes, mainly on verbs taking the genitive and ablative, requires little comment. It may be based on one of the longer treatises.

10 strenkyth wyth coplicase: i.e. 'the strength to take the same case after the verb as goes before it'.

18 be: sc. 'be construed with'.

Notes to text KK

4 Perotto: See also lines 82-4. The reference is to the Cornucopiae of Niccolo Perotto (1429-80), printed at Louvain in 1486 for the English market. (See N.I. Orme, English Schools in the Middle Ages, London 1973, p. 106. The relevant passage is printed on p. 95 of my Catalogue. The inclusion of a reference to such a writer immediately places the text within the

NOTES TO TEXT KK

Renaissance tradition, but it should be noted that the references to Perotto are framed as additions, and that the flavour of the text as a whole – as is characteristic of the work of John Stanbridge with whom this text has been associated – is one of traditional material sprinkled with references to and examples from the new Italian grammarians, rather than one of thoroughgoing revision.

9 Englyshed 'to be att': English is very much used as the key to the Latin constructions in this text.

11 Assui cene: the examples also place an immediate distance between this work and the earlier texts. They attempt to use classical idiom, and in two cases represent themselves as quotations (from Pliny and Seneca) although the layout of the manuscript page shows that the attributed examples are probably afterthoughts.

48 This passage is reminiscent of the earlier grammars (e.g. X329–34) and points to the conservative nature of the present text, despite its use of the new grammar.

75 Also he hath many mo significacions: a reminder of the elementary nature of this text.

Notes to text LL

1 It is clear from the opening phrase onwards that although the sixteenth century writer of this text has some pretensions to the new grammar, much of what he writes is closely dependent on the fifteenth century texts.

3 As with text KK, the examples represent a departure from the earlier tradition. The writer of this text, is far less judicious in his attempts to restore classical usage, witness such a peculiarity as Franciscus formosus est pusus at lines 4–5.

35 The dependence on the earlier tradition is particularly marked in this paragraph.

42 Alongside the previous traditional paragraph, we now find a section replacing that tradition with more modern analysis.

106 The proscription of quod with the indicative in favour of the accusative and infinitive is an obvious sign of

NOTES TO TEXT LL

modernity, but no reason is offered for it.

142 The spaces here and in lines 146 and 258 suggest that the writer was copying and could not understand his original.

292 This stylistic rule again takes us out of the world of the medieval texts. Although the writer does not cite him in this text, it is clear from other texts in the same manuscript **probably written by him** that he was familiar with the work of Robert Whittington (see my Catalogue, p. 257) from whom he could have derived much of his new teaching.

296 Telos: the characteristic and pretentious colophon of the writer of this manuscript.

GLOSSARY

This glossary lists all the grammatical terms used in the texts, with the equivalent modern term or a simple explanation. Where a word or sense is not in the MED (for words to 'noun(e') or OED (before 1500) it is marked with an asterisk, and a sample occurrence cited. Headwords are given in the MED form where possible.

ABLATIF adj. + n. Ablative.
ABSOLUT ppl. Absolute; not governed by the main syntactical
              structure of the sentence.
*ABSOLUTLI adv. Outside the main syntactical structure of
                 the sentence. KK70
ACCIDENCE n. A system of functional endings or inflections.
*ACCIDENTAL adj. Subject to s system of ACCIDENCE. B35
ACCORD n. Concord.
ACCORDEN v. To be in ACCORD.
ACCUSATIF adj. + n. Accusative.
ACTIF adj. + n. Active.
ADJECTIF adj. + n. Of nouns: qualifier, adjective. Of
                    verbs: not SUBSTANTIF (contra MED).
ADVERBE n. Adverb.
ADVERBIALLI adv. By means of an adverb.
ADVERSATIF adj. Of a conjunction: expressing opposition.
*AFFIRMATIF adj. as n. (A noun) standing without a negative.
              BB30
ANTECEDENT adj. + n. Antecedent.
ANTITESIS n. The substitution of one case for another.
APPELLATIF adj. Of a noun: common.
*APPONENT adj. Of the nominative: used in the complement.
APPOSICIOUN n. Apposition. Setting alongside (K204).
ARTICLE n. Article.
ASKING(E ger. Noun of - : an interrogative.

*BEREN v. To - case: to inflect for case. W212
BITOKNEN v. To denote or mean.
BITOKNINGE ger. Meaning.

CAS n. Case.

GLOSSARY

CASUEL adj. + n. (A word) having grammatical case.
 Also = CAUSEL.
CAUSAL adj. Of a conjunction: causal.
CERTAIN adj. Specifying a particular person.
CIRCUMLOCUCIOUN n. Periphrastic construction.
CLAUSE n. A short section of discourse, not necessarily a clause in the modern sense.
COLLECCIOUN n. The use of a collective noun.
COLLECTIF adj. Collective. *Also = COLLECCIOUN LL105.
COMMUN(E adj. Of a noun: common. Of a pronoun: having a common form for **two or more genders**. Of a verb: using the same forms for active and passive.
COMPARATIF adj. + n. **Comparative.**
COMPARISOUN n. Comparison.
COMPOSICIOUN n. Composition, compounding.
COMPOUNED ppl. + n. Compound.
CONCEIVEN v. Of inflections for number, case and person: to over-ride other inflections and determine the concord in CONCEPCIOUN.
CONCEPCIOUN v. The construction of one word with a group of others with only one of which it is in formal agreement; syllepsis.
*CONCORD(E n. Concord. A331
CONJUGACION n. Conjugation.
CONJUNCCIOUN n. Conjunction.
CONJUNCTIF adj. Subjunctive.
CONSTRUCCIOUN n. Construction; syntactical formation.
CONSTRUEN v. To be part of a syntactical structure; to form, analyse or translate such a structure.
*COPLICASE n. The power of taking the same case after a word as stands before it. JJ10
COPULATIF adj. + *n. (A conjunction) expressing connection. A308
*COUPLEN v. To connect, in a syntactical structure. Q20
*COVENABLI adv. Congruously. EE138

DATIF adj. + n. Dative
DECLINEN v. Decline, conjugate.
*DECLINING **ger.** Declension. X306
DECLINSON n. Declension.
DECOMPOUND ppl. Doubly compound.
DEDE n. The action indicated by a verb.
DEFAUTE n. - of gender: not differentiating gender in all cases.
DEFECTIF **adj.** Of a verb: lacking some inflectional forms.

282

GLOSSARY

DEGRE n. - of comparison: degree of comparison.
DEMONSTRATIF adj. + n. Demonstrative.
DEPONENT adj. Deponent.
DERIVATIF adj. + n. Derived from another word.
DISCORD(E n. Faulty concord.
DISJUNCTIF adj. + *n. Of conjunctions: indicating choice
    or alternatives. A308
DISTRIBUCIOUN n. The use of a distributive construction.
DISTRIBUTIF adj. + *n. A distributive (pronoun). D112
*DOUBLE adj. - accusative: **double** accusative. T149
*DRAUEN v. - out of: to derive from. C117
DUBIE adj. + n. (The class of nouns) of uncertain gender.

EKING ger. - of a word: suffix, ending.
ENDEN v. To take a final inflection.
ENDING(E ger. A final inflection.
ENGLISH n. The English equivalent of a Latin expression;
    an English example for translation.
ENGLISHEN v. To translate into English.
*ENORMAL adj. Of a verb: not following the usual rules of
    conjugation. C449
EPICEN(E adj. Epicene; of a name of an animal: used of
    both sexes but having only one gender.
EVOCACION n. The specification of the referent of a
    first or second person pronoun.
*EXCEPT ppl. as adj. a verbe of - action: an impersonal
    verb of the weather. B357
EXPLETIF adj. + *n. Of a conjunction: introducing a clause
    which expounds or develops the meaning of
    the main clause. A308 (see note)
*EXPONENT adj. Of a nominative: the subject of the active
    construction which is equivalent to and
    expounds an impersonal construction. HH22
EXPOUNEN v. To expound a construction by periphrasis.

*FAILEN v. To be lacking in a conjugation. T232
*FEMINE adj. Feminine **in gender.** KK114
FEMININ(E adj. + n. Feminine in gender.
FIGURE n. The formation of a word. Also, by abbreviation,
    = figure of speech.
FUTUR(E adj. Future (tense)

GENDRE n. In nouns and pronouns: gender. In verbs: voice.
*GENERAL adj. Of nouns: **not specific,** abstract. X215 + note
GENETIF adj. + n. Genetive.
GERUNDIF n. Gerund. (In some late texts) gerundive.
*GOVERNAUNCE n. The requiring of a certain case in a word

GLOSSARY

     by another.
GOVERNEN v. To govern (a case); to require a certain case in a dependent word.
GOVERNING(E ger. The requiring of a certain case.
GRAMERE n. Grammar

*HAVEN v. Govern, take. V25
*HONGINC(E ppl. as adj. Not governed by another part of the sentence. Y298

IMPARFIT adj. Imperfect (tense).
IMPERATIF adj. Imperative (mood).
IMPERSONAL adj. +*n. Of **verbs**: impersonal. T373
*IMPERSONALLI adv. In an impersonal construction. FF122
INDECLINABLE adj. Indeclinable, not inflected.
INDICATIF adj. Indicative (mood).
INFINITACIOUN n. The use of an infinitive construction.
INFINITIF adj. Infinitive.
INTERJECCIOUN n. Interjection.
INTERROGATIF adj. Interrogative; used in asking a question.
INTRANSICION n. Agreement of the relative pronoun with its complement rather than its antecedent.
*INVARIABLI adv. Without inflection. HH141 (Not Anglicised?)

KINDE n. Gender.

*LATIN n. A Latin word or phrase set for construing or translation. V6
LETTRE n. Letter of the alphabet.
LONG adj. Of a vowel: long in sound.

*MANERE n. - of speche: part of speech. B1
MASCULIN(E adj. + n. Masculine (gender).
*MATER(E n. An English expression to be translated into Latin. T16
*METONOMIA n. Metonymy; making one word stand for another. B 163 (Not Anglicised)
MOD(E n. Mood (of a verb).
*MULTITUDE n. noun of -: a collective noun. LL58

NEGACIOUN n. A negative assertion.
*NEGATIF n. A negative particle. Z16
NEUTRE adj. + n. Neuter (gender). Of verbs: neither active nor passive in meaning.
*NEUTRE-PASSIF adj. Of verbs: quasi-passive. T411 (see note)
NOMBRE n. Number.
NOMINATIF adj. + n. Nominative.

GLOSSARY

NOUN(E n. Noun.

*OBLIQUE adj. as n. (Word) not in the nominative. F99
*OPTATIF adj. Optative. A170
*ORDRE n. - of construccion: word order. V2 Of conjunctns: pre- or post-position. A307
*PART n. Part of speech. W212
*PARTICION n. The use of a partitive construction. BB131
PARTICIPUL n. Participle.
*PARTITIF adj. + n. Partitive. C621, A62
*PASSEN v. To exceed (by possessing an extra element). O102
PASSIF adj. + *n. Passive. A201
*PERFIT adj. Perfect (tense). C420
*PERSON n. (Grammatical) person. A121
*PERSONAL adj. Of verbs: personal. HH23
*PLUPERFIT adj. Pluperfect (tense). C421
PLURAL adj. + n. Plural.
*PLURAR adj. = PLURAL. C70
*POSITIF adj. + n. Positive (degree of comparison). A29, O17
*POSSESSIF adj. + n. Possessive. D271, D216.
*POUER n. - of coniunccion: category of conjunction. A306
PREPOSICION n. Preposition.
PRESENT adj. Present (tense).
*PRETER adj. Preterite (tense). A247
*PRETERINPERFIT adj. Imperfect (tense). A215
PRETERIT adj. Preterite (tense).
*PRETERITPLUSQUAMPERFIT adj. Pluperfect (tense). Y377
*PRETERPERFIT adj. Perfect (tense). A215
*PRETERPLUPERFIT adj. Pluperfect (tense). A216
*PRIMATIF adj. + n. Of a word: not derived from another word. Y225, A215
*PRINCIPAL adj. Of a verb: the main verb in a construction. T21
*PROLEMPS(IS) n. Prolepsis; the construction where something is stated first in general, and then in parts. EE22
*PRONOUN(E n. Pronoun. A2
PROPRE adj. Of a noun: being the name of a person or place.

*QUALITE n. Denotation, in nouns common or proper, in pronouns definite or indefinite, in verbs of mood and aspect. A21 + note.
QUESTION n. Question.
*RACIONAL adj. + n. Of conjunctions: introducing an inference or the statement from which an inference has been made. D513, A309
*REFERREN v. To refer, of a relative to its antecedent. U61

GLOSSARY

*REHERSEN v. To restate, as a relative does its antecedent.
U42
*REHERSING ger. Restating, as of an antecedent by a
relative. U43
*RELACION n. The use of a relative construction. EE17
RELATIF *adj. + n. Relative (pronoun). X37
*RESOLVED ppl. Of a construction: made explicit in meaning
by transformation into another construction.
FF86
RESQUN n. Sentence; piece of English for translation.
*REULI adv. Following grammatical rules. P97

*SENTENCE n. The sense of a sentence or clause. W28
SHORT adj. Of a vowel: short in sound.
SIGNIFICACION n. Meaning. Of participles: voice.
*SILEMPSIS n. Syllepsis; the construction in which two words
which agree in sense do not agree
grammatically. EE51
SILLABLE n. Syllable.
*SIMPLE adj. Of a word: not compounded. BB624
*SIGNE n. - of a case: the word in an English construction
having the same function as, and translated
by, a certain Latin case. U410
SINGULER adj. Singular.
SINODOCHE n. Synecdoche; usually applied to the con-
struction now labelled accusative of respect.
*SINTECIS n. A category covering constructions in which
two nouns are set alongside each other.
EE117
SOUN n. Sound.
*SOUNEN v. To pronounce, sound. O40
*STRENGTHE n. Ability to be used in certain constructions.
U80
SUBSTANTIF *adj. + n. Of nouns: not adjective; of verbs:
copulative. A14; T78
*SUBSTANTIFLI adv. Of adjectives: as a substantive. Z31
SUPERLATIF adj. + *n. Superlative (degree of comparison).
O82
*SUPINE n. Supine. furst -: accusative supine; latter -:
dative supine. A69; T209; T219
*SUPPONENT adj. Of a nominative: used for the subject of a
personal verb. HH12
*SUPREME adj. (?)Superlative (degree of comparison). LL172

*TAKEN v. Of a word: to take an ending. A200
TENS n. Tense.

GLOSSARY

*TIME n. Tense. A168
*TRANSICION n. Transitivity. EE285
*TRANSITIF adj. Transitive. A68
*TURNING ger. Replacing one construction by another equivalent one, or into a form which allows for direct translation into the idiomatic construction of another language. X247

*UNCERTAIN adj. - person: not referring to a specific person or persons; hence - qualite: the notional quality of such reference. A135
*UNDECLINED ppl. Not declined. A4
*UNDERSTOOD ppl. Not given explicitly. U267
*UNREULI adv. Not following the rules of grammar. P53

*VERBAL adj. noune -: gerund. FF147
VERBE n. Verb.
VOCATIF adj. Vocative (case).
VOIS n. (Grammatical) voice.
VOUEL n. Vowel.

WORDE n. Word.
*WORTHI adj. more -: in CONCEPCIOUN, taking precedence over another element in the determination of the concord. BB399

*ZEUMA n. Zeugma; here the grammatical figure in which a verb has two subjects but agrees with only one of them. EE117

For Product Safety Concerns and Information please contact our EU
representative GPSR@taylorandfrancis.com
Taylor & Francis Verlag GmbH, Kaufingerstraße 24, 80331 München, Germany

www.ingramcontent.com/pod-product-compliance
Lightning Source LLC
Chambersburg PA
CBHW071802300426
44116CB00009B/1173